Multimodality, Cognition, and Experimental Literature

Alison Gibbons

Routledge
Taylor & Francis Group
NEW YORK   LONDON

First published 2012
by Routledge
711 Third Avenue, New York, NY 10017

Simultaneously published in the UK
by Routledge
2 Park Square, Milton Park, Abingdon, Oxfordshire OX14 4RN

First issued in paperback 2014

*Routledge is an imprint of the Taylor & Francis Group,
an informa business*

Typeset in Sabon by IBT Global.

Library of Congress Cataloging-in-Publication Data
Gibbons, Alison.
 Multimodality, cognition, and experimental literature / Alison Gibbons.
  p. cm. — (Routledge studies in multimodality; 3)
 Includes bibliographical references and index.
 1. Modality (Linguistics) 2. Discourse analysis, Literary. 3. Cognitive
grammar. 4. Literature, Experimental—History and criticism. I. Title.
 P99.4.M6.G53 2011
 401'.4—dc22
 2011015293

ISBN 978-0-415-87361-1 (hbk)
ISBN 978-1-138-80976-5 (pbk)
ISBN 978-0-203-80321-9 (ebk)

gnition, and

rature

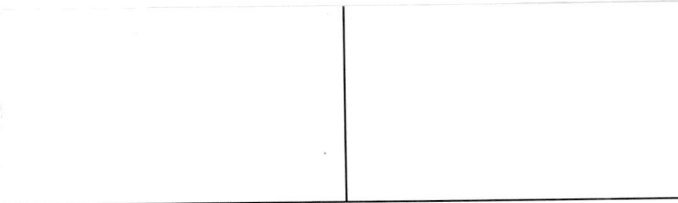

Routledge Studies in Multimodality

Edited by Kay L. O'Halloran, *National University of Singapore*

This is it.

Contents

Figures

Permissions

CHAPTER 4

Figures 4.6 and 4.7, as well as quotations from the novel, are reproduced from *House of Leaves* by Mark Z. Danielewski, published by William Heinemann Ltd. Copyright © 2000 by Mark Z. Danielewski. Used by permission of Pantheon Books, a division of Random House, Inc. Reprinted by permission of The Random House Group Ltd.

Earlier versions of parts of Chapter 4 appeared in the form of journal articles and edited chapters, and I am grateful for permission to include them here:

Gibbons, A. (2010) 'Narrative worlds and multimodal figures in *House of Leaves*: "-find your own words; I have no more"', in Grishakova, M. and Ryan, M-L. (eds.) *Intermediality and Storytelling*, Berlin: Walter de Gruyter.

Gibbons, A. (2011) 'This is not for you', in Bray, J. and Gibbons, A. (eds.) *Mark Z. Danielewski*, Manchester: Manchester University Press.

Gibbons, A. (forthcoming) 'Multimodality and cognition: Reading word and image', in Baldry, A. and Montagna, E. (eds.) *Interdisciplinary Perspectives on Multimodality: Theory and Practice*, Campobasso: Palladino.

CHAPTER 5

Figures 5.1, 5.2, 5.3, 5.4, 5.6, 5.7, 5.8, and 5.11, as well as quotations from the novel, are reproduced from Steve Tomasula, *VAS: An Opera in Flatland: A Novel*. Art and design by Stephen Farrell. Chicago: University of Chicago Press, 2002. Copyright © 2002 by Steve Tomasula. Used by permission of the author.

Earlier versions of parts of Chapter 5 appeared in the form of journal articles and edited chapters, and I am grateful for permission to include them here:

Gibbons, A. (2008) 'Multimodal literature 'moves' us: Dynamic movement and embodiment in *VAS: An Opera In Flatland*', *HERMES* 41: 107–124.

Gibbons, A. (2009) '"I contain multitudes": Narrative multimodality and the book that bleeds', in Page, R. (ed.) *New Perspectives on Narrative and Multimodality*, London: Routledge, pp. 99–114.

CHAPTER 6

Figures 6.3 and 6.5, as well as quotations from the novel, were reproduced from *Extremely Loud & Incredibly Close* by Jonathan Safran Foer (Hamish Hamilton, 2005; Penguin Books, 2006) Copyright © 2005 by Jonathan Safran Foer; Excerpt from *Extremely Loud & Incredibly Close*: A novel by Jonathan Safran Foer. Copyright © 2005 by Jonathan Safran Foer. Reprinted by permission of Houghton Mifflin Harcourt Publishing Company. All rights reserved.

Figure 6.6 was reproduced by permission of the student in question, Emma Penny, who was at the time (2009) studying at the University of Nottingham.

Figure 6.8 was reproduced from the novel *Extremely Loud & Incredibly Close* by Jonathan Safran Foer, Penguin Books, 2005, by permission of the original photographer, Lyle Owerko, copyright © 2001/Polaris.

CHAPTER 7

Figure 7.1 was reproduced from Graham Rawle's website: www.graham-rawle.com. Figures 7.2 and 7.4, as well as quotations from the novel, are reproduced from *Woman's World* by Graham Rawle, Atlantic Books, 2005. Copyright © 2005 by Graham Rawle. Used by permission of the author.

Acknowledgements

This book developed from my doctoral thesis, and so I have many of the same people to thank along with newly accumulated debts. My foremost thanks must go to my PhD supervisor, Joanna Gavins, who was everything one could wish for in a supervisor. I am also greatly indebted to the examiners of that PhD, David Herman and Dan McIntyre, whose comments and advice was invaluable. The encouragement and support of my editors also deserves mention here: Kay O'Halloran as series editor and Erica Wetter at Routledge (who must have the patience of an angel), thank you.

Multimodality, Cognition, and Experimental Literature has been a 'labour of love'. I am in awe of Mark Z. Danielewski, Steve Tomasula, Jonathan Safran Foer, and Graham Rawle, whose novels I have only grown to admire more through thinking and writing about them. I am particularly grateful to Graham Rawle for his enthusiasm in the project and to Steve Tomasula for his generosity and support.

The academic communities I have been privileged to be a part of have been a continuous source of support: the University of Sheffield, the University of Nottingham, De Montfort University-Leicester, the Poetics and Linguistics Association (PALA), amongst others. My students at various institutes have often been a source of inspiration and intellectual stimulation, particularly Jack Brooks, Hannah Gibbons, Chloe Harrison, Jessica Mason, Andrew Straiton, and Isabelle van der Bom.

I have been fortunate to have friends and colleagues willing to read and/ or discuss the work with me at various stages: the anonymous reviewers of this book when it was just a proposal and Anthony Baldry, Joe Bray, Dominic Head, Carmen Daniela Maier, Ruth Page, and Michael O'Toole. My thinking has been sharpened by members of the Interdisciplinary Research Group (IRG) and by members of the Cognitive Poetics Research Group (CPR), both based in Sheffield: Sam Browse, Dan Carroll, Mel Evans, Sam Kirkham, Julie Millward, Dave Peplow; by Andrea Macrae for introducing me to cognitive poetics and by Peter Stockwell for writing the book in question; and by Tom Stafford for kindly allowing me to pick his archival brains about cognitive psychology from time to time. Alice Bell and Sara Whiteley deserve special mention as my PhD Mentor and Mentee respectively: Alice has been a rock in her advice and friendship while the, sometimes alcohol-fuelled, academic debates between Sara and I have challenged and affirmed my thinking in equal measure.

Good friends continue to keep me sane: I am thankful to those who volunteered for the empirical study in this book, as well as Gina Benson, Steven Blackmore, Sarah Carter, Melanie Chalk, Katie Chipperfield, Brittany Cooper, Anne-Marie Evans, Amy Fulstow, Phillipa Harriett, Joanna Hastwell, Hannah Jaggard, Stephen Macrae, Christina Parren, Lara Yates, Emily Lewis, Vicky May, Hannah Spencer, Elisa Tudisco, Jonny Wilkins, Amanda Zacharzewski, and many more. Sarah Clow and Tom Chapman didn't just keep me sane, they also kept a roof over my head for a while and I cannot thank them enough for that.

Last, but never least, my greatest thanks go to my family. My brother Anthony kindly shared his bioscience know-how with me. My parents, Peter and Wendy, have always believed in me, even though they often refused to listen to me talk about my research. I feel that I will never be able to repay them—emotionally and financially—for all they have done for me, and I suspect my thesis, when finished, will be the most expensive book they have ever owned. With love,

Alison Gibbons, January 2011

1 Introduction

1.1 EXPERIMENTAL LITERATURE AND MULTIMODALITY

Novels that feature graphic elements are by no means a recent development in literary innovation. An early, canonical example of a novel with graphic elements is, of course, Laurence Sterne's (1967 [1759–1767]) much celebrated and sometimes berated *The Life and Opinions of Tristram Shandy, Gentleman*. The book plays with the very form of the novel itself, in both a visual and narratological sense, a facet made all the more remarkable in recent revisionings such as the (2010) release of the book by Visual Editions. One might therefore expect that as writers have been experimenting with the inclusion of images in narrative for so long, a critical vocabulary for examining such experimentation and design would be established. Regrettably, this is not the case. Inevitably, literary criticism has instead favoured the word, and often not as the *written* word, focusing instead upon the thematic and conceptual facilities of discourse. However, as White puts it, "Literature has a physical context which criticism should not ignore: the printed book" (White 2005: 24). Indeed, even within mainstream publishing, the period surrounding the turn of the millennium has seen an increase in the inclusion of typography and illustration in fiction for adults.

This book concentrates on the experimental genre of multimodal printed literature. Novels in this generic grouping employ multiple semiotic modalities, primarily the verbal and the visual. As such, the term 'multimodal printed literature' can be seen to be rather broad in its scope. The decision to include the word 'printed' necessarily excludes all forms of multimedia literature, such as hypertext, DVD novels, and film. However, 'multimodal printed literature' could nevertheless be seen to include graphic novels and children's picturebooks. It is also important to acknowledge other creative multimodalities, such as forms of shaped texts like concrete poetry. While the form of experimental literature that is the focus of this book does, to greater and lesser extents, share commonalities with other text-types such as these, on the whole multimodal printed literary fiction is treated as a genre in itself.

Within what is more conventionally considered to be literature, there is still a great deal of scope and variety for multimodal fiction. Novels that use pictures in an illustrative fashion, such as Alex Garland's *The Coma* (2004) and Marisha Pessl's *Special Topics in Calamity Physics* (2006), for instance, could strictly speaking be considered as multimodal printed literature. This book will concentrate solely on multimodal literary novels that utilise a plurality of semiotic modes in the communication and progression of their narrative. More importantly, in the novels examined in this book, the different modes of expression are located on the page not in an autonomous or separate fashion, but in such a way that, while these modes have distinct means of communicating, they constantly interact in the production of narrative meaning. As such, one mode is not privileged, but rather narrative content, type-face, type-setting, graphic design, and images all have a role to play. My use of the phrase 'multimodal literature' will subsequently refer to these forms of composite and integrated texts.

Multimodal novels are starting to receive greater critical attention, in part due to the publishing success of certain books. However, many examples of multimodal literature are not to be found on the shelves of book shops, tending to be considered as 'clique' or 'cult' books which are 'obscure' or 'ambitious' in their design and demands upon the reader. It is therefore worth outlining some of the formal features that consistently appear in multimodal novels (taking the inclusion of images for granted):

(1) Unusual textual layouts and page design.
(2) Varied typography.
(3) Use of colour in both type and imagistic content.
(4) Concrete realisation of text to create images, as in concrete poetry.
(5) Devices that draw attention to the text's materiality, including metafictive writing.
(6) Footnotes and self-interrogative critical voices.
(7) Flipbook sections.
(8) Mixing of genres, both in literary terms, such as horror, and in terms of visual effect, such as newspaper clippings and play dialogue.

Such novels are highly sophisticated art forms, both in terms of their self-consciousness (using metafictional and intertextual reference, foregrounding materiality, innovative typographical textual layouts) and the invitations and demands they issue to readers. Connections to literary movements can certainly be made; for instance, the self-consciousness associated with postmodern writing and the related genre of metafiction. Multimodal printed literature is not entirely divorced from these contexts, yet in analysing such works I have treated them separately for two reasons. Firstly, as these are works published since the turn of the millennium I am reluctant to see them as part of the literary movement of postmodernism and/or of the epoch of postmodernity. As I see it, the turn of the millennium as well as the events of September 11, 2001, are the impetus for a paradigm shift, a fundamental change in the way we see the world and our place within it. As such, literature, including the multimodal printed literature central to this investigation, reflects such a change. Secondly, postmodernist and meta-fictional works are characterised by certain dominant features, and while multimodal printed literature adopts some of these (self-consciousness, a questioning of ontological stability, metafictive writing, mixing of genres), it nevertheless disregards others (questionings of historiography and the grand narrative, explorations of urban space).

There are no *rules* for writing or identifying a multimodal text, and unlike pulp manifestations of literary genre there is no definitive or repeated narrative structure or pattern. The preceding list of elements should not be taken as a checklist, particularly since I do not claim this list to be absolute. Moreover, any given multimodal novel may use any combination of the features since each fiction is unique in its manifestation of multimodality. In short, I see multimodal literature as a spectrum within which there are more and/or less prototypical examples. At one end of the spectrum, imag-istic content has a more illustrative role in the narrative, while in its most central manifestation, the modalities are integrated and of equal impor-tance to the reading experience.

1.2   RESEARCH PARAMETERS

For my analyses in Chapters 4 to 7, I have selected prototypical examples of multimodal printed literature: Mark Z. Danielewski's (2000a) *House of Leaves*; *VAS: An Opera in Flatland* by Steve Tomasula with art and design by Stephen Farrell (2002); Jonathan Safran Foer's (2005a) *Extremely Loud & Incredibly Close*; and Graham Rawle's (2005) *Woman's World*. All of these novels were published in the first decade of the twenty-first century. In itself, this is interesting since, as van Peer (1993: 59) and Verdonk (2005: 235) suggest, increase in the popularity of multimodal forms is closely tied to the zeitgeist of their era of creation. More specifically, multimodality generally takes on new strength in periods of significant communicative and technological development. Van Peer asserts, "new media require new forms for dealing with language and literature" (1993: 59). The develop-ment of new media consequently leads to a "tension between the text and the specific medium in which it is produced" (1993: 59). The twenty-first century is a multimodal era and it is therefore beneficial to analyse multi-modal artefacts from the period.

Delimiting the cultural and historical moment of the case study texts is also of great value from both a multimodal and a stylistic perspective. In a social-semiotic approach to multimodality, Kress (2010: 8–9) points to the importance of cultural specificity. He quite rightly states that "differ-ences between societies and cultures means differences in representation and meaning" (2010: 8). As such, analysts must study forms of representation and multimodal communication within the context (historical, social, cultural) of production. In addition, a central concept in stylistics is deviance, an aspect of foregrounding (Mukařovský 1976, 1977; van Peer 1986), whereby deviances from the 'norm' warrant attention. By ensuring that all four texts for analysis come from the same cultural and historical position, that is they are all post-millennium Western texts, certain 'norms' can be assured. In other words, there exist certain standard and expected patterns within the conventions of Western reading, such as type-set block text which is read in a linear fashion from left to right across each line starting at the top of the page and working downward.

Since I have been justifying my chosen texts and their cultural contexts, it is also useful to clarify my employment of the term 'reader'. Reception-sensitive studies often struggle with the concept of what Head calls the "notional 'general reader'" (2008: 6). Head, in fact, calls for academic critics to acknowledge the "possibility of the reader's sophistication" (2008: 6). Narratology has long categorised types of readers through critical vocabularies aimed at describing speakers and receivers of narrative texts. Iser's (1974) conception of the 'implied reader', taken up by Booth (1983), has been particularly influential. Discussing notional readers in relation to literary texts with graphic elements, White (2005: 38) suggests that critical approaches to such texts "depend on a concept of an active, determined and adaptable actual reader. This reader is implied and encoded in the text but at the same time, actual and external to it". This book similarly depends on this dual notion of the reader. My usage of the term 'reader' will therefore reference a sophisticated implied reader, but one that, crucially, is seen to physically engage with the novel in an actualised way.

1.3   METHODOLOGICAL APPROACH

The study of multimodality is centrally concerned with texts, in the broadest sense, which contain a multitude of semiotic modes. Primary attention has been paid to texts that employ the verbal and visual modes with most frequent investigations looking at magazines, webpages, and school textbooks. Word and image have principally been considered as distinct forms of communication, conveying meaning to *either* reader or viewer, respectively. Yet in practice, literary texts are often 'multimodal', using combinations of expressive modes in their narrative. Multimodal texts therefore call for new systems of analysis proficient in realising and describing the rapport between expressive modes. This book seeks to answer this call by investigating multimodal novels using a progressive transdisciplinary approach that is theoretically aware and rigorous in practical analysis.

Two central disciplines are used in my explorations of novels that employ both verbal and visual modes: these are multimodality studies and cognitive poetics. While both of these disciplines are introduced in Chapters 2 and 3, at this point I make a few brief comments about the methodological approach taken in this book and its position within multimodality studies more generally. The study of multimodality is a broad and diverse field; its impact can be seen in a number of disciplines from medical discourse to literacy studies. As Page puts it, multimodality is a "pluralistic enterprise" (2009a: 4). In the humanities and communication studies, multimodality refers to the multiplicity of semiotic resources within a particular artefact or event. It insists on combination and integration in semiosis, rather than on modes working in isolation. Moreover, it signals a move away from seeing language and the linguistic as the central means of communication; rather language is another semiotic resource among many, "nestled and embedded within a wider semiotic frame" in Jewitt's words (2009b: 2).

Kress identifies an implicit problem to the term multimodality when he states, "Multimodality names both a field of work and a domain to be theorized" (2010: 54). In other words, *multimodality* as a term seems to refer to an academic discipline as well as a formal entity or composition (hence my use of 'multimodality studies' to clearly designate the former). Such disciplinary anxiety can also be seen in Jewitt's introduction to *The Routledge Handbook of Multimodal Analysis*: "Multimodality, it could be argued, strictly speaking, refers to a field of application rather than a theory, although the on-going development of theories that account for the multimodal is an imperative to support high-quality research" (2009b: 2). Such slippage between theory and practice is, within an undeniably multimodal age, somewhat inevitable, making the best remedy for scholars working within multimodality studies one of academic clarity. As Kress goes on to say, "Anyone working multimodally needs to be clear what theoretical frame they are using; and make that position explicit" (2010: 54). One could argue that in this particular articulation, Kress's use of 'multimodally' as a post-modifying adverb has the same disadvantage: does this mean working practically to create multimodal texts? Or working to theorise and/or analyse multimodal texts? Nevertheless, his point is valid. Transparency of academic approach and methodology is vital, particularly in a field which is home to as great a host of theoretical positions and disciplinary variety.

In her introduction to the different approaches to multimodality, Jewitt (2009a: 28–39) outlines what she perceives to be the three central approaches within multimodality studies: the social-semiotic approach (seen most clearly in Kress and van Leeuwen's work 1996; 2001), a discourse analysis approach (typified by O'Toole's 1994 and O'Halloran's work 1999; 2000; 2004; 2005), and an interaction analysis approach (with principle works by Scollon and Scollon 2003; Norris 2004). This book is none of those. Rather, this book advocates a *multimodal cognitive poetics*. Multimodal cognitive poetics, as detailed in Chapter 3, is a critical synthesis, driven by cognitive poetics and supported by frameworks from multimodality studies (discussed in section 2.5 of Chapter 2). Such a radical interdisciplinary exploration has the potential to yield rich insights into, with durable implications for, the literary field and for everyday experience.

Cognitive poetics is the driving force in the approach to multimodality taken in this book. Like all work undertaken in cognitive poetics, it is interested in relating the structure of a work of art to psychological effect and cognitive experience. The composite nature of multimodal texts raises new challenges for cognitive poetics, but such an approach promises to reveal the meaning-making strategies of multimodality as well as the ways in which readers of multimodal texts reach interpretations. In taking a cognitive-poetic approach, therefore, this book is unique. Moreover, exploring literary fiction takes the study of multimodality into a new artistic arena. In doing so, I hope to expand the perception of what multimodality is and what it can be, as well as develop a genre-specific understanding of literary multimodal word–image unions. This book is highly interdisciplinary and is pertinent to the fields of cognitive poetics and stylistics, multimodality studies, narratology, and literary criticism.

1.4 STRUCTURE OF THE BOOK

The book is structured in eight chapters. The present chapter has introduced the aims and motivations of the book. Chapters 2 and 3 offer more detailed introductions to the two central disciplines, multimodality studies and cognitive poetics. In the latter, I detail a proposed augmentation between the two disciplines, an integrative approach to multimodal printed literature I call *multimodal cognitive poetics*. I advocate this as a more efficient approach with which to account for the cognitive implications of multimodal novels.

Chapters 4 to 7 put multimodal cognitive poetics into practice through analysis of literary texts. These analyses allow for the identification of shared multimodal techniques, and are also sensitive to each text's uniqueness. In all of these chapters, I take an analytical journey through the novels, investigating narrative episodes in the chronological order in which a reader would encounter them.

Mark Z. Danielewski's (2000a) *House of Leaves* is the focus of Chapter 4, which acts as a platform for the succeeding analyses of Chapters 5, 6, and 7. Throughout the analysis of *House of Leaves* I am interested in the ontological instability of the boundary between the actual world and the world(s) of the novel, as well as consideration of how ontological slippage might contribute to the experience of *House of Leaves* as a horror fiction. The chapter shows that multimodal literary narrative has a primary impact upon the reader's physical and conceptual relationship to both book and storyworld.

In Chapter 5, I engage with Steve Tomasula (2002) *VAS: An Opera in Flatland* with art and design by Stephen Farrell. The principal concern of the analysis is the way(s) in which the materiality of multimodal novels such as *VAS* foregrounds the embodied dimension of all literary experience. Extending Chapter 4's interest in the relationship between actual and fictional worlds, it is argued throughout this chapter that multimodality creates doubled experience, foregrounding the physical context of reading as well as allowing for the conceptual capacities of immersive narrative experience. The chapter also investigates multimodal manifestations of metaphor, and consolidates terminology in providing a cognitive account of its cerebral processing.

The analysis in Chapter 6 focuses on Jonathan Safran Foer's (2005a) novel *Extremely Loud & Incredibly Close*, which engages through fiction with the traumatic repercussions of 9/11. Section 6.2 is devoted to a discussion of the implications of 9/11 literature for a cognitive approach. In response to this, the analysis in the chapter presents a context-sensitive approach to the multimodal literary text. Drawing on trauma theory and narrative studies of trauma, I demonstrate that fictional representation, and in particular multimodal representation, can act as traumatic testimony. Moreover, I argue that the reader is placed as a cowitness to the testimony offered by the novel.

Chapter 7 presents a study of Graham Rawle's (2005) *Woman's World*. The entire narrative is constructed through the 'cut and paste' of 1960s women's magazines, and the chapter considers the novel's privileging and foregrounding of its textual surface. An additional concern of the chapter related to the novel's formal design is a focus on the way in which typography serves to trigger particular meanings, including its effect on the reading experience. Moreover, unlike the preceding textual analysis chapters, Chapter 7 features an empirical study (sections 7.2.5 through to section 7.2.7) which explores the reactions of real readers to multimodal literature.

Finally, the conclusion reviews the accomplishments of the analytical explorations of the book. In section 8.2, I examine the way in which multimodal novels position the reader in the literary experience. In section 8.3, I discuss the ontological and narratological implications of multimodality in literature, and in section 8.5. I review the advancements made to existing cognitive frameworks, as offered by the analyses in this book. Section 8.6 considers the potential scope of application for a multimodal cognitive poetics by suggesting future directions for further research.

2   Multimodality

2.1   WHAT IS MULTIMODALITY?

Multimodality, in its most fundamental sense, is the coexistence of more than one semiotic mode within a given context. More generally, multimodality is an everyday reality. It is the experience of living; we experience everyday life in multimodal terms through sight, sound, movement. Even the simplest conversation entails language, intonation, gesture, and so forth. Indeed, many of its theorists have acknowledged that, strictly speaking, there is no such thing as a monomodal text (for instance, see Baldry and Thibault 2006: 58). Notably, the development of the academic study of multimodality was catalysed by the rise of digital technologies, provoking increase in multimodal products, which can now be created cheaply and easily. After all, this is the epoch of the internet, of hyperfiction, of the iPod, even of the Sony Reader whose marketing slogan announces, "Finally, the digital book has come of age". Indeed, the twenty-first century can be perceived as a quintessentially multimodal era. Therefore, in today's world, consideration of multimodality in academic research seems to have become even more urgent and even more relevant.

The practice of multimodality is long-standing. Nevertheless, multimodality as a field of academic research is still at an embryonic stage. In this chapter, I first consider what is meant by the term 'mode'. I then survey prominent research in multimodality studies, including works on typography. I conclude this survey with a discussion of criticisms of the field as it stands. The chapter ends by highlighting analytical tools from multimodality studies that will feature in multimodal cognitive poetics.

2.2.   WHAT IS A MODE?

Since any definition of multimodality centres on the notion of a 'multitude of modes', the question of just what qualifies as a mode is an important one. In recent literature, several scholars have sought to clarify 'mode'

(Forceville 2006, 2009; Jewitt 2009c; Kress 2009, 2010; Page 2009a), but as Forceville (2006: 382; 2009: 22) states, "This is no easy task, because what is labelled as a mode here is a complex of various factors". Initially, Forceville turns to the sensory perceptual system for categorisation, thus modes are connected to each of the five senses. For a cognitive approach, this seems to provide a useful foundation for understanding and identifying modes, yet nevertheless it is not without problem since, as Forceville goes on to discuss, it implements "too crude a categorization" (2006: 382; 2009: 22). This is because connecting modes "one-on-one" with each of the five senses is too generalising and overlooks crucial differences between signifying systems. For instance, the visual mode would encapsulate both written communication (which is verbal) and pictorial communication (which is imagistic), and evidently these two forms do not convey meaning through the same means. As such, the question "what is a mode?" is a slippery one; as Kress puts it, it is a question to which "there is no straightforward answer" (2010: 87).

There are varying understandings of 'mode' within the field of multimodal studies. Jewitt (2009c) perceives such variation among the three central approaches to multimodality: the social semiotic, discourse analysis, and interaction analysis. In the latter (e.g. Norris 2009), mode is not such a pivotal issue since gesture is understood as a communicative mode with the analyst's interest being on how that mode is utilised. The discourse analysis approach, which Jewitt aligns with the work of O'Halloran (2005) and O'Toole (1994; see section 2.3.1. of this chapter), works on the premise of semiotic resources rather than modes. In doing so, it takes a somewhat broader perspective. Jewitt explains, "Semiotic resources consist of systems of meaning that realize different functions, and therefore, meaning becomes a matter of choice from the systems of meaning from different semiotic resources, and how these choices integrate in multimodal phenomena" (2009c: 21–22). In this view, language, for instance, is a semiotic resource which can be realised through a number of different modes, such as the written and the oral.

The third approach is the social semiotic, associated with the work of Kress and van Leeuwen (1996, 2001; Kress 2010; see section 2.3.2 of this chapter). The social-semiotic approach grounds the notion of 'mode' in its cultural and material uses, or, as Jewitt phrases it, "in a specific context (time and place) modes are shaped by the daily social interaction of people" (2009c: 21). Kress (2009, 2010) interrogates the notion of mode in more detail, arguing that in order to identify a mode, there are two important questions: The first is social—*does a community-group regularly use the resources of that mode?* The second question is formal—*does the mode fulfil the three communication functions of ideational meaning (states, actions, events), interpersonal meaning (social relations), and textual meaning (formal entities)?* Only if a mode meets these requirements can it, for Kress, indeed be classified as a mode. Such a narrow definition also has its downfalls: there are consequences to affording the status of mode to any signifying system. As Kress ultimately resigns, "what is needed are categories at a level general enough and abstract enough to encompass all the meanings of contemporary social life in the multimodal communicational world" (2010: 92).

Forceville (2006: 383; 2009: 23), whose discussion of 'mode' opened this section, does not entirely resolve the matter either, though he eventually concludes that modal categories include, at least: (1) pictorial signs; (2) written signs; (3) spoken signs; (4) gestures; (5) sounds; (6) music; (7) smells; (8) tastes; (9) touch. Page (2009a), in the introduction to the edited volume *New Perspectives on Narrative and Multimodality*, opts for an even broader definition, evident in her own list of potential modes:

> The modes described in multimodal analysis refer specifically to semiotic modes (as opposed to other, specialist uses of the term). Thus a mode is understood here as a system of choices used to communicate meaning. What might count as a mode is an open-ended set, ranging across a number of systems including but not limited to language, image, color, typography, music, voice quality, dress, gesture, spatial resources, perfume, and cuisine. (6)

What is valuable about Page's definition is her carefully worded designation, "what might count as a mode is an open-ended set", since it allows for modal categories to shift according to usage. She continues, "Given the fluid nature of modes, central questions are how, why, and to what extent some modes become privileged in certain contexts" (2009a: 6). Keywords here are 'fluid' and 'contexts'. The implicit understanding of 'mode' taken in this book is mostly closely aligned to Forceville's and Page's classification, and could perhaps be called a cognitive-narratological approach. Modes are fluid, and determining what counts as a mode must be based on their context of use. In addition to this, it may be helpful to consider the ways in which different signifying systems are perceived, cognised, and interpreted. For instance, in both Chapter 4 on Mark Z. Danielewski's *House of Leaves* and Chapter 6 on Jonathan Safran Foer's *Extremely Loud & Incredibly Close*, I discuss the use of code. The former is created through written language while the latter works through written numerals. In Forceville's terms, these would both be manifestations of the written mode, though I am inclined to see linguistic writing and numerical writing as differing systems. However, if we take the latter example, the numerals in Foer must be translated into alphabetical equivalents and thus 'reading' this code is different to reading 'normal' or at least more naturalised language or numbers. As such, since the act of reception is different, we have a different mode of communication at work, at least within this particularly literary context.

2.3 MULTIMODALITY IN THEORY

In this section of the chapter, I survey prominent works in multimodality studies, focusing on those which have been most influential in developing the thinking behind the approach taken in this book. Further to this, I provide a summary of related work on typography.

2.3.1 The Language of Displayed Art: Michael O'Toole

An early work in multimodality studies is Michael O'Toole's (1994) book *The Language of Displayed Art* (strictly speaking, it presents an approach to the visual arts and not to multimodal art). While O'Toole does not use the term 'multimodality' or engage with multimodal pieces as such, his work is important since it presents an analytical approach to works of art, from painting to sculpture and architecture. The seminal nature of O'Toole's project is clear from the outset in which he creates a captivating imaginary scenario for the reader: "You've come a long way to see this painting. It's beautiful—much more beautiful than those hundreds of copies you've seen of it—but you don't know what to say about it" (1994: 3). O'Toole develops the scenario, continuing to exploit the engaging power of the second-person pronoun, by explaining that you are viewing the painting (Botticelli's *Primavera*) with three companions, all of whom are at ease talking about the painting. Each companion does so from a different perspective: mythology, art history, and composition. Interestingly, O'Toole states:

> The trouble with these sets of observations about the painting is that they don't make contact with each other at any point. They are monologues, and they fail either to relate different aspects of the painting to each other or to help their speakers relate to each other. And although the comments are all rather impressive—as they were designed to be—they don't seem to convey how these various people relate to the painting itself. They involve extensive information from outside the painting—mythology, social history, and technique—all of which might be relevant at some stage of talking about the work, but not now. Your friends are all wasting precious time talking about things that can be read up in a library, and not about how *they* perceive and respond to the painting in all its original, recently restored splendour. (3–4; original emphasis)

O'Toole's criticism of previous, and still current, approaches to art are equally true of much work in literary criticism: there is a general neglect to relate the structure of the work of art (including the literary text) to the reception of the work. Literary and artistic criticism should not be, in Stockwell's (2008) words, "eccentric, impressionistic, irrational, circular, pretentious, amateurish and faddish". It should not be idealistic, stylistically impenetrable, or deliberately obscure; most importantly, it should not be utterly divorced from the reality and experience of real viewers of art and real readers of literature. O'Toole thus sets himself the task of constructing a discursive analytical framework with which to examine works of art, a framework that is capable of accounting not only for the work itself (including those existing forms of academic dialogues), but also for its immediate impact on the viewer. *Multimodality, Cognition, and Experimental Literature* shares such an ideal.

O'Toole's approach stems from Halliday's social systemic functional grammar (1978, 1979, 2004). Systemic Functional Linguistics assumes that all communication is founded on three metafunctions: the ideational/experiential function, the interpersonal function, and the textual function. The ideational/experiential function is concerned with the representation of reality (processes, events) and connected to the linguistic system of transitivity; the interpersonal function is concerned with social relations, in particular those between producers and receivers of texts, and is connected to linguistic mood; finally, the textual function is concerned with the construction of texts, including cohesion. O'Toole modifies these somewhat, making them more pertinent to the semiotic practices of art, sculpture, and painting. For art and sculpture, he speaks of the representational function (ideational/experiential), the modal function (interpersonal), and the compositional function (textual) while he uses Halliday's original functions for architecture. Further to this, he outlines an analytical structure which divides the metafunctions into constituent parts: for instance, the ranks of school/genre, picture, episode, figure, and member are used for painting. The rank scale differs somewhat from genre to genre. On one hand, this can be seen as beneficial, since it recognises that each artistic form communicates in different ways. On the other, it means that O'Toole's approach is not totally uniform and thus not as replicable as might be preferable.

Later developed by O'Halloran (1999, 2000, 2004, 2005), this discourse analysis approach maintains strong links with its Systemic Functional foundations. This is clear in a later article by O'Toole which develops from *The Language of Displayed Art* and focuses on the Sydney Opera House:

> Like a clause in language, a building incorporates Types of Process and their Participants; its specific functions are modified in terms of material, size, colour and texture; and its component elements are organized taxonomically like lexical items in the vocabulary of our language. (2004: 15)

Also cited by Jewitt (2009a: 32) as evidence of the approach's Systemic Functional tradition, this paragraph highlights in explicit terms the predominance of language and of linguistic analytical thinking. Admittedly, O'Toole views architecture as "more similar to language than to the purely contemplative visual arts" (1994: 85), a reason he uses to justify his use of

Halliday's original functions to analyse this genre, yet there is a danger in equating the two. For one thing, it runs the risk of privileging the linguistic as a semiotic system. While O'Toole's analyses throughout *The Language of Displayed Art* are careful in this regard, work in multimodality studies has not escaped this impediment, as I discuss in the next section. Overall, O'Toole's study is compelling. Most significantly, it is an important precursor for multimodality studies, paving the way for later research.

2.3.2   Visual Grammar and Social Semiotics: Gunther Kress and Theo van Leeuwen

The explicit study of multimodality originates with the work of Gunther Kress and Theo van Leeuwen. Kress and van Leeuwen's (1996) *Reading Images: The Grammar of Visual Design* brought multimodality to academic attention, referring to "composite or *multimodal* texts" which they define loosely as "any text whose meanings are realized through more than one semiotic mode" (183). In approaching multimodal texts, ranging from children's drawings to magazine articles and film stills, Kress and van Leeuwen (1996: 5) perceive their own project as an extension of existing semiotic analyses of non-linguistic communications (for instance, see Barthes 1977 [1964], 1977 [1968]; O'Toole 1994). Kress and van Leeuwen also draw upon the work of Charles Sanders Peirce (1940), whose work they see as having been adopted by semiotics as it is "generally taught in the Anglo-Saxon world" (1996: 5).

Most significantly, in *Reading Images*, Kress and van Leeuwen utilise the work of Halliday (1978, 1979, 2004) and Systemic Functional Linguistics. As such, they adopt the concept of 'metafunctions' (Halliday 1978; 2004: 29–31), using the three categories: ideational/experiential, interpersonal, and textual. The metafunctions become structural components in both Kress and van Leeuwen's visual grammar and the organisation of the book. The ideational function allows Kress and van Leeuwen (1996: chaps. 2 and 3) to look at images as either narrational or compositional, building upon Halliday's (2004: 168–305) transitivity system; the interpersonal function is concerned with the relationships between the object or 'participant' in the representation and the viewer (1996: chaps. 4 and 5); while the textual function moves Halliday's focus on language structure to an interest in the composition of the image (1996: chaps. 6 and 7). It is this aspect of Kress and van Leeuwen's work, their use of Systemic Functional Linguistics, which represents the most controversial aspect of their approach as I shall explicate in the following.

Kress and van Leeuwen (1996) clearly state their aim in the following manifesto:

> We seek to be able to look at the whole page as an *integrated* text. Our insistence on drawing comparisons between language and visual

communication stems from this objective. We seek to break down the boundaries between the study of language and the study of images, and we seek as much as possible, to use compatible language, and compatible terminology in speaking about both, for in actual communication the two and indeed many others come together to form integrated texts. (183)

Although implicit in their adoption of Halliday's linguistic framework, I'd like to highlight their "insistence on drawing comparisons between language and visual communication". This relationship of comparison is clearly referenced in the title of their work, through the word *grammar*. Kress and van Leeuwen discuss the formal character of grammar and the word's etymology, but as they themselves acknowledge, their interest in grammar and language is in a general sense; that is, grammar as "an inventory of elements and rules underlying culture-specific verbal [or visual] communication" (1996: 3). Nevertheless, while Kress and van Leeuwen do differentiate language and image as separate systems of communication, when investigating multimodal texts, particularly the images involved, their interpretation is often dependent upon linguistic structures. This is evident in their application of 'given and new' to issues of layout and their comparison of visual vectors to action verbs in language.

The concepts and structures of Systemic Functional Linguistics, such as those mentioned earlier, do not transfer as adequately to images as Kress and van Leeuwen imply. For instance, taking the former topic, Kress and van Leeuwen employ Halliday's (2004: 87–94) notion of information structure, whereby sentences typically present the given information in the first position of a clause (the theme) and the new information in the second part (rheme). When applying this to images and multimodal compositions, Kress and van Leeuwen (1996: 186–192) suggest that what is represented on the left of the image is given and what is positioned on the right is new information. Relating their conceptualisation of given and new with Halliday's, they argue:

> there is a close similarity between *sequential* information structure in language and *horizontal* structure in visual composition, and this attests to the existence of deeper, more abstract coding orientations which find their expression differently in semiotic modes. (1996: 188)

While I would be keen to find 'deeper, more abstract coding orientations', a phrase suggestive of underlying cognitive process, between verbal and visual meaning-making, Kress and van Leeuwen are too quick to find similarity between the two forms in terms of information structure. In doing so, they do not consider how the transfer of conceptual structure (from linguistic formation to image composition) might be problematic.

To my mind, Kress and van Leeuwen overlook the issue of reading paths. Linguistic structure has a different relationship with time and space to the image: sentences, in Western cultures, are necessarily read from left to right, from given to new, whereas images do not impose an equivalent and compulsory structural linearity. Admittedly, Kress and van Leeuwen include the notion of salience, visual foregrounding, as a signal of new information in support of their formulation of visual and multimodal given and new. Nevertheless, it is evident that Kress and van Leeuwen employ linguistic concepts that are not always seamlessly applicable to images, thus resulting in some unsubstantiated claims for the success of their 'visual grammar'.

Kress and van Leeuwen's (1996) work has come under attack for its reliance upon linguistic paradigms (see Forceville 1999; Bateman 2008). Admittedly, the authors counter such criticism in the preface to the second edition of the book, suggesting that although Halliday's work was a starting-point for their study, they "attempted to use its general semiotic aspects rather than its specific linguistically focused features as the grounding for our grammar" (2006 [1996]: vii). Although Kress and van Leeuwen's response is sensible, *Reading Images* has repeatedly been found at fault on two main issues. Firstly, and as mentioned, language and image are treated analytically as corresponding structures, and, secondly, unlike in linguistics proper, their visual grammar has not been subjected to any form of empirical testing with which to support its claims. Indeed, Forceville (1999) and Bateman (2008) note both these weaknesses. My own reflections on *Reading Images* are consistent with their views. Additionally, it strikes me that despite wishing to "break down the boundaries between the study of language and the study of images" (Kress and van Leeuwen 1996: 183), Kress and van Leeuwen's investigations of multimodal texts remain focused upon visual elements, including the integration of text but *within* issues of layout. When their attention turns to the written word it is in terms of positioning, colour, typography, content, rather than upon linguistic structures or the poetics of reading and meaning.

Of course, in *Reading Images* their focus is the visual; yet, if meaning is created by integrative and multimodal means, any analysis of those meanings should be similarly integrative as well as able to account for such composite meaning-making. Most significantly in light of the aims of this book, from a cognitive point of view, and to quote Forceville in his review of the book, Kress and van Leeuwen "compare visual structures too much with surface language instead of with the mental processes of which both surface language and images are the perceptible manifestations" (1999: 170). Despite such drawbacks, it cannot be denied that *Reading Images* maintains a central place in the canon of multimodality studies and deservedly so. It is a pioneering work that, despite building upon existing work in semiotics, launched 'multimodality' as an academic research enterprise.

In a later co-authored book (2001) *Multimodal Discourse: The Modes and Media of Contemporary Communication*, it is the social-semiotic aspect of multimodality that becomes Kress and van Leeuwen's focus. Here, the authors advocate "a view of multimodality in which common semiotic principles operate in and across different modes" (2001: 2). The use of the word 'common' is disconcerting since in *Reading Images* they were careful to stress the status of verbal and visual communication as two independent code systems.

In *Multimodal Discourse*, Kress and van Leeuwen move away from the notion of grammar to consider what multimodality comprises using four domains of practice: Discourse (socially constructed knowledge), Design (the conceptual aspect of expression, including the combination of semiotic modes), Production (the actual material used), and Distribution (the way in which the product reaches the public). In doing so, they attend to classroom teaching, clothing, sound symbolism, and music. By acknowledging the production processes and technologies of multimodal texts, *Multimodal Discourse* demonstrates the breadth of focus in multimodal studies and presents a useful development for the study of multimodality in an increasingly digital age.

One of the most recent books on multimodality is Kress's (2010) *Multimodality: A Social Semiotic Approach to Contemporary Communication*. This work has much more in common with *Multimodal Discourse* than *Reading Images* since, as the subtitle suggests, it too foregrounds the social-semiotic approach. It concentrates on texts, from street signs and children's drawings to kitchen implements, in sociological contexts of use, and in particular how the modal resources of a given text or object are used. In both Kress and van Leeuwen's *Multimodal Discourse* and Kress's *Multimodality*, the multimodal texts of interest become more socially grounded; they are more obviously socially shared artefacts, and therefore less relevant to this book, the interest of which is focused in the literary arts.

2.3.3   Transcription: Anthony Baldry and Paul Thibault

Baldry and Thibault's (2006) *Multimodal Transcription and Text Analysis* can be viewed as both a departure from and an extension of Kress and van Leeuwen's work. Baldry and Thibault begin by articulating, "The term *multimodality* covers a diversity of perspectives, ways of thinking and possible approaches. It is not a single principle or approach. It is a *multipurpose* toolkit, not a single tool for a single purpose" (2006: xv). Baldry and Thibault's acknowledgement that there are many potential avenues for the analysis of multimodal texts is encouraging. However, Baldry and Thibault's methodology, like that of their predecessors, is also drawn from Systemic Functional Linguistics, although such frameworks are seen in a new light when applied to multimodality to "encourage a critical rethinking and reformulation" (2006: 1) of text, society, and traditional critical terminology. This revision of Systemic Functional Linguistics forms the main theoretical body of Baldry and Thibault's work. In addition they draw on Peircean Semiotics (1940) in much the same way as Kress and van Leeuwen (1996).

Baldry and Thibault's (2006) book is structured with an introduction that sets out their 'toolkit', followed by genre-specific chapters: the printed page, webpage, film texts. However, the printed texts under discussion are scientific textbooks, and as such generically very different from the focus of this book—multimodal fiction. In the introduction, Baldry and Thibault supply two significant ideas: the resource integration principle and the meaning compression principle (2006: 18–19). The former, the authors suggest, "lies at the heart of multimodality" (2006: 4) and refers to the fact that meaning is created through the interrelations of modes within a given text. The latter, the meaning compression principle, "refers to the effect of the interaction of smaller-scale semiotic resources on higher scalar levels where meaning is observed and interpreted" (19).

Baldry and Thibault put forward 'cluster analysis' (2006: 31) as a tool for understanding the way in which these smaller-scale resources make meaning and how they work within the text as a whole (see section 2.5 of this chapter for more details of cluster analysis). Bateman (2008) has criticised this aspect of Baldry and Thibault's (2006) approach since, as he sees it, the authors do not suggest *how* clusters can be identified. In other words, identifying clusters is reliant upon the analyst's intuition. To my mind, cluster analysis is a useful approach to multimodal texts, allowing analysts to look at multimodal meaning-making at both micro and macro levels, and in a flexible way.

To resolve the potential drawback of cluster analysis, that is, the lack of a rigorous means of identifying each cluster, the approach to multimodality taken in this book relies upon the structures of visual perception (see section 3.4.3 of Chapter 3). Understanding the faculties of visual perception (Gordon 1997; Haber and Hershenson 1973; Posner and Raichle 1997; Styles 1997), such as the ways in which features of colour and size capture attention or how similarities between objects enable perceptual grouping, allows for greater specificity in cluster analysis.

From the perspective of studying multimodal literature and multimodal literary experience, a weakness in using Baldry and Thibault's (2006) work is their emphasis on transcription, which through the course of their analyses often becomes a case of cataloguing the multimodal make-up of a text. As such, it is in places both clinical and overzealous in its undertaking to identify the semiotic resources at work, resulting in a lack of consideration of the effect such multimodal semiosis has upon the recipient. Although Bateman doesn't explicitly cite this as a flaw in Baldry and Thibault's work, his explanation is telling: "Transcription entails providing more or less sophisticated 'labelling', or description, of each element found in a multimodal artefact" (2008: 53). Indeed, Baldry and Thibault (2006) are more interested in the structure of the texts, how they make meaning through the combination of semiotic modes, than they are in how those meanings are understood, processed, and experienced. Nevertheless, it must be acknowledged that such transcription may be a necessary process in approaching other forms of multimodal texts, such as film and human interaction.

From a cognitive standpoint then, *Multimodal Transcription*, like Kress and van Leeuwen's work, does not account for the reception of multimodal texts. This weakness, emerging as applicable to both Kress and van Leeuwen's (1996, 2001) and Baldry and Thibault's (2006) work, is a crucial justification for the development of a cognitive approach to multimodality. The application of cognitive poetics to multimodal literature that is central to this book therefore is an essential undertaking. This book augments the understanding of multimodality by relating the surface structure of multimodal texts to perceived cognitive effect.

2.3.4   The GeM Model: John A. Bateman

Bateman's (2008) *Multimodality and Genre: A Foundation for the Systematic Analysis of Multimodal Documents* places itself within the Systemic Functional tradition, or what Bateman calls 'multimodal linguistics'. However, despite this connection, Bateman is critical of the approaches of both Kress and van Leeuwen and Baldry and Thibault, principally because of a lack of empirical provability. To counter this weakness, Bateman integrates corpus-based linguistics into multimodal study and specifically into what he calls the 'GeM Model', a model of 'Genre and Multimodality', which "defines several layers of description for multimodal documents" (2008: 15). These layers are the base (basic elements on the page), layout (how the page is spatially composed); rhetoric (relationships between the basic elements and what they communicate); navigation (elements involved in the 'movement' around the page and how it is used); and genre (the semantic patterns that enable texts to be grouped by type) (2008: 108). In the course of the book, Bateman suggests that such an approach provides a foundation for developing a corpus of multimodal documents and thus advances empirical work on multimodal meaning-making. This is indeed the case, allowing Bateman to show his GeM Model as a replicable analytical method.

Bateman's work is more reception-sensitive than previous research in multimodality since in his account of how a multimodal page is construed, Bateman (2008: 21–106) identifies four perspectives from interpretation and visual perception (reception-based) to empirical processing methods and production (text-based). However, perception and interpretation are a lesser, if not often absent, feature of GeM analyses. Moreover, by breaking a multimodal composition into layers, the GeM Model understands multimodal texts in a very artificial way. That is, readers do not process multimodal texts according to a division of information into base, layout, rhetoric, navigation, and genre. While the identification of these layers enables Bateman as an analyst to dissect and examine multimodal documents in a systematic manner, it is antithetical to readers' real experiences of interpreting those multimodal texts. Indeed, cognitive and neuroscientific studies are increasingly reaching the conclusion that cognitive processing is integrative as opposed to isolated in its treatment of different phenomena (for instance, see my discussions of multisensory perception in section 3.4.1 and embodiment in section 3.4.2 of Chapter 3).

For example, in *Multimodality and Genre*, Bateman's analytical model is somewhat depleted in dealing with the navigational layer (2008: 269–271). Defined as "the elements that contribute explicitly to navigation and access in the page, supporting 'movement' around the document in various ways" (2008: 108), the navigational layer ultimately identifies 'pointers', items such as hypertextual nodes or visual vectors, that direct the reader/user towards certain action and/or eye movement around the document. As such, the navigational pointers are not related to the meaning production of other layers. Moreover, the actual movement (physical or visual) experienced by the reader/user in relation to the text is not brought into consideration in the GeM Model.

The central problem of the GeM Model for an analyst primarily interested in the cognitive understanding of multimodality is, therefore, that it produces a somewhat mechanical analysis that fails to recognise the active and cognitively sophisticated potentials of the recipient/user of multimodal documents. Additionally, another drawback of Bateman's book with regards to this study is that Bateman sensibly delimits his generic focus to page-based static multimodal texts. These are all documents in that they are fact-based (e.g. instruction guides, encyclopaedic entries, information booklets), and therefore notably different from multimodal novels. As such, while Bateman's work is significant in the field of multimodality studies, it will not feature in the critical synthesis adopted in this book.

2.3.5. Multimedia: Anne Cranny-Francis

In *Multimedia: Texts and Contexts*, Cranny-Francis (2005) presents a study of multi*media* texts. Although she does not explicitly differentiate her vocabulary, multi*modal*ity and multi*medial*ity are not equivalent terms. Indeed, Kress and van Leeuwen make this clear when they state, "multimodality and multimediality are not quite the same thing" (2001: 67). Multimodality is a broader phenomenon, related to the coexistence of semiotic modes, whereas multimediality is created through the combination of media technologies. Cranny-Francis states:

> This study focuses on the kinds of cultural literacies employed in multimedia artefacts—whether they are digitally-generated multimedia (such as web sites and computer games) or composite forms of multimedia texts (such as films, museum exhibitions, performance art). Both forms are essentially multi-modal in that they employ different

modalities of text—writing, visuals, sound, movement, spatiality—in their construction and meaning-making. (2005: 2)

Although Cranny-Francis is correct in categorising multimedia texts as multimodal, clarification of terms would have been helpful here, particularly for readers not familiar with multimodal or multimedia study.

Cranny-Francis' approach differs from existing work since, rather than drawing principally on the multimodal Systemic Functional tradition, Cranny-Francis adapts ideas from critical theory, particularly Bakhtin's (1981, 1984) notion of heteroglossia, Kristeva's (1986) related conception of 'intertextuality', and concepts of postmodernism (e.g. Baudrillard 2001; de Certeau 1984). *Multimedia*, therefore, presents a refreshing take on multimodal, multimedia objects, though this is not to say it is without problems.

The breadth of Cranny-Francis' critical influences often results in both the lack of a replicable approach and a lack of consistency in her analyses; in her chapter on visuals for instance, she moves from using the ideas of Bakhtin (1981, 1984) and Foucault (1977) to characterise multimedia artefacts as socially and culturally constructed to examining compositions in terms of information structure. Furthermore, neither Cranny-Francis' use of critical theory nor her use of multimodal linguistics serves to illuminate her objects of study. Rather, critical theory serves more as descriptive cultural grounding, while she takes on Kress and van Leeuwen's (1996) employment of information structure and vectors without question, resulting in further descriptive accounts. Thus, the interpretive capacity of Cranny-Francis' work is significantly reduced.

An aspect of Cranny-Francis' work I do endorse is her continual emphasis upon the interactivity of the user with the multimedia artefact. To my thinking, this is a significant aspect of multimodality, as will become clear through the course of the book. Cranny-Francis' interest in textual interaction results in a chapter dedicated to movement. Regrettably, although there is mention of 'embodiment', the term isn't used in a clear and/or cognitively substantiated way. Moreover, since *Multimedia* is concerned with the technological, Cranny-Francis deals with the interaction of a user with computer and web-based texts. Thus, such interactive experiences cannot be drawn upon for direct comparison or support in the analysis of embodied and/or interactive experience with multimodal printed narratives.

2.3.6   Typography

In the introduction to his (2005) article on typographic meaning, van Leeuwen speaks of *Reading Images*, the book he co-authored with Kress, resigning:

this work did not touch at all on typography, and it is only in the last few years that I have come to realize what a fundamental oversight this was, because clearly, it is above all and in the first place through calligraphy and typography that visual communication and writing form an inseparable unity. (2005: 138)

Van Leeuwen's words are admirably honest here, expressing a regret at having neglected typography. Indeed, "[t]ypographic communication is *multimodal*" (van Leeuwen 2005: 141; original emphasis), and as such, van Leeuwen calls for a semiotics of typography, a systematic understanding of the way typographic forms express meaning.

Van Leeuwen begins this project in a (2006) article, 'Towards a Semiotics of Typography'. Continuing the social-semiotic approach to multimodality, van Leeuwen maintains the centrality of the three metafunctions. More importantly, however, he develops a list of distinctive typographical features, creating what he calls a kind of 'typographical profile'. These features are: weight (how bold or heavy a type-face is), expansion (how narrow or wide a type-face is), slope (how upright or slanted a type-face is), curvature (how angular or rounded a type-face is), connectivity (how connected or unconnected the letters of a type-face are), orientation (how tall or flat a type-face is), regularity (how regular or irregular a type-face is), and flourishes (whether type-faces have flourishes and/or additions). Machin (2007: 93) astutely points out that that these features work in combination with other semiotic dimensions such as colour, and their meaning potential is only realised when used and considered within a specific context.

Highlighting that van Leeuwen describes his own work as 'a first attempt at identifying the distinctive features of typography' (2006: 147), Nørgaard (2009b) develops van Leeuwen's project by disregarding flourishes and adding colour to the features list. Nørgaard also suggests three categories for the way in which typography creates meaning. These can be seen in Figure 2.1, the top half of which reproduces Nørgaard's (2009b: 145) own table, while the three semiotic principles of typographical meaning have been appended on the bottom half, definitions of which have been provided. However, it is worth clarifying the semiotic principles. Iconic meaning is closely linked to what in semiotics and stylistics is called iconicity, that is, the resemblance of form to meaning. Van Leeuwen (2005: 140), for instance, talks of the way in which roundness can be interpreted as 'organic' or natural', while Nørgaard (2009b: 150) gives the example of capitalisation being used to suggest shouting. Thus, the latter example shows the "iconic use of visual salience to create the meaning of sonic salience" (2009b: 150). With iconic meaning, it is important to remember that the relationship between form and meaning is not arbitrary but alters in different contexts. As such iconic meaning is the result of perceived similarity on the part of the reader-viewer.

The distinctive features of letterforms:

- **Weight:** bold ↔ light
- **Expansion:** condensed/narrow ↔ expanded/wide
- **Slope:** sloping ↔ upright
- **Curvature:** angular ↔ rounded
- **Connectivity:** connected ↔ disconnected
- **Orientation:** horizontal orientation ↔ vertical orientation
- **Regularity:** regular ↔ irregular
- **Colour**

The three semiotic principles of typographical meaning

- **Icon:** typeface visually resembles its meaning (iconicity)
- **Index:** typeface visually resembles its own mode of production
- **Discursive Import:** typeface associated with a particular media context is imported into a different context in which it did not previously belong (intermedial transposition)

Figure 2.1   Typographical meaning (based on Nørgaard 2009b).

Indexical meaning bears a visual relationship to its mode of production. Nørgaard suggests that one of the most straight-forward examples of typographic index is the use of facsimile reproductions in books since a facsimile directly "invokes the material origin of its coming into being" (2009b: 148). A second, more complex, example provided by Nørgaard is the use of handwriting in Foer's *Extremely Loud & Incredibly Close* (see section 6.3.3. of Chapter 6 in this volume for a discussion of the episode in question) in which she states that the "graphological signifiers function as fictional indices of the people who produced them" (2009b: 149). It is the fictionality of the literary context which complicates this second example. Nevertheless, there is a clear reference to the fictional mode of production in the form of handwriting.

The final semiotic principle is discursive import, in which a type-face associated with a particular media context is imported into a different context in which it did not previously belong. This category often also involves indexical meaning, since the type-face suggests its own mode or media of production, be it fictional or otherwise. In intermediality studies, a related field to multimodality (for instance, see connections made between the two in Elleström 2010; Gibbons 2010), this is known as 'intermedial transposition' whereby one media is represented in another media form. Nørgaard suggests that the most prototypical example of discursive import in literature is the use of the Courier type-face. The typewritten look of the Courier font indexically suggests its creation by a typewriter (though this is an illusory index since it was not in fact produced on a typewriter). Since in contemporary book production, typewriters are not in use, when used in literature to signify typewritten text, it provides an example of discursive import. This is the case in Danielewski's use of the Courier font in *House of Leaves*, which I discuss briefly in the introduction to Chapter 4.

This book follows Nørgaard's (2009b) system for understanding typographic communication, in particular because the system has been adapted specifically for an understanding of multimodal typographic meaning-making within literary contexts. As mentioned, typographical communication is discussed briefly in reference to Danielewski's *House of Leaves* in Chapter 4. Typography is a stronger focus, though, in Chapter 7 on Rawle's novel *Woman's World*.

2.4 MULTIMODALITY: CRITICISM AND CONTRIBUTION

The previous survey of multimodality has so far reviewed principal book-length studies in the field and discussed recent work on typography. While aspects of these works have been criticised, they are nevertheless important studies with constructive insights into multimodal practice. O'Toole (1994), Kress and van Leeuwen (1996, 2001), Baldry and Thibault (2006), Bateman (2008), and Cranny-Francis (2005) to a lesser extent, all provide approaches rooted in Systemic Functional Linguistics. A number of further investigations in multimodality reflect this trend, most of which are collected in edited volumes and conference proceedings (Baldry 2000; Carlsson, Løland, and Malmgren 2005; Jewitt 2009d; Levine and Scollon 2004; O'Halloran 2004; Royce and Bowcher 2007; Ventola, Charles, and Kaltenbacher 2004). There are also introductory texts: Machin (2007) has written an account of Kress and van Leeuwen's work on multimodality, while Burn and Parker (2003) follow Kress and van Leeuwen (2001) in their social-semiotic approach, providing new analyses to exemplify existing methods. Despite the predominant Systemic approach, multimodality is an expanding field, with work being undertaken in the area of literacy and education (Jewitt 2005; Jewitt and Kress 2003; Kress 2003; Kress et al. 2001) as well as everyday interaction (Adolphs and Carter 2007; Herman 2004, 2009c; Norris 2004) and corpus studies (Baldry 2005, 2007; Baldry and Taylor 2004; Baldry and Thibault 2001; Knight and Adolphs 2008).

Throughout this review, the Systemic Functional approach has been criticised for its dependence upon linguistic structures. Such reliance upon linguistic structure runs the risk of exacting monomodal analyses of multimodal texts. Moreover, such treatment conflates verbal and visual modes, dealing with the two as identical in their meaning-making strategies. While I do believe underlying factors of similarity can be ascertained between word and image, such factors are concerned with perceptual and cognitive process and are thus not accounted for in existing approaches. Another consequence of what Bateman (2008) calls 'multimodal linguistics' is that because it is so committed to identifying the semiotic resources at work in multimodal texts, transcribing and dissecting them in the process, it concentrates on the textual formation of multimodality at the expense of gaining an understanding of the user's and/or recipient's experience of those modal combinations.

My own approach to multimodality seeks to investigate the cognitive implications of such composite texts. This is the primary concern of this book, which explores multimodal meaning-making in the specific context of literary fiction. Little work has been done in this arena, with only a few articles existing such as the essays by Nørgaard (2009a) and myself (Gibbons 2009, 2010, 2012) to fill this gap in the field.

2.5 TOWARDS A MULTIMODAL COGNITIVE POETICS: TOOLS FROM VISUAL COMMUNICATION AND MULTIMODAL STUDIES

In this chapter, I have reviewed work in multimodality studies, showing that a predominant approach prevails which uses Systemic Functional Linguistics. While this is a rigorous linguistic methodology, it was suggested that the application of frameworks designed for language were often not always suited or most beneficial in the exploration of visual and/or multimodal texts. Moreover, the customary use of Systemic Functional Linguistics generally results in a privileging of the surface structure of the text, and a consequent neglect of the cognitive and experiential dimension of multimodal experience for the user/reader/viewer.

In the next chapter, I introduce cognitive poetics before detailing important frameworks to be used in a critical synthesis, which I call *multimodal cognitive poetics*. Multimodal cognitive poetics is driven by the cognitive approach but is crucially supported by tools from visual communication and multimodality studies. Visual Communication (Lester 2000; van Leeuwen and Jewitt 2001) is concerned with how messages are communicated through images. It looks at patterns, shapes, layout, etc., analysing these forms in terms of how successful they are at controlling/manipulating the eye and therefore getting the viewer to behave in a predictable manner as dictated by the designer. Consequently, visual communication plays a significant role in the media and marketing communication industries. I utilise three main devices from visual communication, all used in multi-modal analysis. These are cluster analysis, vectors, and reading paths.

Cluster analysis is a method used by Baldry and Thibault (2006) to enable the examination of multimodal texts at both a micro level and on a larger scale. A cluster refers to "a local grouping of items" (Baldry and Thibault 2006: 31). Thus, clusters alter as the viewer/reader's attention alters, and subsequently enable an analyst to perceive both the impact of smaller-scale clusters and the combined cluster relationships within the visual field. Since the continuity of the reading process is not guaranteed, particularly when the visual dynamic of a text makes a significant contribution to meaning-making, Baldry and Thibault use the term 'cluster hopping' (2006: 26) to signal the eyes' movement between and across clusters. To extend this idea and relate it to figure and ground, in cluster hopping, most notably from clusters at a local or micro level to the cluster which represents the entire visual selection under analysis, the eye is enacting the dynamism of the fig-ure-ground process, executing the ability to flip perception from one view to another unconsciously and at will. Baldry and Thibault find the term 'cluster hopping' particularly useful when the eyes' movement breaks with a linear reading path.

A reading path (Baldry and Thibault 2006; Kress and van Leeuwen 1996) simply describes the eyes' movement around a text, so in the majority of novels the reading path is linear—left to right and top to bottom. Read-ing paths can be influenced by vectors (Baldry and Thibault 2006; Kress and van Leeuwen 1996). These are elements in a text that influence the eyes' movement and reading path. Thus, vectors harness such properties as dynamic force, directionality, and orientation (see Baldry and Thibault 2006: 35–36).

While these three devices will be central to my analyses, other aspects of visual communication and multimodality studies may become impor-tant. For instance, in Chapter 6 I refer to Kress and van Leeuwen's (1996) concept of 'naturalistic coding orientation' when analysing the opening images to *Extremely Loud & Incredibly Close*. In such instances, new frameworks are introduced as they arise in analysis. Details of important cognitive frameworks to be employed within multimodal cognitive poetics are provided in the next chapter.

3 Towards a Multimodal Cognitive Poetics

3.1 WHAT IS COGNITIVE POETICS?

A recent 'cognitive turn' in literary studies has been noted by many scholars, and cognitive poetics is part of this movement. Cognitive poetics is a discipline in its infancy, as Stockwell attests when he refers to it as "one of the first disciplines to have emerged within the internet age" (2005: 267). It draws on a range of findings from disciplines within the cognitive sciences: cognitive psychology, cognitive science and neuroscience, and cognitive linguistics. Cognitive poetics is also strongly affiliated with stylistics. Stylistics, as a literary linguistic subject, concentrates upon the formal features of language and how these features are used within literary texts. Building upon this, cognitive poetics seeks to look at form, style, and language in literature in context but through the conviction that structures of language and literary devices are expressions and materialisations of patterns of human thought. Thus, as Gavins and Steen put it, literature is "a specific form of human experience" (2003b: 1) and as such its study may reveal to us the cognitive practices by which we not only read literature but perceive and understand the world.

A primary concern of this book is not simply how novels create meaning through their formal modal synthesis, but also how these modal integrations are processed, understood, and experienced by readers. As a reception-sensitive discipline, cognitive poetics offers a dynamic account of reading, which focuses not simply on "the artifice of the literary text alone, or the reader alone, but the more natural process of reading when one is engaged with the other" (Stockwell 2002a: 2).

3.2 FRAMEWORKS IN COGNITIVE POETICS

In the textbook *Cognitive Poetics: An Introduction* (2002a), Stockwell, a leading figure in cognitive poetics, identifies areas of cognitive research to represent the discipline. Along with its companion volume (Gavins and Steen 2003a) *Cognitive Poetics in Practice*, Stockwell's introduction represents cognitive poetics in its then-current state and proposes future directions. As Stockwell predicted, some of the areas he identified have flourished, while others seem of less cognitive importance.

Today, cognitive poetics continues to encompass an array of cognitive approaches, which as I see it (drawing on but not totally in keeping with Stockwell) are:

- figure and ground
- prototypes
- schema poetics
- cognitive grammar
- cognitive deixis
- conceptual metaphor
- conceptual integration
- Text World Theory
- contextual frame theory
- more broadly, cognitive narratology

A further development is the psychological focus upon personal and emotional investment in literary narrative, in the forms of projection, self-implication, and emotional response. Detailing each and every framework would take this chapter too far afield. However, I would like to draw attention to the cognitive-poetic frameworks that will be of most use in the task of understanding multimodal literary experience through a cognitive lens. While these will be introduced here, their application in cognitive-poetic analysis in Chapters 4, 5, 6, and 7 will display their application and reveal their importance for a multimodal cognitive poetics.

3.2.1 Figure and Ground

Figure and ground was first observed by Danish psychologist Rubin (1958 [1915]), later charted by Gestalt psychologists (Beardslee and Wetheimer 1958; Koffka 1935; Köhler 1947; Wertheimer 1958 [1923]), and is a phenomenon of visual perception. In section 3.4.3, I provide a detailed outline of figure and ground in visual perception and attention studies. However, a brief definition is required here in order to explain the framework in cognitive poetics: figure and ground is the division of attention into an object of focus, the figure, and the ground upon which it is set. Figure and ground has been developed in cognitive linguistics and in cognitive poetics. In the literary environment, figure and ground is most closely related to the stylistic study of foregrounding (van Peer 1986) and thus entails deviation (disruptions in readers' literary and/or linguistic expectations) and parallelism (patterns of equivalence and/or regularity created through devices such as repetition and alliteration) for the creation of dominant textual features.

Stockwell (2002a, 2003) extends the salient and figure-constituting elements in literary texts from those considered in foregrounding to more visually oriented aspects, such as colour. These catch reader attention and are thus called *attractors*. In textual terms, attractors are characterised by newness or 'currency' (Stockwell 2004). That is, by a continual rejuvenation of literary patterns, a creative magnetism that obtains and replenishes reader interest. Stylistically, they are prototypically expressed in active verbs since such linguistically referenced action instils the figure with dynamic motion, which is thus attention grabbing. Attractors may also be created by items that are adjectivised within the field of the narrator/speaker, thus attracting attention by being the focus of the narrative.

Stockwell considers visual figuration through linguistic reference. For instance, in his (2003: 23) remarks on bright and dark imagery in André Breton's poem 'They Tell Me . . .' images of brightness, like the 'great peak smoking with snow / Under a second sun', are seen to produce a foregrounding effect. While cognitive poetics has not explored figure and ground in a literal visual sense, since it takes its cue from visual perception, the apparatus is available (see section 3.4.3 for further details). Moreover, the visual basis of figure and ground as a cognitive-poetic framework makes it an essential element of multimodal cognitive poetics since it is applicable to both verbal and visual communication.

3.2.2   Cognitive Grammar

Cognitive grammar is a framework that seeks to model the cognitive mechanisms and mental representations inherent in linguistic structures. As such grammatical word classes are seen to have a conceptual basis (see Evans and Green 2006 for a detailed and accessible introduction). Cognitive grammar is a cognitive linguistic framework developed by Langacker (1987, 1991, 2008). Significantly, cognitive grammar also treats figure and ground. In cognitive linguistics, figure and ground relations are often made evident through locative relationships, which can be understood as 'image schemas'. Image schemas are embodied mental representations for idealised cognitive models, such as journey or container, and are often expressed through spatial prepositions. Cognitive grammar provides an account of how figure and ground are treated in language. The linguistic equivalents of figure and ground are trajector and landmark respectively, and these are aspects of cognitive grammar's theory of *profiling*.

The best way to elucidate the profiling system is to examine it in practice. Consider the following sentence:

Alison sits on a chair

Alison, as a human subject, is the figure, the linguistic *trajector*, positioned on top of the chair, which is the *landmark*. There is necessarily a relational rapport between trajector and landmark, through a *path* which connects them as an image schema. An image schema is a mental representation linked to bodily experience. In this instance, the path is expressed through the preposition on.

It is worth mentioning that image schemas are pictorial by nature, however abstract, and are often granted pictorial representation in analysis (Langacker 1987). To demonstrate, both of the pictorial representations below symbolise 'Alison sits on a chair'.

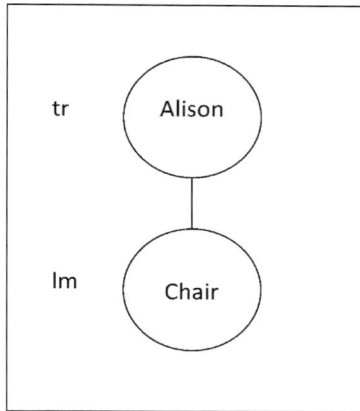

Figure 3.1a   Relational nature of profiling: ON.

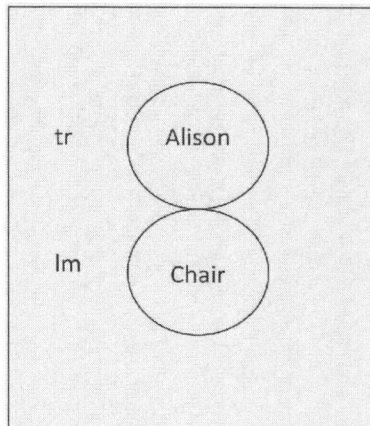

Figure 3.1b   Physical contact of profiling: ON.

Figure 3.1a highlights the relational nature of the profile while Figure 3.1b shows that Alison is in physical contact with the chair.

Profiling is, of course, not the only framework within cognitive grammar (though detailing the entirety of cognitive grammar would merit a study in its own right). It is, however, the most significant in this study due to its relationship to figure and ground and image schemas. Where other aspects of cognitive grammar become relevant in textual analyses of this book, they are explained as they are used.

3.2.3 Cognitive Deixis

Cognitive deixis was first introduced in an edited volume by Duchan, Bruder, and Hewitt (1995). It stems from traditional linguistic studies of deixis, whereby linguistic elements encode a language user's position in the world. Pronouns, demonstratives, and adverbs are representative deictic elements. These linguistic items are typical, in that they point towards their meanings. As Rauh articulates, the name hints at "the function of deictic expressions to *point at* their referents" (Rauh 1983: 10; original emphasis). For instance, the pronoun 'you' changes meaning in context depending on the speaker's addressee.

'I', 'here', and 'now' represent the 'origo', the zero-point or deictic centre of perceptual, spatial, and temporal deixis respectively, and show the egocentric nature of deixis. However, cognitive deixis has developed the concepts of deictic projection and deictic shift to account for the human imaginative capacity to cognitively relocate into another projected deictic stance (Galbraith 1995; Stockwell 2002a). For instance, when reading literary texts readers are able to experience the narrative from the perspective of a character. Such deictic shift is not a stable process throughout a narrative. Indeed, textual cues may cause readers to *shift* their deictic orientation. Galbraith suggests two forms of deictic shift:

> One may emerge from one deictic plane to a higher or more basic onto-logical-level plane, as in awakening from a dream or looking up from reading. Borrowing a computer science term, I call this process *pop-ping*. Conversely, one may submerge from a basic level to a less available deictic plane, such as episodic memory (known as "flashback" in fiction), fictional story world (this may be a fiction within the fiction), or fantasy. I call this submersion a *push*, the term paired with *pop* in computer science. (1995: 47; original emphasis and capitals)

McIntyre (2006: 111) has been critical of the terms *push* and *pop*, viewing them as inaccurate metaphors, rather than as stylistic tools. He also suggests, "More explanation is needed to distinguish between shifting between the real and the fictional world and shifting between deictic fields" (2006: 111). Given that this book is concerned with creating a cognitive approach to multimodality, this is not the place to engage in a critical exposition of terminology. Nevertheless, I do broadly agree with McIntyre's concerns. While deictic positioning is not the central concern of this study, I explore how the multimodality of my chosen texts influences a reader's deictic relationship with and in the narrative.

3.2.4   Conceptual Metaphor

Conceptual Metaphor Theory has been a substantial research area in cognitive science, linguistics, and poetics since the 1980s, suggesting that human conceptual patterns are metaphorical by nature. As Lakoff and Johnson phrase it, "metaphor is not just a matter of language, that is, of mere words. [. . .] on the contrary, human thought processes are largely metaphorical" (1980: 6; original emphasis). Researchers (Lakoff 1987; Lakoff and Johnson 1980, 1999; Lakoff and Turner 1989; Steen 1994; Turner 2000 [1987]) working in this area have sought to catalogue and provide evidence for the pervasiveness of metaphor in the structuring of thought. As such, they find that some metaphors are so pervasive that they become naturalised in cultural understanding, and are thus 'dead' or constitutive metaphors.

A central example of a conceptual metaphor is life is a journey, which can be gleaned from everyday surface expressions such as 'We're at a crossroads'. In conceptual metaphor, abstract domains, known as the target, are understood by reference to a basic-level domain, known as the source. The source is basic in that it is often more familiar and grounded in bodily and/or everyday experience. In life is a journey, the understanding of the source journey is mapped onto the target life. Cognitive-poetic accounts explore how conceptual metaphors are meaningful in the context of literary and poetic experience.

Conceptual metaphor is particularly suited to participation in multimodal cognitive poetics since, as it underlies the way in which human thought is organised, conceptual metaphors should be articulated and perceptible within all forms of human representation. Indeed, Crisp states, "Metaphor can be expressed in different modalities because its underlying reality is conceptual and so not confined to any single mode of expression" (2003: 100). Notably, recent work has started to move in this direction as I discuss in the next section.

3.2.5   Multimodal Metaphor

Forceville's work on pictorial metaphor (1994, 1995, 1996, 2000, 2002) and multimodal metaphor (2006, 2007) significantly opens up the study of conceptual metaphors, by attending to them in multimodal contexts. Forceville's own account of multimodal metaphor develops from Conceptual Metaphor Theory and more directly from Black's (1962, 1979) interaction theory of metaphor. More recently, Forceville has co-edited with Urios-Aparisi a collection of essays in the (2009) book *Multimodal Metaphor*. The book is organised into seven clusters, dividing the chapters by genre: advertising (cluster II); political cartoons (cluster III); comics, manga, and animation (cluster IV); spoken language (cluster V); music and sound (cluster VI); and film (cluster VII); with the opening section creating the foundations for the studies which follow. The first section features a position paper by Forceville which is a reprint of a previously published essay (2006) used to provide coherence and establish an understanding of multimodal metaphor. The editors explain in their introduction, "it was suggested that all contributors take their cue for the definition of multimodal metaphor from the position paper by Forceville (2006/this volume) or else they make clear why and how they deviated from it" (2009: 5). Forceville provides the following definition: "multimodal metaphors are metaphors whose target and source are each represented exclusively or predominantly in different modes" (2009: 24). Thus, for a metaphor to be classed as multimodal, the source domain must be encoded in one mode (e.g. a visual element) while the target domain must be encoded by another (e.g. a verbal form).

To my mind, two important issues are raised by this definition. The first of which concerns what qualifies as a conceptual metaphor. Forceville advocates the relevance of concrete is concrete metaphors in pictorial and multimodal forms (2009: 27–8). Earlier in the same chapter, he provides a fictive example of a visual/multimodal manifestation of the metaphor cat is elephant (further examples of concrete is concrete occur in subsequent chapters). Evidently, this is not a prototypical form. It does not feature in the human conceptual system in the same was as a structural metaphor like life is a journey. Rather, it seems to work as a literalisation of what Lakoff and Turner call 'image metaphors' (1989: 89–96), where the structure of a (verbal-) image is mapped onto the structure of another. Comparing structural conceptual metaphors with image metaphors, they articulate:

> The proliferation of detail in the images limits image-mappings to highly specific cases. This is why we refer to them as "one-shot". [. . .] They contrast with robust conceptual mappings such as life is a journey, where rich knowledge and rich inferential structure are mapped from the domain of journey onto life. One-shot image mappings characteristically do not involve mapping of such rich knowledge and inferential structure. Moreover, life is a journey is used unconsciously and automatically over and over again in reasoning about our lives. But one-shot image-mappings are not involved in daily reasoning. (1989: 91)

As such, the principal difference between a prototypical conceptual metaphor (be it structural, orientation, etc.) and an image metaphor, including visual/multimodal concrete is concrete forms, is significant. The distinction needs to be much clearer since it has fundamental ramifications for noting consistencies in the creation and use of multimodal metaphors.

The second problem centres on the definition offered by Forceville which dictates that source and target of a multimodal metaphor must be encoded in different modes. Admittedly, he follows his definition with an acknowledgement: "The qualification "exclusively or predominantly" is necessary because non-verbal metaphors often have targets and/or sources that are cued in more than one mode simultaneously" (2009: 24). Although it provides a precise method of procedure for the analyst, this narrow definition or pure version of a multimodal metaphor is unnecessarily restrictive; several of the articles seem to grapple with this in various ways (for more details, see my review of the book in Gibbons 2011). Consequently, it may be more productive to think of multimodal metaphors as occurring from the interaction and integration of modes (for instance, see Gibbons 2009) in a broader definition, suggested briefly by Eggertsson and Forceville as cueing "target and/or source in more than one mode simultaneously" (2009: 430). In this book, I show that multimodal manifestations of conceptual metaphors can be much more integrative than Forceville's definition suggests.

Such reservations, it must be noted, are secondary to the immense value of such a volume, which explores multimodal metaphor across genres and cultures. Each chapter substantiates its findings through empirical methods, such as corpora, case studies, and reader-responses, justifying the conclusions drawn by the editors in the introduction. *Multimodal Metaphor* is a crucial development for the study of conceptual metaphor. This book adds to that development. In section 4.2.7 of Chapter 4, and sections 5.2.3 to 5.2.5 of Chapter 5, I identify multimodal metaphors at work in multimodal fiction.

3.2.6 Conceptual Integration

Conceptual Integration Theory or Conceptual Blending Theory developed later than Conceptual Metaphor Theory and seeks to explain how conceptual domains and mental spaces, including metaphor, are merged to create new meanings. Thus, the input spaces, which in metaphor terms would consist of the source (input 1) and the target (input 2) are united in a blended space. Resulting from this is an emergent structure, which also contains any meanings or inferences that are perhaps unexplained by the blend (and generic space which holds the common features of the inputs) or come from the reader's unique experience. This is, therefore, a different approach to Conceptual Metaphor Theory, amalgamating and integrating conceptual arenas rather than transposing one onto the other.

Conceptual Metaphor Theory is primarily interested in metaphors that structure and underlie everyday thought processes. As such it is less able to deal with novel or innovative metaphors, such as those that may be found in literary and poetic works. Conceptual integration, in part, seeks to resolve this, as an advancement from Conceptual Metaphor Theory. Indeed, Dancygier states, "blending as a theory makes us better at describing just how new meanings can be creatively constructed out of the existing knowledge structures" (2006: 6).

Conceptual integration has been a great benefit for cognitive-poetic approaches to literature, and has started to facilitate analysis of other forms of texts. Conceptual integration is important for my approach to multi-modal texts, since it is able to account for the manner in which meaning is made through the blend of conceptual domains or mental spaces, and through multiple modes of expression.

In section 4.2.6 of Chapter 4, I employ Conceptual Integration Theory to illuminate the way in which multimodal graphic design may blend with narrative content to produce an emergent meaning that reconceptualises readers' interactions with the book itself. Further to this, in sections 5.2.3 to 5.2.5 of Chapter 5, I examine a multimodal metaphorical blend, showing that such innovative multimodal meaning-making has a transformative effect on readers' perception of the originating conceptual domains and mental spaces.

3.2.7   Text World Theory

Text World Theory is based upon the premise, in Gavins's words, that "human beings understand all discourse by constructing mental representations" (2005a: 90). The theory was the creative vision of Paul Werth (1994, 1995, 1999), whose seminal book on the subject was published posthumously in 1999. Since Werth's death, a new generation of academics (Gavins 2000, 2005a, 2005b, 2007b; Hidalgo Downing 2000, 2003; Lahey 2004, 2006) have maintained the theory, developing and refining aspects.

The theory uses the powerful conceptual metaphor of text as world to articulate the way in which readers understand any given discourse by producing a cognitive realisation of it, an imaginative construal which may appear so vividly as to take on a world-like quality. A text-world is therefore a mental construct that Werth describes as "a coherent and joint effort on the part of its producer and its recipients" (1999: 20). With literary works, text-worlds are produced between writer and reader(s). Moreover, there are a number of conceptual levels within which these worlds operate. The preliminary level is the context in which the communicative event takes place. This is called the 'discourse-world', referring to the external and immediate situation of the participants. In literature, there is most often a 'split discourse-world' since writer and reader occupy different temporal and spatial positions. The second level is the 'text-world' itself which, as previously mentioned, is the cognitive representation of the communication. Significantly, Werth insists, this is "dependent on the resources of memory and imagination, rather than direct perception" (1999: 17). Section 6.3.2 of Chapter 6 provides a traditional Text World Theory analysis of the opening to *Extremely Loud & Incredibly Close*, illustrating the way in which language facilitates text-world construction, but focusing upon the creation of hypothetical text-worlds.

In his initial hypothesis, Werth begins by speaking of "conceptual scenarios containing just enough information to make sense of the particular utterance they correspond to" (1999: 7). He later expounds, "the reader must envisage a mental picture" to assist comprehension (1999: 8). In her recent book, Gavins provides a complementary definition:

> Text World Theory is a model of human language processing which is based on the notions of mental representation found in Cognitive Psychology and which shares the experientialist principles of Cognitive Linguistics . . . It is a discourse framework . . . concerned not just with how a particular text is constructed but how the context surrounding that text influences its production and reception. (2007b: 8)

In these descriptions, both Werth and Gavins emphasise the language used in the communicative process and its realisation in the mind's eye of the receiver. Thus, in seeking to formulate a strategic awareness of the way in which discourse is understood by listeners or readers, Text World Theory is built upon a complex critical equilibrium between actuality and imagination. With literature, linguistic mechanisms such as deixis and modality serve to point toward and evoke fictional worlds in the mind of the reader. Indeed, it is the highly personal imaginative realm, rather than the words on the page, that becomes most significant for the reader during the literary experience. In this sense, Text World Theory implicitly treats language as a facilitator to literary experience, the printed words functioning as a sort of portal into the imagined world of the novel, that is, into the text-world itself. In sections 5.2.8 through to 5.2.11 of Chapter 5, I use Text World Theory to track the reader's perceptual and imaginative movements between the realm of imagination and the discourse-world.

Text World Theory is a discourse framework, focusing upon how linguistic structures trigger different and various text-worlds. This is a strength since Text World Theory is therefore a rigorous account, in terms of it systematic application, of the way in which texts are constructed and comprehended by readers. However, in terms of the needs of the present study, it presents a challenge. For instance, in Hidalgo Downing's (2003) cognitive examination of advertising discourse, she acknowledges that addressees must interpret both "the linguistic and visual clues provided in the advertisement," but subsequently refrains from accounting for those optical elements since, as she says, "a detailed analysis of the visual aspects would require a different approach". Hidalgo Downing exacts an interesting analysis of the discursive text-world of the advertisement leading to an informative conclusion in which she reports that deictic terms and subsequent deictic parameters contribute significantly to the world-building process, enabling the addressee to both create a vivid sense of the world of the advert and track the advert's movement through the scene. Nevertheless, one might wonder whether she has only partially been able to account for the way in which receivers (re)construct this world since television adverts work not just through the verbal means which she interrogates. In fact, one might argue that adverts are predominantly visual, relying upon a variety of images to explain, enhance, or even subvert the verbal discourse. Thus it is through the "complex relations between textual and visual components of ads" (Hidalgo Downing 2003) that an addressee assembles the meaning of the advert as well as its text-world.

Hidalgo Downing's (2003) study suggests that Text World Theory requires some expansion for analysing multimodal elements. I employ Text World Theory throughout Chapters 4, 5, 6, and 7, using it to account for the complex positioning of readers by multimodal texts. In particular, in Chapter 4, Text World Theory is used in sections 4.2.2 and 4.2.3 to account for the complex cognitive processing of negation. In section 4.2.9 of Chapter 4 and section 6.3.6 of Chapter 6, I augment Text World Theory to facilitate a better understanding of the ontological intricacies, both in terms of narrative levels and the reader's relation to the text, of multimodal fiction.

3.2.8 Cognitive Poetics and the Cognitive Sciences

As mentioned in the introduction to this chapter, cognitive poetics has a close relationship with the cognitive sciences. All branches of cognitive science, particularly neuroscience and psychology, are concerned with continually advancing their models of cognitive processing through improved experimental technique and corresponding interpretation. Many of the frameworks of cognitive poetics, such as Conceptual Metaphor Theory, are grounded in cognitive science. Thus, in order to remain accurate and up to date, cognitive poetics should ideally host a parallel commitment to considering the consequences and applicability of such advancements to models of cognitive processing for literary analysis.

Many central figures of cognitive poetics are not trained in cognitive science (e.g. Stockwell, as mentioned, is a stylistically trained cognitive poetician) and therefore not trained in the field from which their frameworks are drawn. As such, if cognitive-poetic analysts do not also continually revise their understandings of its frameworks and of the relevant cognitive-scientific findings, they run the risk of carrying out less valid analyses since their arguments may be based on work which has been succeeded or refined. This is a palpable challenge for analysts, but for those who are conscientious about their cognitive-scientific research, it can lead to ever more accurate readings and greater insight into literary experience.

In this book, I draw, where possible, on recent cognitive findings, seeking to develop my cognitive-poetic approach to multimodality alongside contemporary scientific data. This is most evident in section 4.2.8 of Chapter 4 and section 5.2.6 of Chapter 5, where I draw on cognitive-scientific and neuroscientific research concerned with the relationship between linguistic processing and embodied understanding.

3.3   COGNITIVE POETICS: CLAIMS AND DISCONTENTS

As a recent academic endeavour, practitioners of cognitive poetics are still very much in the process of declaring and defining the discipline. The advantage of this is to allow scope for scholarly freedom, making it an exciting and evolving field of research. In their introduction to *Cognitive Poetics in Practice*, Gavins and Steen make the following assertion:

> The appeal of literature has been challenged by new art forms directed at new groups of audiences through new media, and it has become inevitable to consider the resemblance and difference between these art forms and literature in terms of their psychological and social effects. This is precisely what cognitive poetics promises to bring into view, by relating the structures of the work of art, including the literary text, to their presumed or observed psychological effects on the recipient, including the reader. (2003b: 1)

Gavins and Steen's description of the goal of cognitive poetics shows that the discipline is conceived as applicable to all forms of artistic expression and, by implication, that all forms of artistic expression exhibit and demonstrate the cognitive capacities of human nature. This is indeed true, and is made evident by the breadth of disciplines that have also taken the 'cognitive turn'. As Turner puts it, "The cognitive turn in the humanities is an aspect of a more general cognitive turn taking place in the contemporary study of human beings" (2002: 9). *The Artful Mind* (Turner 2006), for instance, is an edited volume of essays exploring art from a cognitive perspective. However, unlike cognitive poetics, such work is often most centrally concerned with the neurological functions of the brain in viewing art, rather than with a phenomenological and experiential dynamic (for instance, see Lakoff 2006).

Since cognitive poetics has a literary-linguistic inclination, most of its applications have been to literature and to its use of poetic and linguistic devices while relatively little attention has been given to other art forms. The visual aspect of literary experience has, on the whole, been overlooked by cognitive poeticians and as a result is an area which cognitive poetics needs to address. Oatley asserts that the domain of cognitive poetics "is literature, including texts that are read, movies and plays that are seen, poetry that is heard" (2003: 162). This is all very well with regard to reading and hearing, and to verbal/linguistic modes in general, but in reality cognitive poetics has yet to address in any consistent way the mental processes involved in our experience of movies, plays, or any kind of literature that embraces the visual.

Oatley's (2003: 162) avowal of cognitive poetics' application across the literary arts is not only unfounded for the critical arena in general. It is not applicable to the studies contained in the very book in which his assertion is contained (Gavins and Steen 2003a). A possible explanation for this is that the tools of cognitive poetics are not totally equipped to consider the visual, thus spurring a tacit belief (such as that articulated by Hidalgo Downing) that cognitive poetics has either reached its limit when faced with images or that other theoretical apparatus are needed in order to extend analysis into the optical domain. Stockwell states:

> cognitive poetics is only worth anything if it is able to be addressed to more than just literary texts that seem amenable to it [. . .] we should also be tackling more difficult and challenging texts, the ones which do not fit easily into cognitive poetic theory. Those are the situations in which we will be forced to develop new frameworks for cognitive poetics. (2002a: 10–11)

It seems reasonable to suggest that literary and artistic texts that encapsulate both words and images do indeed pose a challenge to cognitive poetics and may subsequently play an important role in its advancement.

Cognitive poetics is conceptualised not simply as an approach to literature, but as an approach concerned with our cognitive capacities to interpret and feel involved in literary reading. Furthermore, it claims that these capacities and feelings are direct manifestations of the way in which the human mind comprehends, experiences, and represents the world; a world that is encountered not just linguistically, but visually, audibly, physiologically, and so forth. Cognitive poetics, therefore, professes a certain universality of mind asserting that many cognitive procedures are applicable and operational across and within the understanding of many different media. For this reason, the lack of cognitive-poetic studies of the visual is discouraging; one might even call it a weakness. As a discipline with an underlying cognitive inclination, cognitive poetics ought to be able to account for interpretive practice in its entirety, regardless of communicative mode.

While Oatley may indeed express this desire, declaration is not equivalent to deed. Of course, as cognitive poetics is a discipline in its youth, Oatley's words are admirable in their desire to take cognitive poetics into the visual realm. Even so, if cognitive poetics is to outlive the 'cognitive revolution', cognitive poetics must expand its borders to include the visual arts. In doing so, cognitive poetics will reveal itself not simply as an invaluable approach to literature and literary understanding. Its discoveries will be of worth and significance across the humanities.

3.4   TOWARDS A MULTIMODAL COGNITIVE POETICS . . .

The weaknesses of present methods for analysing texts that encapsulate the interface between the verbal and visual are twofold. There is a current persistence either to divide words from images in order to focus upon one's favoured means of expression or to use a single theory, inherently catered to a single mode, to explain the effects of both. While work in stylistics and literary criticism has tended to suffer with the former, visual analysts are often guilty of the latter, looking at multimodal forms, such as magazines, but focusing upon the visual components, thus treating written discourse as secondary information. Often these academic perspectives fail to discuss the interplay between modes and when they do, the so-called secondary mode is characterised in terms of its subjugator. In most cases, one mode becomes subservient to the other. Thus, present approaches to multimodality struggle to reach an understanding of the intricate effect of word and image collaborations upon textual interpretation.

In developing my cognitive-poetic approach to multimodal literary narratives, I will draw on many of the discipline's central components, and in particular figure and ground, cognitive grammar, cognitive deixis, conceptual metaphor and conceptual integration, Text World Theory, and cognitive narratology. Cognitive poetics, however, is "a field that has borders only where you want to draw them" (Stockwell 2002a: 175). Indeed, my approach will be a critical synthesis. In the final section of the previous chapter, I highlighted important tools from visual communication and multimodality studies that would be important for such a critical synthesis, namely, cluster analysis, vectors, and reading paths. In addition to this, there are broader cognitive principles, multisensory perception and embodiment, as well as an understanding of visual perception, which influence this critical synthesis.

3.4.1   Multisensory Perception

Current research in neuroscience demonstrates a renewed interest at the interface of modality, sensory perception, and cognition. Recently, there has been a paradigm shift in conceptions of the human mind whereby the modular view, in which sensory modalities were thought to be processed separately, is being replaced by the belief that the brain handles sensory input in an interactive and integrative manner (Pavani, Murray, and Schroeder 2006; Thesen et al. 2004). While the traditional view saw the brain as a collection of unisensory modules, the emerging evidence of what Ghazanfar and Schroeder term "the multisensory nature of most, possibly all, of the neocortex forces us to abandon the notion that the senses ever operate independently during real-world cognition" (2006: 278). This suggests that the practice of reading multimodal literature can be seen as closer to our experiential processing of reality when compared to more conventional novels. Of course, this is not to say that more traditional forms of literature are not received in a multimodal fashion. Such a statement would be a reductive account of literary experience, failing to acknowledge the imaginative (potentially visual) capacities of the reader, as well as the physical and locative context of reading in which the body is situated in relation to the book as an artefact.

Rather, multimodal novels in their employment of multiple sensory stimuli are self-conscious of their material form, playing upon the integrative nature of cognition. Ghazanfar and Schroeder conclude:

> it is likely that neither the brain nor cognition develops one sensory modality at a time. The world is a barrage of sensory inputs, our perception is a unified representation of it, and the neocortex is organised in a manner to make the underlying processes as efficient as possible. (2006: 278)

Another important finding in neuroscientific research suggests that even the most basic combination of two senses appears to result in an enhanced neurological response (Stafford and Webb 2005). This undoubtedly holds implications for the readerly reception of multimodal novels. Although neuroscientific classification may deem both word and image as forms of visual stimuli in the reading process, Khateb et al.'s (2002) study of their recognition and resulting written and pictorial processing in the brain verifies that the two modalities do not take the same neural pathways. In fact, while there are areas of similarity, Khateb et al. deduce that "brain regions engaged during verbal and pictorial recognition are different. More specifically, words and word-like recognition involved more dominantly left-hemisphere regions while image recognition involved more dominantly right hemisphere areas" (2002: 211). Therefore, word and image, as disparate phenomena where neural activity is concerned, may indeed be considered as distinct modalities of literary expression.

For responsive neurological enhancement to occur, the two modalities must be construed as part of the same event, an outcome that is usually the result of a "horizon of simultaneity" (Stafford and Webb 2005: 187) or 'co-occurrence' (Bertelson and Gelder 2004: 141). In other words, the sensory stimuli must be congruent (Ghazanfar and Schroeder 2006: 282). Admittedly, since reading is a practice grounded in temporal progression, the necessity of co-occurrence may seem to undermine any significance that multisensory processing may have for the reception of multimodal fiction. However, I contend that word and image act in synchronicity, engaged in the production of a shared textual meaning. Their narrative congruence is thus perceived as contributing to a joint event. Consequently, multimodal novels may create more intense narrative experiences. The intensity of multimodal literary experience is a central concern of my analysis of *House of Leaves* in Chapter 4.

3.4.2 Embodiment

Embodiment is a crucial concept in cognitive science and cognitive linguistics. Both consider mind and body as a syndicate through which conceptual information is understood. As Gibbs articulates:

> Cognition is what happens when the body interacts with the physical/ cultural world. Minds are not internal to the human body, but exist as webs encompassing brains, bodies, and world . . . "embodiment" refers to the dynamical interactions between the brain, the body, and the physical/cultural environment. (2005: 66–67)

Thus, it is the body's physical, sensory, and perceptual interactions within the world that influence the way in which the mind structures and conceptualises human experience. The view of embodiment as pervasive in cognition and experience is known as 'experiential realism' and is explained by Lakoff as experience construed as "the totality of human experience and everything that plays a role in it—the nature of our bodies, our genetically inherited capacities, our modes of physical functioning in the world, our social organization, etc." (1987: 166).

As a central tenet of the cognitive sciences, embodiment is therefore also fundamental to cognitive poetics, underlying conceptual structures, as shown by Conceptual Metaphor Theory and image schemas, for example. Even though it is an underlying factor in cognitive experience, embodiment has not been treated directly in cognitive-poetic analysis. By drawing attention to this, I am not necessarily pointing to it as a failing. However, since multimodal texts accentuate their materiality, the bodies of the book and of the reader are more noticeably engaged in multimodal literary reading. In his seminal work, *The Body in the Mind*, Johnson states:

> The centrality of human embodiment directly influences what and how things can be meaningful for us, the ways in which these meanings

can be developed and articulated, the ways we are able to comprehend and reason about our experience, and the actions we take. Our reality is shaped by the patterns of bodily movement, the contours of our spatial and temporal orientation, and the forms of our interaction with objects. It is never merely a matter of abstract conceptualizations and propositional judgements. (1987: 5)

Since embodiment is fundamental to human understanding and experience, it seems logical to suggest if the body is more involved in the act of reading, then that particular reading may become more meaningful, or loaded with greater significance, as a result.

Given the nature of multimodal novels, cognitive embodiment is an important consideration in my analyses. In section 4.2.8 of Chapter 4 and section 5.2.6 of Chapter 5, I suggest the ways in which multimodal texts accentuate the connections between language and embodied understanding. Moreover, in sections 4.2.9 and 4.2.10 of Chapter 4 and sections 6.3.6 and 6.3.7 of Chapter 6, I consider the reader's direct embodied relationship with the text and how this impacts upon literary experience.

3.4.3   Visual Perception

Originating with Rubin (1958 [1915]) and developed by Gestalt psychologists (Beardslee and Wertheimer 1958; Koffka 1935; Köhler 1947; Wertheimer 1958 [1923]), figure and ground still holds recognised currency in contemporary research into attention (Gordon 1997; Gregory 1970; Haber and Hershenson 1973; Posner and Raichle 1997; Styles 1997). As previously mentioned in section 3.2.1, figure and ground is a cognitive mechanism which enables us to discriminate between subjects or objects of focus, figures, and the background against which they are presented. As Haber and Hershenson put it, "any inhomogeneity in the retinal projection leads to a perceptual segregation of the field into one part called a figure and another part called a ground" (1973: 184).

A brief illustration will elucidate. In Figure 3.2, which shows the famous image devised by Danish psychologist Rubin (1958 [1915]: 201), whether we see a black vase on a white background or two white faces in profile upon a black background depends upon which image we take as our figure and which we hold as our ground. This image was used by Gestaltists to reveal the dynamism of the figure–ground process, making people aware of the ability to *flip* our perception from one view to the other unconsciously and at will (noted by Stockwell 2002a: 2; Ungerer and Schmid 1996: 158).

Rubin's vase, therefore, is an image of a special order, since the figure and ground segregations we experience on an everyday basis are more clearly segregated.

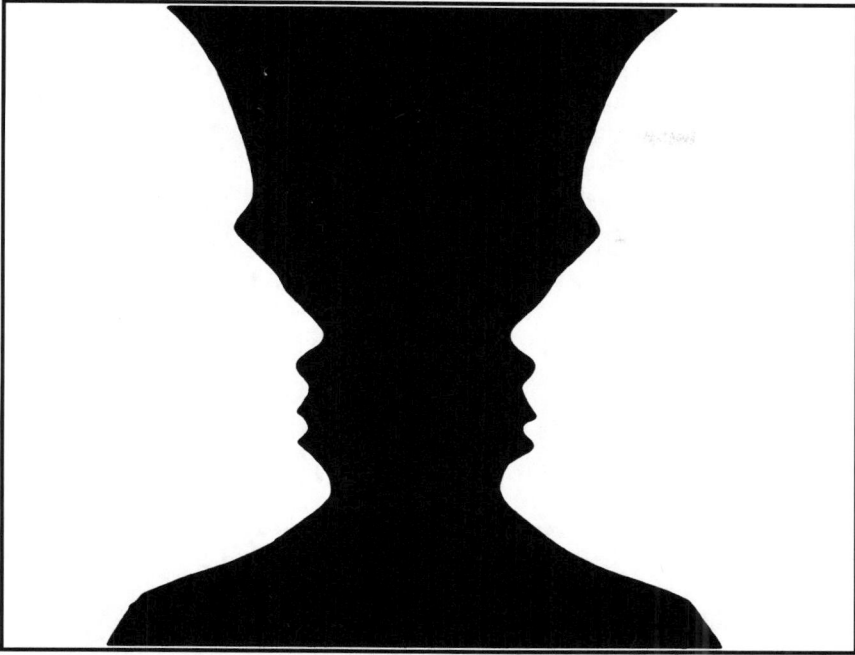

Figure 3.2   Rubin's vase from Stockwell (2002a: 14). Original from Rubin (1958 [1915]: 201).

Studies in attention have refined figure identification. The main visual qualities that often result in figure creation are:

- self-containment; well-defined edges
- movement in relation to a static ground
- preceding the ground in time or space
- salient features; detail, brightness, colour, large size, etc. (see Stockwell 2002a: 15; 2003: 15)

Figure and ground enables depth perception and thus three-dimensional sight. Connected are the cognitive-psychological notions of *interposition* and *occlusion*: "Interposition is the occlusion of a far object by a nearer one", articulate Andrade and May (2004: 23). In figure identification, one object occluded by another results in the latter being perceived as being further away. Figure and ground is part of human perceptual organisation.

Principles from Gestalt psychology are also relevant to figure identification and to understanding how and why certain visual structures are perceived as related and/or meaningful. Gestalt psychologists were principally concerned with the holistic aspect of visual perception, under the law of Prägnanz. The law of Prägnanz is a fundamental yet unconscious process of visual perception, explaining how humans impose order upon the perceptual field—that is, the cognitive restructuring of our perceptual environment in order to make sense of it and perceive Gestalt wholes. A Gestalt whole is a 'good' shape. By the word 'good', Gestalt psychologists were referring to properties of shape and form.

Under the law of Prägnanz, a set of Gestalt principles suggest the properties which cohere to make a Gestalt whole. These principles were first outlined in Wertheimer's (1958 [1923]) laws of perceptual grouping. It is generally agreed that five of the laws are of greatest import:

> *The Principle of Proximity*: Elements which are closer together are generally perceived as belonging together.

> *The Principle of Similarity*: Elements with similar qualities are perceived as belonging to the same group.

> *The Principle of (Good) Continuity*: There is a perceptual preference for continuous patterning of elements as opposed to abrupt changes or disruptions. Thus the visual system has a predisposition to perceive continuity, through connection and cohesion.

> *The Principle of Closure*: The perceptual system enables us to complete forms even though parts may be missing. This is also related to Continuity.

> *The Principle of Smallness:* Smaller elements are generally perceived as objects or figures against the ground.

Of these five Gestalt principles, the latter is evidently a quality of figure identification.

The Gestalt principles are a useful aspect of multimodal cognitive poetics, since they aid analysis in showing how elements of multimodal texts are perceived as working in synchronicity. Figure and ground fits perfectly into a multimodal cognitive poetics since, although I have recounted figure and ground as a phenomenon of visual perception, it "occurs in all sensory modalities" (Gordon 1997: 65) and is already employed by cognitive poetics in a linguistic context. Figure and ground analysis, both linguistic and visual, can be seen most clearly at work in section 4.2.7 of Chapter 4.

3.4.4　The Goals of Multimodal Cognitive Poetics

Multimodal cognitive poetics is an interdisciplinary critical synthesis. The driving force in this critical collective is cognitive poetics. Within cognitive poetics, I have identified the most relevant components, namely, figure and ground, cognitive grammar (and particularly the system of profiling), cognitive deixis, conceptual metaphor, conceptual integration, and Text World Theory. These are all framed by an overarching concern with embodiment, and the awareness of neuroscientific research into the multisensory nature of perception. I combine my cognitive approach with visual perception (drawing on studies of attention and Gestalt psychology), and tools from multimodal studies (cluster analysis, reading paths, and vectors).

The critical combination united in multimodal cognitive poetics presents a new approach to the study of multimodality. While the theoretical merger is original and exploratory, it is also ambitious. At the heart of all of the disciplines involved exist two shared goals. Firstly, they seek to uncover the structures of meaning-making within texts, and secondly they are all driven by an essential desire to relate to general human experience. Crucially, this new approach primarily aims to explore multimodality from an experientialist perspective, leading to greater understandings of the way in which we see, read, and make sense of both literature and the world around us.

3.5 CONCLUSION

In this chapter, I have introduced the discipline of cognitive poetics as well as highlighted the frameworks from cognitive poetics, visual perception, and multimodal studies that I employ in my exploration of multimodal literary print narratives. This critical synthesis looks at *both* the surface of multimodal novels, their graphic design and composition, and how such multimodality impacts upon readers' experiential and cognitive encounters with those novels. In doing so, this book will be pioneering new ground for cognitive poetics. It also enhances our understandings of multimodal experience through a multimodal cognitive poetics. The four chapters which follow put multimodal cognitive poetics into practice in the analysis of multimodal printed novels, beginning with the exploration of Mark Z. Danielewski's *House of Leaves* in Chapter 4.

4 Crossing Thresholds and the Exploring Reader of *House of Leaves* by Mark Z. Danielewski

4.1 INTRODUCTION

Mark Z. Danielewski's (2000a) debut novel *House of Leaves by Zampanò with Introduction and Notes by Johnny Truant* is a central example of a multimodal fiction, having achieved 'bestseller' status soon after its publication. The novel's success has resulted not only in it being cited by Boxall as a 'must-read' book (2006: 888), but also in it amassing a cult following, spurring a number of fansites and discussion boards on the internet (e.g. see Website 2, Website 3, Website 4 in References; and Thomas 2011 for an academic discussion of these forums).

As a multimodal object, *House of Leaves* is brimming with typographical trickery and inventive visual designs that share many commonalities with concrete poetry. In many of the novel's narrative sequences, text traverses the page, frequently changing direction and page-location or forming imagistic designs, all of which bear relevance to the narrative action within the present moment of reading. The material reality of the novel is also a point of emphasis, since the book is an epic seven-hundred-page read, its almost squarelike shape making it a 'door-stop' of a book that is heavy in a reader's hands. Indeed, these features lead Hayles to speak of *House of Leaves* as "so profound it becomes a new kind of form and artefact" (2002b: 112) when compared to so-called 'traditional' printed literature. Importantly, the multimodal attributes of *House of Leaves* are vital both to its narrative and to the reader's cognitive experience of the novel.

House of Leaves is not only challenging in terms of its multimodality and materiality, but it is narratologically intricate. It weaves multiple storylines together into what McCaffery and Gregory (using McHale's 1987 structural category) call a "Chinese-box novel" (2003: 100), that is, a recursive narrative structure composed of embedded or nested worlds. In an interview with Cottrell, Danielewski admits, "I believe the structure of *House of Leaves* is far more difficult to explain than it is to read" (no date). As such, my summary of the novel's complicated plot is accompanied by illustrative diagram (see Figure 4.1).

At the heart of *House of Leaves* is the central plot of "The Navidson Record". Will Navidson is a Pulitzer Prize–winning photojournalist who decides to create a film documenting his family's move to, and new life in, their new home on Ash Tree Lane. However, all is not as it seems, and the video takes a sinister turn when the internal measurements of the house appear to grow and an unfamiliar door opening into a dim corridor emerges in the master bedroom. A series of explorations into these strange and shifting proportions take place, conducted by Navidson, his brother Tom, and friend Bill Reston, as well as a team of professional hunter/ explorers—Holloway, Jed, and Wax. "The Navidson Record" is the name of the video, documenting the mysterious occurrences in the house and the explorations of its dark interior.

Since "The Navidson Record" is a docu-film, the reader does not, of course, have direct access to it. Although it forms a narrative layer in terms of the novel's ontological landscape, this layer is not concrete or tangible, but rather one that is recovered through narrative mediation. In fact, the reader learns of "The Navidson Record" through a character named Zampanò. Zampanò is an old blind man who documents the video through written narrative description and academic commentary, the completed manuscript of which is also named "The Navidson Record". It is worth mentioning that Zampanò's visual disability troubles the video's ontological status (Does it really exist? How could the old man have ever *seen* it?).

Zampanò's commentary is itself encased within the narrative of Johnny Truant, a crude tattooist with a Los Angeles lifestyle who, after Zampanò is found dead in his apartment, becomes the owner of the manuscript compiling Zampanò's reflections on "The Navidson Record". Truant's narrative begins in the novel's Introduction, after which it exists in the form of footnotes, sometimes brief and sometimes spiralling into large passages of text that take over the narrative for several pages.

Framing Truant's narrative is the text of the anonymous editors, who occasionally add footnoted remarks, often pertaining to the fact or fictionality of the book and/or functioning in a similar way to a disclaimer. For instance, their words appear on the text's actual copyright page, they author the short foreword, and an example of their commentary within the novel can be found on page 54: "[66]Mr. Truant declined to comment further on this particular passage.—Ed." (Danielewski 2000a: 54). To differentiate the latter three authors and layers of narrative, each is assigned a different type-face, made explicit in the anonymous editors' footnote on page 4 of the novel. While this chapter reproduces these (as closely as possible) in quotation, the device itself can be seen as a visual representation of narrative voice. Moreover, in terms of Nørgaard's (2009b) three semiotic principles of typographic meaning, iconic meaning, indexical meaning, and discursive import can be seen at work. Pressman (2006) explains:

> Each of these narrative voices is identified by a different font and associated with a specific medium: Zampanò's academic commentary appears

in Times Roman, the font associated with newspapers and the linotype; Truant's footnotes are in Courier, imitate a typewriter's inscription, and thematically identify him as the "courier" of the manuscript; the terse notations from the Ed. are aptly presented in Bookman.

Interestingly, McIntyre's (2007) brief remarks on the encoding of point of view in a graphic novel suggest a comparable representation. Considering an unreadable speech bubble which stems from two characters located in the distance, McIntyre argues that this "suggests that the reader's position within the fictional world is one where the men pictured are too far away for the reader to hear clearly what they are saying" (2007: 122). As such, he concludes that the unreadable speech bubble is a "graphological equivalent of what Semino and Short (2004), in their work on discourse presentation, refer to as the 'narrative report of voice'" (2007: 122). The fonts in *House of Leaves* can be seen as a similar phenomenon. Font choice does not work like narrative report of voice, but instead functions like the reported clauses of direct speech, signalling the character who speaks.

In addition to the aforementioned narrative worlds, *House of Leaves* also contains three appendices, the contents of which are attributed to the three storyworld authors, respectively, and, unusually for a novel, an index. Figure 4.1 depicts the relationship(s) between these and the more central narratives with dotted connecting lines originating from the border of the narrative world that claims ownership. Due to the recursive narrative structure of the novel, characters in framing worlds have narrative access to the appendices of the world(s) they encase. For instance, both Truant and "- The Editors" have ontological access to Zampanò's appendix, but only "- The Editors" have access to Truant's appendix. Those who have access are thus able to comment upon these lower level appendices, such as "- The Editors" note at the beginning of "The Three Attic Whalestoe Institute Letters" in part E. of Truant's Appendix. Not insignificantly, "The Three Attic Whalestoe Institute Letters" is a collection of letters to Truant from his mother Pelafina, an extended version of which has also been published separately (see Danielewski 2000b). Pelafina's letters introduce, therefore, another author to *House of Leaves* who also has her own font and narrative voice.

Since *House of Leaves*, Mark Z. Danielewski has published two other fictional works, *The Fifty Year Sword* (2005) and *Only Revolutions* (2006). Both of these novels continue Danielewski's commitment to literary multimodality. As he perceives it, he is "creating something that goes beyond books" (Danielewski in Miller 2006), exploring the formal and imaginative properties of the novel and its textual space. The multimodality of *House of Leaves* foregrounds the book as a physical artefact and challenges the reader's most basic suppositions concerning what the book is as an object and how it should be interacted with during the reading experience. Along with its bestseller status, this makes *House of Leaves* a good starting-point for my study of multimodal fiction from a cognitive-poetic perspective.

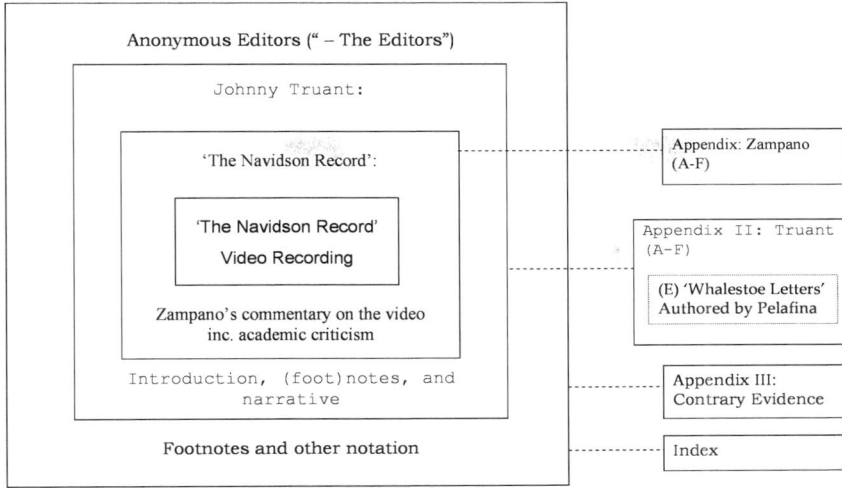

Figure 4.1   Narrative levels of Danielewski (2000a) *House of Leaves.*

As a starting-point for the development of a multimodal cognitive poetics, the analysis in this chapter firstly demonstrates the suggested critical synthesis in practice, using tools from visual perception, communication, and multimodality studies alongside cognitive poetics. Secondly, *House of Leaves* as a multimodal text necessarily provides challenges for cognitive poetics. Thus in the process of analysis, I augment existing cognitive models to better account for the reading experience such texts create.

4.2 ANALYSIS

House of Leaves is often classified as a horror fiction. Pressman justifies this by stating that the novel is "shelved in the horror section of bookstores" (2006). Fordham (2002), however, seems uncertain, commenting that a friend of his found the novel too fearsome to read while he found it unthreatening. I am not suggesting here that readers will react in one way or another. Rather I will take cue from the novel's cult following: 'real' readers consistently refer to the novel as a horror or an object of horror. For instance, one customer review on Amazon.com calls it an "obsessive house of horrors" (see Website 1 in References). Furthermore, there are numerous threads on the book's official online forum (see Website 4 in References) that discuss such fear-related topics as its scariest episode and its provocation of nightmares and/or insomnia. One user starts a thread called "Scared me to the point of NOT SLEEPING". Comments and confessions such as these attest to the success of the novel as a powerful reading experience, regardless of its generic categorisation. By studying the multimodal features using a cognitive-poetic approach, this chapter reveals why *House of Leaves* becomes such an intense literary encounter for many of its readers. I substantiate this reaction to the text through rigorous analysis, demonstrating how Danielewski manipulates the reader physically and psychologically through ontological instability and transgressions of the boundary between fictional worlds and discourse-world(s).

In *Postmodernist Fiction*, McHale touches upon the notion of 'semipermeable membranes' (1987: 34–36), referring to the flexible boundaries between narrative worlds and/or levels. He articulates, "Fiction's epidermis, it appears, is not an impermeable but a semipermeable membrane" (1987: 34). The concept of the semipermeable membrane does not in fact originate with McHale, but can be traced to Goffman's (1961) enquiry into social interaction. Nevertheless, McHale is suggesting that the metaphor can be applied to literary experience by signifying the possibilities for transgressions between and across narrative worlds.

In terms of effect, McHale claims semipermeation "foregrounds ontological boundaries and ontological structure" (1987: 35). Bell's (2006, 2007) stylistic investigation of the possible worlds of hypertext fictions endorses this understanding. Looking at the crossings between actual world and textual world(s), Bell (2006: 103) concludes that such transgressions between worlds expose the boundary and reinforce the worlds as distinct domains in ontological terms. By foregrounding this boundary and emphasising the ontological separation between actual and textual worlds, for Bell semipermeation also alienates the reader from the textual world by imposing ontological distance. Bell's stance on the function of semipermeable membranes in hypertext is sound, yet the permeations in *House of Leaves* do not result in a comparable distancing of the reader.

Danielewski's ontological manoeuvres, breaches of the semipermeable membrane, work not to fortify the boundaries between worlds by foregrounding the artificiality and fictionality of the text, but instead to obscure, and to some extent conceal, these boundaries. This is crucial to the intensity of the novel as a reading experience. By this means, *House of Leaves* utilises both narratological instability and multimodal design to generate subjective parallels between readers and characters and, crucially, bring the reader into play in the narrative. The reader's role is fundamental to the novel's opening, which I begin to explore in the following section.

4.2.1 Open the Door

House of Leaves opens with the extraordinary admonition, "This is not for you" (Danielewski 2000a: ix). This caution initially appears to be a strange tactic by the author designed to deter readers; in which case, the demonstrative pronoun 'this' refers to the novel, the object of the book itself as well as the reading experience it entails. Locating the deictic referents of the opening sentence in the context of the reading experience leads to an interpretation of the perceptual deictic 'you' as an address to the reader of the novel. Fludernik states, "*You*, even if it turns out to refer to a fictional protagonist, initially always seems to involve the actual reader" (1995: 106). Her observation of readers' initial reaction to *you* is apposite to Danielewski's provocative opening, endorsing a reading of it as a direct address.

In order to understand the full impact of the opening sentence, further consideration of both readerly cognitive process and multimodal design is required. Examination of linguistic negation, pronoun usage, and the effects of these on text-world creation, leads to a more intricate understanding of the meaning-making layers encapsulated in this aperture.

In Text World Theory, written communication usually incurs a split discourse-world, as participants involved in the communication normally occupy different spatio-temporal locations. Boundaries between worlds have been referred to by Young (1987) as 'edgework'. The entrance to any storyworld is an important boundary. Segal states:

> When the first sentence of the first chapter of a novel or short story is being read (or the curtain opens on a play, or the words "feature presentation" are replaced by a scene at the movies), a reader usually responds by anticipating that what comes next will represent a new entity. The objects and events represented by the discourse following the boundary are to be instantiated in the space made available. (1995: 75)

McIntyre (2007) concurs with Segal, explaining that when "we start to read the novel, the first deictic shift we make is to recentre ourselves within the text-world as opposed to the actual world" (128). The opening to a novel represents a significant boundary or piece of edgework across which a reader takes a cognitive step from their side of the split discourse-world into the shared text-world of written and fictional communication.

The first sentence in *House of Leaves* prohibits text-world entry, thus presenting a challenge to the customary creation of and shift into the text-world. Despite familiarity between participants being established by direct address, the negative adverb 'not' works to alienate the actual reader. In "This is not for you", with 'this' signalling the novel *House of Leaves*, Danielewski performs an act of prohibition, suggesting that the reader should not read the book. The effect is that "This is not for you" appears to traverse the discourse-world divide, achieving semipermeability in McHale's (1987) terms, in an effort to obstruct the reader's entrance into the text-world of the novel. At this point, semipermeation does foreground ontological divides. However, since the boundary is strengthened though narratorial obstruction, readers who continue reading in effect may potentially negotiate the strength of that boundary.

Danielewski's prohibiting aperture is intriguing. It is a radical move for an author to deny the reader access into the narrative world, especially before the novel has even begun. Of course, in making the latter statement I am being somewhat crude. Danielewski is not simply denying access to the narrative as his use of direct address works antithetically by inviting reader engagement.

This paradox is a deliberate strategy, the motivation for which will be revealed in the course of my consideration of "This is not for you". At present, the paradox presented to the reader suffices to demonstrate that Danielewski does not write escapist fiction. Rather, with the opening sentence to *House of Leaves*, he issues readers a number of complex cognitive challenges.

I offer an extensive analysis of the linguistic elements and stylistic features employed in "This is not for you". This reveals that Danielewski imposes upon his readers many complicated processes of psychological negotiation before they may enter the narrative world and proceed in reading *House of Leaves*.

4.2.2 Do Not Enter

One such negotiation rests upon the sentence's uses of negation. Negation, the linguistic and conceptual denial, absence or non-being of something, is signalled in this sentence through its essential reliance upon the explicitly negative word 'not'. As Hidalgo Downing explains, words such as 'not' "are negative in meaning, they are marked morphologically for negation and they follow co-occurrence restrictions that single them out as syntactically negative" (2000: 42). This latter label of 'syntactic negation' follows Givón's (1979, 1993) terminology to indicate that explicitly negative words carry meaning in the context of a syntactic construction. For instance, in the sentence 'you do *not* want to read this chapter', the negative lexeme serves the syntactic function of inverting the meaning of the verb phrase (want to read), thus working in coordination with the sentence rather than isolation. Linguistic negation necessarily demands complex cognitive operations. Hidalgo Downing states that "negation as a structure involves the formation of a complex structure with regard to the corresponding affirmative" (2000: 36). Clark and Clark (1977: 108, 110), in their book on psycholinguistics, cite empirical studies to show that negative assertions take longer to process precisely because they involve this conception of a supposition first at its affirmative pole followed by the cancellation of it. Cognising "This is not for you", therefore, is only possible by interpreting it alongside and in comparison with "This is for you".

In text-world terms, Werth (1999: 249–257) classifies negation as a foregrounding process that creates a subworld. Gavins (2007b: 102) builds on this, suggesting that negation produces a negative text-world whose contents must be conceptualised before they can be translated into an exclusion in and from the separate positive text-world. For Gavins, then, while this negative world can impact upon the positive world, there is an implication that the negative world is part of a conceptual route rather than a simultaneous and equally realised domain. Thus, while there is an ontological tension between positive and negative worlds, these worlds do not ever exist in a state of concurrent stability.

The text-worlds involved in processing "This is not for you" can be identified and represented by Figure 4.2.

TEXT-WORLD		NEGATIVE TEXT-WORLD
'This' (*House of Leaves*)		'This' (*House of Leaves*)
'you' (the reader)		'you' (the reader)
neg		

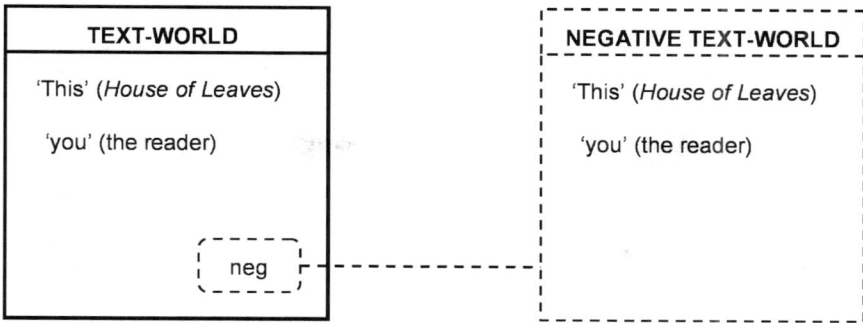

Figure 4.2   Text-world and negative text-world in "This is not for you".

The negation in the opening to *House of Leaves* serves to create a fleeting negative text-world in which 'This is for you' is foregrounded in the reader's mind. In Werth's words, "to deny the existence or presence of an entity, you have to mention it. The very act of denying it brings it into focus" (1999: 251). This process enables the negation in the originating text-world to be conceptualised.

Nørgaard claims that a negated proposition, like "negatives in general, ultimately entails two (incompatible) viewpoints" (2007: 39), albeit perceived consecutively—the positive presence of a thing followed by its absence. Danielewski takes cognitive incompatibility beyond the complex cognitive operations demanded by the cerebral processing of linguistic negation. The author also generates cognitive dissonance for the reader. Cognitive dissonance, as formulated by Festinger, is "the experience of nonfitting relations among cognitions" (1957: 3). Individuals experiencing cognitive dissonance will be actuated to seek resolution or, as Festinger posits, "The existence of dissonance, being psychologically uncomfortable, will motivate a person to try to reduce the dissonance and achieve consonance" (1957: 3). Cognitive dissonance can occur not just between conflicting knowledges, but also between a held belief and a behaviour or action. Festinger's original example is that of the smoker who continues the habit despite knowing that smoking is bad for one's health. When behaviour and belief are in conflict like this, the forces inducing desire to diminish dissonance are considerable.

In relation to the opening of Danielewski's *House of Leaves*, a reader encountering this sentence has presumably bought or borrowed the book and therefore decided that it is a novel s/he wants to read. Effectively, readers hold the belief that 'this is for them'. In consequence, "This is not for you" takes on a great magnitude of dissonance since incongruity arises between the primary narrative statement and the reader's preceding actions and belief. Furthermore, the inference communicated is dissonant with a reader's impulse and intent to read on. Readers must therefore find a means with which to reconcile the dissonance between their habits in the practice of reading and the semantic implication of the sentence.

I must acknowledge that other interpretations of the opening sentence than the one explicated so far are possible. It would be easy enough to consider the author's words as disingenuous. In doing so, a reader is able to disregard the semantic impact of the sentence in favour of understanding it as sensationalist shock tactic rather than sincere forbiddance. Arguably, this in itself is a way to avoid or decrease cognitive dissonance on the part of the reader, preventing the arousal of tension between the semantic implication of the sentence and the exercise of reading.

Related to cognitive dissonance is another cognitive behaviour, cognitive reactance. Theorised by Brehm (1966), this social-psychological behaviour plays a significant part in a reader's cognitive experience of "This is not for you" as well as in a reader's response to it. Crawford et al. (2002) define reactance in the following way:

> Reactance theory holds that there exists a set of free behaviors from which an individual can potentially choose. When any of these free behaviors is eliminated or threatened with elimination, the individual experiences psychological reactance, a motivational state directed toward the reestablishment of the free behavior. (56)

In other words, we react against overt attempts to persuade us or to delimit our choices. Thus, the popular concept of reverse psychology relies upon reactance as by insisting upon the implementation of a particular behaviour or course of action, it aims to induce a person to perform the opposite. What distinguishes reactance from reverse psychology is its emphasis upon choice and behavioural freedom, thus making reactance a more subtle and sophisticated psychological model. Notably, the new trend in marketing known as reverse psychology or anti-marketing (Sinha and Foscht 2007) is implicitly informed by the notion of reactance. Its efficacy relies not upon 'push' marketing strategies, which are likely to cause reactance and resistance on the part of the consumer, but through an understated 'pull' dynamic, often making products seem unreachable in order to heighten their allure.

Baron and Byrne (2003) relate the theory of reactance in accessible terms, explaining that, when we are persistently asked or told to do a particular thing, we are more likely to resist. In their words, we "change our attitudes (or behaviour) in a direction exactly opposite to that being urged of us" (2003: 140). For this reason, being issued with the negative statement "This is not for you" is likely to provoke an adversative effect; the reader becomes more adamant that the experience of reading *House of Leaves* will be something s/he welcomes and expects to appreciate.

Considering schematic meaning adds weight to this assertion. Discussing prepositional phrases formed through the combination of preposition and noun phrase such as 'to me' and 'on the floor', Evans and Green (2006) suggest that constructions of this kind are underwritten by the "highly schematic meaning, DIRECTION OR LOCATION WITH RESPECT TO SOME PHYSICAL ENTITY" (117). As 'for you' is a prepositional phrase of this format, it is evident that this schema is highly applicable. Since in order to understand the negated meaning, a reader must initially cognise that which it negates, directional schematic meaning is both valid and pertinent in regard to constructing any conclusions of a cognitive nature. Acknowledging this meaning also enables comparison with the negative variation.

'Not' has a noticeable impact upon both the semantic and schematic content of the sentence. 'Not' almost appears to reverse the oriented movement suggested by the preposition. Admittedly, such reversal would be an oversimplification, yet when we imagine the phrase in use it is often accompanied not by giving as in the un-negated form but with taking away. Indeed, it is somewhat reminiscent of the forbidding words of a parent to their child as they move a potentially exciting object away from the child and out of reach. Since negation involves the foregrounding of the content of the negative text-world followed by its exclusion in the positive text-world, one could argue that Danielewski is linguistically presenting the reader with a gift, the book, tantalising the reader before forbidding them to read it. This gives rise to a tension between the reader as the intended recipient of the book (signalled by the second-person direct address) and as a persona non grata, thus contributing to readerly cognitive reactance. As such, the schematic meaning and reactance triggered by Danielewski's opening strengthens the paradox of "This is not for you" as both invitation and prohibition, increasing the tension it entails, both in terms of meaning and psychological affect. In the next section, I consider how readers may reduce this tension.

4.2.3   Negotiate the Lock

In order for a reader to reduce the dissonance that "This is not for you" creates, the meaning of the perceptual deictic personal pronoun 'you' can be negotiated. In the English language, the second-person pronoun can be used to indicate a number of referents. Wales (1996) describes personal pronouns in general as "multi-functional in their roles in different contexts, which is tantamount to a kind of polysemy" (7). Herman (1994, 2002), in his exploration of 'textual *you*' in fictional second-person narrative, points to at least five functional types of textual *you* which he terms as: (1) generalised *you*, (2) fictional reference, (3) fictionalised (= horizontal) address, (4) apostrophic (= vertical) address, and (5) doubly deictic *you* (1994: 381; 2002: 345). As I interpret these categories, type two, fictional reference, signifies a protagonist in the storyworld through what Herman, drawing on Margolin (1984, 1986–1987), calls 'deictic transfer' in which the narrative *you* is "convertible to the first or third person" (Herman 1994: 382).

While generalised *you* seems rather self-explanatory in referring to the indefinite plural form of the second-person pronoun, Herman cites it as "another species" of deictic transfer (1994: 380), this time shifting from the individualised participant to this impersonal form. The third category, fictionalised address, diverges from fictional reference since although it still functions within the storyworld, it involves address to and/or by fictional characters in much the same way direct address functions in real-world conversation. Apostrophic address, in comparison, transcends the boundaries of the fiction and "directly designates the audience comprising readers of (or listeners to) a fiction" (Herman 1994: 387).

Before considering Herman's final type of textual *you*, it is useful to pause and consider "This is not for you" in light of the pronoun's polysemy. Thus far, this analysis has defined the use of second-person pronoun in "This is not for you" as direct address, emphasising its apostrophic sense. However, *you* is a polysemous pronominal and can also be reinterpreted as a generalised *you* for dissonance-reducing purposes. This would enable manipulation of the referential ambiguity of 'you' to reason that it does not in fact involve the reader. Instead, the reader can actively disassociate, perceiving 'you' to refer to a group of 'others', perhaps unworthy readers, from which s/he is exclusively omitted. As a result, the text-world in which the absence of the reader exists is re-established. As depicted in Figure 4.3, it can now be seen to contain 'others'. Such reinterpretation causes the enhanced foregrounding of the negated text-world in which the reader and novel are synchronised.

As demonstrated by the shift from dotted to solid boundary lines, the negative text-world, in which 'This is for you' is conceptually realised, evolves from the fleeting negative world usually triggered by negation into a more stable conceptual space.

Herman's final functional type of *you* is the doubly deictic *you*. For Herman, this signifies that "on some occasions *you* functions as a cue for

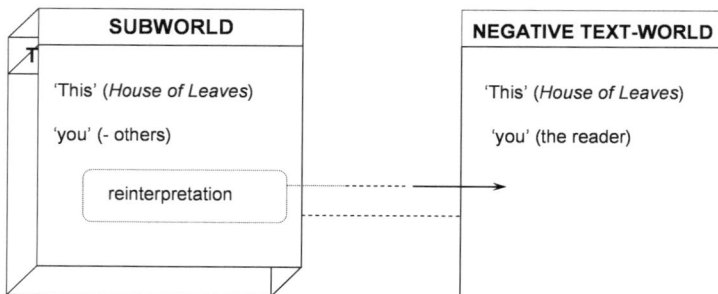

Figure 4.3   Reinterpretation of originating text-world and subsequent foregrounding of negative text-world in "This is not for you".

superimposing two or more deictic roles, one internal to the discourse situation represented in and/or through the diegesis and the other(s) external to that discourse situation" (1994: 381). As Herman himself acknowledges, a doubly deictic you, conflating virtual (storyworld) and actual (real-world) reference, is often difficult to pinpoint. I would be quick to concede that Danielewski's 'you' is not of this order since both construals are positioned in the actualised domain. Nevertheless, Herman's concept of a personal deictic category signalling double situatedness, revisited in section 4.2.9, is valuable. Although Danielewski points to two meanings of 'you' both of which are modes of what Herman calls vertical address, there is a recognisable capacity for interpretive movement between them. In Herman's terms, this subtle perceptual shift can be seen as a case of oscillating deictic transfer between apostrophic and generalised you.

Discussing the second-person pronoun from a cognitive linguistic and discourse analysis perspective, Lee (2001: 177) suggests that the potential ambiguity of 'you' can be manipulated by speakers, and utilised for rhetorical purposes. Wales also notes:

> The fact that standard (English) English does not formalise the distinction between singular and plural sometimes has an advantage. In advertising language, for example, where *you* occurs so frequently in direct if simulated 'personal' address, empathy is heightened by ambivalence: a mass-consumer relationship is simultaneously an individual singled out. (1996: 74)

Danielewski's employment of 'you' also utilises the pronoun's referential multiplicity, creating a slippage between its individualised and generalised meanings. In short, he exploits two senses in the semantic network of *you* for literary effect. However, Danielewski's skilled usage of the pronoun differs from the examples given by Lee and Wales. Instead of heightening subjective affinity through a blurring of the individual and the plural, Danielewski creates distance and desirability.

As a result of reinterpreting 'you' to signal its generalised meaning and then disassociating from this grouping, the reader now appears to occupy a unique subject position (as embodied in the text-world of 'This is for you'). This subject position takes on an uncharacteristic quality of exclusivity, such as that promoted by anti-marketing strategies (Sinha and Foscht 2007). In such marketing campaigns, the desirability of a product is enhanced as a direct consequence of its limited availability. Therefore, an implicit conclusion that can be drawn from Danielewski's crafted employment of the second-person pronoun is that the referential slippage it facilitates creates an appealing subject position for the reader to adopt, one distinct from those encapsulated by the now interpreted generalised *you* in "This is not for you".

4.2.4   Choose to Trespass

The multimodal dimension of "This is not for you" has yet to be considered, but it too has a part to play in the intricacies of the novel's initial statement. It is therefore worth considering the positioning of the sentence upon the page. These five words are the only imprint upon a single page. In fact, upon a double page spread. A reader who experiences reactance to this negated assertion must turn the page in order to encounter succeeding text in the form of the (fictional) introduction. While this is not exactly a demanding task, proceeding to read *House of Leaves* would be easier if further linguistic content appeared upon the same page. Had this been the case, the 'choice' either to continue or stop reading would have been rather less noticeable or significant, since most readers are likely to proceed out of habit. As a result, the white space of page takes on a less innocent façade. This 'emptiness' of the remainder of the page transforms the normally unremarkable operation of turning the page into a defiant performance of reactance, one which works to reassert the reader's free behaviour. In light of McHale's (1987) notion of semipermeability, while the initial meaning of "This is not for you" reinforced the divisions between the reader's discourse-world and the worlds of the novel, the act of turning the page effectively exhibits force, refusing to be obstructed and breaking down the boundary in the process.

Another multimodal consideration affecting the meaning of "This is not for you" is its positioning, not just upon the page but within the book more generally. Since it is placed between the foreword and introduction, we are able to read it as the opening of the narrative, and thus experience the effects described above. However, an additional knowledge frame that could apply is that of the dedication. In his work on paratextual features, Genette states, "the canonical site of the dedication has obviously been at the head of the book, and today, more precisely, on the first right hand page after the title page" (1997 [1987]: 126). In *House of Leaves*, the preceding foreword complicates this, enabling "This is not for you" to be read as both opening sentence and dedication. Dedications usually occur in the ellipted form, '[ ] For [proper noun/noun phrase]'. The resulting implication is that Danielewski's "This is not for you" is a form of negative dedication.

Genette's discussion of dedicatees can be used to enhance an understanding of the subversive potential of Danielewski's negation. Within what Genette considers a "no doubt playful set" of dedicatory subjects, he lists self-dedication, dedication to the hero, and dedication to the reader—"that is, to the real addressee of the work" (1997 [1987]: 133). The dissident nature of a dedication of this sort can be seen from example. Consider the following dedication from Neil Gaiman's (2005) *Anansi Boys*:

> You know how it is. You pick up a book, flip to the dedication, and find that, once again, the author has dedicated a book to someone else and not to you.

Not this time.

Because we haven't yet met/have only a glancing acquaintance/are just crazy about each other/haven't seen each other in much too long/ are in some way related/will never meet, but will I trust, despite that, always think fondly of each other. . .

This one's for you.

With you know what, and you probably know why.

Clearly, Gaiman is toying with the conventional boundaries of the dedication format. The first sentences employ *you* in an active voice using simple present tense. Combined with the generic descriptions, this creates a *you* that embraces both a definite and indefinite audience, encouraging readerly self-implication. Gavins (2007b: 85–86) discusses this form of transcendental address in which a connection is made between an implied author (or author-enactor) and an apostrophically addressed reader, commenting that the "closer the resemblance between the life of the text-world enactor and the life of the real world reader, the more likely it is that the reader will comfortably inhabit the new projected text-world persona" (2007b: 86). Gaiman cleverly avoids readerly disengagement by making his dedication maximally applicable, as evident in the semantic alternatives punctuated by the use of the '/' punctuation mark. What I find most interesting in Gaiman's dedication is his explicit mention of a book dedicated 'to someone else and not to you', shortly succeeded by the unembedded 'This one's for you', which is foregrounded as a result of the semantic contrast. Gaiman's concluding sentence is also remarkable in its proximal and repeated use of interrogatives functioning as ambiguous pronouns.

Gaiman's dedication is a fitting contrast to Danielewski's negated adaptation. Unfortunately, Genette does not consider the possibility of a negative dedication, but he does speak of the author's choice not to include a dedication: "the absence of dedication, in a system that includes the possibility of one, is significant as degree zero. 'This book is not dedicated to anyone'— isn't such an implied message loaded with meaning?" (1997 [1987]: 135). Genette's rhetorical question assumes an affirmative response, though I would argue that this is only the case when the absence is noticed by the reader. Danielewski, in exposing his subversive intent, exhibits the agency of his intention and harnesses the potency of such literary insurgence.

As an explicit negated dedication, "This is not for you" is without question charged with semantic value. By using negation to create dissonance and reactance, alongside the referential slippage of the pronoun *you*, Danielewski heightens readerly desire to read the novel. While multimodality is restricted in this extract, its importance must be acknowledged in enhancing the psychological intensity and complexity evoked by the opening sentence.

Genette speaks of paratextual features as "thresholds", that is "the literary and printerly conventions that mediate between the world of publishing and the world of the text" (1997 [1987]: xvii). Danielewski's literary (-linguistic and -multimodal) manoeuvres entice readers inwards. His use of direct address brings semipermeability into effect, working not to alienate the reader through ontological distancing, but to engage them in an active performance. Turning the page of *House of Leaves* in this sense is a performance by the reader through which they gesture toward an ontological transgression in the direction of the text-world from the discourse-world: turning the page is an act of 'entering', moving toward the narrative world of the novel and into the house.

The creative aperture that has focused the analysis so far acts as a threshold to the novel, a door into the *House of Leaves*. Yet, paradoxically, it is an entrance into a place we are being forbidden to enter. By both inviting and prohibiting the reader, the opening possesses a tension of meaning that Danielewski employs to create a sense of discomfort for the reader to take with them as they turn the page. The paradox and feeling of discomfort are crucial for a novel often cited by critics as belonging to the horror or gothic genre. In *The Mysteries of Udolpho*, a foundational gothic novel, Radcliffe writes of imaginatively evoked fear; "a terror of this nature, as it occupies and expands the mind, and elevates it to high expectation, is purely sublime, and leads us, by a kind of fascination, to seek even the object, from which we appear to shrink" (1966 [1794]: 248). Danielewski's "This is not for you" tempts us to trespass, luring us inside the *House of Leaves*.

4.2.5 Cross the Threshold

The novel's Introduction, which in the storyworld has been written by Johnny Truant, follows "This is not for you". Truant recounts how he was woken at three in the morning by a phone call from his friend Lude. Lude informs Truant that he has found Zampanò dead in the old man's apartment. After police and paramedics have left the scene, Zampanò's body removed, Truant travels across Los Angeles and he and Lude enter the apartment to investigate. Inside, they encounter four long claw marks etched onto Zampanò's floor and a manuscript.

For the most part, this narrative is written in the past tense, providing a retrospective account of events from the fictional moment of narration. It is also homodiegetic, though the second-person pronoun does appear. In the first instance, it is used in rhetorical question: "Ever see yourself doing something in the past and no matter how many times you remember it, you want to scream stop, somehow redirect the action, reorder the present?" (Danielewski 2000a: xiv). In this rhetorical question, the second-person pronoun is used three times; firstly it is used reflexively and in the second and third usages, it is generalised, its usage including the speaking 'I' too. It therefore does not engage the reader into a full identification nor does it interrupt or redirect the first-person narration. This part of the narrative (Danielewski 2000a: xi–xvii) thus invites the reader to project into its deictic centre, the character of Johnny Truant; through this conceptual repositioning, the reader experiences the narrative events through his focalising perspective.

The homodiegetic narration that commences the Introduction creates a centre of orientation that aligns the reader's textual experience with Truant's focalising perspective. However, a dramatic separation of the character Truant and the reader occurs when Danielewski unexpectedly reinstates the second-person pronoun as a form of apostrophic address to the reader. Truant reflects, "What did I know then? What do I know now? At least some of the horror I took away at four in the morning you now have before you, waiting for you a little like it waited for me that night, only without these few covering pages" (xvii). This paragraph entails continual deictic shifts in the reading process. Although I have mentioned pronoun usage prior to revealing the quotation, I will unravel Danielewski's perceptual, temporal, spatial, and textual deictic manoeuvres as they occur in the extract, and thus in reader consciousness, before returning to the relationship between character and reader.

Truant's reflection begins in simple past tense, with past temporality emphasised through the addition of the deictic adverb 'then'. This is in keeping with the preceding narrative in which Truant relates the events of the night on which he first discovered the manuscript. In the second sentence, the same rhetorical question is repeated, but altered to simple present tense with the deictic adverb changed from 'then' to 'now'. This phrasal repetition is a case of syntactic parallelism. Moreover, it has a foregrounding effect; the repetition and parallelism focus attention while the exchanged adverb becomes deviant. It thus works to accentuate the occurring deictic shift and mark a clear separation in time between the night in which Truant first took possession of Zampanò's manuscript and the moment of narration.

The third and final sentence is the longest and most complex. It is in this sentence that apostrophic address recurs with the use of the interpersonal pronouns. The first-person singular continues to refer to Johnny Truant, the narrating character and perceptual deictic centre of the discourse. Employing first-person in conjunction with second-person pronouns, Danielewski creates a situational context that produces the impression of dialogue between character and reader. Consequently, the reader 'pops' out of the focalising perspective of Truant.

Speaking of 'the horror', Truant reveals to the reader his emotional state after leaving Zampanò's apartment. Furthermore, the temporal and spatial deictic markers linked to 'the horror', which in turn trigger textual deixis, generate a double semantic layering. Truant takes the horror *away* at *four in the morning*. The temporal locative refreshes the beginning of Truant's tale in the mind of the reader. This acts as a narrative frame recall (Emmott

1994, 1997), mentioning information about a previous narrative episode to prompt readers to recollect and reinstate knowledge of that episode for use in present literary understanding. The recall is prompted by the specificity of the time. It is exactly one hour after Truant has informed the reader he was woken by Lude's telephone call. The locative therefore contextualises and clarifies the event under discussion. In doing so, it prompts a comprehension of the spatial adverb *away* to construe a path moving from Lude and Zampanò's apartment block. Subsequent to this, 'the horror' is signified as an entity that readers "now have before you". As the temporal and spatial parameters employed are in reference to the 'you', it is the reader's real-world situation being called into play in the interpretation of these deictic markers.

'Before' makes the most significant contribution in characterising 'the horror' since the object *before* the reader in their physical and spatial environment, and the object of their attention, is of course the book, Mark Z. Danielewski's *House of Leaves by Zampanò with Introduction and Notes by Johnny Truant*. Thus, the temporal and spatial indicators give rise to textual deixis by unveiling 'the horror' as a reference to the text itself, a reference supported by the closing mention of 'these covering pages' or, in other words, Truant's penned introduction. The use of the definite article aids this reference by seeming to concretise the abstract noun 'horror' as an existential preposition. Accordingly, the deictic elements disclose the double semantic layering of the phrase 'the horror' which is simultaneously invested with emotional and physical meaning. Its linguistic treatment is therefore underwritten by the conceptual metaphor, EMOTIONS ARE OBJECTS.

I have already indicated that Danielewski constructs a dialogic parameter through the use of first-person narration and apostrophic address. The profusion of deictic markers in this short paragraph reinforces the shift from Truant's recollection to this situational context and facilitates reader self-implication and identification with 'you' since the text-world's spatio-temporal centre of orientation has been aligned with the actual reader's in the discourse-world. Moreover, the use of 'I' and 'you', 'you' and 'me', along with their close linguistic proximity connects the interpersonal pronouns, creating a sense of shared intimacy. The subordinate clause 'waiting for you a little like it waited for me that night' sustains this relationship between reader and character, 'you' and 'me', through syntactic parallelism and explicit comparison. Additionally, this clause complements the interpretation of 'the horror' as concrete entity rather than abstract emotional experience.

The verb 'waiting' suggests the respite prior and leading to dynamic action, as in the phrase "waiting to pounce" or "waiting to attack", endowing 'the horror' with the potential for animation. The threat of animation the verb contains is heightened by Danielewski's use of continuous aspect, making the anticipated potential act seem inescapable for the 'you' it relates to. Lastly in connection with this, the recent frame recall, bringing to mind how Truant found Zampanò's manuscript, enables the reader to draw on the sense of animation instilled in 'the horror' and the manuscript it signifies to cognitively revisit and reinterpret the daunting claw marks Truant and Lude encountered in Zampanò's apartment. Another embodied conceptual metaphor of emotion is at work here then: EMOTION IS A WILD ANIMAL (Gibbs 2006: 242).

In conjunction with shifting the deictic centre of the text-world into a *here* and *now* which seemingly parallels the discourse-world(s) of readers, Danielewski's employment of apostrophic address creates a cognitive illusion: Truant's introduction breaches the ontological divide between text and discourse-world, fiction and reality, to engage with each and every actual reader in their own time frame. Ultimately, this transgressive union is deceptive. An enactor of the reader is engaged with the character of Truant. Arguably, too, the textual deictic mention of 'these few covering pages' shifts Truant's narrating act into the past, causing a 'crackle' or 'flux' in direct communication. Nevertheless, I contend that the combination of deictics in this paragraph serves not only to forge parallels between Truant and the reader, but also to anthropomorphise the character of Truant, so that both he and his narrative seem all the more real and, along with 'the horror', all the more disturbing.

Discussing the use of narrative apostrophe in fiction, Kacandes asserts that if readers accept the position of "direct addressee, the desired other of the narrator, [they are] positioned to feel the emotional force of the relationship created" (2001: 179). Danielewski's employment of apostrophic *you* has exactly this effect, constructing a textual encounter that encourages the reader to develop an affinity with Truant, thus drawing the reader deeper into the world(s) of *House of Leaves* and motivating his/her emotional investment into the narrative.

As a final comment on the paragraph analysed above, it is useful to draw a brief comparison with the opening sentence to the novel. The book as an object is not explicitly named, but signalled through the use of deictic expressions and the seeming concretisation of the abstract noun 'horror' as an existential preposition. Similarly, in the novel's opening sentence, the demonstrative 'this' stands for the novel. The disinclination to name explicitly *House of Leaves* adds to a building sense of mystery surrounding it via its fictional origin in Zampanò's manuscript.

Following the paragraph analysed above, Truant attempts to calm readers' anticipation and trepidation concerning the enigmatic nature of Zampanò's manuscript, demystifying the novel through description:

```
As I discovered, there were reams and reams of it.
Endless snarls of words, sometimes twisting into mean-
ing, sometimes into nothing at all, frequently break-
ing apart, always branching off into other pieces I'd
```

come across later—on old napkins, the tattered edges of
an envelope, once even on the back of a postage stamp;
everything and anything but empty; each fragment completely covered with the creep of years and years of ink
pronouncements; layered, crossed out, amended; handwritten, typed; legible, illegible; impenetrable, lucid;
torn, stained, scotch taped; some bits crisp and clean,
others faded, burnt or folded and refolded so many
times the creases have obliterated whole passages of god
knows what—sense? truth? deceit? a legacy of prophecy or
lunacy or nothing of the kind?, and in the end achieving, designating, describing, recreating—find your own
words; I have no more; or plenty more but why? and all
to tell—what? (xvii)

This paragraph functions not only as a lengthy, and sometimes contradictory, account of Zampanò's manuscript. It also enables Danielewski to prepare the reader for the text and the reading experience ahead. At the start
of this quotation, Danielewski gestures towards the size of both manuscript
and book, using hyperbolic language ('reams and reams', 'endless', 'always',
'years and years') to emphasise the vast scale of the novel. These are assimilated with progressive verbs of motion ('twisting', 'breaking', 'branching')
which endow the words of the text with ongoing agency and dynamism,
while the mention of 'snarls', an animalistic sound, ties in with the claw
marks on Zampanò's floor and the carnivorous undertone attributed to
'the horror'.

In comparison to the verbs of motion, the verb chain that comes after the
extensive list of contradictory descriptions (achieving, designating, describing, recreating) is instead concerned with the ideational. This sequence, from
action to signification, suggests the way in which the multimodal designs of
the text, which shift and alter through the novel, result in meaning-making
as well as what might be called an unmaking of meaning. These verbs of
ideation are at odds with the action verbs. Similarly, each adjective used to
describe the text is consistently paired with a contradictory adjective (e.g.
'legible, illegible; impenetrable, lucid'), thus creating an effect similar to
negation by suggesting a meaning, and then cancelling it out and therefore
denying a definitive meaning to emerge.

Importantly, like the contradictory descriptions and the close of the
passage which denies definitive conclusions, the meaning arising from the
multimodality of the text is not singular and prescriptive but multiple and
thus open to readerly interpretation. To this end, the inconclusive nature
of the passage denies any narrative or descriptive closure. Instead, it gives
way to interrogatives that challenge the reader to take on an editorial
and/or interpretive task, and find their own individualised meaning in
the text. As mentioned, the conclusion affords no ending, trailing off into

unanswered questions. Truant's experience of 'the horror', his relationship to Zampanò's manuscript, is obsessive and unceasing. The description of the novel that Danielewski provides in this passage hints at what
is to come for the reader of *House of Leaves* and how his/her relationship
with the novel is to evolve . . . for what is obsession but a preoccupation
without end? In the next section, I begin to consider the novel's graphic
design and textual layout, which bear out Truant's description of Zampanò's manuscript, quoted earlier.

4.2.6   Explore the House

At the centre of *House of Leaves'* recursive narrative structure is the
embedded world of "The Navidson Record". The 'video recording' and
Zampanò's commentary feature the Navidson family in their new home
on Ash Tree Lane. As the strange shifting proportions of the house become
conspicuous, "The Navidson Record" develops into an account of a series
of six explorations into the dark depths of the house's ominous interior.
Exploration A is the first investigation, undertaken and recorded by Navidson alone. After Navidson nearly gets lost in the vast darkness, a team of
professional explorers, lead by Holloway Roberts, are called in and from
this point onwards the explorations are numbered #1–#5. With each exploration, the explorers delve deeper into the darkness.

Interestingly, as their explorations become successively more extensive, Danielewski's representation of them becomes increasingly multimodal, peaking with #4 and #5 and in a sense fulfilling the dynamic
description of the text in Johnny Truant's Introduction, quoted earlier.
As multimodal compositions, these 'explorations' require the reader to
construct a coherent narrative from the multitude of semiotic modes in
use. The multimodal representation of Exploration #4 and Exploration
#5 creates a design template founded upon a conceptual integration of
the domains house and book. In capitalising these, I am treating them as
conceptual domains. As Langacker explains, "Domains are conceptual
entities: mental experiences, representation spaces, concepts, or conceptual complexes" (1987: 147).

The integration of house and book is suggested by the novel's title and
made most evident in its French title, *La Maison des Feuilles*. Like many
French words, 'feuille' has a double meaning as both 'leaf' and 'sheet of
paper'. (This meaning is pointed to on page 564 of the novel in Appendix
F. 'Poems'. The page is titled *La Feuille*, written in French, and features
an Apollinaire poem.) Thus, 'House of Leaves' references not just the
Ash *Tree* Lane house at the centre of the novel. It is also a self-referential
detail, blending the concept of house with the book of paper pages. This
blend, which is at play during the more extensive explorations, is part of
a single-scope network (Fauconnier and Turner 2002: 126–131), shown
in Figure 4.4.

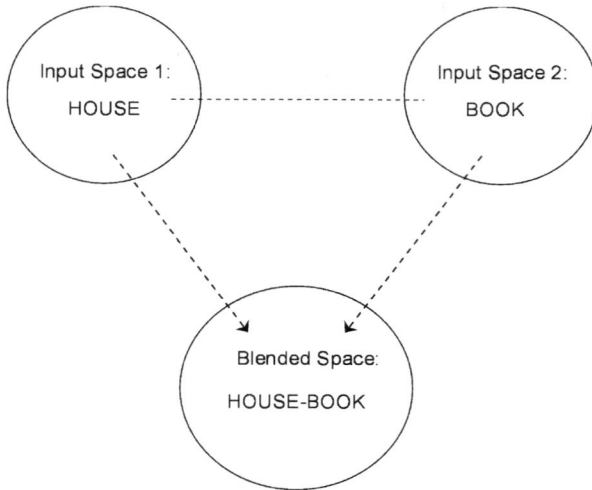

Figure 4.4   HOUSE-BOOK single-scope blend.

Fauconnier and Turner suggest that this form of integration, the single-scope network, fits the model of source to target mapping, whereby one domain, the target, is reinterpreted as a result of the blend (2002: 127). In the single-scope network identified here, the HOUSE input is the organising frame. What this means in practice is that the concept of HOUSE, as framing input, acts to structure the new meanings that emerge from the blend (emergent meaning). In contrast, the concept of BOOK acts as the focus input, with elements from this domain reframed by the HOUSE structure. The emergent blend, therefore, sees the book taking on properties of the HOUSE domain, such as corridors, doorways, windows, and so forth. The blend is achieved multimodally, in that these corridors and doorways are created through the diagrammatic organisation of text upon the page, their visual shape and layout producing an abstract, structural analogy of HOUSE.

In addition, since the interior of the house takes on a labyrinthine structure, it could be said that prior to the aforementioned blending process, the domains of LABYRINTH and HOUSE are also blended. In this case, the conceptual integration that takes place entails multiple blending. The first conceptual blend involves LABYRINTH and HOUSE. This is again a single-scope blend, since the concept of LABYRINTH works to organise the concept of HOUSE. The further blend, therefore, occurs between the emergent blend from the first conceptual integration, LABYRINTHINE HOUSE, and the new input or conceptual domain of BOOK, as shown in Figure 4.5.

Although the emergent blend consequently involves all three domains, throughout this chapter I will refer to the blend of HOUSE and BOOK,

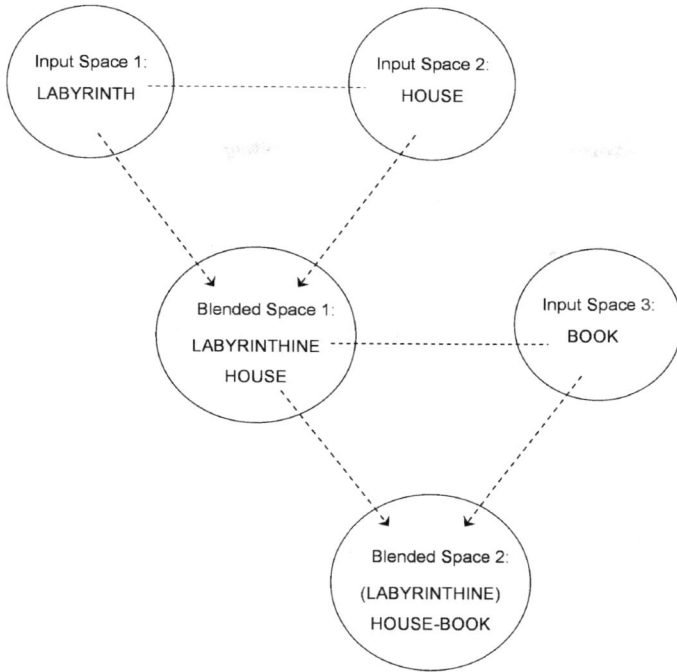

Figure 4.5   Multiple blending network of LABYRINTH, HOUSE, and BOOK.

since both of these domains are initially focus inputs in their respective blends, and therefore most significant to the final emergent blend.

Explorations #1–#3 are relatively brief, both in terms of Danielewski's descriptions of them and their storyworld duration (Exploration #1 is said to last just one hour, while Exploration #3 takes twenty hours). Moreover, Holloway and his team make little progress through the mysterious interior space, and by the end of the third exploration, their discoveries are still minimal. They have moved through what originally seemed like an endless corridor reaching a seemingly bottomless staircase leading downwards. Exploration #4, on the other hand, is both extensive and dramatically mul-timodal. Shortly after Exploration #4 begins, the textual design of the page alters, columns of text forming 'corridors' of words. These corridors are composed of some of the different discourses which make up the novel: the description of Exploration #4 from "The Navidson Record", footnotes and intertextual references, Truant's idle comments. As shown in Figure 4.6, these labyrinthine configurations do not conform to the prototypical type-setting of Western literature, and thus cause greater awareness of the visual surface of the page.

As Exploration #4 progresses, the number of corridors increases and the text traverses the page in different directions. Each corridor can be seen as

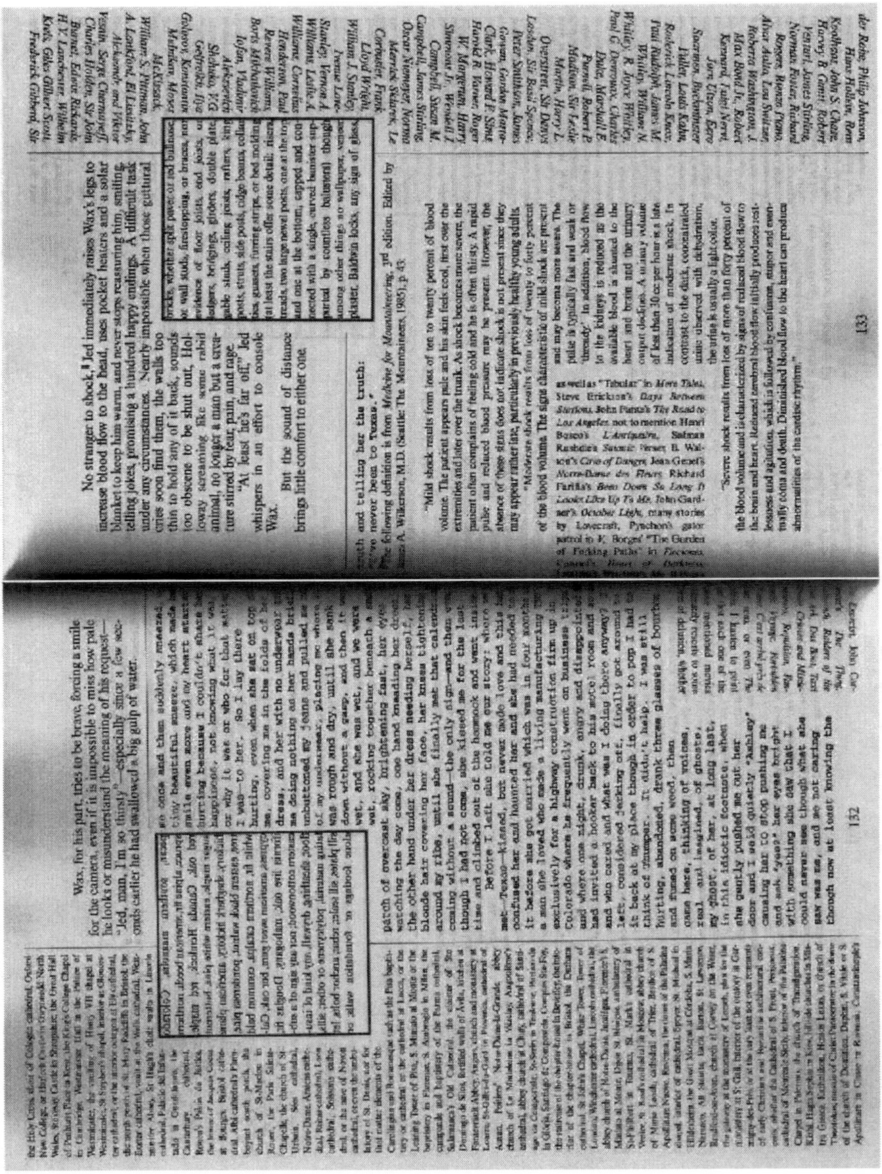

Figure 4.6   Danielewski (2000a) *House of Leaves*: 132–133.

a cluster, spatially confined by either a border or some white space of page with the typography of that discourse and the direction of text making each cluster distinct.

As I have already implied, the chief way in which the multimodal integration of house and book is realised is through textual layout—the imagistic design of the book being informed by the structural elements of a house. Since the windows, rooms, and columns hold text written in divergent directions, readers must rotate the book in order to read the various clusters. In doing so, the integration is furthered by creating a correlation between the reader of the book and the explorers of the internal house. Fordham also reaches this conclusion, though without reference to conceptual integration, stating "the narrative content is being projected into the reader's experience of the text" (2002: 14). Just as Holloway and his team turn corners in the dark corridors, discovering additional spaces and/ or rooms, the reader revolves the book to read the text. While Fordham may reach a similar conclusion about the correlation between reader(s) and explorer(s), multimodal cognitive poetics, and in particular the use of Conceptual Integration Theory, substantiates such an observation. It not only provides support for this interpretation of the text, but it also shows that multimodal conceptual integration (here realised by *House of Leaves*' textual design) evokes an emergent structure which brings together textual form, reader cognitive process, and resulting effect in the context of the reading experience.

Admittedly, some clusters have more semantic importance than others. The corridor that occupies the far-right column of the right-hand page on almost every double page spread of Exploration #4, for example, is an italicised list, printed upside down, of names of architects and patrons of buildings. This eight-page list, offering little semantic or narrative content, is not likely to attract reader attention enough to motivate the rotation of the book for every double page spread in Exploration #4. Still, this does not detract from the conceptual integration since in the process of elaboration, or running the blend, these unread columns can be made analogous to untravelled routes or corridors. Similarly, if readers begin reading the column only to become unresponsive to it, it can be neglected and treated as a 'dead end'. Interestingly, in an interpretive explanation which confirms my proposal of the house-book blend, Slocombe interprets the content of the many 'corridors' or footnotes in Chapter IX accordingly:

> These are not "footnotes" but rooms within a house, sometimes empty (the blank boxes), sometimes full of people (lists of people such as the "authors of buildings" section on page 121). They also include store cupboards (the supplies and objects of footnote 144, pages 119–42) and libraries (footnote 167, pages 131–35, on "literary hauntings," including texts by Erickson, Pynchon, Borges, and Rushdie). (2005: 97–98)

In addition, the textual configurations of Chapter IX alter slightly from page to page, reinforcing the reader's correlation with the novel's explorers by multimodally representing the shifting proportions of the space and thus emulating in the reader a parallel sense of disorientation to that the characters are inferred to feel as they become lost and unsettled.

The initial visual transformation of the page at the start of Exploration #4 starts with the appearance of an unusual box to the right containing footnote[1]44. Footnote 144 is a list of items that do not appear in the dark interior of the Ash Tree Lane house. Indeed, Fordham describes it as a "list of 'subtractives' rather than 'additives', just like the other footnotes which all describe the house or the film, in terms of what it is *not*, of negation" (2002: 15). As discussed in the opening analysis (see section 4.3.2), negation is a foregrounding device, thus the list emphasises all of the material objects that the house's mysterious centre lacks.

In terms of the HOUSE-BOOK conceptual integration, footnote 144's list of items not in the house can be seen to temporarily disintegrate the blend. Instead of emphasising emergent structure or shared properties between the inputs of HOUSE and BOOK, the footnote points out unselected properties, points of difference. In this way, it leads to a decompression of the blend, partially separating the inputs and in the process causing an uncanny tension between the physicality and conceptuality of literary texts; while the reader may be rotating the book and interacting with it in a very material way, unlike an actual house and the material objects mentioned in the footnote, literature is a transcendental and abstract endeavour, the objects of which exist in the imagination. Ironically, this tension is suggested by the footnote's final line of text: "~~Picture that, In your dreams~~" (141). This in itself is interesting for the visual strike-through device places its text under erasure, yet leaves it legible underneath. As such, this can be seen to work like negation, foregrounding that which is negated.

Hayles (2002a, 2002b) has discussed footnote 144, focusing on its materiality. The footnote begins in the box on page 119 and runs through every identically located box, positioned on the right-hand page of the double page spread, to end on page 145. The text, in fact, ends on page 141, but the box continues for the further four pages. As such, the footnote appears to tunnel through the pages. Moreover, for the majority of this 'ductnote', as Fordham calls it (2002: 14), the right-hand side of each double page spread displays the previous page's text in reverse, as can be seen in Figure 4.6. Hayles analyses this structure as follows:

> The box calls into question an assumption so commonplace that we are not normally aware of it: book pages are opaque, a property that defines one page as separate from another. Here the back of the page

---

144   "Not only are there no hot-air registers . . ." (Danielewski 2000a: 119).

appears to open transparently onto the front, a notion that overruns the boundary between them and constructs the page as a leaky container rather than an unambiguous unit of print. Treating the page as a window. (2002a: 792; 2002b: 123)

Hayles is concerned with the way in which the reversed text challenges readers' basic presuppositions of how a book is supposed to look and behave. Notably, the simile of her final comment feeds into my contention that the multimodal design of *House of Leaves* forms a conceptual integration of HOUSE and BOOK. The subversive illusion of transparency used to represent footnote 144 visually creates an ironic accompaniment. Working multimodally through text and image to create the impression of a window, footnote 144's visual design complements its negated content, since there are also no windows inside the dark and daunting area.

4.2.7   Climb the Stairs

Exploration #5 is the final exploration of the novel and the one that Navidson obsessively takes alone, after the team of professional explorers and his brother have all become lost inside or devoured by the house's interior darkness. Danielewski's representation of this exploration is erratic, with the page designs constantly altering in accordance with the narrative. More significantly, my analysis exposes a new dimension of the multimodal literary experience.

The spatial arrangement of pages 440–441 is particularly striking and will provide a valuable point of analytical departure. Arranged across a double page spread, the words sit vertically, meaning that the book must be rotated in order for the pages to be read. The narrative delivers the following episode:

> Slowly but surely, hand over hand, Navidson pulls himself up the ladder. But after presumably hours and hours of climbing with only brief stops to take a gulp of water or have a bite of some high-caloric energy bar, Navidson admits he will probably have to tie himself to a rung and try to sleep. This idea, however, is so unappealing he continues to push on for a little longer. His tenacity is rewarded. Thirty minutes later, he reaches the last rung. A few more seconds and he is standing inside a very . . . (440–441)

At this point, the narrative stops and the reader must turn the page to continue the sentence and find out where Navidson is standing.

From a cognitive-linguistic perspective, the first sentence immediately creates figure and ground relations. Initially, the focus is placed upon Navidson's hands, utilising a synecdochical mapping, before drawing back

standing inside a very
seconds and he is

rung. A few more
he reaches the last

Thirty minutes later,
tenacity is rewarded.

for a little longer. His
continues to push on

unappealing he
however, is so

sleep. This idea,
rung and try to

tie himself to a
probably have to

admits he will
bar, Navidson

high-caloric energy
have a bite of some

gulp of water or
stops to take a

with only brief
of climbing,

hours and hours
after presumably

the ladder. But
pulls himself up

Navidson

hand over hand,

Slowly but surely,

'above and below'.

exchange the words
and Hell, cannot

believe in Heaven
long ceased to

those who have
the word 'up'. Even

and the power of
the word 'above',

due to the force of
redemption. That is

mountain reflects
The climbing of a

meanings:
comments on the force of vertical
berge (Frankfurt, 1960, p. 95)
Erich Kästner in *Oberste Wesn-*

An idea Fischer beautifully sub-
verts in *House of Stairs*, disen-
chanting his audience of the
gravity of the world, while at the
same time enchanting them with
the peculiar gravity of the self.

441

440

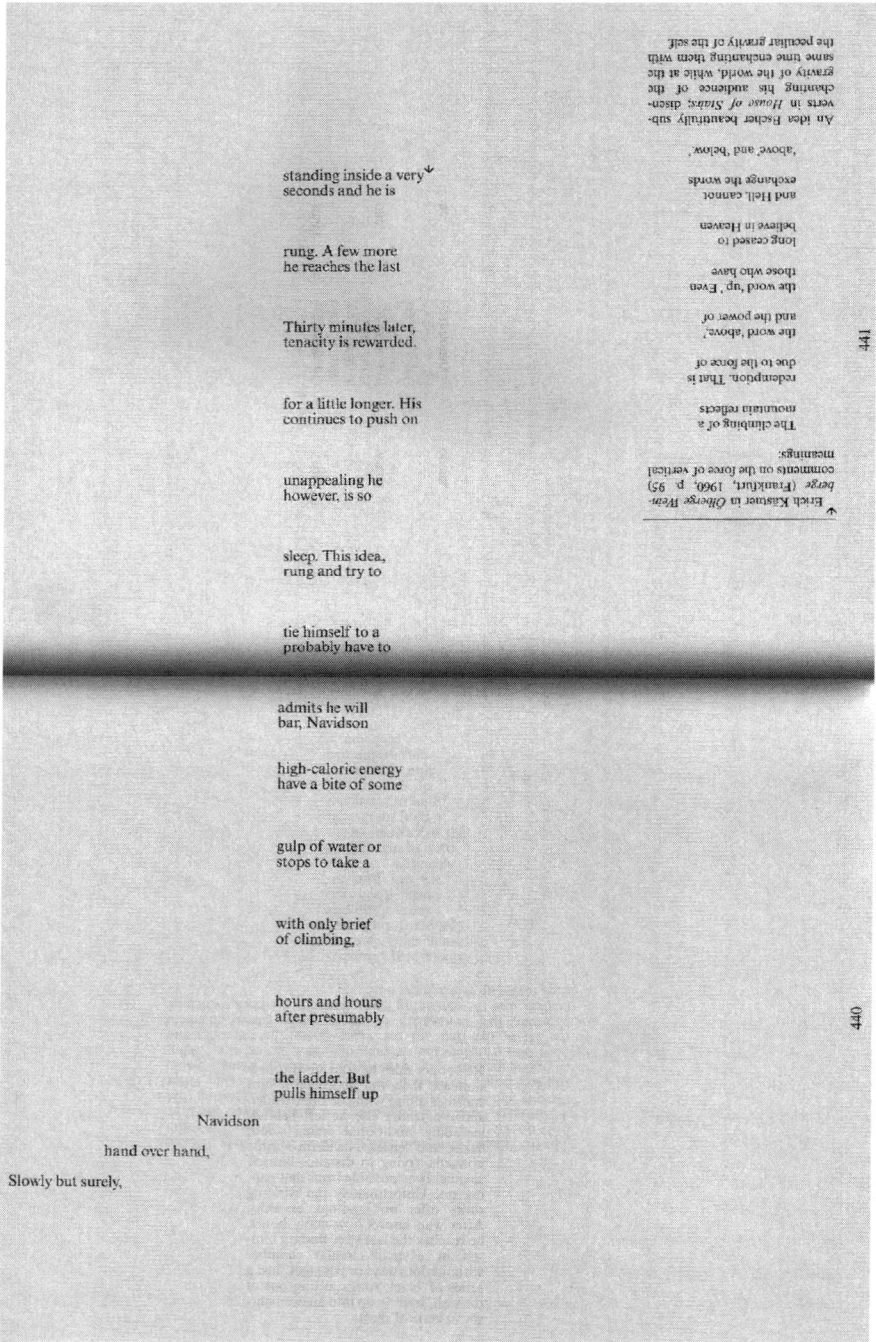

Figure 4.7   Danielewski (2000a) *House of Leaves*: 440–441.

to Navidson himself. Navidson, occupying the subject theme position and invested with agency and motion, is profiled as the trajector while the ladder is marked as landmark in the narrative world. His movement is part of an UP image schema whereby his path is one of ascent. This linguistic configuration, in effect, transcends its static manifestation (as words on a page), instilling dynamism and animation into the narrative world.

Figuration can also (and clearly) be identified visually in this extract. The iconic spatial arrangement, viewed as a whole, creates a ladder that bridges horizontally across the pages. This ladder is obviously a deviant visual design when compared with conventional Western literary textual arrangement. Each rung of the ladder is formed by and as a cluster of two short lines of words positioned in tight proximity and surrounded by white space. The words, printed in dark black type, stand prominent against the pale scape of blank page, just as in life a real ladder would occupy the figural position when leant against a wall.

The ladder, its sequence of words and their spatial location, dictates the reading path that must be taken. Even when the book has been rotated, the apparent starting-point is in its original top left corner. However, the physical revolution of the book forces a less familiar eye motion. The first three lines, each moving horizontally from left to right toward the next, create vectors that signal reading direction. These 'stairs' push the eyes' path upward, step by step, toward the rungs of the ladder where the unconventional rising of textual fragments makes for a somewhat uncomfortable and awkward reading process. This ascendant design results in a deviant reading path. The upward accumulation of rungs, another vectorial patterning, forces the eye to leap across the spaces, visually 'cluster hopping' (Baldry and Thibault 2006: 26) despite the linearity of verbal narrative.

In the process of cluster hopping, the eyes perform a kind of 'kinetic occlusion' (Gibson 1966: 203–206). The notion of kinetic occlusion originates in the work of perceptual and ecological psychologist, J. J. Gibson (1966: 203–206) and has been developed by Scarry (2001) in relation to literary experience. Starting with the imagined narrative world of *House of Leaves*, Navidson's climbing movement involves "hand over hand" on alternate rungs of the ladder. From an objective side-view, as the forehand passes before the back hand to reach for the higher tier, there would arise within the text-world a brief instance of kinetic occlusion where the forehand blocks the rear from sight. Returning to *House of Leaves'* visual structure, each rung of the ladder, as it is read, attracts the reader's attention, throwing the previous into relief. Unlike the literal process of kinetic occlusion, that is, of seeing one object pass before another object, these rungs create occlusion through the eyes' motion, as the rung being presently read, the currency of that cluster, overshadows the former. This process, as Scarry points out, "specifies durability" (2001: 13): the previous rungs, while no longer in focus, continue to exist below, and in the eyes' journey to the top of the ladder, create a layering, an accumulation of lower tiers. Additionally, one may perceive the grammatical constructions of "Slowly but surely", "hand over hand", and "hours and hours" as creating a similar effect, using lexical repetition, parallelism, and sound patterning to echo this layering and emphasise Navidson's monotonous climbing activity, continuous throughout the lengthy temporal duration.

The reading path involved in this extract creates a subjective resonance. The reader's eyes and the character Navidson become counterparts through upward motion and discomfort. The reader's physical and visual encounter with the text parallels the narrative depiction of climbing and by extension the actual exercise in the real world. This visual representation, enhanced by the linguistic use of present tense, thus forces the eyes to enact a conceptual metaphor: LITERARY EXPERIENCE IS PHYSICAL MOVEMENT. This links neatly to Gerrig's (1993) idea of narrative experience as akin to transportation. He speaks of the reader "*being transported* by virtue of *performing* that narrative*" (1993: 2; original emphasis). This is, therefore, by no means a newly revealed conceptual metaphor; yet, I believe, the performance of this metaphor in *House of Leaves* is distinct. By 'performance', Gerrig refers to a purely imaginative and emotional endeavour whereas this reading path adds another performative dimension, that of literal ocular movement and participation parallel to that in the world of the text. The manifestation of this conceptual metaphor, produced by the interplay of word and image, is the shared endeavour of the writer, deciding and organising the visual layout according to narrative content, and the reader whose optical journey realises LITERARY EXPERIENCE IS PHYSICAL MOVEMENT. Had the visual aspect of this extract not been taken into account, the performance of this visual conceptual metaphor may not have been considered.

Moving to the right-hand page of the extract, there is a second ladder. Positioned at the top of the larger primary ladder, the book must again be rotated in order to facilitate reading. Running left to right from the top downwards, this ladder including the top and bottom platform reads:

> Erich Kästner . . . comments on the force of vertical meanings:
> The climbing of a mountain reflects redemption. That is due to the force of the word 'above,' and the power of the word 'up.' Even those who have long ceased to believe in Heaven and Hell, cannot exchange the words 'above' and 'below.'
> An idea Escher beautifully subverts in *House of Stairs*; disenchanting his audience of the gravity of the world, while at the same time enchanting them with the peculiar gravity of the self. (441)

The reflection upon the words 'up', 'above', and 'below' is essentially a meditation on the related conceptual metaphors good is up and bad is down in which psychological judgements are explained via reference to the experience of elevation. The discussion of the 'power' and 'force' of these words implies their importance in the structuring of thought. In other words, good is up and bad is down have become constitutive metaphors, and are vital to the process of human understanding. This visual ladder and the reading pattern it implements generate a twist in the construal of this observation. good is up suggests a cognitive expectation concerning what happens when one reaches the top of a ladder. Conversely, the reading path journeys downwards, thus creating a paradox. The disparity between the verbal and the visual spawns a tension of meaning: does the directionality of reading invert the meaning of the linguistic content? Furthermore, before turning the page to discover Navidson's next location, the ladders have taken the reader upwards and downwards respectively. This conflict, left unresolved, creates a 'cliff-hanger' effect, raising anxiety over the nature of the page-turning location overleaf.

At the top of each ladder on pages 440–441 can be seen two small arrows. Both point back down their respective ladders. While one may be tempted to characterise these as indexes (like the pointing finger), they seem not to be directing the reader to a particular object, thus rendering this category inapplicable. Neither do they signal reading direction as the reader's first encounter with an arrow is at the top of the central ladder that s/he has just 'climbed'. One possibility is that they are in fact connected with reading direction, but acting more like visual vectors, the first pushing the reader's eye toward the top of the second ladder from where to begin reading in the direction the second arrow points. Another possibility is that the arrow at the top of the first ladder, pointing downward to the floor so to speak, is designed to act as a diagrammatic reminder of the possibility of falling. This cognitive possibility, when contemplated, coupled with the vectorial instinct to follow the direction pointed to by the arrow-head, may influence the reader's eye to journey back down the ladder in a form of literary 'freefall'. In this case the arrow has, through a combination of indexical and iconic sign, along with the reader's complicit optical descent, stood in for the snake in the popular children's game *Snakes and Ladders*. This displays the innovative and playful nature of the novel, yet it also functions to heighten narrative anxiety, suggesting the dangerous route that Navidson, and through a parallel relation the reader too, has taken.

4.2.8   Move Around

In considering how the multimodal composition of the extract affects the reader's interaction with the novel, it is important to take into account both cognitive and corporeal dimensions of the encounter. Reflecting upon the reader's corporeal experience to begin, it is significant that at the start of the extract Danielewski focuses upon 'hand over hand' in the climbing process. Not only are 'hands' mentioned on multiple occasions in the novel, as the book's index evidences, but the phrase 'hand over hand' is in fact employed verbatim (Danielewski 2000a: 283) within another account of an earlier exploration.

Neuroscientic findings demonstrate a strong connection between sensorimotor process and linguistic comprehension. It has now been evidenced using functional imaging experiments that action words also trigger similar patterns of activation in the brain (Rizzolatti and Craighero 2004; Tettamanti et al. 2005), thus demonstrating that language comprehension is an embodied process. Drawing on these conclusions, it can be deduced that in the *House of Leaves* extract, the movement implied by the preposition 'over' and the explicit linguistic coding (and repetition) of hands generates activity in readers' corresponding sensorimotor cells of the same sort as that generated in executing the action. Many neuroscientists believe that 'motor resonance', the phenomenon associated with the mirror-neuron system, is a skill which functions to enable prediction and control of one's own actions, thus facilitating "a useful shortcut" (Zwaan and Taylor 2006: 2) to the action in question, should performance of it be required. In the extract from *House of Leaves*, then, the linguistic priming of 'hand over hand' has a strategic relationship to the physical act of rotating the book, which, unusually in Western literature, the reader must perform as he or she proceeds through this exploration.

Reader involvement in the narrative world of *House of Leaves* is intensified by corporeal encounter. While the phrase 'hand over hand' primes readerly movement, the reader's actual movement is in itself a device of engagement. Indeed, Gallese and Lakoff (2005: 456) highlight the connectivity of action and imagination when they state, "Imagining and doing use a shared neural substrate". Glenberg's (2008; Glenberg and Gutierrez 2004; Glenberg, Jaworrski, and Rischal 2007) empirical studies into embodied learning reveal the significance of readerly physical activity for literary experience. The foundation for Glenberg's experiments is the indexical hypothesis, an embodied account of language comprehension. To quote Glenberg, Jaworrski, and Rischal (2007: 231–232), the indexical hypothesis suggests:

> meaning arises from creating or simulating the perceptual/action situation described by sentences. These simulations are determined by the properties of the objects referred to, that is, the affordances of the objects, not the properties of the words.

The indexical hypothesis has been successfully tested in classroom contexts with regards both to children's linguistic comprehension of narrative texts and mathematical story problem solving. By providing children with toy objects that have iconic relation to entities in the narrative text or mathematical story problem, it was ensured that children index the words to real-world objects, integrating first- and second-hand knowledge and preventing semantic 'emptiness' through what Glenberg and Gutierrez call "a meaningless exercise in word calling" (2004: 427). They conclude, "manipulation and imagined manipulation can greatly enhance young children's reading performance, as reflected by both their memory for what they have read and their ability to derive text-based inferences" (434).

Although these results apply to children in an educational context, they do bear relevance to the reader's physical manipulation of the book of *House of Leaves*. Readerly physical activity such as rotating the book and 'climbing' the ladder can be seen to endow *House of Leaves* with cognitive impact, heightening narrative conception and making it more memorable as a result of corporeal encounter. In the following section, I suggest how the reader's corporeal encounter with the text impacts upon the process of text-world creation.

4.2.9   Experiencing the House

The reader's physical interaction with the book, his or her need to rotate it to facilitate reading, is a product of the multimodal arrangement and conceptual integration of house and book. The words on the page replicate the shifting architecture of the house's dark interior and as a result the characters' journeys through it too. In Exploration #5, it is Navidson's solo expedition that is represented and followed by the reader. As shown in the preceding analysis, this pursuit creates parallel relations between the reader and the character Navidson. By this means, I argue, a form of doubly deictic subjectivity is created. To recall and extend Herman's definition of the doubly deictic *you*:

> the audience will find itself more or less subject to conflation with the fictional self addressed by *you*. The deictic force of *you* is double; or to put it another way, the scope of the discourse context embedding the description is indeterminate, as is the domain of participants in principle specified or picked out by *you*. (1994: 399)

According to the latter sentence of Herman's articulation, the ambiguous reference of *you* is at the heart of this subjective conflation.

In this extract from Exploration #5, the second-person pronoun is not in use, yet a convergence of character and reader does nevertheless transpire. While I cannot therefore call this an instance of doubly deictic *you* per se, I advocate it as an example of doubly deictic subjectivity, built upon a similar "superimposition of virtuality (the fictional protagonist) and actuality (the reader)" (Herman 1994: 387), only in this case it is triggered not by pronominal polysemous reference but by multimodal imposition. The reader is at once both an observer of the fiction and powerfully involved in that fiction.

The combination of physical activity with doubly deictic involvement in *House of Leaves* alters the customary creation and experience of the text-world. In the passage analysed in section 4.2.7, the central ladder is the prominent text-world, as shown in Figure 4.8.

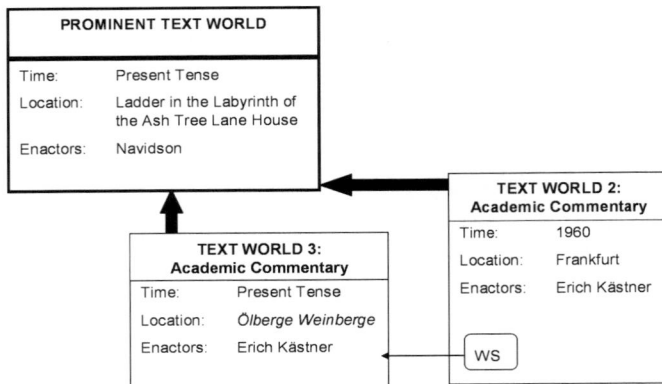

Figure 4.8 Text-worlds of Danielewski (2000a) *House of Leaves*: 440–441.

The smaller ladder, holding academic commentary, creates a second separate text-world with a further embedded text-world in the form of direct quotation from Erich Kästner. Due to the corresponding visual designs of the ladders, among other factors, the reader makes cross-world inferences, that is Erick Kästner's comments on the words 'above' and 'below' influence the reader's understanding and interpretation of Navidson's climbing of the ladder in the prominent text-world, as demonstrated in the earlier analysis. In Figure 4.8, the larger arrows represent the way in which meanings from text-world 2 and text-world 3 feed into the prominent text-world.

In terms of the extract's text-world structure, I am most interested, however, in how a multimodal novel like *House of Leaves* creates further ontological layers. As a multimodal novel, *House of Leaves* accentuates the reader's involvement in text-world creation, demanding physical interaction with the book as object and positioning the reader doubly deictically through a subjective resonance with the character of Navidson. Unlike theories of literary identification that claim readers may imaginatively assume the role of a character, I am arguing that only a partial identification with Navidson is encouraged by Danielewski, since the text also dramatises the reader as participant. The reader is not just projecting into the world of the text, but playing a more active and corporeal role.

In an article on multimodality and imagination, Hall suggests that multimodal children's books affect the relative positioning of the imaginative domain to the actual text, since the imagination no longer operates in "a separate and bounded world" (2008: 137). Rather, drawing on Marsh's (2005) work on children's performance and engagement with media texts, Hall speaks of "imagination as action, triggered not through words or looking into receptacles but through deep commitment to an object" (2008: 138). *House of Leaves* requires such deep commitment from its readers, too, the impact of which leads to the construction of what I term a 'figured trans-world'.

The concept of the figured trans-world stems from Holland et al.'s (1998) studies of identity construction in cultural environments as well as one of their sources, Vygotsky's (1978) work in the arena of children's play. Holland et al.'s study makes a case for the existence of cultural worlds in which identities are constructed through collective imaginings and active participation. These worlds are called 'figured worlds'. Holland et al. provide the following definition:

> By "figured world," then, we mean a socially and culturally constructed realm of interpretation in which particular characters and actors are recognized, significance is assigned to certain acts, and particular outcomes are valued over others. [. . .] These collective "as-if" worlds are sociohistoric, contrived interpretations or imaginations that mediate behavior and so, from the perspective of heuristic development, inform participants' outlooks. The ability to sense (see, hear, touch, taste, feel) the figured world becomes embodied over time, through continual participation. (1998: 52–53)

As examples of such worlds, they cite academia, Alcoholics Anonymous meetings, and romantic dating practices amongst others.

Material objects and artefacts are central to figured worlds, acting as 'pivots' in Vygotsky's (1978) terms. Holland et al. summarise Vygotsky's hypothesis:

> Describing how children develop the ability to enter into an imagined world, Vygotsky speaks of a "pivot", a mediating or symbolic device that the child uses not just to organise a particular response but to pivot or shift into the frame of a different world. (1998: 50)

With regard to figured worlds, pivots are employed synonymously: "Artifacts 'open up' figured worlds" (Holland et al. 1998: 61). In reference to literature, the book as an object is a mediating artefact that evokes, and enables a shift into, its imaginative world. However, it does not generate a figured world since, although literature is a cultural and collective endeavour, it does not produce an analogous shared experience, nor does it depend upon equivalent active participation and/or performance. Multimodal texts, however, emphasise the embodied nature of the reading experience. As Kress, in his book *Literacy in the New Media Age*, articulates, "imagination in the sense that it is required by the demands of design—the imposition of order on the representational world—is a move towards action in the outer world" (2003: 60).

The concept of the figured trans-world that I am presenting here is not identical with Holland et al.'s (1998) socially grounded notion of figured worlds. In my conception, a figured trans-world is generated when the reader is required and/or directed by the text into a performative role in the discourse-world, a role that calls upon corporeal activity and insinuates, to greater or lesser extent, active reader involvement in the narrative. In the 'ladder' extract from *House of Leaves*, the multimodal design of the book results in it being rotated and handled as an object. Executing these affordances of the book is a performance that emulates Navidson's movements, creating doubly deictic subjectivity. Likewise, in Exploration #4, multimodal designs provoke movement of the book which reiterate the actions and movements of the explorers. Used thus, the book as a material artefact acts a pivot, opening up the text-world for figuration. Crucially, this process forges a concretised form of trans-world projection for the reader, an embodied connection between participant and enactor.

As a *trans*-world, this idea has the benefit of maintaining the rigid ontological boundaries between text-world and discourse-world that are fundamental to Text World Theory. The figured trans-world encompasses the reader's performance in the discourse-world, that is, their figured representation of the action in the narrative of the text-world without assuming absolute 'transportation' or compression of worlds.

Crucially, it accounts for the reader's self-awareness and heightened involvement with the book as object, as narrative, and as literary experience.

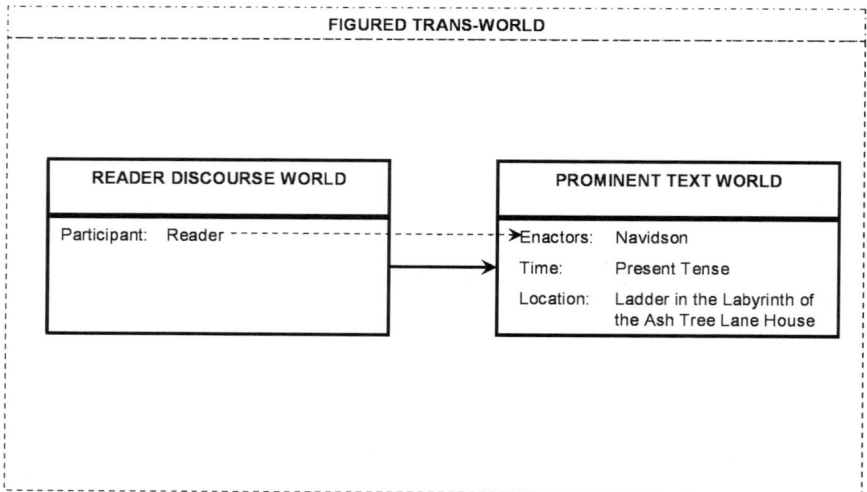

Figure 4.9 Figured trans-world of Danielewski (2000a) *House of Leaves*: 440–441.

Through cognitive-poetic analysis of the explorations, I have shown that the design of *House of Leaves* and its multimodal conceptual integration of house and book affect the reader's literary encounter. The combination of doubly deictic subjectivity, enactive performance, and the creation of figured trans-worlds leads yet again to infringements of the semipermeable membrane. Indeed, speaking of doubly deictic *you*, Herman suggests that fictions which utilise the effect of double deictics, "by formally encoding (features of) the contexts in which they are or might be read, in turn prompt reflection on how contexts permeate and modify the narrative structures anchored in them" (2002: 350).

In fact, the figured trans-world itself can be seen as vital to this effect, since although text-world and discourse-world maintain their ontological separation, the readerly impression of enactive participation augments the blurring of the boundary or, in other words, the membrane itself. The discourse-world and the text-world are distinct worlds in ontological terms, yet by dramatising the reader's relationship with the book through performance, Danielewski provokes concretised trans-world projection, making the boundary itself seem almost indistinguishable. The reader of *House of Leaves* does not just 'read' the novel. Like Navidson, and aligned with him through subjective and corporeal resonance, s/he seems to actively explore it.

4.2.10   Leave Your Mark

Figured trans-worlds, and the embodied projection relations between reader and character(s) they create, do not only arise within the explorations of "The Navidson Record", but can be seen to occur in other layers of the narrative and throughout the novel as a whole. In narrative terms, Pelafina's letters to Johnny Truant, collected in Appendix E and reprinted and extended in *The Whalestoe Letters* (Danielewski 2000b), also invite the reader to participate in a figured trans-world. Unlike the previous example, the figured trans-world that is generated here is not the product of readerly movement that emulates narrative action. This instance, therefore, provides further details of the figured trans-world and its creation.

The Whalestoe Letters are written by Pelafina, Truant's mother, who at the time of writing was a committed patient at the psychiatric facility, the Whalestoe Institute, and date from 1982 until 1989 when Pelafina dies from "self-inflicted asphyxiation" (Danielewski 2000a: 643). The letters begin as tender communications from mother to son, but as they progress, Pelafina becomes increasingly paranoid about the institute's new director to the extent that she suggests he may murder her. Her paranoia culminates in a brief letter dated April 27, 1987, when she writes (Danielewski 2000a: 619):

Dear, dear Johnny,

Pay attention: the next letter I will encode as
follows: use the first letter of each word to build
subsequent words and phrases: your exquisite
intuition will help sort out the spaces: I've sent
this via a night nurse: our secret will be safe

Tenderly,

Mom

This letter provides Johnny and the reader with a cipher with which to decode the next letter (Danielewski 2000a: 620–623), indeed encrypted as Pelafina describes.

The next letter read by its surface text, that is, in its coded form, makes little semantic sense. Thus in order to recover meaning the reader must make use of the cipher to translate the letter. This is a relatively undemanding process that, although I am reluctant to disclose the exact text, reveals a disturbing message concerning Pelafina's experiences in the Whalestoe Institute. What is interesting from the perspective of this study is the necessity of reader participation for the narrative exposé.

According to Holland et al., a figured world is "an abstraction, an extraction carried out under guidance" (1998: 53). In the figured trans-world, the text directs the reader as to their enactive participation. While in Exploration #5 the multimodal arrangement acted as a guiding tool, in Pelafina's letters, the reader is provided with instructions in the form of the cipher; "use the first letter of each word to build subsequent words and phrases". In actively deciphering Pelafina's letter, the reader enters into a figured trans-world. Rather than merely reading Truant's letters from his mother, the reader performs the decoding operation, in the process suggesting a doubly deictic subjectivity aligned with Truant. Crucially, the reader acts upon the text, paying attention to its surface, and inscribing the secret message to create an alternative surface, written in the reader's own hand.

Figured involvements founded in textual inscription, as in decoding Pelafina's letters, were hinted at in the description of the book that Truant provides in the Introduction. As cited in section 4.2.5 of this chapter, after an exhaustive and at points conflicting list of features possessed by the novel, Truant resignedly writes, "find your own words; I have no more" (Danielewski 2000a: xvii). From what appears to be a flippant comment, there emerges a poignant truth, one whose meaning is an implicit directive for the generation of a figured trans-world. Technically, in deciphering Pelafina's letter, the reader is finding Pelafina's words, rather than their own. Yet in doing so how does one keep track of Pelafina's horrific admission? Perhaps it is scrawled into the thick margins of Appendix E; perhaps it is scribbled on a scrap of paper, a leaf, and then folded into the pages of the book.

Furthermore, considering figured involvement in the novel as a whole, as academics, students, or inspired readers willing to take on Truant's challenge, temptation may have us writing notes into the empty spaces of the page. While such a reaction may seem more closely aligned to an academic readership, 'real' readers of the novel have confessed to also behaving in this way. For instance, in an Amazon.com review of the book, a customer named Laura A. admits, "Only a few pages in (hooked), I made the executive decision to arm myself with those little page-marker sticky notes so I could go back and re-visit things of interest" (see Website 1 in References).

The full title to Danielewski's novel is *House of Leaves, by Zampanò with Introduction and Notes by Johnny Truant*. Truant's footnotes interspersed throughout the novel, presumably sprawled onto the pages of Zampanò's manuscript, are his textual inscriptions. If we mark our copy of the book with literary and/or personal comment, we create a doubly deictic alignment with Truant and therefore another figured trans-world. In short, we do add our own words; we carry out Johnny's plea. In the process, we create an additional layer to the novel (shown in Figure 4.10), so that it becomes our rendered copy of a book introduced and noted by Truant, and written by Zampanò. In many novels, this act would not carry the same semantic weight, but *House of Leaves*, with its recursive narrative structure and multiple authors, turns this act into a significant narrative event. As 'writers', we are caught up in constructing a further narrative encasing,

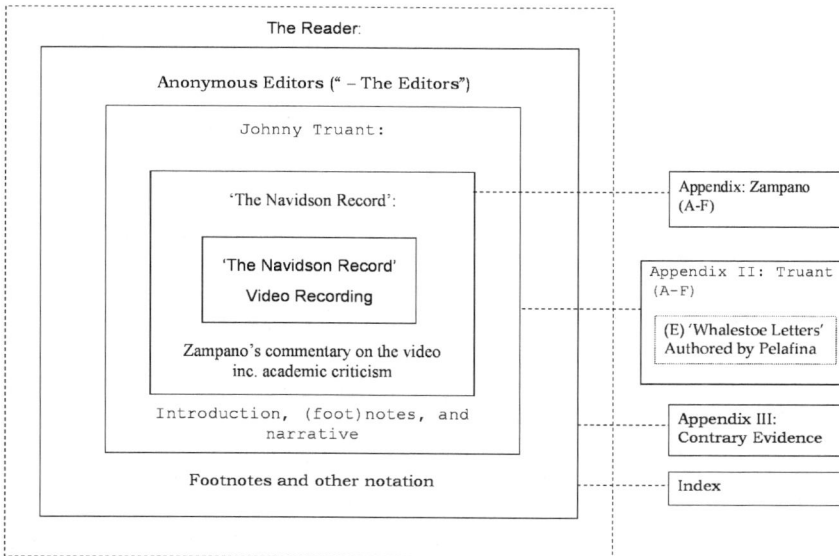

Figure 4.10   Narrative levels of *House of Leaves*, including readerly 'figured' layer.

through doubly deictic involvement in a figured trans-world, in which we do have a degree of agency. The content of our scribblings is not dictated but highly individual, more so because the discourse-world of the reader is brought into play, and the act of reading and interpreting is itself dramatised by the narrative. As Brick puts it, "*Personal experience* is at the heart of Danielewski's book" (2004; original emphasis).

4.3   CONCLUSION

As a form of gothic or horror novel, Mark Z. Danielewski's *House of Leaves* is highly successful, and the intensity the novel demands as a reading experience is crucial to this success. By analysing *House of Leaves* from a cognitive-poetic perspective, I have been able to account for the ways in which it creates this intensity though transgressions of the semipermeable membrane between the fictional text-world and the reader's discourse-world. From its use of second-person pronoun to trigger cognitive reactance or provoke affinity with characters to its demand for physical action and superimposition of subjectivity, the novel motivates intense engagement from its readers—not least because readers are led into figured trans-worlds which call for enactive participation and engender highly personal and corporeal encounters with the world(s) of the text.

In his comparison of *House of Leaves* with modern and postmodern novels, Fordham claims:

> The reader maneuvers through it, operates it, explores and chases the notes it has made to itself, in a series of obsessive and eccentric activities. These subversively make the reader identify with the several obsessive questers of the book's narratives. (2002: 15)

Fordham's claim that the reader 'identifies' with all of the novel's central characters is problematic in its absoluteness. I would hesitate to suggest a complete identification with any of the characters since I consider the reader's autonomy as vital to the intensity of the literary experience that *House of Leaves* entails. Nevertheless, through doubly deictic subjectivity and figured trans-worlds, the boundaries between text-world and discourse-world are obscured in a way that implicates readers in the materiality and the narrative structure of the novel. In consequence, it is as though we, as readers, become the next in line of a legacy, just as Danielewski's use of parallelism and explicit comparison between Truant and the reader in the Introduction intimated. The figured trans-world of the reader's own writing appears to manifest this literary interpretation of their relationship to the novel as part of an obsessive reality—the writing upon the book has occurred in relation to the text-world, as part of a figured trans-world, and, vitally, as the reader's indelible action in the discourse-world. Moreover, the length, weight, and time it takes to read this seven-hundred-page novel triggers within readers an uncanny sensation reminiscent of Truant's daunting account of having begun to "feel its heaviness, sensed something horrifying in its proportions, its silence, its stillness" (Danielewski 2000a: xvii).

Just as it grows into an obsession for Truant, and Zampanò before him, reading (and writing) this novel becomes an exhaustive preoccupation, consuming the reader's thoughts and time. The only question left being: will you be able to put it down? In Truant's Introduction, many of the themes and effects of the novel, its intensities, are suggested. In his closing, Truant warns:

> With a little luck, you'll dismiss this labor, react as Zampanò had hoped, call it needlessly complicated, pointlessly obtuse, prolix—your word—, ridiculously conceived, and you'll believe all you've said, and then you'll put it aside—though even here, just that one word, "aside" makes me shudder, for what is ever really just put aside?—and you'll carry on, eat, drink, be merry and most of all you'll sleep well.
>   Then again there's a good chance you won't.
>   This much I'm certain of: it doesn't happen immediately. You'll finish and that will be that, until a moment will come, maybe in a month, maybe a year, maybe even several years. You'll be sick or feeling troubled or deeply in love or quietly uncertain or even content for the first time in your life. It won't matter. Out of the blue, beyond any cause you can trace, you'll suddenly realize things are not how you perceived them to be at all. For some reason, you will no longer be the person you believed you once were. You'll detect slow and subtle shifts going on all around you, more importantly shifts in you. [. . .]
>   And then the nightmares will begin. (xxii–xxiii)

Undoubtedly, for the many readers who form the novel's cult following, contributing to online forums, creating websites in homage, and zealously collecting books to which it intertextually refers as well as paratextual products like Poe's intertextual album *Haunted*, putting this book down is not an easy task. The indelible performative acts in the discourse-world which the book provokes and the presence of real-world entities, these inter- and paratextual objects which exist beyond the book's covers, continue to add to its narrative, meaning that the possibility of completing an exploration of *House of Leaves* is remote.

5 Embodiment and the Book that Bleeds

VAS: An Opera in Flatland
by Steve Tomasula with
Stephen Farrell

5.1 INTRODUCTION

VAS: An Opera in Flatland (2002), written by Steve Tomasula and designed (in collaboration with Tomasula) by Stephen Farrell,[1] is described by the publisher as an 'imagetext' novel. As this compound neologism suggests, the novel uses words or text as well as images throughout. As in *House of Leaves*, concrete poetic designs abound in *VAS*, and similarly these designs are never used merely for aesthetic or poetic conceit. Rather, they have a central and vital role in the meaning-making of their particular novelistic context. Tomasula's inclusion of images extends well beyond concrete poetry and typographical experimentation. While both of these devices are in use, *VAS: An Opera in Flatland* is a constantly mutating multimodal artefact. Its visual appearance, typographical layout, and image positioning change frequently, so that as the reader turns the pages, he or she is continually faced with new and remarkable graphic designs. Indeed, the most consistent feature of the novel's design is a single line or series of vertical stencilled lines that run down the page, acting like a margin identifier. Meanwhile, there are sections reminiscent of graphic novels; there are scientific graphs, DNA chains, and family trees; at other times, photographic images, commercial advertisements, and illustrations punctuate the narrative. These multimodal innovations have resulted in the novel being spoken of as defying categorisation (Thacker 2006: 166), as an "unforgettably unique reading experience" (Olsen 2004: 133), and as a "generous and original design experiment [. . .] a beguilingly intricate, immaculately crafted labour of love" (Poynor 2003).

The novel's narrative is equally convoluted. Set in an unspecified future time, the main plot centres upon a character named Square, who agonises over the decision to undergo a vasectomy at the request of his wife, Circle. Notably, these characters, along with their daughter Oval, are named using shape nouns. This is significant as the subtitle of *VAS* is an intertextual allusion to Edwin A. Abbott's (1998 [1884]) short novella, *Flatland: A Romance*

---

1. When referring to VAS' textual narrative or conceptual design, I reference Steve Tomasula alone, thus showing his authorship, while in instances where I am interested in the graphic design of the novel as well, I acknowledge Stephen Farrell's contribution.

of Many Dimensions by A. Square, which conceives of a world populated by two-dimensional shapes. Abbott's *Flatland* is considered to be his defining work, functioning both as a social satire and a creative science fiction. The latter is underpinned by mathematical laws and abstract conjectures on time and space (the presence of a fourth dimension) which foreshadowed the scientific concerns of its period, particularly in the arena of theoretical physics. *VAS: An Opera in Flatland* engages with many of the topics of Abbott's novella, reflecting upon contemporary American society while also extending Abbott's concern over scientific ethics by inspecting contemporary subjects of controversy. As Thacker puts it, *VAS* "makes use of Abbott's narrative as a kind of allegory for the way in which we are all making the shift from 'human' to 'posthuman'" (2006: 166). That is, the 'Flatland' in which the narrative of *VAS* is set is a world that is becoming progressively postbiological, with its culture of surgery, cloning, biological patenting, genetic commerce, and bio-robotics. The book's structure augments these themes by utilising scientific quotation, facts, and figures about the human genome and evolutionary process as well as including multimodal elements and/or graphics that relate to cloning and DNA testing.

    VAS: An Opera in Flatland was Steve Tomasula's debut novel, followed by *In&Oz* (2003) and *The Book of Portraiture* (2006). *In&Oz* (2003) is not a multimodal novel per se, but it does feature some multimodal elements such as illustrations and typographical deviance. *The Book of Portraiture* (2006), on the other hand, is comparable to *VAS* in its status as an imagetext novel. Indeed, its publisher describes it as "a postmodern epic in writing and images". Additionally, Tomasula's latest artistic offering is a creative multimedia project, a DVD novel called *TOC* (2009), the title of which suggests it is a development from a previously published short fiction (Tomasula and Farrell 1996), also a collaboration with Farrell.

    Tomasula's literary oeuvre reveals that multimodality is a recurring feature of his fiction. Writing in a special edition of *The Review of Contemporary Fiction* devoted to contemplating the future of the novel, Tomasula (1996) suggests that novels are always a product as well as reflective of the period in which they are created. Considering the process of writing *VAS*, Tomasula connects the novel to the media-saturated environment and highly visual culture that has developed into the twenty-first century:

> I never really thought I was writing a hybrid novel, per se, while writing it—I guess I didn't think about it except to think that this was a way to write that seemed natural, given the times we live in, i.e., given all the graphics, collaged video etc. in something as pedestrian as the nightly news; this just seemed to be plain old realism to me—the way we communicate today—and I remember being surprised the first time someone suggested that it wasn't. (personal correspondence, March 16, 2007)

In part, Tomasula's employment of multimodality is a way to connect the reading experience of *VAS: An Opera in Flatland* to readers' real lived experience(s). The aforementioned inclusion of adverts and commercials in the novel is one method for doing this. In addition, Tomasula utilises multimodality to call attention to the materiality of *VAS* as a book and the reader's own bodily relationship to that book.

Building upon my use of a critical synthesis designed to form multi-modal cognitive poetics in the analysis of *House of Leaves* in Chapter 4, the present chapter contributes to this aim through continued application. More significantly, I develop cognitive models, particularly in terms of per-ceptual processing and conceptual integration. I also continue to consider the doubled experience, seen in the previous chapter through double deixis and the figured trans-world, promoted by multimodal texts.

5.2 ANALYSIS

In considering a multimodal cybertext, Ensslin asserts, "we need to turn our attention to the interplay of corporeal and psychological func-tions at work during the receptive process" (2009: 156). Like virtual forms including hyper- and cybertexts, multimodal printed novels such as Tomasula's *VAS: An Opera in Flatland* foreground their material-ity and the receiver's embodied participation in the process of literary experience. *VAS* brings the reader's body into play in the process of liter-ary world-creation by involving it in the meaning-making process, for instance, by transforming the act of turning the page into an act which directly affects the narrative. Tomasula thus exploits physicality and cor-poreality to heighten awareness of the embodied nature of not merely reading, but also being, cognising, and imagining.

My analysis of *House of Leaves* indicated that the concrete-poetic multimodality of the book directed the reader into active participation, which in turn led to the creation of figured trans-worlds and doubly deictic subjectivity. Both of these processes superimpose the reader's world with the narrative in such a way that one could perhaps suggest that *House of Leaves* enables new experiences built upon enactive imagi-nation, in the process creating projection relations between reader and character. This is not always the case. Ensslin, considering the phenom-enological implications of 'physio-cybertexts', speaks of 'double situ-atedness' (2009: 158). By this, Ensslin means that readers are at once "direct receivers" of the text as well as psychologically involved with the represented narrative. Since it does not necessarily entail a convergence of reader and character, Ensslin's 'double situatedness' differs from my notion of doubly deictic subjectivity. However, it is similarly focused on the sense of literary experience as a doubled (at least) locative phenom-enon. This sense of double situatedness is present in all reading experi-ences but multimodal texts, like the cybertexts that are Ensslin's focus, place emphasis on this dual positioning.

The striking and unusual graphic designs of multimodal print narratives, such as those found in *VAS*, consistently trigger an awareness of their physical substance, of the words and images printed on the page and of the book as a literary artefact through which readers can access the virtual world of the text. In addition, these novels induce kinaesthetic and proprioceptive engagement. In this chapter, I employ multimodal cognitive poetics to analyse the ways in which *VAS* brings about double situatedness for the reader. As a result, it is shown that readers of *VAS* and of multimodal novels receive and experience these narratives at the embodied and ontological interface of actual and virtual, corporeal and cognitive. I begin to do this in the next section, focusing on the novel's opening.

5.2.1   First the Body, then the Text

Tomasula's (2002) *VAS: An Opera in Flatland* is a novel with an unusual narrative inception:

First Pain.

Then knowledge: a paper cut. (Tomasula 2002: 9–10)

Importantly, this opening sets up the theme of embodiment, which is so central to the novel. As outlined in section 3.4.2 of Chapter 3, embodiment is a central tenet of cognitive science and poetics. Its thematisation in *VAS* is especially interesting as the novel's multimodality ensures that embodiment is not merely a literary trope, but an integral aspect of the act of reading. Reading is always an embodied activity, though literary criticism does not usually explicitly recognise it as such. *VAS* utilises multimodality to fuse both virtual literary meaning with actual literary experience in the reader's narrative understanding of embodiment.

The initial sentence of Tomasula's novel reflects embodied understanding, by bringing a physical encounter (through injury) into direct relationship with cognitive awareness using the enumerative conjunct 'first' and temporal coordinating conjunction 'then'. Moreover, the mode in which the two clauses are represented contributes significantly to the communication of the theme of embodiment. As can be seen in Figure 5.1, Tomasula's opening sentence spans two pages, starting on a right-hand page and continuing overleaf.

The depiction of "first pain" utilises forms from graphic novels. The capitalisation and bold typography of the words combined with their positioning within the rectangle suggests that this information should be interpreted as a 'narrative box' (McGlothlin 2003) or 'caption' (Saraceni 2003), a convention used to comment upon the visual frame. Its proximal positioning to the star-burst shape heightens cognitive association between the

Then knowledge: a paper cut.
He kissed his finger, a gesture of
'shhh' making him both Judas and
first-and-truest lover to his body?—a kiss,
like hers—for hers—comforting as he lay
down with the scalpel?

bright and shining

On the page in his lap, the
world he'd been writing into existence was

truth

shining membranes

dead-skin white—paper sans corpuscles—
nothing more—the bubble of presence its
people and dramas had occupied pricked
by less than a sting and he buried them
beneath the hospital form he had cut
himself on.

so effortlessly
that it would be bloodless

His daughter's science experiment took
technique's first baby steps on the coffee
table before him: a white carnation in
water dyed a lurid TV-red no flower could
be. Except this one, already turning color,
capillary action manipulated by the
insertion of a dye doing the trick.

He had already written his name where it said:

FIRST PAIN.

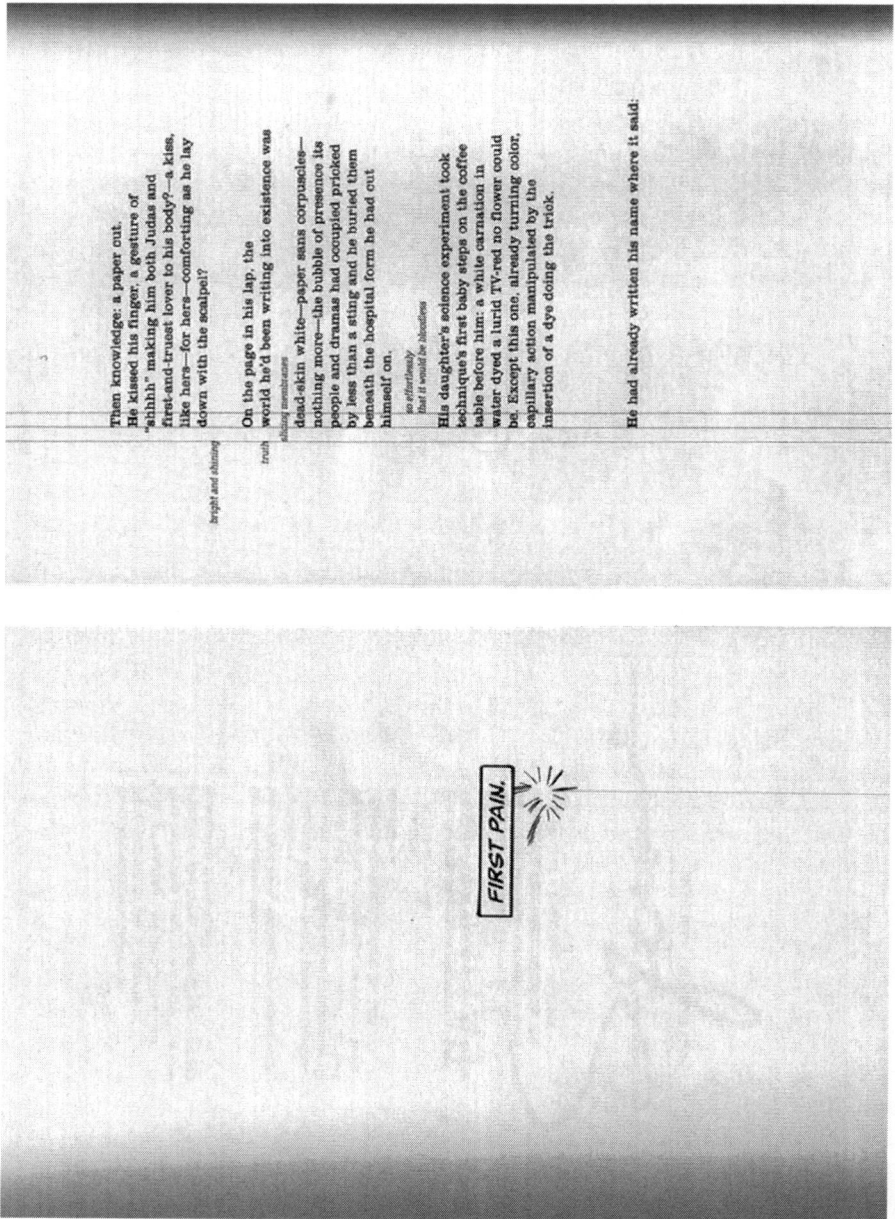

Figure 5.1   Tomasula (2002) *VAS: An Opera in Flatland*: 9–10.

two elements. The star-burst shape is characterised by strokes that are visually akin to 'action lines' or 'motion lines' (Lander 2005). Lander explains that artists of graphic novels and comics "add motion lines and shading to indicate movement, speed, and direction to assist the reader" (2005: 115). The action lines in *VAS* thus suggest that not only is that area a site of pain, it is instilled with action and impact too. The completion of Tomasula's first sentence overleaf sheds new light for the reader on the first page's graphic realisation. The vertical line on the initial page can be construed as the edge of a piece of paper, or indeed a page, while the star-burst shape comes to signify the spatial point at which the paper cut was received.

The paper cut, although visually represented by the star-burst shape or action lines on the opening page, is not accompanied by a drawing of a character to whom the injury can be attributed. In fact, neither does the linguistic structure of the sentence disclose who has received this injury. In this way, the sentence can be seen as deviant since the indefinite paper cut presupposes someone to have experienced it. Using the system of transitivity from Halliday's (1978; 2004: 168–305) Systemic Functional Linguistics, the deviance of the opening sentence can be explained. Moreover, this system offers an account of readers' experience and interpretation of the sentence. As Simpson suggests, "the transitivity model provides one means of investigating how a reader's or listener's perception of the meaning of a text is pushed in a particular direction" (1993: 104).

Considering how the experience of a paper cut would ordinarily be recounted linguistically, one might say something like 'I received a paper cut'. In the categories dictated by Systemic Functional Linguistics, this would be a 'material supervention process', which is itself a subcategory of 'material action processes' (Halliday 1978; 2004: 179–197). Material processes are composed of an actor, a process, and a goal. Looking at our invented example, then, we can see that it neatly fits this configuration:

ACTOR	PROCESS	GOAL
I	received	a paper cut

It is a material supervention process because the actor does not intentionally take up the action. As Gavins phrases it, material supervention processes "have no deliberate will behind them and can be seen as relating to actions which seem to take place by accident" (2007b: 56). Returning to the opening sentence in light of the structures set out in Halliday's (2004) transitivity model, it is clear that the sentence is deviant because although the goal is linguistically explicit, the sentence lacks both actor and process. Instead, the first part of the sentence is composed of two units of coordinator and abstract noun and the second part merely contains the goal of 'a paper cut'.

In Text World Theory, worlds are produced by discourse chiefly through a combination of world-building elements and function-advancing propositions. The former are deictic terms—time, place, people, location—all of which "collectively gives us the basic deictic arrangement of the text world" (Werth 1999: 181) and enable imaginative visualisation. Function-advancing propositions on the other hand move the narrative forward. Gavins (2007b) refines this aspect of Werth's original theorisation using Systemic Functional Linguistics and transitivity. Both world-building elements and function-advancing propositions are sparse in Tomasula's opening sentence. Consequently, imagining the scene—its location and character—cannot be achieved in definite terms. Adding to this 'sparseness', the absence of an actor in the sentence and in the graphic realisation of the paper cut thus opens up the text-world for the reader to implicate him- or herself into. This possibility is enhanced by the sense of impact and movement that the action lines on the first page imply as well as the positioning of the vertical line in parallel with the edge of the actual page that it can be said to represent. By echoing the real-world situation of the fiction's actual reader, the line comes close to encouraging what Olalquiaga (1992), in relation to contemporary culture, and Hansen (2006), in relation to the virtual, call 'psychasthenia', that is, "a state in which the space defined by the coordinates of the organism's own body is confused with represented space" (Olalquiaga 1992: 2). The visual immediacy of the representation of the paper cut thus induces the reader to envisage the paper cut in relation to his or her self. In doing so, the graphic designs of the first page, in particular the vertical line and the action lines, work with the deviance of the sentence (its lack of actor and process) to invite the reader to momentarily self-implicate (Kuiken, Miall, and Sikora 2004) into the narrative action.

The second page, starting "then knowledge", is printed in a more familiar manner, with text left aligned in an unremarkable font, its appearance according with reader assumptions of 'conventional' novels. This suggests its primary aim is the communication of conceptual information concerning the story. Like the experience of receiving a paper cut in which pain is felt initially and realisation follows, the temporal sequence and multimodal arrangement of Tomasula's primary sentence enacts this process. The opening page symbolises the physical experience while the information on the second page elucidates and makes comprehensible the preceding imagistic design. This enables Tomasula to introduce the theme of embodiment through a multimodal form of narrativity that emphasises both the conceptual and physical realms of literary experience.

The narrative continues with the phrase "He kissed his finger". The third-person pronoun cataphorically (re)orientates the construal of the first sentence, providing an actor whom the paper cut relates to. Indeed, as the narrative progresses, it becomes clear that at the story level, it is the main character Square who has given himself a paper cut. Interestingly, this means that readers for whom the multimodal immediacy of the first page's opening design resulted in self-implication into the narrative *subsequently* find themselves in a relation of doubly deictic subjectivity (see section 4.2.9 of Chapter 4 for definition; and Herman 1994, 2002 on 'doubly deictic you'), having their own initial self-implication successively superimposed onto Square's experience. In addition to retrospective doubly deictic subjectivity, the third-person pronoun instigates a deictic 'pop', shifting from a personalised self-implication towards a more distanced perspective upon Square as a character. The immediate construal of Tomasula's opening sentence promotes double situatedness, while the second sentence's subjective reference to a 'he' enables a subsequent refinement of this double situatedness into a retrospective form of doubly deictic subjectivity.

In consequence, *VAS* is exemplary of multimodal novels in that from its immediate opening, the book draws attention to its material status, causing a shifting awareness between the actual and the immersive, a fusion of virtual and physical. The following section presents an analysis of a narrative episode which plays with the boundary between the actual world of the reader and the virtual world of the narrative.

5.2.2   Fusing Bodies

In an early scene from the novel, Square's mother-in-law is narrating the story behind the famous opera, *La Traviata*, to her granddaughter, Oval. There are three acts to *La Traviata*. Act I concludes with the uncertain possibility of a blossoming romance between the young Alfredo and Violetta. Act II "opens with the couple living together" (Tomasula 2002: 24). Clearly, between these two acts there is a disjuncture in time and narrative progression, glossing over the development of Alfredo and Violetta's relationship and leaving the reader to 'fill in the gaps' of the plot. In *VAS*, there are three pages inserted between the descriptions of these two acts. The first includes an example of one of the many appearances of scientific quotation that pervade the novel. This entry is from *The Naked Ape* by Desmond Morris, and details the evolution of sexual intercourse in the advancement of human society from Neanderthal man:

> For pair bonding and therefore civilization to develop, the naked ape had to acquire a capacity to become sexually imprinted on a single partner. It did so by linking sex to identity through evolutionary changes that favored face-to-face copulation. . . . Copulation is most commonly performed with the naked male over the naked female, with the female's legs apart. (Tomasula 2002: 21)

Further down the page, which is shown in Figure 5.2, a peculiar diagram can be seen. It would be possible to overlook this puzzling image, yet it is important to an understanding of what occurs overleaf. Through a relationship of visual likeness, this illustration is an icon for the book itself.

Its identity as *VAS* is signalled through the black semicircles on the edges of pages that appear throughout the novel, like thumb tabs in dictionaries and encyclopaedias, referencing the name of the scientist or philosopher quoted on that page (the one on page 21, for example, spells MORR for Morris). The curved dotted line represents the movement trajectory of the page as it is lifted. Significantly, there are two arrows beside it, pointing in each page-turning direction. The structure of Western literature and its reading patterns usually ensures that each page is moved from right to left as it is turned and, unless the reader revisits pages to check information, the movement is repeated, page after page accumulating on the left as reading continues. The lower arrow, then, is intriguing since one would not usually expect to move the page back from left to right, or alternate its movement in a fanning motion.

The significance of this diagram becomes apparent when the reader turns the page to be confronted by a double-page spread in which the image of a faceless naked male on the left page is reflected by the image of a faceless naked female on the right. Existing text is written in the form of scientific report (some of which, the thumb tabs suggest, was authored by Morris) and describes the physical reactions of the body and actions of the male and female in the act of copulation. At the bottom of the right page are found the words, "The partner's genitals may also become the target for repeated actions. Often rhythmically. Often rhythmically. Often rhythmically . . ." (Tomasula 2002: 23), and so on; the repeated words producing an inferred auditory mapping between their visual and heard replication and the sexual rhythm of a couple in intercourse. Furthermore, given the scientific context with which this design is framed, the mechanical rhythm of the repetition echoes Morris's phrase to suggest a perfunctory, routine kind of sex.

The positioning of the figures, their stilted bodies, adds weight to this suggestion. In other words the diagram represents "copulation" as Morris put it—sex serving the interests of human reproduction and procreation rather than fulfilling sexual desire. Interestingly, it is worth noting that the noun 'copula' and adjective 'copulative' refer in linguistics to the connection of words and clauses. Thus, copulation carries a double entendre of biological (sex for procreation, in this case) and linguistic meaning. More significantly, it is concerned with connection, a notion particularly pertinent in a book that brings together word and image, verbal and visual, in the communication of its narrative. Either through following the diagram's visual instructions, or by turning the page in order to continue reading, the pages are brought together, fulfilling the act of intercourse for the naked textual lovers.

To return to *La Traviata*, Tomasula employs this device to satisfy the narrative gap between Acts I and II of the described opera, verifying the reader's narrative inference that Alfredo and Violetta have consummated

> *For pair bonding and therefore civilization to develop, the naked ape had to acquire a capacity to become sexually imprinted on a single partner. It did so by linking sex to identity through evolutionary changes that favored face-to-face copulation. ....Copulation is most commonly performed with the naked male over the naked female, with the female's legs apart.*
>
> **DESMOND MORRIS**
> *The Naked Ape,* 1967

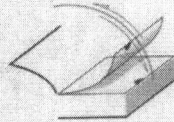

Figure 5.2   Tomasula/Farrell (2002) *VAS: An Opera in Flatland*: 21.

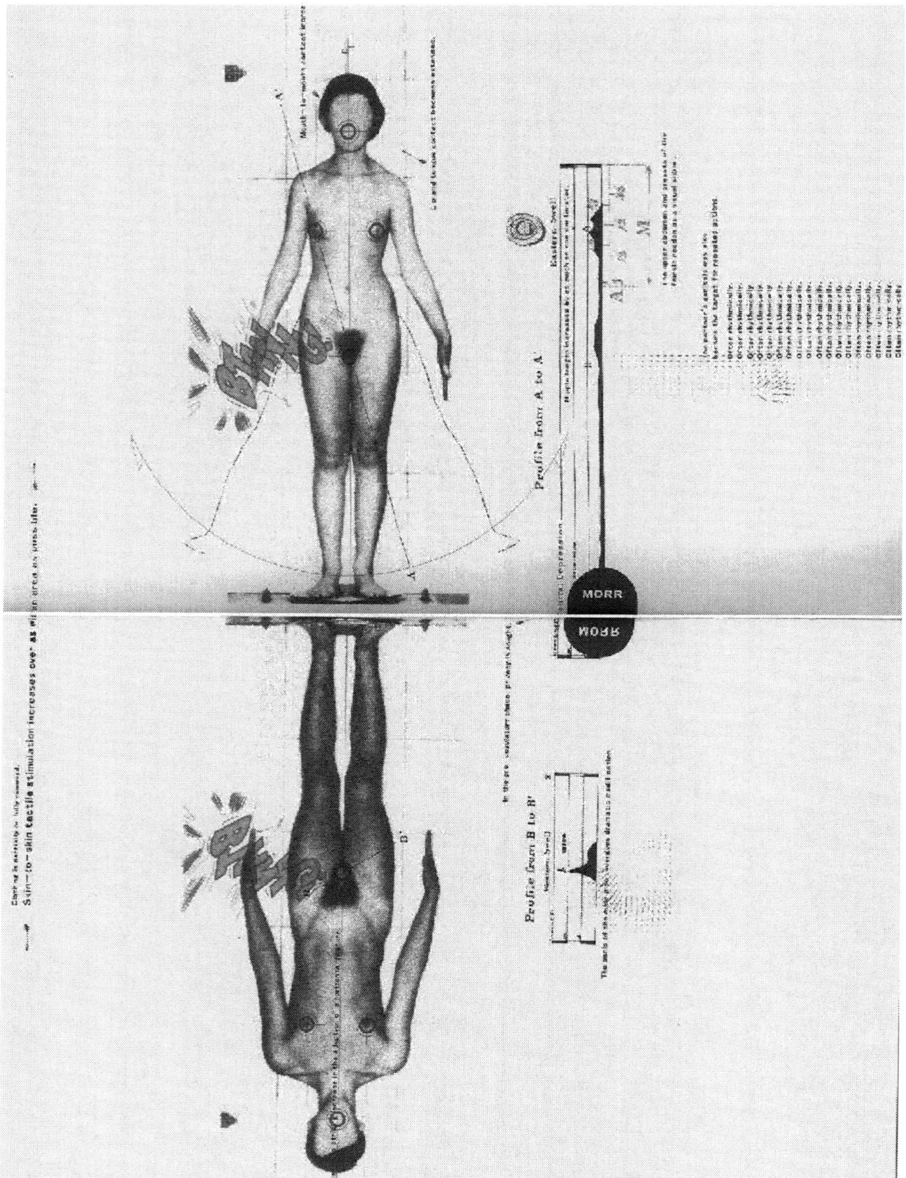

Figure 5.3   Tomasula/Farrell (2002) VAS: An Opera in Flatland: 22–23.

their relationship. Beyond the fiction, it could be said that just as the lovers are moved into a more active intimacy in their textual sexual act, the reader is drawn into a bodily relation with the novel. Indeed, in this instance it is the reader's physical and kinaesthetic interaction with the book as a material object that discloses the development of Alfredo and Violetta's relationship and thus accomplishes the narrative effect.

In terms of sensory modalities, the physical body is part of the haptic sense. As cognitive scientists Lederman and Klatzy explain, "People use the haptic system to perceive and interact with the world of concrete and virtual objects" (2001: 71). Marks also offers a definition, affirming the haptic sense comprises "the combination of tactile, kinesthetic, and proprioceptive functions, the way we experience touch both on the surface and inside our bodies" (2002: 2). Media critic Marks (2002) and art theorist Fisher (1997) consider haptic perception in relation to cinema, and art and exhibition spaces, respectively. In considering artistic forms and genres that utilise a 'haptic aesthetic' as Fisher (1997) might term it, they share a promising ideal of the effect such works have on the reception process. Marks' thoughts on haptic cinema, video media which explores and underlines the viewer's tactile and physiological presence, are particularly apt. With Tomasula's novel *VAS* in mind, consider Marks' comments on how haptic cinema recognises the viewer's corporeality:

> by appearing to us as an object with which we interact rather than an illusion into which we enter, [it] calls on [a] sort of embodied intelligence. In the dynamic movement between optical and haptic ways of seeing, it is possible to compare different ways of knowing and interacting. (2002: 18)

Marks and Fisher both conceive of a haptic or bodily oriented aesthetics which is not solely immersive or illusory, but rather utilises the visual and virtual as well as the haptic and embodied. In the episode from *VAS* discussed earlier, ontological realms are fused since the reader's bodily enaction in the discourse-world is the source of narrative consequence in the world of the text.

In their work on synaesthesia in poetic language, Shen and Cohen (1998: 125; 2008: 108) discuss the organisational ranking of modalities along a scale from high to low. Sight is the 'highest' modality, followed by sound, smell, and taste, with the 'lowest' modality being that of touch. Following Lakoff and Johnson's (1980, 1999) ideas on embodiment, they convincingly argue that concepts belonging to lower modalities are more accessible since they "involve a more direct, less mediated experience of perception" (1998: 128). Therefore, by tapping into the lower modality of (haptic) touch using the immediate contact of the reader with the text through bodily experience, Tomasula enhances the accessibility of the narrative world, making *VAS* a more vivid and dynamic reading experience.

The next section takes my analysis of *VAS* in a new direction by exploring the extended metaphor at the heart of the novel, both in terms of narrative content and multimodal design.

5.2.3 Blending Bodies

A recurring motif within *VAS* is the metaphorical rapport between the book and the body. This isomorphism is clearly related to a conceptual metaphor. The conceptual metaphor in question is people are books, or, as Manguel phrases it in his account of the metaphors of reading, "Human beings, made in the image of God, are also books to be read" (1997: 169). In this metaphor, the target, people, is reinterpreted through reference to an experiential knowledge of the source, books. This conceptual metaphor is easily recognisable in everyday language, in phrases such as 'You can read him like a book' or 'She's an open book' (Thompson and Thompson 1987: 201).

The metaphor has a long-standing history in literature (see Manguel 1997; Thompson and Thompson 1987, 2005) and has been used by William Shakespeare, detailed by Thompson and Thompson (1987), Walt Whitman, evidenced by Manguel (1997), and Mary Shelley, noted by Marchessault (2000), among many others. It has also experienced a revival in postmodern writing with the development of post-structural thinking (Foucault 1977). Jeanette Winterson's (1992) *Written on the Body* is an example of a postmodern novel in which the people are books metaphor is apparent. Winterson's novel is told through the eyes of a narrator whose gender is left indeterminate, manifesting the postmodern take on the fluid unstable body which is simultaneously a discursive product. Moreover, the narrative focuses on the loss of a lover to cancer and at one point in the novel the narrator deals with this loss by inscribing in block capitals the anatomical details of cancer upon the body onto the pages of the book (Winterson 1992: 115–139).

In *VAS*, simply identifying the conceptual metaphor people are books as a thematic trope does not result in an adequate account of the cognising and/or meaning-making processes of the various manifestations of that metaphor. Consider the book's materiality. The cover is a dappled peach colour, added to which are lines of greyish-blue. Undoubtedly, this is representative of skin and underlying veins. Additionally, the pages are printed in the colours of flesh and blood; they are an off-white shade, while text and image are presented in black, beige, or red. Furthermore, just like a human body, this book will age: as it is read, the spine will crease and it will effectively develop 'wrinkles'. Therefore, the book's visual design, and the book itself as a material object in the actual world, acts not just as a metaphorical mapping, but as a corporeal realisation of the blending or conceptual integration of two conceptual domains, book and body.

Conceptual Integration Theory developed later than Conceptual Metaphor Theory, and is conceived as a broader approach. As Grady, Oakley, and Coulson explain, Conceptual Integration Theory seeks to "unify the analysis of metaphor with the analysis of a variety of other linguistic and conceptual phenomena" (1999: 103). In this chapter, I follow Grady, Oakley, and Coulson (1999) and Brandt and Brandt (2005) in perceiving conceptual metaphor and conceptual integration as complementary cognitive accounts of expressive meaning-making, as well as Hiraga (2005), who uses the two in conjunction for the analysis of iconic (and multimodal in my terms) poetic works. Cognitive-poetic analysis of the extended metaphor of book with/and body in *VAS* reveals that multimodal integrations can require a complex negotiation of domains from the reader, who must comprehend metaphorical relations through cognitive blending practices.

In Conceptual Metaphor Theory, metaphorical relations are delimited by the 'Invariance Hypothesis' (Lakoff 1990; Lakoff and Turner 1989; Murphy 1996; Stockwell 1999; Turner 1990), which dictates that conceptual metaphorical mapping is unidirectional. In other words, meaning may only be transferred from source to target, rather than functioning in a bipolar manner. Interrogating this restriction, Stockwell has suggested that the source and target of a metaphor may have a relation of 'interanimation' (1999: 129–142) rather than irreversible transposition. Describing the process with regards to idealised cognitive models, Stockwell suggests that it would "entail that the total meaning is generated by first understanding the target in terms of the base, *and then* dialectically revising your view of the base in light of the new experience of the metaphor just read" (1999: 129–131; original emphasis). Interanimation, as Stockwell acknowledges in his own reading of a poem, has the potential to "alter perception" (1999: 136), sometimes irrevocably. In *VAS*, I believe the multimodal manifestations of the book and body metaphor are inclined to interanimate. This is in part due to the fact that visual and multimodal forms of metaphor do not presuppose a specific temporal arrangement in the way language does. Thus, source and target do not have the same currency in multimodal manifestations of the metaphor as they do in linguistic versions. That is, in multimodal realisations, the temporal sequence of the interanimation process suggested by Stockwell (source to target; target to source) is less applicable. Using conceptual integration is advantageous in this respect since it developed in part to overcome the restraint placed on metaphorical mapping by the invariance hypothesis. However, this is not to say that Stockwell's (1999) notion of interanimation is surplus. In fact, I believe it is an important aspect, if not a consequence, of some conceptual integrations, as will be elucidated in section 5.2.5 of this chapter.

In section 4.2.6 of Chapter 4, I identified a conceptual integration in *House of Leaves*. However, the blend of book and body, which occurs in *VAS*, differs from the blend of house and book found in *House of Leaves*. The latter blend was a single-scope network whereby one domain/input

acted as organising frame. In comparison, the blend of book and body in
VAS is a double-scope network (Fauconnier and Turner 2002: 130–135)
because it does not possess an integration hierarchy of framing input and
focus input. Instead, the blend is organised by both domains, in a sense
making it more integrative.

There are numerous manifestations of the book and body metaphorical blend in *VAS*, many of which are analysed through the course of this
section and section 5.2.4 of this chapter. Nevertheless, as I begin to make
claims about the prominence of the metaphorical blend in the novel at this
point in the chapter, it is useful to supply a few examples. For instance, in
considering his impending vasectomy, Square thinks of it as "rewriting his
body" (Tomasula 2002: 193) and as "a little editing" (312), transforming
the concept of the body into both an inscription surface such as a page as
well as a discursive product. Another more multimodal instance is provided by pages 202–227 in which Tomasula has inserted the entire genetic
sequence for Chromosome 12. Here, the book becomes a coded body written in the genetic alphabet.

The reader's first encounter with the book and body metaphorical blend
is through Square's endeavours to compose a story in which the blend is
introduced linguistically:

> Square stopped writing to look at the whorls of his fingertips, little
> miracles of line, their repetition a swirling reification of his mother
> and father and their mothers and fathers and their mothers and
> fathers and their mothers and fathers and their mothers and fathers
> and their mothers and fathers and their mothers and fathers and
> their mothers and fathers and their mothers and fathers back through
> 125,000 generations to the ape, written in a language of four base
> letters, AGCT, which combined into words—CAG|ATA|AGG—the
> words forming double-helix sentences of genes which filled pages of
> chromosomes within the cells which made up the book of his body.
> And he marveled at the malleability of the system—people, orchids,
> amoebas, elk—all cognate. (51)

Significantly, given that this is the metaphor's initial appearance within
the novel, the blending of the conceptual domains of book and body
effectively comes to pass through the course of the quotation. At the
start, book and body are distinct entities; Square actively shifts his
attention *from* his creative writing *to* his body, admiring his own finger-
prints, or rather admiring the biological lineage and individual genetic
character the friction ridges signify. The visual patterning of fingerprint
lines, "their repetition", is mirrored linguistically in the repetition of the
phrase "and their mothers and fathers". Though repetition is a type of
foregrounding, due to its duration this lexical reiteration eventually has
a converse effect.

Stockwell points out that "'newness' is the key to attention" (2002a: 18) and that when items become predictable or expected, they become 'redundant' and no longer capture attention. The extensive repetition of "and their mothers and fathers" thus results in it becoming redundant. The recurring phrase becomes prosaic and it consequently loses the reader's attention, almost seeming to 'pale back' in cognitive terms. Since it was previously the target of Square's focalisation, the fingerprint is thus refreshed as foregrounded object, giving a parallel conceptual effect of the "mothers and fathers" melding into Square's fingertips. To conclude this merger, Tomasula continues by intermingling biomedical terminology (e.g. double-helix, gene, chromosome, cells) with nouns associated with language and literature (e.g. sentence, page, book). In the linear process of reading this passage, an impression of movement toward conceptual integration transpires. At the start of the (admittedly lengthy) sentence, the domains of book and body in the form of Square's writing and his body, synecdochally represented by his fingertips, are separate. By the end of the sentence, the associated biological and linguistic discourses are interrelated, thus the relation between book and body is repositioned as Tomasula blends the two originally disparate domains.

Interestingly, the relationship between DNA code and the alphabet has been remarked upon by evolutionary biologist Richard Dawkins:

> DNA messages are written in a true alphabet . . . the DNA alphabet is a strictly limited repertoire of symbols with no self-evident meanings. Arbitrary symbols are chosen and combined to make meaningful messages of unlimited complexity and size. (2004: 22)

Avowing the status of genetic code as a writing system in its own right, Dawkins makes terminological analogies by presenting equivalencies. Consequently, the DNA code is itself seen as an alphabet, a codon is a word, strings of codons are sentences, and there is even an item comparable to a punctuation mark.

Dawkins's comparison of DNA code with language is clearly metaphorical, and serves to show that the donor metaphor PEOPLE ARE BOOKS is a conventional metaphor. Indeed, Thompson and Thompson cite PEOPLE ARE BOOKS as an "everyday structural metaphor" (2005: 60). Certainly, Dawkins (2004) is not alone is using the analogy in a scientific context. It has also been noted, for instance, by Marchessault (2000) and van Dijck (2000). In fact, van Dijck's (2000) article directly addresses metaphorical understandings associated with genetic research. He states that the "most popular metaphor for DNA is that of 'language' or 'alphabet'" (2000: 66). He continues:

> Out of the language metaphor an extensive web of semantically related images emerged, such as the "book," the "library," "reading" and

"writing." Naturally, this semantic frame was not exactly new in the 1960s; ideas like the "legibility of nature" or "the book of life" have been traditional topoi in literature and science. (66–67)

Evidently, the people are books conceptual metaphor and its associated metaphors and integrations reach beyond literary contexts into culture generally.

In section 5.2.4, I look at another instance of the metaphorical conceptual integration of book and body. This particular instance is overtly multimodal.

5.2.4   The Double Helix

The concept of 'double-helix sentences' (Tomasula 2002: 51) is, in fact, reified later in the novel. The extract in question occupies a trifold foldout page in which two of the frames show DNA chains (Tomasula/Farrell 2002), as shown in Figure 5.4.

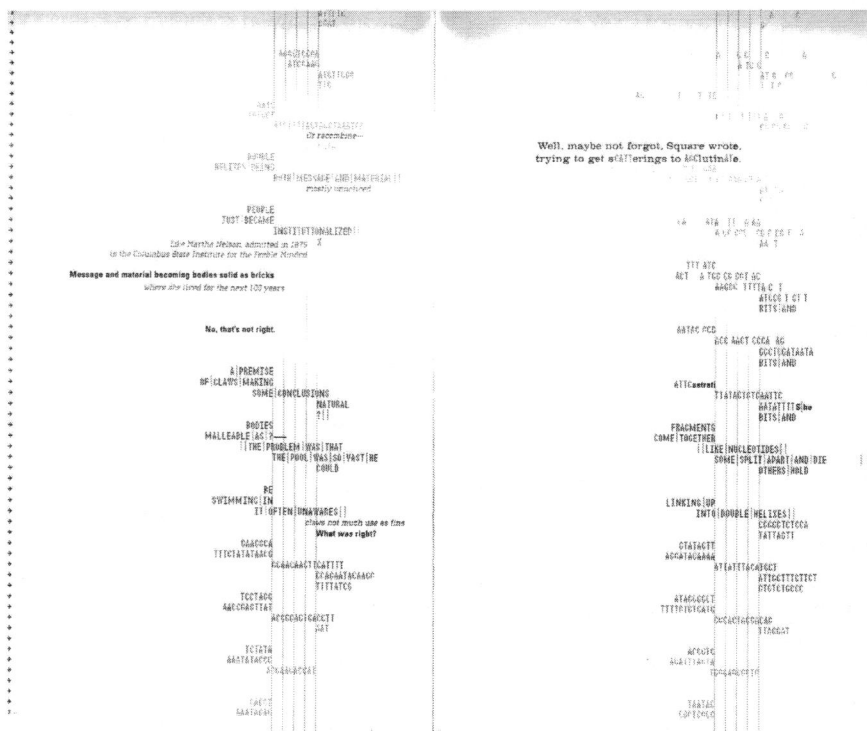

Figure 5.4   Two frames from Tomasula/Farrell (2002) *VAS: An Opera in Flatland*: 58.

DNA stores information using a four-letter code: C, G, A, and T. In these strange configurations, strings of the base letters are strewn around stencilled vertical lines, along with chains of words that form sentences. Consequently, DNA code and words as linguistic units become almost interchangeable. In this transposition, language is merged with the genetic alphabet. Language and lineage are blended through their shared status as signifying systems; just as we may tell a story using words, our genetic bodies narrate our personal and biological histories.

To facilitate reading, the words in this extract are printed in darker type, foregrounding them visually. The first word phrase to emerge is:

DOUBLE

HELIXES|BEING

BOTH|MESSAGE|AND|MATERIAL| |

The separation of words using a line follows a scientific convention. The lines are used to create what is known in scientific discourse (Russell 2002) as a 'reading frame' representing 'codons' (Dawkins 2004: 22; Johansen Mange and Mange 1999: 103, 108) which are tri-nucleotide sequences or, in other words, a series of three base letters that specify an amino acid. This is relevant to the theme of embodiment since amino acids are important to nearly every chemical process in the body that affects both physical and mental functioning. The final word phrase in this spread also mentions the double helix:

BITS AND

FRAGMENTS

COME|TOGETHER

| |LIKE|NUCLEOTIDES| |

SOME|SPLIT|APART|AND|DIE

OTHERS HOLD

LINKING|UP

INTO|DOUBLE|HELIXES| |

Reference to the double helix as the start and end of linguistic information in this extract provides a vital clue for the reader about the visual design. The way in which the letters and words weave around the vertical cords mimics the interlacing of two polynucleotide strands, winding around each other to form a double helix.

The visual arrangement of words into diagonal contours directs the reader's eye; the eyes are swept along the cluster before doubling back to the start of the next cluster of words. Through this ocular movement, the reader takes a spiralling pathway through this part of the text, as though tracing a polynucleotide strand. Indeed, there is a structural similarity between the double helix and the visual design of this section of *VAS*. Comparable to the double helix, which consists of the interaction of two tightly associated strands, the shared act of literary construction is foregrounded through the reader's involvement in the helix shape. This is what Cranny-Francis (2005: 37) calls the 'visceral reading' of multimedia texts, indicating the "relationship between the text and the embodied practice of reading".

Literature is always a joint venture, the cognitive compromise between the intentions of the writer and imagination of the reader. The analogy of the interweaving structure of DNA with the reading process constructs another blend of book and body, reliant upon their shared property of mutual creation: our DNA shows that each one of us is the genetic combination of mother and father, while the text is the product of writer and reader.

Toward the top of the right frame (please refer back to Figure 5.4), Square is described, in the act of writing, as "trying to get sCATTerings to AGGlutinATe". The capitalised letters in the words, 'scatterings' and 'agglutinate', are written in the same font as the DNA chains, and are letters from the base code, integrating the genetic and linguistic alphabets further. The word 'agglutinate' carries a specialised meaning in both scientific and linguistic discourse. In biochemistry, 'agglutination' is the formation of a mass of particles, such as red blood cells, by the action of antibodies, while in linguistics it is the building up of words from component morphemes in such a way that these undergo little or no change of form or meaning. Thus, in a similar way to the use of the word 'copulate' discussed in section 5.2.2, in each discourse, it is a case of bringing things together to make something new from the constituent parts. In *VAS*, word and image agglutinate, creating both formal and conceptual emergent blend(s) of the book and the body. Section 5.2.5 considers a few more examples to demonstrate the pervasive nature of this conceptual integration throughout the novel.

5.2.5   Refunctionalising the Body

As I have demonstrated, the metaphorical conceptual integration of BOOK and BODY is a consistent feature of the novel. It is what is known as an 'extended' (Nowottny 1962; Werth 1994), 'sustained' or 'megametaphor' (Werth 1999), a metaphor which is conceptually "developed through a *discourse*, e.g. an entire poem, play or novel" (Werth 1994: 80). Werth states that the "fact that metaphors can [. . .] be *sustained*, as a kind of 'undercurrent', over an extended text allows for extremely subtle conceptual effects to be achieved" (1999: 323; original emphasis). In *VAS*, the cumulative undercurrent of the isomorphism of BOOK and BODY not only projects an emergent structure that is a synthesis of BOOK and BODY. Each conceptual domain is also reassessed in light of its parallels to the other. The body can be rewritten through cosmetic surgery for instance, while literature takes on a life of its own. Indeed, discussing the history of the PEOPLE ARE BOOKS metaphor, Manguel notes, "the act of reading serves as a metaphor to help us understand our hesitant relationship with our body, the encounter and the touch and the deciphering of signs in another person" (1997: 169). Interestingly, Gavins's (2007b) development of Text World Theory details a comparable occurrence in literary and poetic reading whereby metaphors produce what she calls "blended worlds" (146–164) that transpire alongside a prominent text-world, influencing a reader's imaginative reconstruction of that principal world.

In section 5.2.3, where I introduced Conceptual Metaphor Theory and Conceptual Integration Theory in relation to the metaphor PEOPLE ARE BOOKS and the integration of BOOK and BODY, I suggested that it was useful to employ both frameworks together. Furthermore, I outlined the limitations of the Invariance Hypothesis (Lakoff 1990; Lakoff and Turner 1989; Murphy 1996; Stockwell 1999; Turner 1990), and Stockwell's (1999) proposal to conceive of metaphorical mapping not as unidirectional from source to target but as a process of 'interanimation'. Stockwell is not alone in noting the interconnected nature of metaphorical meaning-making among source and target. Looking to theorists working on conceptual integration, the work of Coulson (2001) is also relevant. Coulson objects to the unidirectionality proposed in traditional accounts of conceptual metaphor since in her words "nothing inherent to cross-domain mapping mandates mapping from source to target" (2001: 178). As such, Coulson develops conceptual integration to include what she calls "retrospective projections" (2001: 178–199). Essentially, this is the bidirectional possibilities of metaphorical mapping including those which take place in a metaphorical conceptual blend.

On the surface, this would seem to account for the cognitive reassessment of both domains, in the case of *VAS*—BOOK and BODY, in light of their metaphorical relation and the emergent blends they create. However, the analyses presented by Coulson to demonstrate retrospective projection show the process occurring in *either* one direction *or* the other. At one point, she questions, "why do such *asymmetries* in the direction of projections arise in the first place?" (2001: 191; emphasis mine). In order to answer the question, she does not consider the possibilities of symmetry, that is, of interanimation in Stockwell's (1999) terms, but instead suggests a justification behind the motivation of the unconventional mapping from target to source.

In *VAS*, I am arguing that while conceptual integration takes place, it is consequently also useful to consider BOOK and BODY not simply as input spaces to be fed into a blend, but as conceptual domains (in the sense used in Conceptual Metaphor Theory) which re-emerge from the blend intact yet cognitively reconsidered. With regards to terminology, then, I propose that the reconsideration of *each* domain is part of a process of *retrospective*

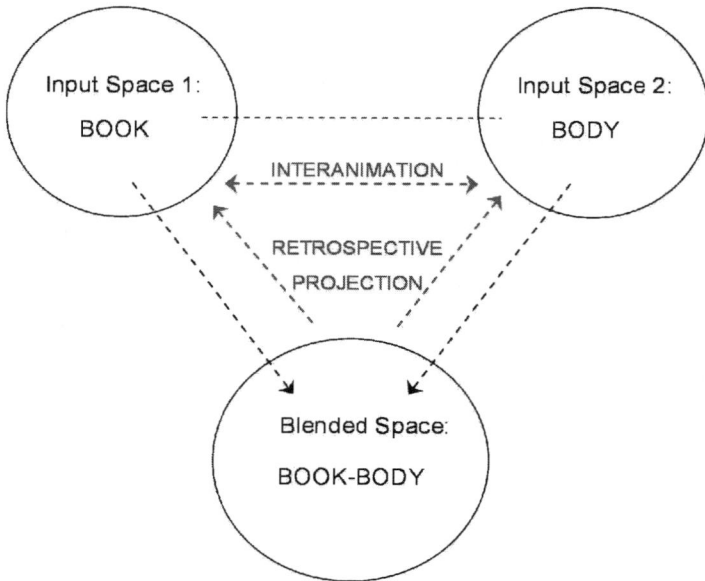

Figure 5.5   Retrospective projection and interanimation of metaphorical integration in *VAS*.

projection (Coulson 2001) whereby meanings in the emergent blend refract upon the inputs, following which the input domains, source and target, *interanimate* (Stockwell 1999) to bring about refreshed and altered perceptions of those domains. Figure 5.5 shows the process. The outer arrows represent the blending operation itself while the inner arrows depict the processes of retrospective projection and interanimation that occur.

The multimodal metaphors and integrations in *VAS* not only revise the domains of BOOK and BODY as conceptual spaces and represented entities. They also serve to refunctionalise both domains in concrete terms, including the perceived potentialities between them. That is, our understandings of our bodies and of how we interact with books are revised.

Our physical interaction with *VAS* as a book is the topic of the next section, which considers the relationship between such physical activity and linguistic comprehension.

5.2.6   "Still, It Moves"

At the end of a highly political discussion of genetic development, ethnic cleansing, and U.S. legislation, the nature of the universe of the book is suddenly referenced: "astronomers concluded, the universe . . . must be . . . flat" (Tomasula 2002: 139). The last linguistic content of this page appears in a very small elaborate font. More unusually, these final words are upside down: "*ᵐᵐᵐᔑᕁ ᔑ ᵐᵐᔐ*". Due to the diminutive type size and ornate script-like font, it is difficult to read this clearly without rotating the book. On doing so, one is able to decipher the text as "Still, It Moves".

The word 'move' is, obviously, associated with dynamic action. Even when the word 'move' is used metaphorically, such as expressing that we 'feel moved by' something, the conceptual metaphor underlying it (EMOTION IS MOTION) relies on our experiences of physical manipulation and activity. This is in line with the tenets of cognitive linguistics, which conceives of all abstract thinking, particularly metaphor and image schemata, as grounded in bodily experience (Gibbs 2005, 2006; Johnson 1987; Lakoff and Johnson 1980, 1999; Sweetser 1990). As mentioned in section 4.2.8 of Chapter 4, research in cognitive science and neuroscience demonstrates that embodied experience is vital to linguistic processing and comprehension, particularly in the use of action verbs such as 'to grasp'. This is the case both when action verbs are used literally such as in the sentence 'He grasped the handle' (de Vega et al. 2004; Gallese and Lakoff 2005; Glenberg 2007; Glenberg and Kaschak 2002; Hauk, Johnsrude, and Pulvermüller 2004; Pulvermüller 2005; Pulvermüller et al., 2005; Rizzolatti and Arbib 1998; Tettamanti et al. 2005; Zwaan et al. 2004; Zwaan and Taylor 2006) and when they are used metaphorically, for instance, in the phrase 'He grasped the idea' (Wilson and Gibbs 2007). The former research evidences that when reading action-related sentences, some of the same regions in the brain are activated as when performing the action, thus priming the neurological circuitry for the linguistically referenced movement. Although this research looks at action verbs that are specifically related to parts of the body (e.g. 'grasp' is associated with the hands), it nevertheless suggests that "real bodily action is at the root of meaning conveyed by language" (Glenberg and Kaschak 2002: 563). Thus, the word 'moves' in *VAS*, like all uses of this word, has an undeniably concrete and corporeal motoric dimension.

It is significant that the reader must physically move the book in order to read "Still, It Moves". Motor resonance and the priming operation of language for action also work in reverse; language which refers to a said action can be processed with increased speed and ease if a subject has previously performed that same action. This can be inferred from Glenberg and Kaschak's (2002) results, as well as Pulvermüller et al.'s (2005), who show that "sensorimotor areas can play a specific functional role in recognizing action words" (795). Wilson and Gibbs (2007) also reach a similar conclusion, which Gibbs (2005: 88) summarises: "performing an action facilitates understanding of a figurative phrase containing that action word, just as it does for literal phrases". Consequently, the kinaesthetic movement of rotating the book primes the concept of 'movement' and assists the linguistic comprehension of "Still, It Moves", with 'moves' interpreted with a literal construal.

In analysing "Still, It Moves", I have thus far paid little heed to the word 'Still', yet this too is significant. In fact, I believe that its most significant semantic contribution works alongside the visual feature on this page (shown in Figure 5.6).

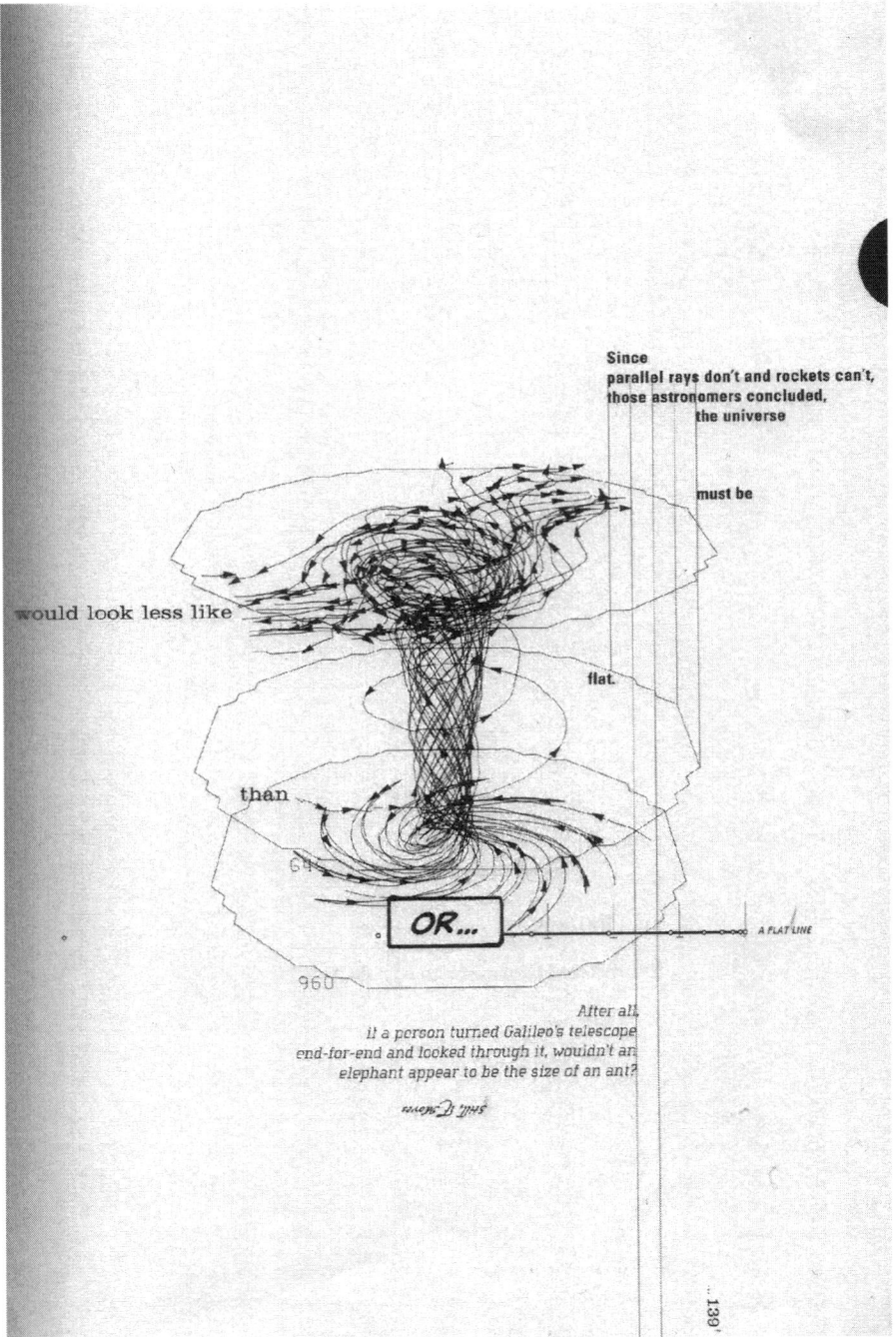

Figure 5.6   Tomasula/Farrell (2002) *VAS: An Opera in Flatland*: 139.

The image is a diagrammatic swirl of arrows, which resembles the shape of a tornado. As such, these may also contribute to motor resonance and the priming operation discussed in relation to the word 'moves' earlier. The arrows appear to be acting under a centripetal force, thus creating the impression of rotary motion. In this way, the diagram may be a form of pictorial priming for rotational movement. As for the word 'Still', even in conjunction with the reader's actual rotation of the book, the impression of movement created by and in this diagram is, in effect, just that—an impression. If the word 'Still' is taken in its literal meaning, it may allude to the fact that the movement suggested by the image is not actual, but merely the result of the reader-viewer's perceptual inferences, as influenced by the linguistic narrative. This idea is supported by work in cognitive neuroscience, which demonstrates that static images with implied motion engage the same brain areas as the processing of actual motion (Bertamini 2002; Kourtzi and Kanwisher 2000). Thus, static images, such as this diagrammatic swirl of arrows from *VAS*, trigger implied dynamic information processing. "Still, It Moves" is therefore a multimodal inscription, the reading of which cognitively and neurologically unites word, image, and physical kinaesthetics.

Above the words "Still, It Moves" is written: "After all, if a person turned Galileo's telescope end-for-end and looked through it, wouldn't an elephant appear to be the size of an ant?" (Tomasula 2002: 139). This hypothetical and rhetorical question is concerned with perception—looking at something in a different way or from a different vantage point results in a different vision. This is relevant to readers' experience of "Still, It Moves" since it is only by altering their approach to the text, physically rotating it as with Galileo's telescope, that the words are comprehended.

The reference to Galileo becomes even more important overleaf where on the right-hand page "Still, It Moves" is repeated (Tomasula 2002: 64), having been imprinted in exact replication of its previous appearance. Above this appear a series of vertically aligned circles and the words "Eppur, Si Muove", shown by Figure 5.7.

The lowest line of this inscription seemingly authenticates the material with a date (April and the year in roman numerals) and signatory, Galileo, enabling the reader to infer that the mysterious words, "Eppur, Si Muove" belong to the seventeenth-century astronomer and physicist Galileo Galilei. "Eppur, Si Muove" is, in fact, an Italian phrase, more or less translatable to "Still, It Moves". Galileo is reported to have muttered these words at the close of the inquisition of 1633 as he rose from his knees after having recited the abjuration in which he was forced to retract his belief in the Copernican solar system, namely, that the earth (and all planets) move in orbit around the sun (Fahie 1903: 324; Næss 2005: 177). Although historians and biographers, who consider it inaccurate, have discarded this speech, it nevertheless holds magnitude for a reading of *VAS*.

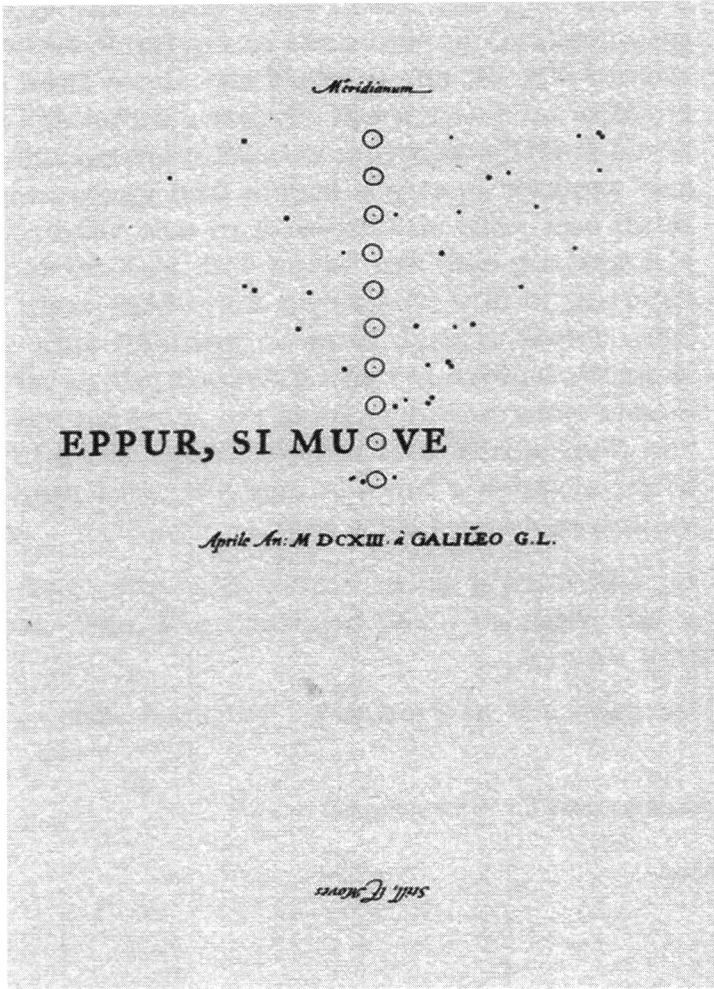

Figure 5.7   Tomasula/Farrell (2002) *VAS: An Opera in Flatland*: 141.

To begin with, the 'o' in "Eppur, Si Muove" is not realised in the same typography as the rest of the words. It is actually created using one of the vertical circles. These circles, ten in total, can be said to represent nine planets and the earth's moon in the solar system, an idea confirmed by the heading word 'Méridianum'. This is a version of the word 'meridian', which refers in astronomy to an imagined circle passing through the celestial poles and zenith of a given place, enabling astronomers to plot the positions of stars and planets. In effect, the reader holds in their hands a solar system, albeit a two-dimensional 'flatland' version. More-over, since "Still, It Moves" once again sits upside down at the bottom of the page, the book requires rotation. Those readers who choose to revolve the book in this manner, rather than lazily reading it wrong way up, take on the role of the sun spinning the planets, putting them into orbit, so to speak. This physical interaction produces a multimodal sin-gle-scope conceptual blend in which the notion of the sun is transposed upon the reader. Thus in its emergent meaning, like the sun for the earth, the reader is a life-giving force for the novel, bringing it 'alive' in cogni-tive terms. Significantly, the conceptual blend at work here is produced not just by the synthesis of graphic design and linguistic content. It is the reader's kinaesthetic action, the physical rotation of the book, which instigates and synchronises the blend. Embodied action, therefore, has both a creative role in the conceptual integration process here as well as being used as an element within that integration.

Ultimately, it is the reader's corporeal transaction with *VAS* that enables the interpretation of these circles as planets, and the reader's direct motoric engagement with the book that creates a solar system in action. The reader's movement realises the conceptual integration, interacting with the text and with the book as an object in the world. Moreover, the reader's embodied enaction is responsible for both the narrative mean-ing which is produced as well as an integral component in that emergent (in blending terms) narrative meaning. Therefore, the reader's corporeal effort and role in literary world-creation is not just foregrounded in the discourse-world. The movement is also being placed 'onstage', to adopt a phrase from Langacker (2002 [1991], 2002a), actively narrativised in the world of the text.

In the next section, I analyse a metatextual passage concerned with cre-ative writing and books as material artefacts.

5.2.7   The Body of the Book

Tomasula presumably intended *VAS* to be experienced as a concrete and corporeal entity. This objective is palpable toward the close of the story. As Square and his wife Circle lie in bed together, Square picks up her book from the nightstand:

> The weight of the book surprised him, sex having drained him more than it used to. He ran a palm along its trimmed edges, breathed in the scent of its paper. He wanted to taste it, to put his ear to it like the sea shell so he could, as advised in all the books about "how to write stories," describe it by using all five senses, to make her (and you) experi-ence the text as an object in the world, real as a brick. Only more so because it was more than its material. (284)

The presence of behavioural process verbs (Halliday 2004: 248–252) such as 'breathe(d)', 'taste', and 'experience' in relation to the book as a textual artefact emphasise the role of Square as a participant in a literary encounter that mediates between the cognitive and the physical. The similes comparing the book to a seashell and a brick serve to ground the literary article as a corporeal item with which Square may interrelate in mental, physiological, and material ways. The perceptual deictic shift from 'her' to 'you', emphasised through the close proximity of the pronouns, is also significant. The verb phrase 'to describe' sets up a relationship between Square as a potential speaker and Circle as his hearer/receiver. Conversely, the parenthetical expression 'and you' instigates a perceptual shift from 'her', referring to Circle in Square's point of view, to a generalised 'you' through indefinite reference. This reference and the fact that it is not located in direct speech means it cannot refer to another enactor or receiver in the narrative world. Furthermore, since parenthetical expressions operate in parallel rather than necessarily in conjunction with the text in which they are embedded, the typographical difference in type-size and subsequently depth of colour denotes a change in discourse levels. Due to its visual status and linguistic convention, this use of parenthesis indicates a literary relocation into a domain where 'you' is interpreted as the reader, while the words are assigned by oppositional reference to implied author, an extra-fictional counterpart of Tomasula himself. As Gavins argues in her investigation into readers' mental representations, "The use of 'you' specifies the inclusion of an enactor of the reader at the text-world level, along with an enactor of the author" (2007b: 98). Additionally, in engaging the reader in direct address with the author-enactor, the second-person pronoun gives that address a sense of intimacy: even though it occurs in parenthesis, the address effectively invites the reader-enactor to self-implicate (Kuiken, Miall, and Sikora 2004) into a context that places him or her, both linguistically and within the storyworld, in bed with Square and Circle. The use of subjective deictic reference demonstrates that language necessarily has an orientating function; all language, and all literary language, is embodied.

In his experience of the book, Square contemplates "how to *write* stories", emphasising the connections between reading and writing, as well as the shared human capacity for sensual imagination. The world of the novel, particularly its imaginative creation, is therefore a procreative mutual act between writer and reader. Additionally, not only does the writerly requirement of utilising the five senses fit well with Tomasula's attempt to ground *VAS* as a sensory entity, it is pertinent to contemporary ruminations on the future of the novel. In a recent newspaper article, Marr (2007) passes judgement on the 'ebook', a handheld digital device. While Marr's conclusions are reluctantly positive, he laments what would be the loss of the 'body' of the book and its scent: "my advice to the makers is to refine the page-turning just a little more, offer a battered blue cloth-bound wallet and, above all, make it smell—just a little musty, please. Or dank. You could offer a choice" (2007). *VAS* accentuates corporeal sensory features. By employing parenthesis and typography in the above extract, Tomasula emphasises that multimodal books, and *VAS* specifically, entice readers into a resonantly physical and sensual encounter with narrative.

The physical and sensual literary experiences that multimodal texts provoke are in part created as an effect of their eye-catching graphic designs and textual layouts. In the next section, I explore how this multimodality draws attention to textual surface and impacts upon the reader's perceptual experience of the literary text.

5.2.8   Moving between Worlds

VAS: An Opera in Flatland's multimodal forms repeatedly remind the reader of its materiality, provoking a renewed awareness of its physical as well as metaphysical utility. Considering the experience of reading and the disparity between traditional and more visually innovative literature, designer Stephen Farrell articulates:

> The book is widely conceived as a field for language, for textuality. When the flesh of language—the design—tremors, it disturbs the trance of deep reading. The oft requested antidote—the 'pure language field' or 'neutral' page—is itself costume. It wields a typographic body bearing the mask of unmediated legibility . . . And with the formulation of this 'neutral' page . . . attention is diverted from the fleshy presence of a *thing*, a discursive subject, a theatrical concretion that is a language and an inseparable ingredient of the duck-rabbit dialectic. (1999)

Farrell's words suggest how visual design and multimodality can foreground the textual surface of the novel and prevent a form of complete imaginative immersion. The concluding reference to the 'duck-rabbit dialectic' gestures towards a famous bistable illusion. Studied by perceptual psychologists and neuro-vision researchers, bistable illusions, such as Rubin's vase (discussed in section 3.4.3 of Chapter 3) and the duck-rabbit picture, are constant visual stimuli in which can be perceived two mutually incompatible figures. This results in shifting perceptual experience.

Early cognitive psychological theories of literary experience tend to focus on the immersive nature of the imaginative endeavour. Gerrig's (1993) notion of 'transportation', for example, indirectly accentuates the reader's imaginative relocation into the fictional arena of the text. The same is true of the world metaphor at the heart of Text World Theory. Despite the detailed linguistic focus of Text World Theory, text-worlds and Gerrig's notion of transportation share a dedicated interest in the psychological 'beyond', which indirectly renders the printed words as 'transparent'. The phenomenon of literary language as a transparent medium has been eloquently observed by Merleau-Ponty (1962), who wrote:

> The wonderful thing about language is that it promotes its own oblivion: my eyes follow the lines on the paper, and from the moment I am caught up in their meaning, I lose sight of them. The paper, the letters on it, my eyes and body are there only as the minimum setting of some invisible operation. Expression fades out before what is expressed, and that is why its mediating rôle may pass unnoticed. (401)

Language in literature is certainly a vehicle of 'immersion', aided by the established, and now conventional, appearance of books. Most publications follow similar visual directives, designed with margins, pagination and type-set in block text in accord with strictly coded linear reading paths. Such standardisation in publishing heightens transparency, ensuring that the literal surface of a page is as unremarkable as possible to its reader. Consequently, the design of most fiction presents what Bolter and Grusin (1999) in their work on 'Remediation' have termed 'transparent immediacy', that is, "a style of visual representation whose goal is to make the viewer forget the presence of the medium (the canvas, photographic film, cinema, and so on) and believe that he is in the presence of the objects of representation" (1999: 272–273).

As has been shown throughout this chapter, multimodal (printed) novels like *VAS* complicate the relationship of the concrete to the imaginary, since in contrast to traditional Western literary forms, they are not transparent. They are 'opaque', bearing self-conscious graphic designs that draw attention to their materiality. In doing so, the concrete realisation of word and image upon the printed page participates in the narrative. The innovative appearance of multimodal literature induces the two semiotic modes to collaborate in the literary act, and thus both the verbal and visual influence the reader's creation of, and potential immersion in, an imagined text-world. Moreover, since multimodal novels exploit the visual surface of the page to communicate their story, the readerly performance of transportation from the discourse-world and submersion into the text-world is not as fixed as with traditional literary forms. Rather, a slippage occurs between discourse-world and text-world, in which the surface of the book's pages also becomes a significant conceptual plane. In other words, multimodal texts demand a dynamic reading strategy in which the reader must 'toggle' between the mediating textual surface and cognitive worlds.

Farrell is, in fact, not alone in recalling bistable perception as a metaphor for the shifting perceptual dimension of all literary experience. Lanham's

(1993) theory of bistable oscillation launches a path for investigation into reading multimodal texts as a form of dual vision. Lanham's thoughts on literature are triggered by the rise of digital media and are, moreover, one of the foundations for Bolter and Grusin's (1999) work on 'Remediation'. In opposition to 'transparent immediacy', Bolter and Grusin conceptualise 'Hypermediacy', detailing:

> If the logic of immediacy leads one either to erase or to render automatic the act of representation, the logic of hypermediacy acknowledges multiple acts of representation and makes them visible. Where immediacy suggests a unified visual space, contemporary hypermediacy offers a heterogeneous space, in which representation is conceived of not as a window on to the world, but rather as "windowed" itself with windows that open on to other representations or other media. The logic of hypermediacy multiplies the signs of mediation and in this way tries to reproduce the rich sensorium of human experience. (1999: 33–34)

Drawing attention to itself as the 'windowed' object in addition to opening windows into an intangible realm of imagination, the hypermedial art object encompasses the tension between the material artefact and the abstract representation to which it refers. Multimodal texts are hypermedial, expressing this tension through their 'opaque' and decidedly visual nature. In other words, they encourage double situatedness (Ensslin 2009).

Defining bistable oscillation, Lanham asserts:

> The textual surface has become permanently bi-stable. We are always looking first at it and then through it, and this oscillation creates a different implied ideal of decorum, both stylistic and behavioral. Look through a text and you are in the familiar world of the Newtonian interlude, where facts were facts, the world was really "out there," folks had sincere central selves, and the best writing style dropped from the writer as "simply and directly as a stone falls to the ground," precisely as Thoreau counseled. Look at a text, however, and we have deconstructed the Newtonian world into Pirandello's and yearn to "act naturally." (1993: 5)

It is this perceptual fluctuation between looking *at* the material surface of the page and looking *through* the page to immerse oneself in its content which characterises multimodal literature. Regrettably, Lanham does not develop bistable oscillation into a working model, nor does he suggest a potential route for doing so. It is merely a conjecture, a theoretical observation. Since Text World Theory is grounded in language, which on the printed page forms substantial ocular matter, it presents a pertinent approach within which to incorporate a framework for bistable oscillation.

Tomasula's investigation of literary dimensionality and perspective is most evident in its appropriation of Edwin A. Abbott's (1998 [1884]) short novella. To reiterate and expand the synopsis provided in the introduction, Abbott's original text *Flatland: A Romance of Many Dimensions* is written from the perspective of a square who lives in a two-dimensional world known as Flatland. By the end of the story, Square has experienced the single dimension of 'Lineland' in dream form, as well as discovering 'Spaceland', a three-dimensional realm. These encounters ultimately affect Square's perception of his own plane of existence.

Abbott's voice is present as one of the first of many scientific quotations included in *VAS*, charging readers to "*Imagine a vast sheet of paper on which straight Lines, Triangles, Squares, Pentagons, Hexagons, and other figures move freely about, but without the power to rise above or sink below it, and you will then have a pretty correct notion of my country and countrymen.*" In Abbott's novella, this is the square's direct address to readers, an attempt to aid them in conceptualising his homeland and, of course, the setting of the fiction. Tomasula makes use of Abbott's narrator and employ this quote to manipulate the concept of 'Flatland'. As Farrell expounds:

> These countrymen, sprawled across the country of Flatland, are like Square's words, sprawled across the page. The square speaks in words recorded and confined in tiny letterforms on a page I hold and read. These tiny letterforms colonize the page and transform it into its own flat land. The page is now an inhabited world, a flat world . . . As we writers and designers fashion the surface of flat pages, we form the stuff of flatlands . . . their topologies—and their inhabitants. (1999)

For Tomasula and Farrell, Flatland is the surface of the page, the interposing plane between the writer and designer's craft and the reader's imagination.

One of the most visually challenging sections of *VAS* occurs in its penultimate pages when Square takes his wife Circle to the opera. Circle has been trying to persuade Square to have a vasectomy, and so reluctantly agrees to this outing on the condition that Square fulfils what Circle sees as his 'obligation'. Instantly succeeding Circle's concession to attend appear two unexpectedly dark pages (Tomasula/Farrell 2002: 326–327), the left of which is a monotone block of black while the right-hand page features what looks like an aged photograph of a description plaque or card. These pages are strikingly different and so instantly produce a readerly awareness of the book as a physical object. The subdued colour of the printed description demands a close examination of the writing in order for it to be clearly read. Additionally, the image is swathed with a grainy effect, a look reminiscent of watching old black-and-white film reels. This potential remediation of a poor-quality film or photograph forces the reader to look at the page, while also heightening a realisation of one's self as a reader and viewer of the fiction.

Turning overleaf, shown in Figure 5.8, this visual style is continued, though interspersed with a more familiar literary form, a single white page on which sits a portion of typed text. The passage begins, "The opera was called *The Strange Voyage of Imagining Chatter* and Square and Circle had box seats" (Tomasula 2002: 328). The initial reference to the opera functions as a locative with which to build the text-world. The word 'opera' presupposes a theatre or opera house, enabling the reader to construct a setting for this scene based on his or her existing knowledge structures and experience. Square and Circle's 'box seats' adds further locative detail and deictically positions the characters at the opera as observers of the performance. This is the primary text-world envisaged by the reader as they 'travel' THROUGH the printed words. In the following section, I continue to consider the perceptual tension between at and THROUGH layers of literary experience by exploring the repeated existence of two shape icons in *VAS*. These can be seen on the left hand page shown in Figure 5.8.

Figure 5.8   Tomasula/Farrell (2002) *VAS: An Opera in Flatland*: 328–329.

5.2.9   Beings of Flatland

The existence of two icons, situated above the aforementioned passage on the page, disrupts the permanence of this transportation. The icons, a square and a circle, are likenesses of the two characters based on their names. As such, they are graphic representations of beings from Flatland and serve to displace language's seductive power of transparency, returning the reader's consciousness to (or should I say at) the surface of the page. This is an ontological 'pop' in deictic terms (Galbraith 1995), propelling the reader upwards toward the discourse-world, however momentarily.

The shape symbols of the two central characters are, in fact, not merely iconic renderings of inhabitants from Flatland, but take on greater significance when considered alongside genetic science. American geneticists use standardised symbols when creating 'pedigree charts' (Bennett et al. 1995) such as shapes for people and lines for the relationships between them (Johansen Mange and Mange 1999: 68–69). A pedigree chart is essentially like a family tree used to trace certain biological traits, such as eye colour if necessary. Their most valuable use is, of course, to determine the likelihood of the inheritance of genetic disease or physical abnormality. Not surprisingly given the thematic concerns of *VAS*, in pedigree nomenclature a square is used to represent a male while a circle represents a female. Moreover, in both the representation in question (Tomasula/Farrell 2002: 328) and throughout the novel, Square and Circle are connected using a dotted line rather than an unbroken line. As shown in Figure 5.9, an unbroken line would suggest marriage and Circle and Square are indeed married in the novel. A dotted line, however, signifies illegitimate offspring (Johansen Mange and Mange 1999: 69).

As Circle and Square's daughter Oval is not illegitimate, the use of the dotted line in *VAS* does not strictly follow its coded meaning. Nevertheless, since this connotative meaning is connected to the status of offspring, it seems to have implied significance with regard to Square's pending vasectomy and the tensions placed on his marriage to Circle by his hesitancy to commit himself to the procedure. These uncertainties are therefore realised graphically by the intervallic nature of the line. The exact nature of these symbolic meanings can therefore only be fully comprehended by readers with specialist scientific knowledge. Indeed, Bennett et al. (1995) emphasise, "The pedigree is the

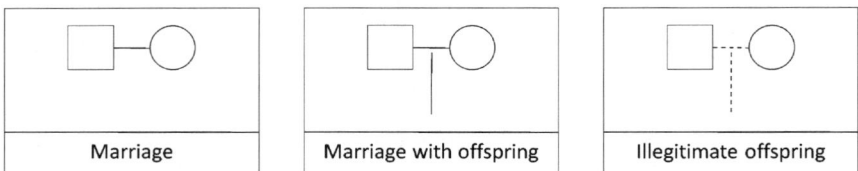

| Marriage | Marriage with offspring | Illegitimate offspring |

Figure 5.9   Genetic nomenclature, adapted from Johansen Mange and Mange (1999: 69).

symbolic language of clinical genetic services and of human genetic research" (747). Furthermore, Bennett et al.'s project to standardise the pedigree nomen-clature in order to avoid confusion demonstrates its unmotivated character.

Pushing back into the narrative of *VAS*, Square and Circle are described as "leaning into each other, holding hands as it began" (Tomasula 2002: 328). This portrayal of the couple creates a sense of intimacy. More remark-ably though, 'leaning' implies a moulding of one's body position and this is not an ability one would attribute to a square or circle, however animate they may be. Neither would one imagine these object-beings to have hands that can be held, or arms for that matter; certainly these limbs aren't pres-ent on the two-dimensional drawings included on this page. Thus the nar-rative undermines its visual accompaniment, the surface of the page and the imagined text-world existing in tension.

As analysis throughout this chapter has suggested, the friction between two- and three-dimensional visualisation, toggling between at and through, occurs consistently when reading *VAS*. This is partly owing to the linguis-tic details provided, but it is also due to human cognitive competence. As dictated by the 'reality principle' (Walton 1990) or 'principle of minimal departure' (Ryan 1991), when we picture a text-world or storyworld it shares much of its identity with the actual world (which is, of course, three-dimensional). To complicate matters further, Square and Circle are personi-fied in the novel, not just descriptively, but also through narrative necessity. Square's deep anxiety over having a vasectomy, for instance, instils his character with complex emotional intelligence, an essentially human trait. Moreover, the shapes—a square and a circle—have cultural connotations that personify them. A square, for instance, often stands in as a signifier for someone who is 'geeky' or in some way 'unfashionable', as in the phrase 'Be there or be square'. It is, therefore, difficult to conceptualise the characters as two-dimensional beings (even when explicitly stated), meaning that the cognitive image of the scene is often in direct conflict with the book's con-crete realisations of Flatland.

In the next section, I utilise Text World Theory to suggest how the per-ceptual oscillation of bistable reading practices can be tracked in a system-atic way that is suitable to a cognitive approach to multimodality.

5.2.10   Blending Worlds

Taking Gavins's (2007b) model of 'blended worlds', this disparity between representations, between the two forms of dimensional visualisation as well as between their literal graphic depiction on the page and the reader's imaginative construal, requires a 'dual vision' (Werth 1977) inherent in bistable oscillation. For Gavins, a blended world is created by the presence of a metaphor in a text, resulting in "a conceptual merger of two otherwise independent text-worlds" (2007b: 149). Figure 5.10 represents how this occurs with *VAS*, and will be explained below.

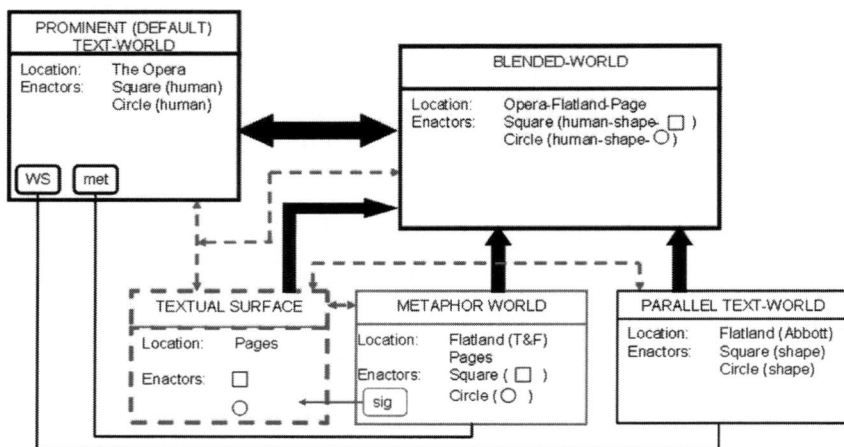

Figure 5.10 Multiple conceptual arenas in *VAS* created by multimodality and metaphor.

In *VAS*, 'Flatland' is employed by Tomasula and Farrell in several ways: firstly, it is a fictional representation as in Abbott's original novella (parallel text-world in diagram); secondly, it is a metaphor for the pages of the book (metaphor world in diagram); and, finally, as a causal effect of the metaphor, it comes to signify the pages themselves (shown as textual surface in the diagram). These layers exist as new text-worlds that feed into an emergent blended world. This input process is represented by the larger arrows. In addition, the large dual-direction arrow shows that the reader's understanding of the blended world impacts upon their interpretation of the prominent text-world containing the immediate narrative action, and viceversa. Both of these are depicted in bolded boxes to show their primary import.

This process, as represented in the diagram of Figure 5.10, creates multiple conceptual arenas, which the reader must cognitively run in parallel, in order to glean the extended metaphor of 'Flatland' that is sustained throughout the novel. Discussing this procedure, Gavins anticipates, "participants in the discourse-world are able to manage all these mental representations simultaneously, toggling between the worlds if necessary" (2007b: 152). In *VAS*, while this is the case, the added dimension of opaque textual surface must be included in this process for the totality of the novel's intricate metaphor to be comprehended by the reader. The pervasive interpretive impact of the textual surface is represented by the pink dual-direction arrows in Figure 5.10.

Werth (1977, 1994) and Gavins (2007b) refer to linguistic metaphor and metaphorical text-worlds as 'double-layered'. As Werth (1977) articulates:

It is this essential trait which I am referring to as "double-vision", or if you want a more impressive term, *diplopia*: the reader, like the viewer of a cubist painting, is allowed, and in fact encouraged, to glimpse two or more aspects of meaning simultaneously. (9)

In *VAS*, and in multimodal literary experience, textual comprehension is even more complex. Ordinarily, metaphor entails diplopic reading, toggling between conceptual worlds. When the textual surface provides a self-conscious contribution to textual comprehension, the reader must bistably oscillate between each individual world and the textual surface too. Thus, another layer of meaning-making is involved. The following section concludes my analysis of bistable oscillation in *VAS*.

5.2.11 Imagining Chatter

Returning to the passage under scrutiny, a colon is placed after the description of Square and Circle's intimate posture; "They leaned into each other, holding hands as it began: a huge projection of artist Charles Willson Peale flickers from a kinescope" (Tomasula 2002: 328). The colon is used in a syntactical-descriptive fashion. Thus, what follows is a detailed description of the opera, cataphorically signalled using the pronoun 'it', which precedes the punctuation. This elaboration begins in the present continuous tense, with the artist "pulling back a tasseled Victorian curtain". It does not require a great leap of imagination to perceive the picture on the right-hand page as a representation of this action and of the opera's opening. This picture is, in fact, a copy of Charles Willson Peale's 1822 self portrait, *The Artist in his Museum*. Peale stands in the fore of the painting, lifting the curtain to reveal the main exhibit room of his natural history museum.

In a contrary move to the visual elements discussed earlier, this captivating and somewhat ghostly image assists readerly immersion. This may be partially indebted to its more realist depiction or its 'naturalistic coding orientation' to use Kress and van Leeuwen's phrase (1996: 170). However, it seems more significant that, unlike previously, this visual works to reinforce, rather than undercut, the linguistic content. Indeed, it is this aspect of the image, its reinforcement of linguistic content, which causes immersion. The image in question does more than cooperate with the narrative. It directly corresponds to the action of the described opera and therefore can be seen to manifest the visual scene witnessed by the characters. It therefore represents and positions the reader to see through the characters' 'point of view' (Simpson 1993). In doing so, it is a considerable 'push' in deictic terms (Galbraith 1995; Stockwell 2002a), moving the reader away from the discourse-world. Coupled with the involving use of present tense, it encourages the reader to project into (through) the text-world, viewing the opera from within the deictic centre of one of the characters, Square or Circle.

As the narrative proceeds, the reader is pushed deeper into the text. Describing the items present in Peale's exhibition room, Tomasula initiates a deictic shift: "—props that he had used for still lifes before they took on a life of their own" (2002: 328). The past perfect tense (had used) and locative preposition (before) instigate a change in deictic parameters, and thus triggers a world-switch into the action of the opera itself. The reader's transportation into the embedded world of the opera is short-lived, since overleaf they are greeted by a new visual format, its unfamiliarity once again retrieving them from their journey THROUGH the language of the novel. This type of formal configuration is repeated for several pages, and is comparable (though by no means identical) to the layout of graphic novels, as can be seen in Figure 5.11. The new design is used to represent the stage action of the opera. As in graphic novels where they tend to contain narration, there is a caption box located at the top of each panel. Considering any caption box from *VAS*, one might at first think that it fulfils the same function. Take one from page 332, for instance: "Musicians in loincloths bring on screeching monkeys." Although slightly bizarre, this nevertheless has a descriptive function encouraging the reader to envisage the described action.

It is also noteworthy that the return to present tense pops the reader back into the primary text-world with Circle and Square watching the opera. While in graphic novels, the rest of the panel would ordinarily display an image, in *VAS* the panel contains words. Given the multimodal nature of the novel, this is a little surprising.

This panel reads, "Images of monkeys swinging through trees projected on a scrim stretching across the stage". On one hand, the movement attributed to the primates foregrounds the creatures and assigns them a prominence which prompts the reader to construct a mental representation. However, the reference to inscription technology (the images projected onto the scrim) has the adverse effect. By mentioning the mediating screen, the passage emphasises that the words are a linguistic replacement for a representation that would normally behave transparently. Consequently, the perspectives of at and through are brought together, though not seamlessly and unnoticeably. That is, the reader must perform a dynamic cognitive balancing act in the form of bistable oscillation.

Figure 5.12 depicts the opera episode currently under analysis, though blended worlds are not accounted for here. In the text-world diagram, the prominent text-world is bolded. Text-world 2 is the world of the opera itself and was created in the narrative of *VAS* through a deictic world-switch. Finally, as in Figure 5.12, the textual surface of the book is contained in another text-world, with dual-direction arrows to show that readers are required to take account of each text-world level, a process which calls for them to alternate cognitive awareness between imaginative immersion and

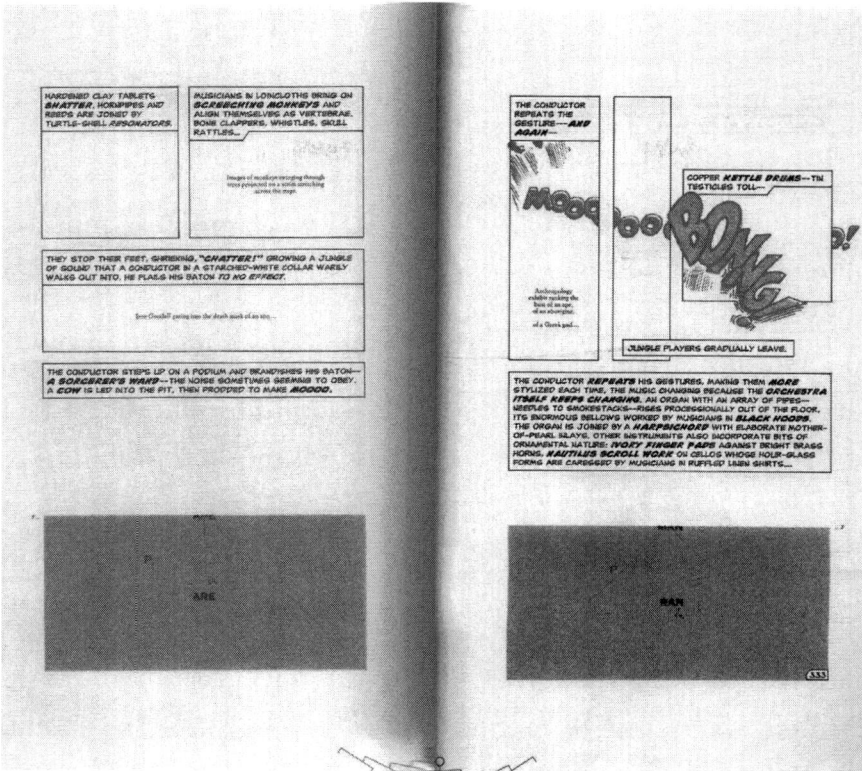

Figure 5.11   Tomasula/Farrell (2002) *VAS: An Opera in Flatland*: 332–333.

a consciousness of the book as a physical entity, ultimately resulting in a mixed reality literary experience.

Fittingly, the title of the opera, "The Strange Voyage of Imagining Chatter", encapsulates the nature of this reading experience, with its reference to a transporting journey, the literary imagination, and the discursive process implied by the word 'chatter'. Its graphic manifestation, both in terms of its typography and pictorial accompaniment, accentuates the multifaceted capacity of *VAS* as multimodal fiction. In the episode analysed in sections 5.2.8 through to 5.2.11 of this chapter, the panels of the novel's opera represented the stage action in an extraordinary two-dimensional fashion. Consequently, it probably will not shock the reader to discover a two-dimensional audience. Central at the bottom of each double page spread in the opera section, Square and Circle can be found (in Flatland form) viewing the performance space. Another remediating visual cue, this is not only a distancing device to prevent transcendental reading. By observing observers observing the opera, the

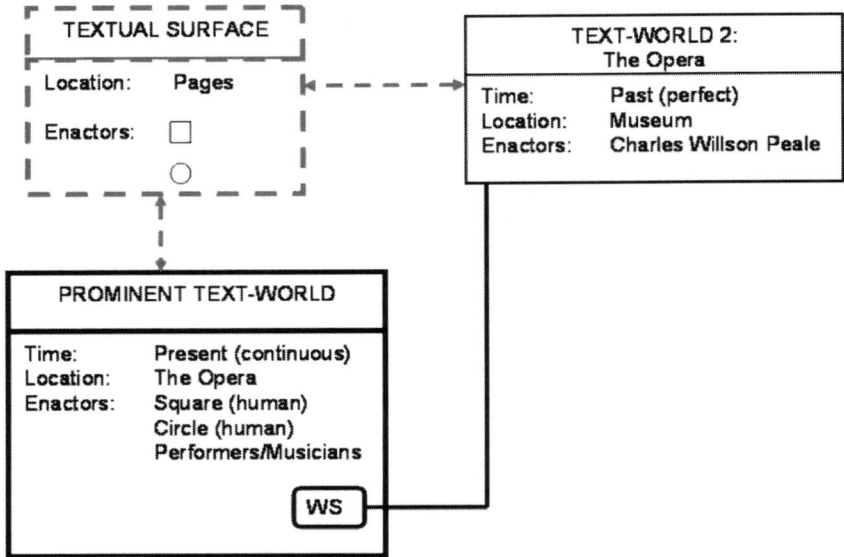

Figure 5.12   Text-worlds and textual surface.

reader is reminded of his or her own corporeality, as a reader reading. Indeed, *VAS* is visually, thematically, and experientially a narrative of embodiment. *VAS* foregrounds and utilises the body and the senses of the reader throughout demonstrating, to quote Klatzy and Lederman (2000), that when "stimulated by movement in different ways, the same receptors can tell different stories" (2000: 236).

5.3   CONCLUSION

Steve Tomasula states, "I'd always wanted *VAS* to be very much an object in the world, an entity rather than a 'dream a reader can get lost in'" (personal correspondence, July 14, 2007). *VAS: An Opera in Flatland* offers a dynamic literary experience, whereby the physical context of reading is continually brought to the reader's attention, thus inhibiting the immersive act of literary transportation(s) (Gerrig 1993). The analysis in this chapter sought to expound the ways in which multimodal novels such as *VAS* continually place the reader in positions of double situatedness (Ensslin 2009) with the text. This occurs both experientially, in terms of the readers' cognitive and corporeal engagement, as well as perceptually in bistable oscillation.

Lanham (1993) uses the phrase *bistable oscillation* to describe the perceptual experience of toggling between looking AT the surface of a text and looking through it in the sense of imagining its narrative world. This chapter employed the Text World Theory framework to track the perceptual processes involved in the bistable reading experience triggered by the multimodality of *VAS: An Opera in Flatland*. Text World Theory analysis of bistable oscillation is rigorous and replicable, and, moreover, exposes some of the devices which assist or impede literary immersion. These devices can be connected to deictic shifts in reading comprehension. For instance, linguistic devices such as present tense and imagistic representations that correspond to the narrative work to push the reader 'lower' down the scale of textual deictic fields (Stockwell 2002a) and deeper into the world of the novel, e.g. from actual reader position into a character deictic centre.

Given that the novel is interested in the politics of genetic modification and cyberbiological advancement, Tomasula's narrative disclosure within the novel is apt:

> My intention is to tell of bodies . . .
>
> . . . of bodies changed to different forms . . .
>
> (2002: 143–144)

Beyond the novel's narrative themes, this statement is made manifest by the way in which the reader must engage with the book. *VAS* encourages an embodied and enactive literary experience, transforming the bodies of its readers in terms of their habitual forms of corporeal being during the activity of literary reading.

A literary trope of *VAS* is the sustained metaphor of PEOPLE ARE BOOKS, and the associated conceptual integration of BOOK and BODY. Both are achieved through linguistic and multimodal means. Using Conceptual Metaphor Theory and Conceptual Integration Theory as complementary approaches made clear that BOOK and BODY integrate in the novel to produce emergent meaning as well as remaining intact as conceptual domains. In light of the blends and in light of their metaphorical analogy, readers of *VAS* experience perceptual alterations in their understandings of BOOK and BODY, an effect explained by the allied notions of retrospective projection (Coulson 2001), understood as the way in which emergent meaning can refract onto the inputs, and interanimation (Stockwell 1999), Stockwell's term for the way meaning can be mapped bilaterally between both source and target. Both retrospective projection and interanimation bring about the revisioning of the original input domains.

Analogous to our bodies, composed of various matter, chains of DNA, and encompassing our genetic histories, *VAS: An Opera in Flatland* is multimodal in its employment of the visual, verbal, and somatosensory factors which collaborate in the production of textual meaning. This is therefore a book that can indeed declare, "I contain multitudes" (Tomasula 2002: 298). By taking on a corporeal quality through multimodal metaphoric blending and emphasising its nature as a material object in the world for our bodies, brains, and minds to interact with, *VAS* leaves a telling impression; if you dissect this book, it is likely to bleed.

6 Cowitnessing Trauma in Reading *Extremely Loud & Incredibly Close* by Jonathan Safran Foer

6.1 INTRODUCTION

Extremely Loud & Incredibly Close (2005a) is the second novel from New York–based author Jonathan Safran Foer. The novel focuses on nine-year-old Oskar Schell, a young boy who lost his father in the terrorist attack on the World Trade Center on September 11, 2001. A year later, still struggling to come to terms with his father's death, Oskar discovers a mysterious key in an envelope in his father's closet. On the back of the envelope, the word "Black" is written. This prompts Oskar to embark on a quest to find the lock in which the key fits by visiting all the New Yorkers with the surname Black.

Oskar is the central narrating character, though his narrative episodes are interspersed with chapters narrated by his grandmother and grandfather. Thomas Schell Senior, Oskar's grandfather, lived through the bombing of his native Dresden and has subsequently lost the power of speech as a result of the traumatic experience. In the storyworld, Thomas Senior communicates by writing on a notebook (pages of which feature in his narrative) as well as through tattoos on his left and right hands of the words YES and NO, respectively. Thomas Senior's chapters are written as letters to 'his unborn child'. This is primarily Oskar's father prior to his birth. It is also the unborn child Thomas Senior was going to father with Anna, his greatest love and Oskar's grandmother's sister, who was killed in the Dresden bombings. Oskar's grandmother's chapters, on the other hand, are written as letters to Oskar. Through these three narrators, the narrative structure essentially divides the novel into two main narrative threads; Oskar's search for the key post 9/11, and Oskar's grandparents' memories of Dresden and its effect on their lives.

The three narrators, Oskar, Thomas Sr., and Oskar's grandmother, all have distinctive narrative styles. Danielewski's novel *House of Leaves* assigns each of its narrators a different type-face, the font thus graphologically representing narrative voice. Foer creates a similar effect through typographical markings such as punctuation. Oskar's narrative is written with standard and correct punctuation; Thomas' narrative is characterised by a lack of full stops; while Oskar's grandmother's letters contain extended gaps and blank spaces between sentences.

Extremely Loud & Incredibly Close has many multimodal features. It won the V&A 2005 Book Illustration Award for which the novel was described as being "as much visual as it is textual". However, in its multimodality, *Extremely Loud & Incredibly Close* differs from Mark Z. Danielewski's *House of Leaves* (Chapter 4) and *VAS: An Opera in Flatland* by Steve Tomasula and Stephen Farrell (Chapter 5) in two main ways. Firstly, although images do not have a merely illustrative function in the novel, word and image are more obviously separated in *Extremely Loud & Incredibly Close*. Where the text in *House of Leaves* and *VAS* is continually transformed by type-setting to create imagistic designs that enhance or subvert verbal meaning, *Extremely Loud & Incredibly Close* is, for the most part, type-set in the conventionalised block fashion. Nevertheless, type-face, type-setting, and images do interact in the progression of the narrative. Secondly, *Extremely Loud & Incredibly Close* has a much higher imagistic content, in terms of its inclusion of photographs. In fact, in the novel Oskar keeps a scrapbook called *Stuff That Happened to Me*, in which he keeps photographic images of personal importance collected from sources such as the internet and newspapers as well as photographs Oskar has taken himself or presumably takes during the course of the novel.

The creative process is also important to *Extremely Loud & Incredibly Close* as a multimodal book. Foer's work with book designer Anne Chalmers is revealing of his multimodal intention. Gerber and Triggs outline this process, quoting Chalmers's words:

> "Jonathan was very interested in how the book was going to look and in the technical aspects of his visual elements," Chalmers says. "He has a very finely tuned feeling of how type is set up on the page and what happens when you turn the pages. He has a strong awareness of books as visual objects." (2006: 65)

Chalmers' discussion of Foer's awareness of books as multimodal artefacts, including the implication her comments hold concerning his authorial intentions, is significant. These remarks suggest that she believes Foer consciously seeks to create certain literary effects (and reader experiences) using multimodality.

Jonathan Safran Foer's literary career began with the success of his debut novel, *Everything Is Illuminated* (2002b). Although not a multimodal novel, *Everything Is Illuminated* does indicate the start of Foer's experimentation with visual features in literature since it contains instances of typographical multimodality (Nørgaard 2009b). In addition, Foer has written several short stories (2002a, 2002c, 2005b, 2006). While not applicable to all his short fiction, some of these stories such as 'A Primer for the Punctuation of Heart Disease' (2002c) and 'About the Typefaces Not Used in This Edition'

(2002a) also play around with multimodality and specifically the material production of fiction. Discussing his use of the visual in *Extremely Loud & Incredibly Close* in interview, Foer explains:

> It felt to me like the most honest way to express what it was like, or what it feels like. I had no interest in doing something experimental. I had no interest in doing something . . . I wasn't playing any games, you know. I really just wanted to tell the story as forcefully as I could. (Guernica 2005)

Elsewhere, he argues that had he not presented the novel through multimodality, it would "diverge from how most people I know experience the world, which is as a collage of different kinds of media, a jumble of sights and sounds and bits of information, in a way that wasn't true even five years ago or ten years ago" (Weich 2006). Like Tomasula (see section 5.1 of Chapter 5), Foer sees multimodality in literature not just as deliberate innovation, but as a response to the changing cultural environment of the late twentieth and early twenty-first centuries. Moreover, in his justification of the multimodality of his novel, Foer implicitly articulates the power of multisensory communication and perception (see section 3.4.1 of Chapter 3), suggesting that his use of multimodality is intended to evoke a powerful emotional response in readers.

This chapter provides further evidence of aspects of literary reading that are emphasised by multimodal novels, such as double deixis and the creation of figured trans-worlds. It also demonstrates the way in which a (multimodal) cognitive-poetic analysis can at once consider readerly experience while also revealing the prominent literary meanings and effects of a given text. Furthermore, since *Extremely Loud & Incredibly Close* is a work of 9/11 literature, this chapter explores the relationship between fiction and readers' real-world knowledge. In the next section, I discuss some of the implications of 9/11 literature.

6.2   LITERATURE AND 9/11

Jonathan Safran Foer is not, of course, alone in engaging with the trauma of 9/11 through literature. Among the novels which deal with the recent literary territory of 9/11 are William Gibson's (2003) *Pattern Recognition*, Frédéric Beigbeder's (2004) *Windows on the World*, Ian McEwan's (2005) *Saturday*, Ken Kalfus's (2006) *A Disorder Peculiar to the Country*, Jay McInerney's (2006) *The Good Life*, Claire Messud's (2006) *The Emperor's Children*, and Don DeLillo's (2007) *Falling Man*, to name but a few.

Many authors initially stepped back from the event in terms of writing fiction. In 'The uses of invention', Jay McInerney discusses the impact of September 11, 2001, on British and American authors:

> Most novelists I know went through a period of intense self-exami-
> nation and self-loathing after the terrorist attacks on the World Trade
> Center. I certainly did. For a while the idea of "invented characters"
> and alternate realities seemed trivial and frivolous and suddenly, horri-
> bly outdated. For a while. I abandoned the novel I was working on and
> didn't even think about writing fiction for the next six months. In fact,
> I was so traumatised and my attention span was shot to such an extent
> that for months I was incapable of reading a novel, or anything much
> longer than a standard article in the New York Times, even though I
> was fortunate enough not to have lost any close friends in the attack.
> (McInerney 2005)

As McInerney suggests, in the immediate after-climate of 9/11 the instincts
of many authors were antithetical to the writing of fiction, but as the grow-
ing number of literary accounts of 9/11 show, writers overcame this initial
reaction. When asked in interview if he felt it was 'a risk' to write on such
an emotionally charged subject, Jonathan Safran Foer responded, "I think
it's a greater risk not to write about it. If you're in my position—a New
Yorker who felt the event very deeply and a writer who wants to write
about things he feels deeply about—I think it's risky to avoid what's right
in front of you" (Shenk 2005).

   In engaging with 9/11 through the medium of literature, authors are asking readers not simply to suspend their disbelief in the imaginative creation
of a fictional world. Readers must also utilise their real-world knowledge
of 9/11 in the literary experience. Of course, most people reading Foer's
novel will not have experienced the event first-hand, and so the 'real' nature
of this knowledge is somewhat unstable. Nevertheless, readers will have
individual memories, such as where they were when they heard the news
or watched the broadcast images of the towers falling, and related personal
feelings that they bring to their reading of 9/11 literature.

   While cognitive poetics perceives context as "a crucial notion" (Stockwell 2002a: 2), Text World Theory is particularly suited to accounting for
contexts of reading and writing. In Text World Theory (Gavins 2007a,
2007b; Lahey 2005; Werth 1999), the discourse-world level encompasses
writer and reader contexts including knowledge and emotions specific to
the participants of the literary experience. Indeed, Werth believed, "situations do not occur in a conceptual vacuum" (1999: 84). Furthermore,
"Speakers are not only equipped with their physical senses, they also carry
a "baggage" of memories and knowledge" (1995: 52). Consequently, Text
World Theory is designed as a context-sensitive approach, attending to the
text, as well as to its contexts of writing and reception. Although all fiction
requires such consideration from a cognitive perspective, 9/11 literature
makes explicit the need for a context-sensitive approach.

   In 'The uses of invention', McInerney (2005) suggests that the novel as a
literary genre provides a unique opportunity to share emotional responses,

reconcile emotional confusion, and make sense of the impact of the event. Speaking on behalf of the general public, he declares:

> It is to the novel, ultimately, that we turn to confirm our own senses and emotions, to create narratives that reveal to us how we feel now and how we live now, to reveal emotional truths that approach the condition of music. We desperately want to have a novelist such as McEwan or DeLillo or Roth process the experience for us.

The novel as a literary form is seen to hold a unique position in terms of its ability to deal with the emotional ramifications of what has been popularly described in the press as an event 'which shook the world'. McInerney quotes the words of British novelist Patrick McGrath from a personal conversation on why McGrath has decided to write a novel dealing with the events of September 11. According to McInerney (2005), McGrath posits, "What we can do, what the novelist can do, is talk about how people have internalised trauma." Foer's novel demonstrates the representation of 9/11 as trauma. Through the course of the ensuing cognitive-poetic analysis, I demonstrate that fictional representation, particularly multimodal representation, can act as a traumatic testimony from the author in which the reader is a complicit witness, both parties struggling with similar psychological trauma stemming from their experience of 9/11.

6.3   ANALYSIS

A thought-provoking approach to the study of trauma in literature is presented by Kacandes (1994b, 2001). In *Talk Fiction*, Kacandes suggests that one way in which literature functions as interaction or conversation between authors and readers is as a form of testimony, or as she puts it, "talk as witness" (2001: 89–140). In line with her notion of 'Talk Fiction' generally, 'talk as witness' asks for 'replies':

> By "reply" I do not mean just the action of reading the text. I mean specific "answerings" to specific matters that have been raised by the text as statement. These may be constituted by the feeling of an emotion, the making of an intellectual connection, the speaking of an utterance, the passing on of a story in the real world beyond it, or the completion of another type of action in the physical world. What distinguishes the communicative circuit from any other literary one is the self-conscious perception by readers that they are formulating a reply invited by some feature of the text. (2001: 24–25)

Some of the responses Kacandes identifies as constituting 'answers' seem problematic, such as the elicitation of emotion from the reader or 'making an intellectual connection'. These are not only difficult to verify and/or isolate but, other than self-consciousness on the reader's part, these reactions cannot be discriminated from the provocation of such reactions in other literary experiences that are not classified as 'talk' in Kacandes's terms.

Nevertheless, I do perceive value in Kacandes's ideas. First of all, in support of the notion of literature as communication of trauma, Kacandes and theorists in the field of trauma studies (Caruth 1996; Felman and Laub 1992; Herman 1992) point to the importance of a listener. Kacandes states, the "listener has to be there so the survivor can re-externalise the event" (2001: 96), re-externalisation being vital to the psychological healing of trauma. As psychiatrist Laub explains, "re-externalisation of the event can occur and take effect only when one can articulate and transmit the story, literally transfer it to another outside oneself and then take it back in again, inside" (1992: 69). Therefore, the reader of *Extremely Loud & Incredibly Close* is a crucial participant in the process of traumatic recovery and rehabilitation as well as an involved cowitness. To quote Caruth's reflections on history and trauma, "history, like trauma, is never simply one's own, that history is precisely the way we are implicated in each other's traumas" (1996: 24).

Secondly, Kacandes continues to suggest that 'Talk fiction requires active readers . . . active readers interpret what they might be feeling, thinking, or doing *as a reply to the move of the text*" (2001: 26; original emphasis). Kacandes's insistence on the active role of readers as well as the way in which texts 'invite' these active reader-responses appropriately corresponds to my assertion that multimodal novels engage readers in dynamic and enactive practices. In the initial quotation provided earlier, Kacandes speaks of "the completion of another type of action in the physical world" (2001: 25). The agency or potential extent of such an action is never made clear by Kacandes, though her conception of 'literary performatives' (2001: 183–185) appears to fulfil this aspect of her theorisation of reader reply. Drawing on Austin (1962), Kacandes sees a literary performative as an "actualisation of the utterance by any reader" (2001: 183), for which she provides the example "You are reading this sentence". The act of reading the sentence necessarily performs its meaning. Literary performatives, therefore, are a feature of second-person fiction and, given the necessity of actualisation, are limited in their occurrence. However, returning to the way in which a reader may respond to a novel by performing an action in the physical world, my notion of figured trans-world involvement, first introduced in section 4.2.9 of Chapter 4, is a suitable example of such activity.

Kacandes speaks of "literary narratives of/as trauma" as constituting "circuits of narrative witnessing" (2001: 95). In doing so, she identifies six circuits of narrative witnessing relevant to the literary text:

1. Intrapsychic witnessing: a character witnesses to the self about the character's own experience.

2. Interpersonal witnessing: two characters cowitness to trauma suffered by one of them.
3. Surrogate witnessing: two characters cowitness to a third character's trauma.
4. Textual witnessing: narrator and narratee cowitness to the trauma of/in the text.
5. Literary-historical witnessing: text and its contemporary reader cowitness to the trauma of/in the text.
6. Transhistorical-transcultural witnessing: text and its later or foreign reader cowitness to the trauma of/in the text. (2001: 97)

In Text World Theory terms, circuits 1–4 are forms of narrative witness that are internal to the text-world, while circuits 5 and 6 are positioned at the discourse-world level. In the course of my analysis I will, naturally, be paying attention to testimony and witness that is thematised by and narrated within the novel. My focus, though, will be on circuit 4 and upon the discourse-world, considering how *Extremely Loud & Incredibly Close* as a multimodal novel narrates the trauma of 9/11 and engages 'real' readers in multimodal reading practices. These practices, I argue, can be seen to function as recognition of and riposte to traumatic experience in a way compatible with Kacandes's formulation. In dealing with the discourse-world 'circuits of witnessing', then, it is worth justifying why considering *Extremely Loud & Incredibly Close* as a textual circuit of narrative witness is important, before pointing to the differences between circuits 5 and 6, as well as explaining how these fit with readers of the novel.

The terrorist attacks on the World Trade Center were witnessed as a global event. People all across the world watched the attack on the twin towers and their resulting collapse. As Schuster et al. state, "Television coverage was immediate, graphic, and pervasive" (2001: 1507). In relation to America, Barringer and Fabrikant note, "television brought disaster into American homes in real time" (2001). The profound distress of the event has also been evidenced in psychological studies of memory and emotion (Budson et al. 2004; Pezdek 2003; Smith, Bibi, and Sheard 2003). Schuster et al. (2001) show that the event caused widespread stress symptoms, and predict that these are likely to lead to post-traumatic stress disorder in large numbers of Americans, irrespective of their proximity and/or personal connections to the event. Consequently, 9/11 must be acknowledged as a traumatic event that was not only witnessed on a global scale, but also caused unprecedented psychological ramifications for the American public, and indeed around the world. As such, any novel that fictionalises 9/11 cannot avoid acting within a circuit of witness. Therefore, not only are the knowledge of readers in the discourse-world and their emotional responses to 9/11 vital to an account of the novel as literary experience, so too is the recognition of the novel as product, response to, and psychological resolution of trauma crucial in a cognitive-poetic analysis.

The two forms of discourse-world 'circuits of witness' are literary-historical witnessing and transhistorical-transcultural witnessing. Kacandes defines the former as "how a text communicates to the actual flesh-and-blood readers of the culture and time in which it was written" (2001: 115), while the latter is aimed at readers "from a culture other than the one in which a text was written and/or from a latter time period" (2001: 116–117). These categories are not unproblematic since Kacandes conflates time-period and culture, though admittedly she does utilise 'and/or' as a way round this in transhistorical-transcultural witnessing. Nevertheless, the lack of a definition of 'culture' and the seeming conflation of time-period and culture poses investigative difficulties. For example, which circuit of witness would be relevant to a reader from the same time-period, but a different culture? This predicament bears relevance in the context of this book. In section 1.2 of Chapter 1, I made clear that my analyses were grounded in Western literary culture due to the need to take heed of Western literacy and literary patterns, such as the standardised left to right reading path, in order to qualify deviation. The notion of 'Western literary culture' comprises both the American and British reading public (among other nations) and, of course, the reaction experienced by these two groups to 9/11 is far from equivalent.

Pezdek (2003) has demonstrated that, based on geographical proximity to the event, the cognitive attachment of emotion to memories of 9/11 varies significantly in participants across the U.S. alone. Smith, Bibi, and Sheard's (2003) study upholds this conclusion, having extended the geographical subject base by assessing a Canadian sample. The temporal proximity of 9/11 and of *Extremely Loud & Incredibly Close*'s publication date means that readers are contemporaneous to the novel and to 9/11. Due to this and the extensive televisual coverage, I will treat the narrative circuit of witness of *Extremely Loud & Incredibly Close* as literary-historical. Even so, it should be kept in mind that reader-responses in terms of traumatic narrative witness will differ somewhat between, and even within, national cultures. As both multimodal novel and trauma text, Foer's *Extremely Loud & Incredibly Close* does 'talk' to readers, seeking responses both in the sense Kacandes identifies and as multimodal responses grounded in the materiality of the text. These 'answerings' to the text, exposed in cognitive-poetic analysis, exemplify active reading both in terms of narrative inference as well as enactive performance within the discourse-world. Crucially, such responses function as a form of psychotherapy, attempting to evoke a coming to terms with the events of September 11, 2001. My analysis begins in the next section, which focuses on the novel's visual opening.

6.3.1   Trying to 'Make Things Out' at First Glance

When readers open the novel to begin reading, they are confronted by an image of a keyhole that takes up the entirety of the first right-hand page.

The inclusion of images is central to the novel (see Foer in Henrikson 2006) and this is, in fact, the first of three successive black-and-white images, all of which are located on the right-hand page of double page spreads. These enigmatic photographs seem to constitute the opening, or even a prologue, to *Extremely Loud & Incredibly Close*. The second of these images is a shot of birds flying, the birds somewhat fuzzy due to motion. The third photograph is also blurred and is an image showing windows in an apartment block. Within the far left middle window, the shadow of a figure might be inferred. As is evident, all three images are photographic and have no anchorage or accompanying text. This means that there are no linguistic 'clues' for the reader to use in order to deduce a specific meaning, in a way comparable to Barthes' (1977 [1964]) theorisations in 'Rhetoric of the Image'. Barthes believed that text serves to "fix" or "anchor" meaning, whereas without accompanying text the potential meanings of an image are too various and multiple. In his words, "all images are polysemous; they imply, underlying their signifiers, a 'floating chain' of signifieds, the reader able to choose some and ignore others. Polysemy poses a question of meaning" (1977 [1964]: 38–39). According to Barthes, then, any meaning readers take from these images, seen before they have begun 'reading' the novel in the traditional (linguistic) sense, cannot be identified in any definitive way.

Actually, each image represents a significant theme or aspect of the narrative of the novel. On one hand, the images may work as primers. As such, they prime idealised cognitive models (Lakoff 1982, 1987; Lakoff and Johnson 1980, 1999; Stockwell 2002a) or frames (Fauconnier and Turner 2002; Fillmore 1977, 1982a, 1982b, 1985), cognitive knowledge structures such as *lock and keyhole*, *birds*, and *house*. As a result, when readers encounter narrative details that relate to these idealised cognitive models they are likely to perceive them to be of greater significance than might have been the case without the opening images. On the other hand, these images only serve to prime these idealised cognitive models at a basic level at this point in the reading experience. It is only with retrospective narrative knowledge that the reader is able to connect the images to the themes to which they relate: the search for the lock into which the key fits, birds, and attempts at communication (Oskar talks to his Grandmother via a walkie-talkie and she leaves notes for him on the window of her third-floor apartment which he can see from his bedroom window). In addition, it is worth noting that the first overleaf page after the three images contains paratext of 'books by jonathan safran foer'. The mention of Foer's (2006) editorial project *A Convergence of Birds* could also lead readers to suspect that the second image, the birds, is a visual intertextual reference and by association, a marketing ploy.

In traditional multimodal study, the three opening images could be said to create what Kress and van Leeuwen call a 'naturalistic coding orientation' (1996: 170). Such orientation is usual in the interpretation of photographs, with naturalism "defined on the basis of how much correspondence there is between the visual representation of an object and what we normally see of that object with the naked eye" (Kress and van Leeuwen 1996: 163). However, these photographs are black and white, thus there is a departure from the naturalism Kress and van Leeuwen describe in terms of colour saturation. This raises awareness of the production choices made in the creation of the novel, particularly as the use of black and white for the photographs contrasts with the intense red used on the novel's front cover.

More significantly, the first image of the keyhole is in close-up, 'incredibly close' one might say. Interestingly, taking a cognitive-grammatical approach to narratological focalisation, Herman (2009a, 2009b) considers the degrees of 'granularity' in the construal of a scene. A detailed image (whether produced through verbal or visual means) such as the close-up of the keyhole exhibits a detailed granular texture. For Kress and van Leeuwen, this granularity might cause the image to be "experienced as 'hyperreal', as showing 'too much detail'" (1996: 163). Factors such as the close photographic concentration on the keyhole and the deliberate blurriness of the third photograph move readers' interpretation of these images away from a naturalistic coding orientation, viewing the photographs not as 'natural' or 'real' but as hyperreal, thus connecting them to the fiction world(s) of the novel. Their hyperreal elements, then, are seen as purposeful, heightening their perceived significance in light of the narrative to follow. The next section studies the linguistic text which opens the novel.

6.3.2　"What The?"

Since the opening images prime idealised cognitive models, which can later be understood as relating to the themes of the novel and the narrative plot, one would anticipate that these would be both present, as well as foregrounded, in the opening text. However, the first page of the verbal text contains the following:

> What about a teakettle? What if the spout opened and closed when the steam came out, so it would become a mouth, and it could whistle pretty melodies, or do Shakespeare, or just crack up with me? I could invent a teakettle that reads in Dad's voice, so I could fall asleep, or maybe a set of kettles that sings the chorus of "Yellow Submarine," which is a song by the Beatles, who I love, because entomology is one of my *raisons d'être*, which is a French expression that I know. Another good thing is that I could train my anus to talk when I farted. If I wanted to be extremely hilarious, I'd train it to say, "Wasn't me!" every time I made an incredibly bad fart. And if I ever made an incredibly bad fart in the Hall of Mirrors, which is in Versailles, which is outside of Paris, which is in France, obviously, my anus would say, *"Ce n'étais pas moi!"*
>
> What about little microphones? What if everyone swallowed them, and they played the sound of our hearts through little speakers, which

could be in the pouches of our overalls? When you skateboarded down the street at night you could hear everyone's heartbeat, and they could hear yours, sort of like sonar. One weird thing is, I wonder if everyone's hearts would start to beat at the same time, like how many women who live together have their menstrual periods at the same time, which I know about, but don't really want to know about. That would be so weird, except that place in the hospital where babies were born would sound like a crystal chandelier in a houseboat, because the babies wouldn't have had time to match up their heartbeats yet. And at the finish line at the end of the New York City Marathon it would sound like war. (Foer 2005a: 1)

Surprisingly, the concepts and objects primed by the photographs do not surface in the opening two paragraphs. Rather, these read like unrelated interior monologue (defined in stylistic terms by Wales 2001 [1990]), using first-person narration in the free direct mode (Leech and Short 2007 [1981]). In addition, Foer employs coordinators (*and, or, but*), subordinators (*so, because*) and relative pronouns (*which, who*), which lengthen the sentences by adding multiple clauses, giving the syntax a 'rambling' feel. The following sentence from the preceding extract is a good example:

I could invent a teakettle *that* reads in Dad's voice, *so* I could fall asleep, *or* maybe a set of kettles *that* sings the chorus of "Yellow Submarine," *which* is a song by the Beatles, *who* I love, *because* entomology is one of my *raisons d'être*, *which* is a French expression *that* I know. (emphasis mine)

Foer's extensive use of simple connectives and conjunctions instils a lack of grammatical sophistication in the passage and consequently works to signal to readers that the focalising character is a child—the central character, Oskar. This child-like narrative voice joins with the surreal and bizarre nature of Oskar's inventions to generate a humorous tone to his narration. The creation of humour from both of these elements is also crucial to the pathos Oskar's narration communicates to the reader. For instance, consider the singing and talking teakettle. On one hand, such an object is reminiscent of characters from children's books or Disney films. However, the teakettle might 'read in Dad's voice' or 'just crack up with me'. Both of these narrative options disguise Oskar's grief and loneliness in their surreal humour.

There is a notable dissimilarity in the cognitive and imaginative effects of the linguistic opening and the initial photographs. This difference can be explained using Text World Theory. Examining the text-world structure of the passage reveals that, in relation to the passage's length, it generates a high number of text-worlds. Starting with the first sentence—'What about a teakettle?' is a rhetorical question, created through the combination of interrogative adverb and preposition. Its rhetorical nature and the fact that it is written in free direct discourse, as previously mentioned, serves to create a text-world based upon the communicative situation context—a textual speech-world, in other words. 'About' is used here as a preposition of thought or in what Tyler and Evans call a "focus-of-attention sense" (2003: 95–96), that is, it is used non-physically in terms of thought and or mental enquiry. The second text-world is therefore a hypothetical text-world that imaginatively centres upon the kettle, and is extended through a further hypothetical construction, "What if . . ."

Figure 6.1 depicts the text-world structure of the first paragraph. Apart from text-world 1, the originating textual speech-world, all the other worlds are hypothetical in nature.

These hypothetical worlds are fleeting, either shifted into a variation of the current hypothetical text-world by the subordinating conjunction *or*, extended into relative clauses by pronouns such as *which* and *who* with the effect of casting the previous imaginative focus into relief (Stockwell 2002a, 2002b, 2003), or simply through the creation of a different and separate imagined worlds. Although these hypothetical worlds contain concrete objects (e.g. kettle, sprout, anus), they are therefore transient. While the photographs in the opening provide sustained focal detail that the reader-viewer can study for any length of time desired, the linguistic opening generates vivid images through concrete noun phrases. Moreover, these conceptualised images are ephemeral, as short-lived as the worlds in which they exist.

The passage also relies heavily upon the epistemic modal auxiliary *could*, which, as Coates articulates, is "primarily used as a hypothetical form"

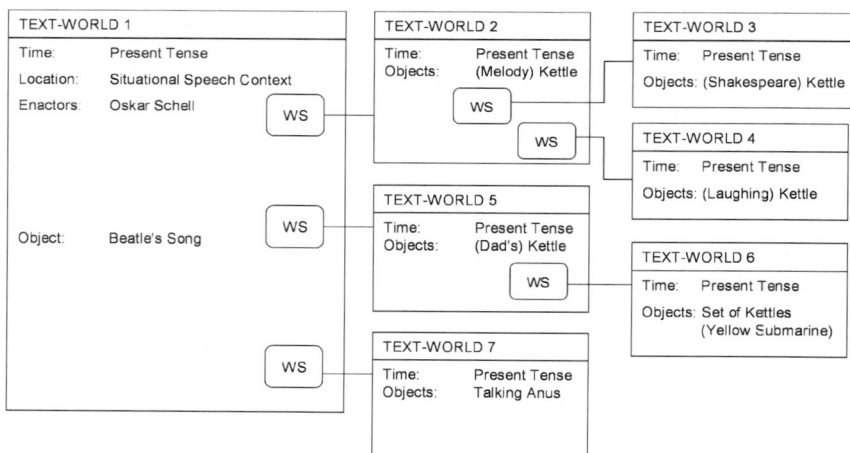

Figure 6.1   Text-worlds for opening paragraph of Foer (2005a) *Extremely Loud & Incredibly Close*: 1.

(1983: 107). Modality has been the focus of many linguistic studies (most influentially Coates 1983; Lyons 1977; Palmer 1986; Perkins 1983) and refers to the linguistic means by which a speaker's attitudes, beliefs, and obligations are expressed. Moreover, it has proven a useful tool for stylistic analysis, helping to craft points of view (Simpson 1993). Epistemic modality encodes the speaker's commitment to a proposition in terms of knowledge and belief. In his original theorisations of Text World Theory, Werth (1999: 244–248) pays particular attention to the way in which epistemic modality generates further text-worlds, worlds of possibility. Gavins (2005a; 2005b; 2007b: 109–125) refines this aspect of Text World Theory to show that epistemic modals, including the auxiliary *could* that is our concern here, create character-accessible epistemic modal-worlds. She also points out a crucial difference between the root modal-worlds (boulomaic, deontic) and epistemic modal-worlds: "While all modal-worlds contain situations that are in one way or another remote from their originating worlds, epistemic modal-worlds often have an added layer of unreality attached to them" (2007b: 112).

Gavins's rethinking of Text World Theory to better account for modality is a useful development in the framework, particularly as it is well suited to understanding the psychological relationship and distance between a character and the proposition they express. A quick glance at cognitive grammar is also beneficial here though, especially as Langacker's (1987, 1991, 2002 [1991], 1999) theoretical framework demonstrates how conceptual constructions are generated though language in a very diagrammatical way. In cognitive grammar, Langacker uses what he calls 'the epistemic model' (1991: 242–243) to deal with tense and linguistic modality. The epistemic model, shown in Figure 6.2 which reproduces Evans and Green's (2006: 628) elucidated diagram, is egocentric and accounts for how time is conceptualised by language.

The present time or 'immediate reality' is represented by the large circle, while the small shaded circle represents the language user. 'known reality' or the past is shown on the left, while the space on the right depicts

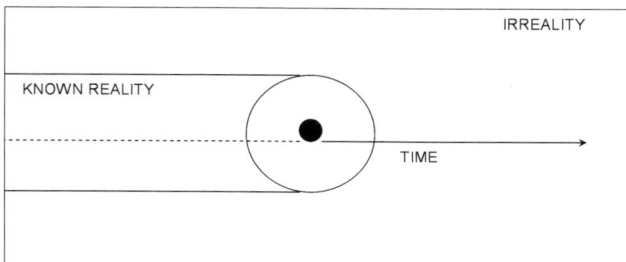

Figure 6.2   Langacker's epistemic model (1991: 242–243) taken from Evans and Green (2006: 628).

what Langacker (1991) calls 'irreality'. 'irreality' comprises "everything other than (known) reality" (Langacker 1991: 243), such as the imagined future.

Langacker's (1991) epistemic model and Gavins' (2005a, 2005b, 2007b) work on epistemic modal-worlds can be related to Foer's use of the modal auxiliary *could* in the opening to *Extremely Loud & Incredibly Close*. Evans and Green (2006: 628) explain, "a modal verb indicates that a speaker construes the event as part of irreality". According to Langacker, "irreality is divisible in any absolute or consistent way into two discrete zones" (1991: 247) and this occurs on the basis on the modal's 'epistemic distance' (Langacker 1991; Simpson 1993; Gavins 2005a; Evans and Green 2006: 394–396), or in other words the language user's epistemic commitment to the proposition in terms of its perceived likelihood. *Could* signifies a distant or non-immediate irreality (as opposed to immediate irreality), or as Evans and Green put it, *could* encodes "a much weaker sense of possibility, a much stronger sense of doubt" (2006: 628). Consequently, most of the text-worlds of the opening are also positioned within distant irreality. From a psychological standpoint, the epistemic modal text-worlds are far removed from Oskar in the originating textual speech-world.

Interestingly, both the opening paragraphs exhibit structural and grammatical similarities. For ease, I have reproduced the first sentences of each (Foer 2005a: 1):

Para 1:

What about a teakettle? What if the sprout opened and closed when the steam came out, so it would become a mouth, and it could whistle pretty melodies, or do Shakespeare, or just crack up with me? I could invent . . .

Para 2:

What about little microphones? What if everyone swallowed them, and they played the sound of our hearts through little speakers, which could be in the pouches of our overalls? When you skateboarded . . .

Both paragraphs begin with a rhetorical question, which is then elaborated through the 'What if' hypothetical construction. A crucial difference between the two paragraphs is their predominant pronouns of use: the first paragraph uses first person and centres on Oskar's non-immediate irreality, while the following paragraph initially references 'everyone', then 'our', and afterwards 'you'. Although interpersonal pronouns are being employed, they are anchored in a generalised narrative context. The generalised *you* can thus be seen to involve the reader, particularly since it occurs along with the inclusive *our*.

In her fourth circuit of narrative witness between narrator and narratee(s), Kacandes suggests that texts that utilise this circuit often "make an explicit request for a cowitness through pronouns of address" (2001: 111). In the examples Kacandes (1994a; 1994b; 2001: 111–114) provides, the text makes continued usage of the second-person pronoun. Kacandes suggests that if readers are prompted to 'take up' the available subjectivity of the pronoun, they are inherently engaging in 'talk' and thus participating in the circuit of witness of the trauma text. The passage of *Extremely Loud & Incredibly Close* under discussion does not relate Oskar's trauma. Nevertheless, it has a specific function in terms of Oskar's traumatic memories as will be expounded below. Thus, for those readers who do take up the invitation to self-implicate (Kuiken, Miall, and Sikora 2004) into the second-person *you* and inclusive *our*, their trans-world projection stands as a 'reply' to the text and becomes an act of cowitness.

The opening to *Extremely Loud & Incredibly Close* continues, "And also, there are so many times when you need to make a quick escape, but humans don't have their own wings, or not yet, anyway, so what about a birdseed shirt?" (2). Not only does this connect thematically to the earlier image of birds, it suggests a motivation for Oskar's creation of hypothetical and irreal worlds. In the storyworld, it transpires that Oskar likes to 'invent' things, partly as an escape from reality and his grief over the loss of his father. Oskar's inventions and imaginings are, therefore, a displacement activity. As becomes clear in the course of the narrative, Oskar's father had a meeting on the morning of September 11, 2001, at Windows on the World, the restaurant on floors 106 and 107 of the World Trade Center's North Tower. Like the 170 people who were believed to be at Windows on the World when the first plane crashed into the tower, Oskar's father Thomas Schell Jr. would have died either in the restaurant at a height of around 1,310 feet or by plummeting to his death like the many victims who jumped from the building. As readers, these narrative details have not actually been made available to us in the narrative (though any reader who has read the novel synopsis on the book's reverse cover will know of Oskar's father's death in 9/11). Even so, Oskar's birdseed shirt invention is a cognitive intervention since the idea of the birdseed shirt is a way for Oskar to imagine a means of rescuing his father from what became his fate. Speaking of Oskar's imaginings, Brauner states, "all his 'what-ifs'—all his extravagant inventions—are sublimation of his desire to rewrite history so that his father does not die in the attack on the twin towers on 9/11" (2007: 208).

In reading the opening, readers cannot avoid entering into the act of imaginative world-creation that the literary experience proscribes, however fleeting and irreal the text-worlds of Oskar's inventions may be. As such, they experience doubly deictic subjectivity, a concept I suggested in section 4.2.9 of Chapter 4 based on Herman's (1994, 2002) notion of the doubly deictic *you*, whereby the reader's actions become superimposed onto a character's actions. Here, the fictional scenes Oskar imagines provide him with a cognitive escape from his reality, while simultaneously readers escape the discourse-world through imaginative relocation, deictic shift, into the text-world(s) of the fictional discourse. Drawing on Goffman (1974), Herman suggests that processes such as that described are processes "by which one set of space-time parameters can be 'laminated' within another" (2009b: 106; 2009a: 131). Herman applies this to two extracts from Joyce's (1967 [1914]) short story 'The Dead' in *Dubliners* where what the character imagines becomes what the reader imagines in the reading process, as is the case in *Extremely Loud & Incredibly Close* with Oskar's imagined inventions becoming the focal imaginative text-worlds for readers. I will attend to Goffman's (1974, 1981) notion of 'lamination' and Herman's (2009a, 2009b) reorientation of it to literature later in section 6.4.6 of this chapter. For the time being, it suffices to say that lamination clearly applies to doubly deictic subjectivity, and figured trans-worlds too for that matter (see Chapter 4, section 4.2.9).

In the opening to *Extremely Loud & Incredibly Close*, lamination and doubly deictic subjectivity mean that readers do not just act as cowitnesses for Oskar's grief, manifested in his displacement activity, by their possible self-implication (Kuiken, Miall, and Sikora 2004) with the subjective pronouns of the second passage. They are also coparticipants in the displacement activity of that grief and trauma. In the next section, I examine how Foer's use of colour in the novel contributes to this dynamic.

6.3.3 Pay Attention to Colour

Having found a key in an envelope with the word "Black" written on it among his father's possessions, Oskar embarks upon a search to find the lock that the key opens. The novel centres on this search and, ironically, while Bird (2007: 563) sees it as displacement activity for Oskar, Codde (2007: 244) speaks of it as "a transparent metaphor for the door that will presumably give access to his father's past". Regardless, Oskar's need to know the meaning of the key motivates his search. Oskar's first move is to visit the locksmith, who is of little use, though he does tell Oskar that it is an old key and guesses that it is probably for a safety deposit box. Oskar's initial thought for the meaning of the word "Black", then, is that it is the name of a company that produces safety deposit boxes. This turns out to be a false guess, however, and so Oskar visits his local art supply store to ask about the word "Black":

> I wanted to know what she could tell me about black, since she was probably an expert of color. "Well," she said, "I don't know that I'm an *expert* of anything. But one thing I *can* say is it's sort of interesting that the person wrote the word 'black' in red pen." I asked why that was interesting, because I just thought it was one of the red pens Dad used when he read the *New York Times*. "Come here," she said, and she led me to a display of ten pens. "Look at this," She showed me a pad of paper that was next to the display. (44; original emphasis)

The facing page represents the page of the pad of paper that the store manager has shown to Oskar. Subsequently, there is another page of narrative text followed by three more pages with images which correspond to those which Oskar sees when he flips through the pad. These pages are iconic representations of what Oskar sees, and thus enhance the focalising perspective (Zubin and Hewitt 1995) of the narrative's employment of the first-person pronoun. In the narrative after the first image-page (Foer 2005a: 46), the store manager explains her interest in the red inscription of the word *black*: "most people write the name of the color of the pen they are writing with". She continues, "So the fact that 'Black' was written in red makes me think that Black is someone's name", an interpretation for which she cites the capitalised *B* in support.

The visual plates, showing the handwriting of customers testing out pens, look very similar. As already mentioned, one purpose of these pages is to enhance the reader's imaginative deictic shift into Oskar's focalising perspective. The first image, therefore, is the first page on the pad of paper shown to Oskar by the store manager, while the following three images represent what Oskar sees when he flips back through the pad. Nørgaard supports this view when discussing the temporal sequence of linguistic narrative and these visual interspersions when she states, "readers read the words and see the handwritten text in the order that Oskar experiences it" (2009a: 117). As such, this could be perceived as another instance of doubly deictic subjectivity and lamination, the multimodality of the novel superimposing the reader's experience of the text onto the character's experience.

The first of these visual plates captures readers' attention. It exhibits a marked contrast from its facing page of black text in standard block type-setting, making it an 'attractor', a term used by Stockwell (2002a: 18; 2002b: 86–89; 2003: 15) and informed by work in visual perception. However, since the following three visual pages look so similar, they do not have the same attracting force. Stockwell justifies such a transition in reader attention in his outline of the cognitive framework figure and ground, explaining that we "tend to neglect features where there is *redundancy*— that is, where the element is stereotypical and expected—in order to focus attention on features that are new to us" (2002a: 19; original emphasis). As such, while the first visual plate in this section seemed 'new' and therefore demanded visual notice, the following three make lesser demands on readers' attention. It is unlikely, therefore, that readers would study or scrutinise these, and they may even scan past them quickly in order to return to the written narrative. The written narrative delivers the following information: "I ripped the last sheet from the pad and ran to find the manager again. She was helping somebody with paintbrushes, but I thought it wouldn't be rude to interrupt her. 'That's my dad!' I told her, putting my finger on his name. 'Thomas Schell!'" (50). Given that these plates have lost attention, it is unlikely that readers will have noticed this detail. As a result, they may have to revisit the last visual page to find the name. Written in red pen, characteristic of Oskar's father in Oskar's recollections, 'Thomas Schell' is indeed written on the final page, just to the left of the centre about a third of the way down. Foer's repetition of similar images creates attentive redundancy. Although the subsequent written text does re-narrate the finding of 'Thomas Schell' in a different mode for readers who failed to see it, this reference ensures that readers become aware that the visual aspect of the book is of equal import to its verbal dimension and to the literary experience.

In the following section, I also consider colouration, namely, the use of red, in one of the letters that Oskar's grandfather, Thomas Schell Sr., has written.

6.3.4   "Not Stop Looking" or "Why I'm Not Where You Are"

The four chapters in *Extremely Loud & Incredibly Close* written by Oskar's grandfather, Thomas Schell Senior, are all titled 'why i'm not where you are' followed by a date. As outlined in the introduction, these are generally written as letters to his child. The first of these chapters highlights its intended recipient immediately, "To my unborn child" (16). In 'why i'm not where you are; 4/12/78', Thomas Sr. recounts his experience of the Dresden bombings. It opens similarly with "To my child" (208). There is a strikingly immediate difference, however, between this letter and the two that precede it. The words, 'my child' are actually circled in red. Such red circling is not isolated to this one phrase. It occurs throughout the letter/chapter.

To deduce the narrative meaning signalled by the red circling, readers are required to draw on information from earlier in the novel. In section 6.3.3, a quotation from Oskar alluded to the fact that his father would use red pen when reading the *New York Times* (44). This information in itself is anaphoric, referring back to Oskar's opening chapter, when Oskar describes his father "marking the mistakes with his red pen" (9). The detail is then made manifest on the following page when Oskar examines the newspaper his dad had been reading for clues in the 'puzzle' his father has set him. In the book, an extract from the newspaper is provided and it shows the words "not stop looking" circled in red (10). The reader can therefore retrieve this information through narrative frame recall (Emmott 1994, 1997) in order to apply it to this episode of the narrative. In doing so, readers can deduce that while, in the storyworld, the letter was written by Oskar's grandfather, Thomas Sr., the red circling was produced by Oskar's father, Thomas Jr.

Oskar's grandfather's letter has been overwritten in places by his son's markings, with both inscriptions existing on the same textual surface. The coexistence of two separate narrative worlds and/or levels upon the same textual surface has noteworthy consequences. Considering 'worlds' broadly at a narratological level, there is a superimposition of the world in which Oskar's father marks the text onto the world in which Oskar's grandfather

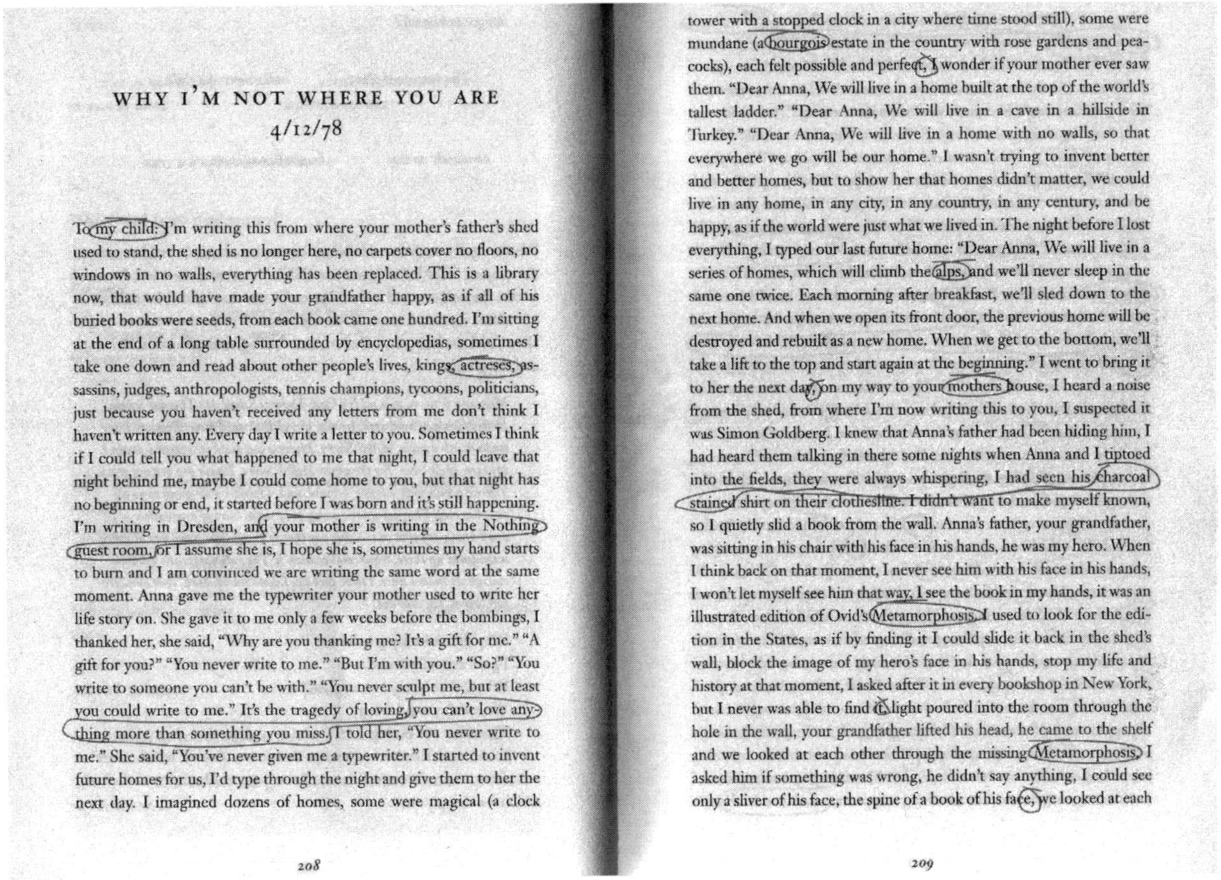

WHY I'M NOT WHERE YOU ARE
4/12/78

To my child: I'm writing this from where your mother's father's shed used to stand, the shed is no longer here, no carpets cover no floors, no windows in no walls, everything has been replaced. This is a library now, that would have made your grandfather happy, as if all of his buried books were seeds, from each book came one hundred. I'm sitting at the end of a long table surrounded by encyclopedias, sometimes I take one down and read about other people's lives, kings, actresses, assassins, judges, anthropologists, tennis champions, tycoons, politicians, just because you haven't received any letters from me don't think I haven't written any. Every day I write a letter to you. Sometimes I think if I could tell you what happened to me that night, I could leave that night behind me, maybe I could come home to you, but that night has no beginning or end, it started before I was born and it's still happening. I'm writing in Dresden, and your mother is writing in the Nothing guest room, for I assume she is, I hope she is, sometimes my hand starts to burn and I am convinced we are writing the same word at the same moment. Anna gave me the typewriter your mother used to write her life story on. She gave it to me only a few weeks before the bombings, I thanked her, she said, "Why are you thanking me? It's a gift for me." "A gift for you?" "You never write to me." "But I'm with you." "So?" "You write to someone you can't be with." "You never sculpt me, but at least you could write to me." "It's the tragedy of loving, you can't love any-thing more than something you miss." I told her, "You never write to me." She said, "You've never given me a typewriter." I started to invent future homes for us, I'd type through the night and give them to her the next day. I imagined dozens of homes, some were magical (a clock

208

tower with a stopped clock in a city where time stood still), some were mundane (a bourgois estate in the country with rose gardens and pea-cocks), each felt possible and perfect, I wonder if your mother ever saw them. "Dear Anna, We will live in a home built at the top of the world's tallest ladder." "Dear Anna, We will live in a cave in a hillside in Turkey." "Dear Anna, We will live in a home with no walls, so that everywhere we go will be our home." I wasn't trying to invent better and better homes, but to show her that homes didn't matter, we could live in any home, in any city, in any country, in any century, and be happy, as if the world were just what we lived in. The night before I lost everything, I typed out our last future home: "Dear Anna, We will live in a series of homes, which will climb the Alps, and we'll never sleep in the same one twice. Each morning after breakfast, we'll sled down to the next home. And when we open its front door, the previous home will be destroyed and rebuilt as a new home. When we get to the bottom, we'll take a lift to the top and start again at the beginning." I went to bring it to her the next day, on my way to your mother's house, I heard a noise from the shed, from where I'm now writing this to you, I suspected it was Simon Goldberg, I knew that Anna's father had been hiding him, I had heard them talking in there some nights when Anna and I tiptoed into the fields, they were always whispering, I had seen his charcoal stained shirt on their clothesline, I didn't want to make myself known, so I quietly slid a book from the wall. Anna's father, your grandfather, was sitting in his chair with his face in his hands, he was my hero. When I think back on that moment, I never see him with his face in his hands, I won't let myself see him that way, I see the book in my hands, it was an illustrated edition of Ovid's Metamorphosis, I used to look for the edi-tion in the States, as if by finding it I could slide it back in the shed's wall, block the image of my hero's face in his hands, stop my life and history at that moment, I asked after it in every bookshop in New York, but I never was able to find it, light poured into the room through the hole in the wall, your grandfather lifted his head, he came to the shelf and we looked at each other through the missing Metamorphosis, I could see only a sliver of his face, the spine of a book of his face, we looked at each

209

Figure 6.3   Foer (2005a) *Extremely Loud & Incredibly Close*: 208–209.

writes the letter. Further to this, the fictional world of reference, namely, the bombing of Dresden as Thomas Sr. remembers it, creates a further narrative layer. In reading this chapter of *Extremely Loud & Incredibly Close* then, readers must utilise bistable reading strategies, by which I refer to Lanham's (1993) term for the way in which texts that foreground their materiality require both a looking at the surface of the pages and a looking through into the imagined world of the narrative.

In sections 5.2.8 through to 5.2.11 of Chapter 5, I began to develop this idea into a model for the analysis of multimodal literature using Text World Theory. I adapted Gavins's (2007b) notion of the blended world, which shows how readers 'blend' the multiple conceptual arenas of metaphorical narratives into a coherent whole as well as toggling between those arenas. I added recognition of the level of textual surface, which must also be managed in the blend and toggled between.

Foer's decision to use bright red circles in/on 'why i'm not where you are; 4/12/78' is a choice which draws attention to the page surface, and therefore provokes bistable oscillation in reading. The extract I analysed from *VAS: An Opera in Flatland* contained metaphorical worlds that fed into an emergent blended world (see section 5.2.10 of Chapter 5). Here, none of the worlds are metaphorical. As a result, the worlds do not 'blend' but instead rigidly maintain ontological autonomy. The foregrounding of the surface of the page therefore causes toggling between the world represented by the red circles at the surface and the world(s) the grandfather occupies.

Another effect of the red circling is to create an apparent hierarchy of worlds in terms of perceived depth since the reader seemingly has to travel through each layer to reach the world 'below'. This hierarchical world structure is shown in Figure 6.4. I have represented these worlds as text-worlds, in keeping with my use of the model throughout this book. However, I must acknowledge that the grandfather's letter in its linguistic make-up would, of course, reference and create multiple text-worlds that are not shown here. Returning to the bistable reading of this chapter, in focusing attention on the page, the red circles 'pop' (Galbraith 1995; Stockwell 2002a) the reader upwards through narrative levels.

The red circles, as with Oskar's description of his father's habits, mark mistakes in the letter-writing. Often these are grammatical mistakes or spelling mistakes, such as the second marking around 'actreses'. On other occasions, though, they are a matter of semantics. The first marking provides a suitable example. Thomas Jr. has circled the words 'my child', presumably because although Thomas Sr. is biologically his father, he did not raise him. Indeed, Oskar's grandfather left his grandmother after discovering she was pregnant. The red circle around 'my child' suggests that while Thomas Senior wrote the letter for Thomas Junior, Thomas Junior refuses to implicate himself into the position of intended recipient. It is the multimodality of the text that creates this

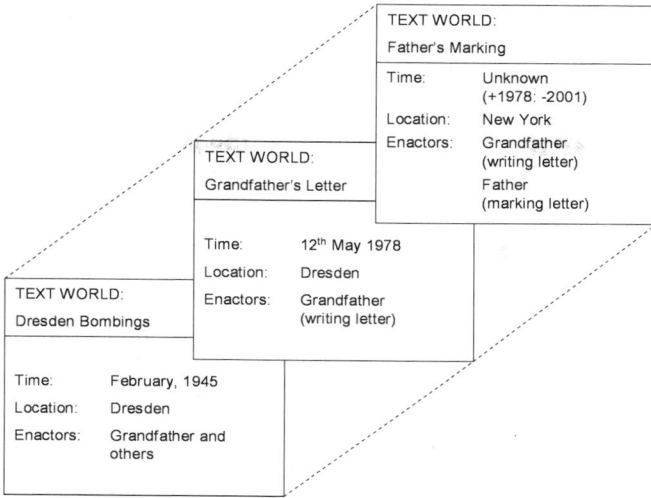

Figure 6.4   Narratological worlds in 'WHY I'M NOT WHERE YOU ARE; 4/12/78' (Foer 2005a).

effect. The red circle foregrounds the words and, along with the narrative implication that 'my child' is a mistake or needs correction, prevents a naturalised association between the words and Thomas Junior, the storyworld author of the red circles.

A similar incident occurs on page 214. Oskar's grandfather writes, "I looked for my parents and for Anna and for you". Given that the context to which the utterance refers is the aftermath of the Dresden bombings, this 'you' could not possibly signify Oskar's father, and must therefore refer to Thomas Senior's unborn child with Anna. In this instance, the red circle symbolises that Thomas Junior is not simply rejecting the subject position offered to him as intended recipient, but that in the context of the narrative to which the sentence refers, *you* rejects him as its referent—that is, the narrative context signals that this 'you' could not possibly signify Thomas Jr. and therefore alienates him as a result. Discussing the potentialities for self-implication with the second-person pronoun, Gavins (2007b: 85–87) suggests that when narrative details do not resemble or closely match the real-world situation of readers, self-implication becomes difficult. Moreover, in an autobiographical account of reading a second-person fiction, Gavins (2007b: 86–87) admits that her negative impressions of the *you* character led to an even stronger subjective response: "my self-implication in the text-world was not just difficult, I was actively resisting it" (87). In 'why i'm not where you are; 4/12/78', Thomas Schell Jr. appears to be both an inappropriately matched referent for the 'you' under discussion as well as actively resisting it in the storyworld, as demonstrated by the red circling.

The referential confusion at work in the second-person pronoun here can also be related to traumatic memory and Thomas Schell's experience of the Dresden bombing. Considering the slippage between Thomas Schell Jr. and the unborn child at work in this employment of *you*, Codde asserts, "Foer creates here a very subtle confusion of time levels (typical of trauma patients), as well as a confusion between the surviving son and the child lost during the moment of crisis" (2007: 251). Indeed, Caruth articulates that the cause of trauma "is a shock that appears to work very much like a bodily threat but is in fact a break in the mind's experience of time" (1993: 25; 1996: 61). The second-person pronoun as used here cannot be construed to include the reader, and therefore readers are less likely to respond to the trauma, as Kacandes (2001) hypothesises by taking up the subject position *you* might offer. However, she also suggests that in textual witnessing, the identification of traumatic symptoms is enough to constitute an act of cowitnessing if readers interpret them as such (2001: 111).

Foer's use of red circling foregrounds certain words and phrases. By highlighting 'you', the temporal confusion at work is made palpable, disposing it for reader interpretation as a sign of trauma in what Herman characterises as "the rupture in continuity between present and past" (1992: 89). Moreover, as a 'pop' in the bistable reading process, the red circle raises awareness of the distinctions between the periods of temporal confusion (the world of Dresden below the world of the letter writing and the world above the letter writing of Thomas Junior's writing) and affects the decompression of time and world. This is a process that occurs in the reader's mind and thus constitutes a 'reply' in the circuit of witness as Foer's multimodality provokes readers to mentally rectify the temporal confusion of Oskar's grandfather's employment of *you*. In the next section, I look at Foer's use of red circling in cognitive psychological terms.

6.3.5   Seeing Red

The use of red circling in 'why i'm not where you are; 4/12/78' can be related to trauma in another multimodal way. In his personal testimony of his experience of the bombing of Dresden, Thomas Sr. narrates:

> One hundred planes flew overhead, massive, heavy planes, pushing through the night like one hundred whales through water, they dropped clusters of red flares to light up the blackness for whatever was to come next, I was alone on the street, the red flares fell around me, thousands of them, I knew. (210)

The red circles which visually punctuate the surface of the text are evocative of the 'clusters of red flares' described in the narrative, which in itself is an imaginative attention attractor (see Stockwell 2002a, 2003 for how linguistically referenced images of brightness and colour can have a foregrounding effect). Moreover, just as bombs impact upon their target, these red circles are imprinted on the page and create sites of visual impact. As detailed in attention studies and by Stockwell (2002a, 2002b, 2003) in his work on figure and ground in literature, the red circles capture attention since they appear brighter and more colourful than the rest of the text, and they appear to be written on top of the letter.

Curiously, Foer's description of the actual bombings and explosions is anything but red. He speaks of "orange and blue explosions, violet and white" (210); "yellow-gray smoke" (211); "silver explosion" (211); and the "bombs kept falling, purple, orange, and white" (213). Nevertheless, though the text-world of the Dresden bombings is filled with bright and various colours, the literal visual effect of this chapter for the reader is an impression of the barrage of red fissures upon the white page with black text. This is unavoidably the case in the final pages of 'why i'm not where you are; 4/12/78', where the frequency of the red circles has increased and thus intensified.

Foer's excessive use of the colour red to mark the page of the text in this chapter is also significant in light of work in cognitive psychology. Birren's (1961 [1950]: 143) book on colour psychology cites red as having common mental associations of 'Hot, fire, heat, blood', and mentions generalised experimental conclusions that red can "irritate and distract" in terms of fundamental physiological effect (122). Interestingly, the other colours present in 'why i'm not where you are; 4/12/78', white and black, are often used in psychological experimentation as control colours. Although Birren's (1961 [1950]) book has been highly influential, recent experimental conclusions (Elliot et al. 2007; Valdez and Mehrabian 1994) concerning the colour red are more reliable by modern scientific measures. Elliot et al. (2007) studied the effect of red on performance, predicting that the perception of red prior to undergoing a performance assessment task would impair performance in that task. Elliot et al.'s (2007) prediction was supported by their results. More significantly, it was grounded on the hypothesis that in such contexts:

> red is associated with danger, specifically the psychological danger of failure. This association is presumed to be the product of multiple sources. Most specifically and directly, the repeated pairing of red with mistakes and failures that is encountered by most children in the educational system (e.g., incorrect answers marked with red ink) teaches them to associate red with failure in achievement contexts. (156)

Relating results from colour psychology, Foer's use of red circles in 'why i'm not where you are; 4/12/78', leads to three significant inferences.

Starting with internal text-worlds, since Elliot et al. (2007) effectively substantiate the association of danger with the colour red, the colour usage on a narrative about the Dresden bombings can be seen to intensify readers' sense of the threat to Thomas Sr.'s life in the 'deepest' text-world, thus raising narrative anxiety. Secondly, the intense psychological and physiological effects of red can be used to support a reading of the letter as a narrative of/ as trauma. By the end of why i'm not where you are; 4/12/78', the use of the colour red has increased dramatically, and seems not just to mark errors. It seems to score anything Thomas Jr. might find incredulous and as such emotionally painful. This is particular evident in the fact that at the close of the letter, Thomas Jr. circles 'I love you', shown in Figure 6.5.

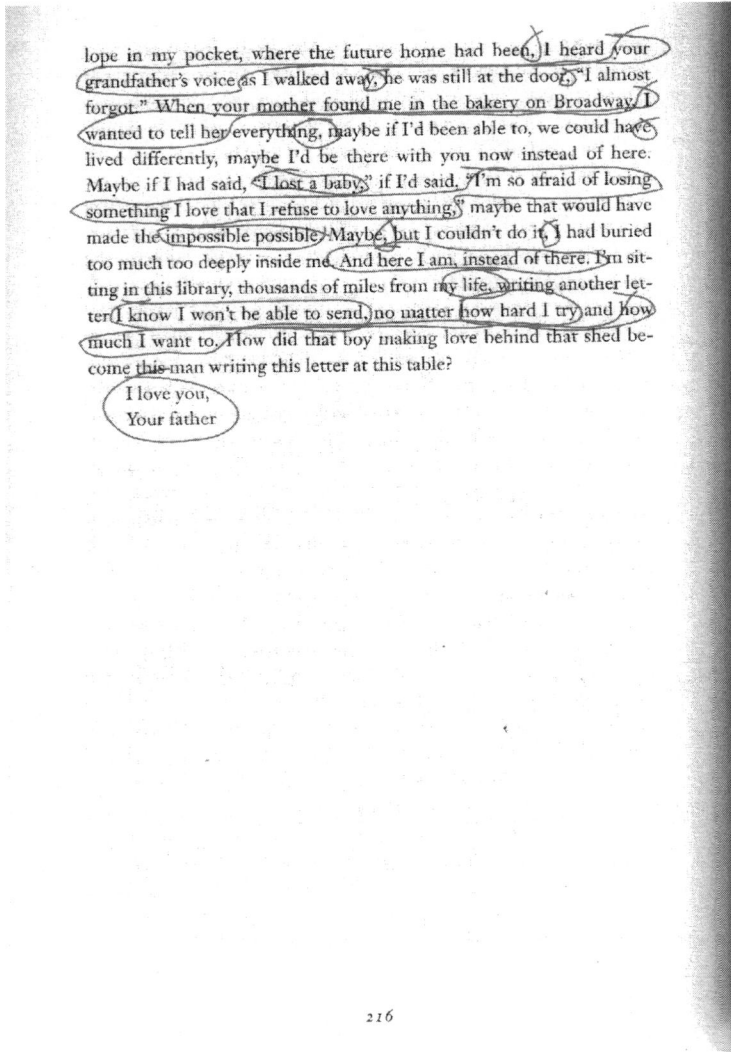

Figure 6.5   Foer (2005a) *Extremely Loud & Incredibly Close*: 216.

It is remarkable that Elliot et al. (2007) cite the use of red in education to high-light mistakes, in effect identical to Thomas Jr.'s use of red pen. As such, the 'natural' cognitive association of red to mark error, enhanced or primed by awareness of this being carried out explicitly in the narrative of the novel, can be seen to generate a cognitive effect upon readers by which their experience of the colour red holds a sense of distress. This in turn may lead to the third inference whereby readers relate their own cognitive impression of red as a sign of distress with Thomas Schell Jr.'s red circling to infer that the red mark-ing communicates its maker's emotional trauma and/or distress in reading the letter. Interestingly, the colours red and white have been discussed in imagina-tive terms by Szollosy (2002: 150–154) as symbolic of traumatic experience in autobiographical writing and the poetic works of Sylvia Plath. Overall, by using red in this way, Foer inserts a narrative of trauma into each narrative level, or each of the text-worlds represented in Figure 6.4, in a circuit of wit-ness that is fulfilled by readers' own experience of the colour. In the following section, I consider how the reader fits into the complex narrative structure Foer has created in 'why i'm not where you are; 4/12/78'.

6.3.6   Joining in the Search

Finally, in relation to 'why i'm not where you are; 4/12/78', it is important to examine the reader's relationship to the narrative worlds of the chapter. In my analysis of Danielewski's *House of Leaves* (see section 4.2.10 of Chapter 4), I demonstrated how the narratological structure of the novel in its use of embedded worlds foregrounds the casings of those worlds, result-ing in a self-consciousness which casts the reader as creating another narra-tive level through any notes they write on their copy of the book. A similar process occurs in this chapter of *Extremely Loud & Incredibly Close*, although unlike *House of Leaves*, narrative worlds are not embedded here but superimposed on top of each other. Many readers, particularly those who come from an academic or scholastic background, write notes into the margins of the novels they read. Indeed, Faber (2005) admits to writing on his copy of the novel when he confesses, "looking back at my jottings in the margins of Foer's new book, I can't deny how frequently and furiously I've scribbled 'Aaaarrghh!'" Moreover, for any sceptics who believe that multi-modal books often evoke a more restrained reaction in terms of notation, Figure 6.6 shows a scan of the opening pages of the chapter taken from one of my student's copies. The student in question brought this book in for a discussion seminar about multimodality and cognition in which they were asked to provide an example of literary multimodality. What I find particu-larly fascinating is that not only did she write upon the pages of the book, and this chapter, but she did so in a way that directly echoed the multimo-dality at work in this part of the novel. She has written using a red biro, and circled the title in much the same manner as Thomas Schell Jr.'s circlings, her own seeming frustration with the novel (judging from her notes) map-ping on to Thomas Schell's emotional frustration in the storyworld.

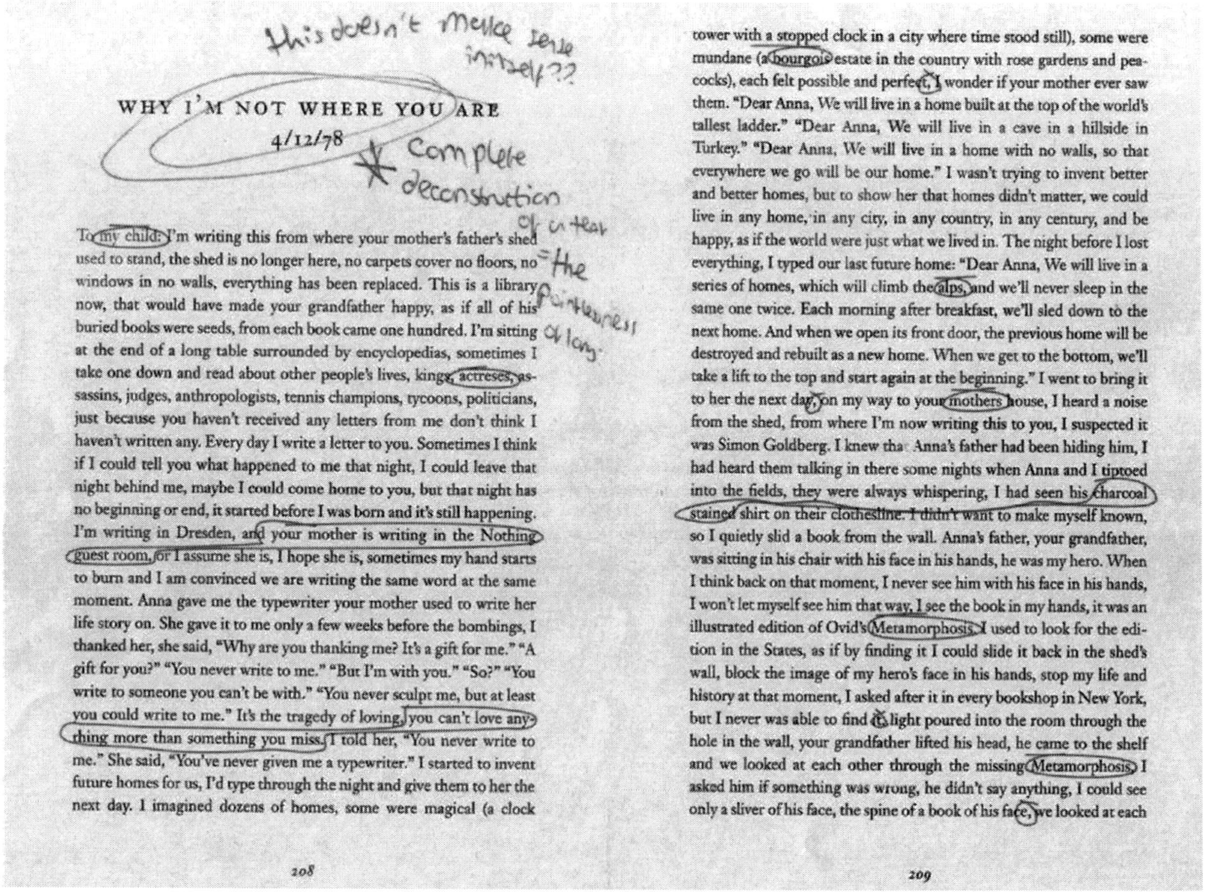

this doesn't make sense though???

complete deconstruction

of a new furniture of loop

WHY I'M NOT WHERE YOU ARE 4/12/78

To my child: I'm writing this from where your mother's father's shed used to stand, the shed is no longer here, no carpets cover no floors, no windows in no walls, everything has been replaced. This is a library now, that would have made your grandfather happy, as if all of this buried books were seeds, from each book came one hundred. I'm sitting at the end of a long table surrounded by encyclopedias, sometimes I take one down and read about other people's lives, kings, actresses, assassins, judges, anthropologists, tennis champions, tycoons, politicians, just because you haven't received any letters from me don't think I haven't written any. Every day I write a letter to you. Sometimes I think if I could tell you what happened to me that night. I could leave that night behind me, maybe I could come home to you, but that night has no beginning or end, it started before I was born and it's still happening. I'm writing in Dresden, and your mother is writing in the Nothing guest room, or I assume she is, I hope she is, sometimes my hand starts to burn and I am convinced we are writing the same word at the same moment. Anna gave me the typewriter your mother used to write her life story on. She gave it to me only a few weeks before the bombings, I thanked her, she said, "Why are you thanking me? It's a gift for me." "A gift for you?" "You never write to me." "But I'm with you." "So?" "You write to someone you can't be with." "You never sculpt me, but at least you could write to me." It's the tragedy of loving, you can't love anything more than something you miss, I told her, "You never write to me." She said, "You've never given me a typewriter," I started to invent future homes for us, I'd type through the night and give them to her the next day. I imagined dozens of homes, some were magical (a clock

208

tower with a stopped clock in a city where time stood still), some were mundane (a bourgeois estate in the country with rose gardens and peacocks), each felt possible and perfect, I wonder if your mother ever saw them. "Dear Anna, We will live in a home built at the top of the world's tallest ladder." "Dear Anna, We will live in a cave in a hillside in Turkey." "Dear Anna, We will live in a home with no walls, so that everywhere we go will be our home." I wasn't trying to invent better and better homes, but to show her that homes didn't matter, we could live in any home, in any city, in any country, and be happy, as if the world were just what we lived in. The night before I lost everything, I typed out our last future home: "Dear Anna, We will live in a series of homes, which will climb the Alps, and we'll never sleep in the same one twice. Each morning after breakfast, we'll sled down to the next home. And when we open its front door, the previous home will be destroyed and rebuilt as a new home. When we get to the bottom, we'll take a lift to the top and start again at the beginning." I went to bring it to her the next day on my way to your mother's house, I heard a noise from the shed, from where I'm now writing this to you, I suspected it was Simon Goldberg, I knew that Anna's father had been hiding him, I had heard them talking in there some nights when Anna and I tiptoed into the fields, they were always whispering, I had seen his charcoal stained shirt on their clothesline, I didn't want to make myself known, so I quietly slid a book from the wall. Anna's father, your grandfather, was sitting in his chair with his face in his hands, he was my hero. When I think back on that moment, I never see him with his face in his hands, I won't let myself see him that way, I see the book in my hands, it was an illustrated edition of Ovid's Metamorphosis I used to look for the edition in the States, as if by finding it I could slide it back in the shed's wall, block the image of my hero's face in his hands, stop my life and history at that moment, I asked after it in every bookshop in New York, but I never was able to find it, light poured into the room through the hole in the wall, your grandfather lifted his head, he came to the shelf and we looked at each other through the missing Metamorphosis, I asked him if something was wrong, he didn't say anything, I could see only a sliver of his face, the spine of a book of his face, we looked at each

209

Figure 6.6 Foer (2005a) *Extremely Loud & Incredibly Close*: 208–209, including readerly layer.

Readers who do write on their copy of *Extremely Loud & Incredibly Close*, and specifically on the pages of this chapter since here the accumulation of worlds is made explicit, add another narrative layer. This can be seen in Figure 6.7.

In section 6.3.2 of this chapter, I briefly touched on Herman's (2009a, 2009b) employment of Goffman's (1974, 1981) notion of lamination in relation to literature. Goffman's work is focused in the field of social interaction. Building on Bateson's (1972) use of the term 'frame', Goffman (1974) conceives of social interaction as composed of various frames defined by parameters of meaning and context. When frames accumulate or are transformed into an alternate frame of interpretation, layering or lamination is said to occur:

> it becomes convenient to think of transformations as adding a *layer* or *lamination* to the activity. And one can address two features of the activity. One is the innermost layering, wherein dramatic activity can be at play to engross the participant. The other is the outermost layering, the *rim* of the frame, as it were, which tells us just what sort of status in the real world the activity has, whatever the complexity of the inner laminations. (Goffman 1974: 82)

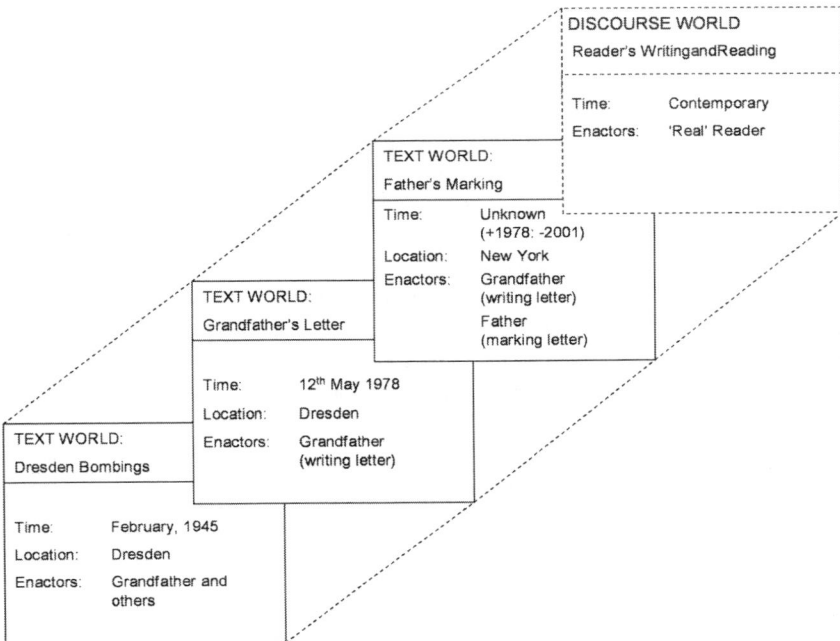

Figure 6.7   Narratological worlds in 'WHY I'M NOT WHERE YOU ARE; 4/12/78' (Foer 2005a), including readerly layer.

Goffman's concept of lamination offers support for bistable oscillation in reading (see my extended discussion of this in section 5.2.8 through to section 5.2.11 of Chapter 5) and is useful in accounting for the layering of frames, including paying attention to the outmost layer. In literary terms, the 'rim' of literary experience is of course located at the site of the reader. In clarifying Goffman's terminology, Schiffrin (2006) explains that lamination can transform the meaning(s) of frames "by adding another layer (e.g. from the outside, akin to another layer) through which the original can still be viewed" (239). This notion of viewing more internal layer(s) through more external layer(s) is apt in relation to 'why i'm not where you are; 4/12/78' since, as mentioned, the multimodality of the chapter creates a sense of perceived depth in terms of its narrative worlds. Moreover, Thomas Jr.'s red circlings do have a transformative semantic effect on his father's letter. Consequently, lamination can be seen to be at work in 'why i'm not where you are; 4/12/78', achieved primarily through Foer's employment of multimodality (the red circles) to signal multiple narrative levels.

By creating a further narrative layer through their own writing, readers' acts of writing and the indelible traces such writing leaves upon the book constitute 'answerings' in Kacandes' (2001) terms to the traumas expressed in the chapter in a literary-historical circuit of witness. This is a multimodal response, both in terms of how Foer uses colour and image to generate a greater awareness of the reader-based 'rim' of the lamination, as well as the way in which readerly physical action in the discourse-world engenders those answers. Potential performative ways of communicating a discourse-world answer to Foer's text is the topic of the following section.

6.3.7   Transmuting a Mute Message

Thomas Sr.'s subsequent and final narrated chapter, 'why i'm not where you are; 9/11/03', is once again written to Oskar's father, but this time after 9/11 and therefore after he has died. Since the bombing of Dresden, Thomas Sr. has lost his ability to talk and has thus developed a number of different strategies of communication, one of which is his daybook, a notebook he carries with him in which to write the words he wishes to speak, pages of which appear in the novel. In his final letter, Thomas Sr. relates his return to America and to Oskar's grandmother. On arriving in the U.S., Thomas Sr. uses a payphone to call Oskar's grandmother, having not thought through how he will speak to her if and when she answers the phone. Foer's depiction of this episode is multimodal:

> "Hello?" I knew it was her, the voice had changed but the breath was the same, the spaces between the words were the same, I pressed "4, 3, 5, 5, 6," she said, "Hello?" I asked, "4, 7, 4, 8, 7, 3, 2, 5, 5, 9, 9, 6, 8?" She said, "Your phone isn't working one hundred dollars. Hello?" (269)

Evident in Oskar's grandmother's repeated "Hello?", this communication is not too successful. As with the red circles in 'why i'm not where you are; 4/12/78', readers are required to use narrative frame recall (Emmott 1994, 1997) to access previous narrative information from Thomas Sr.'s first chapter in which he tells readers, "when I was on the phone I'd dial the numbers—2, 6, 6, 2—so that the person could hear what I couldn't say" (16). Readers hoping to understand this communication could therefore use the telephone keypad as their cipher to decode the message. At first this is not too demanding, Thomas's words to his estranged wife above translating as 'Hello' and 'Is it really you?' However, Oskar's grandmother does not understand what in the storyworld are a series of tonal sounds and hangs up the telephone. Thomas Sr. calls again, this time telling her 'everything': "I broke my life down into letters, for love I pressed 5, 6, 8, 3,' for death 3, 3, 2, 8, 4,' when the suffering is abstracted from the joy, what remains? What, I wondered, is the sum of my life?" (269). After this, the remainder of the page is filled with numbers and this continues for another two pages.

Foer's use of numbers and code in this part of the book directs the reader towards enactive participation and consequently also into the creation of a figured trans-world, first defined in section 4.2.9 of Chapter 4. In Danielewski's *House of Leaves*, a figured trans-world was also created through the use of coded message. In that instance, deciphering the code situated the reader in a doubly deictic relationship with the character Johnny Truant. The code was relatively straight-forward and enabled readers to uncover and inscribe an alternative narrative surface. In *Extremely Loud & Incredibly Close*, the act of decoding the communication is far more challenging since each number signifies the possibility of three letters (so the number 2, for example, could stand for a, b, or c). This makes the act of decoding, particularly when the coded passage is so lengthy, an arduous task that readers will commit to in varying degrees. Such degrees of commitment can, in fact, be seen amongst the authors of literary reviews and criticism of the novel. Updike (2005) describes this part of the text as "two and half pages of numerals that an ideal reader (not me) could decipher". By not participating in the act of decoding Updike does not trigger the creation of or take part in a figured trans-world in his reading of the novel. What's more, Updike's abstinence from performative involvement with the book means that he refrains from acting in a circuit of traumatic witness and refuses to "formulate a reply as invited by some feature of the text" (Kacandes 2001: 25), in this case the coded numbers.

Nevertheless, many readers do enter into the performative act of decoding. My own initial scribblings in the margins of page 269 show the start of my attempt. Gessen (2005) claims that the numerals are "decipherable with the use of cell-phone T9 word-recognition technology. I myself got as far as 'My Name is el heal.' (6, 9, 2, 6, 3, 4, 7, 3, 5, 4, 3, 5, 5 . . .') It would have been helpful had Foer inserted spaces between the words" (2007). Codde (2007) also started to decipher the passage:

> Though I cannot claim even to have tried to decode the entire two and
> a half pages of numerical code (has anyone?), the few sentences in the
> beginning yield interesting results . . . The name [Thomas Sr.] gives
> himself is definitely not Thomas Schell (the best I can come up with is
> "Elie Blum"), which may indicate that Thomas changed his name after
> the war. (253)

Both Codde's and Gessen's accounts show the difficulty of successfully
decoding Foer's numerals. They both reach different conclusions as to the
name Thomas Sr. gives in the message, and both seem to have found the
experience frustrating, clear from Codde's parenthetical question and Gessen's suggestion for how Foer could have aided the process. Certainly, my
own experience endorses the feelings of frustration and textual obscurity,
having repeatedly returned to what felt like an unsolved mystery, a narrative confession I simply could not comprehend, could not lay (co)witness
to in terms of Kacandes's (2001) circuits of narrative trauma and certainly
could not 'answer' in any informed or knowing way.

Effecting this frustration in readers is exactly Foer's goal (Hanks 2008):
the numbers cannot be deciphered because soon after they begin, their
design stops being organised and becomes random. A major theme of the
novel is the failure of personal communication, a theme that this numerical 'code' puts into practice, communicating a message that cannot be
deciphered. For Foer, the frustration experienced by readers who try to
translate the numerals into words "is very much in the spirit of the book"
(Hanks 2008). As I have mentioned, this code creates a figured trans-world,
crucially based on a doubly deictic subjective resonance that I have not yet
explicated: the reader is positioned doubly deictically with Oskar's grandmother. Readers' frustration in trying to understand the linguistic meaning
of the numbers echoes Oskar's grandmother's confusion and inability to
understand the semantic force behind the tonal bleeps created by Thomas
Sr. pressing the telephone keypad in the storyworld.

Doubly deictic subjectivity and the existence of the figured trans-world in
this extract co-occur and cause lamination. Goffman's (1974, 1981) notion
of lamination is highly compatible with my conception of the figured trans-
world since the latter was motivated by Holland et al.'s (1998) 'figured
world', which, like Goffman's frame analysis, is designed to account for
shifting engagements and domains of reference in social interaction. As
with figured worlds, Goffman's frame analysis is commonly applied to children's play (Buchbinder 2008). Moreover, studies such as Jurow's (2005)
analysis of students' commitments to meaningful educational contexts
shows that figured worlds and lamination can be used together fruitfully.
While, as shown in section 6.3.6, the existence of a figured trans-world is
not necessary for lamination to take place, figured trans-worlds unavoidably create laminated narrative framing since they emphasise the reader in
relation to the literary text and its text-worlds, thus bringing into focus the

'rim' of literary experience. Notably, Bell's (2007, 2010) work on the worlds of hypertext fiction and McHale's (1987) study of postmodern fiction both similarly demonstrate the way in which the role of the reader can be foregrounded through self-referential devices.

The combination of doubly deictic subjectivity, figured trans-world, and lamination consequently means that although readers feel unable to formulate an 'answer' to the text of/as trauma in an informed way, their recognition of their doubly deictic subjective positioning and role in the figured trans-world can constitute cowitness in a similar way to that expressed by Kacandes (2001: 112) in readers taking up an available second-person pronoun. The multimodality in *Extremely Loud & Incredibly Close* offers the potential for doubly deictic subjectivity and figured trans-worlds in a call for involvement to readers which enables them to feel 'addressed', while the trans-world projection of the reader is a response of self-implication in relation to that call. In the next section, I begin my analysis of the conclusion to Foer's novel.

6.3.8   Examining the Falling Man

At the end of the novel Oskar's search has been more or less unsuccessful; while he did find the 'Black' to whom the envelope referred and the key belonged, the key has meaning potential for William Black in relation to his own deceased father. Oskar's father had come to own it coincidentally, and so it means very little for Oskar. The final scene of the novel takes place later the same day. At home, Oskar and his mother are for the first time in the novel honest with each other, and share an emotionally intimate moment. After Oskar's mother has tucked him in to bed, Oskar gets out his scrapbook, *Stuff That Happened to Me*, and looks through the pages:

> Finally, I found the pictures of the falling body.
> Was it Dad?
> Maybe.
> Whoever it was, it was somebody.
> I ripped out the pages of the book.
> I reversed the order so the last one was first, and the first was last.
> When I flipped through them, it looked like the man was floating up through the sky. (325)

Before looking at this part of the novel in detail, it is worth mentioning the way in which the image of the falling body haunts the entirety of Foer's novel in repeated references to it both in the book's visual images and verbal narrative. Earlier in the novel in a sequence of photographs supposedly from *Stuff That Happened to Me*, two images of the falling body appear (59, 62), the latter one zoomed in, and another similar photographic image (205) appears during Oskar's visit to see his psychologist. The falling bodies of 9/11 are significant as publicly witnessed icons of the trauma of 9/11 held in collective memory.

The images used in *Extremely Loud & Incredibly Close* evoke the photograph of 'The Falling Man'. This image was widely distributed in the immediate journalistic reporting of the event then later disappeared, along with all the photos of falling bodies, "relegated to the internet underbelly", as Junod (2007) phrases it, in a collective form of media censorship on the grounds of sensitivity. The picture(s) of the Falling Man is famous and notorious, on both counts due to its emotive impact. The Falling Man also permeates Don DeLillo's (2007) 9/11 novel of the same name. DeLillo eloquently describes the affective force of the famous image through one of his central character's perspectives; "Headlong, free fall, she thought, and this picture burned a hole in her mind and heart, dear God, he was a falling angel and his beauty was horrific" (2007: 222).

In the verbal narrative, many of Oskar's inventions and musings—the birdseed shirt (2), Oskar's reflections about the experience of falling (147), discussion of the behaviour of cats when falling and their chance of survival (190–191), metaphors of life and death using skyscrapers (245)—prime 9/11 and the falling body as part of this cognitive frame. Another of Oskar's inventions is the skyscraper that moves up and down rather than having a lift (3). This can be seen as a subversion of basic idealised cognitive models (Lakoff 1982, 1987; Lakoff and Johnson 1980, 1999; Stockwell 2002a). In the scenario, the lift becomes surplus. The idealised cognitive model for *skyscraper*, or even *buildings* more generally, cues up notions of static architectural structures that do not fit Oskar's invention. The cognitive comparison of Oskar's imagined skyscraper with our experiential idealised cognitive model for *skyscraper* shows up the differences between the two. In doing so, it reveals to the reader how Oskar tries to reinvent or subvert the primed 9/11 context.

In introducing trauma and its relation to memory, Caruth states that trauma consists "solely in the *structure of its experience* or reception: the event is not assimilated or experienced fully at the time, but only belatedly, in its repeated *possession* of the one who experiences it. To be traumatised is precisely to be possessed by an image or event" (1995: 4–5; original emphasis). In the storyworld, Oskar's (re)inventions, related to 9/11, suggest that he suffers his trauma in this way, as does the reader of the novel both in the discourse-world if they too find the image of the falling man (generically or as representative of an individual) haunting and in a doubly deictic experience, which draws on their involvement in 9/11 as cultural trauma in relation to Oskar's personal trauma.

Returning to the quotation that opened this section, Oskar wonders, "Was it Dad?" Earlier in the novel, Oskar revealed to his grandfather that he "printed out the frames from the Portuguese videos and examined them extremely closely. There's one body that could be him. It's dressed like he was and when I magnify it until the pixels are so big that it stops looking like a person, sometimes I can see glasses" (257). Oskar's search for tangible knowledge of his father's death in 9/11 is not merely fictional, but reminiscent of the actual responses of many of the people who lost loved ones in the 9/11 attacks. Richard Pecorella, in the 2006 Channel 4 documentary *9/11: The Falling Man*, claims to have done exactly the same as Oskar with the result of finding an image he believes to be of his fiancée. He says:

> It wasn't painful for some reason, it really wasn't. I finally, you know, I have something I can hold on to. This is where she was and this is how she died. She jumped. She didn't burn up. She didn't become dust.
>
> Nothing is more painful than losing her, but not knowing how I lost her was even more painful. So now that I believe that's what took place, its not painful for me to talk about it.
>
> And if she jumped, she jumped.

Pecorella's sentiments are mirrored by Oskar's in the novel: "I want to stop inventing. If I could know how he died, exactly how he died, I wouldn't have to invent him dying [. . .] There were so many ways to die, and I just need to know which was his" (257). In this respect, Oskar's search for the lock has been unsuccessful; it has opened no doors to shed light on the nature of his father's death. In the next section, I consider how the falling man flipbook may provide some form of closure for Oskar.

6.3.9   Recovering the Falling Man

Oskar extracts and reorganises the sequential images of the falling body in his scrapbook so that he is able to flip through them and create the effect of the man 'floating up through the sky'. The verbal narrative extends beyond this, so that the body doesn't just float up in the sky, but moves further backwards through time, reversing daily routine from the morning of September 11, 2001. In the process, the third-person pronoun 'he' is interrupted by the use of the noun 'Dad', so that subsequent uses of 'he' anaphorically reference Oskar's father, enabling Oskar to claim the falling body as his father's (in an attempt to know what happened to him?) and return his dad alive and well. After the verbal narrative ends with the words "We would have been safe", Foer presents readers with fifteen pages of sequential images of the falling body (one of which is shown in Figure 6.8). This is essentially a flipbook section, so that the reader can, in another doubly deictic alignment with Oscar and his trauma, reverse the fate of the falling body.

This flipbook section has been the cause of much controversy in literary review and criticism of the novel. Both Barbash (2005) and Head (2008) view the flipbook as an aesthetic trivialisation of deeply serious subject matter. Head calls the flipbook a "textual trick that lowers the emotional intensity of the closing page" (2008: 141); Barbash declares that the flipbook

Figure 6.8   Foer (2005a) *Extremely Loud & Incredibly Close*: 343.

"lends to the story a horrific and unearned gravity, and at the same time it cheapens a gorgeous and beautifully sad moment at the end of the final chapter" (2007). Evident in both Barbash's and Head's assertions is their belief that the visual accompaniment spoils the emotive effect of the verbal narrative. In part this is due to the role of context. Flipbooks are usually associated with children's books or cartoons, thus seeming to trivialise the deeply non-trivial.

My own critical position is dissonant with Barbash's and Head's opinions, since I see the flipbook as having a very specific function in relation to the novel as trauma text, that can be borne out by cognitive-poetic attention to multimodality. Firstly, I would like to restate that readers who engage with the mechanics of these pages, flipping them to make the figure of the falling man glide upward, align themselves doubly deictically with Oskar. Their actions in the discourse-world emulate Oskar's supposed actions in the text-world and therefore also create a figured trans-world through enactive performance.

Flipping the falling man pages does indeed cause the body to rise in a reversal of temporal reality. For Oskar in the storyworld, by reversing the temporal currency of 9/11 like this, he is able to 'recover' his father from it, cognitively speaking. Reading the flipbook as unified with the linguistic narrative, Codde suggests that Foer's employment of the past conditional mood "indicates the illusory nature of the entire endeavor" (2007: 251). Indeed, in relaying his dad's actions, Oskar's grammatical constructions are all composed, including elliptical forms, as 'He would have walked', though of course Foer changes the main verb as required. For Codde, seeing this part of the novel as ultimately illusory supports his argument that the past, and trauma to a certain extent, too, is inaccessible and so closure cannot be achieved. I do not necessarily disagree with his stance on the "impossibility of closure" (2007: 250), and I certainly value his decision to 'read' Foer's linguistic and visual reversals of time as united in meaning-making, rather than as competing modes and narratives. Nevertheless, I find Codde's claim that Oskar's revisioning of time is illusory dismissive of the intricacies of both the flipbook and of Foer's employment of the past conditional mood, for reasons that will become apparent shortly.

In her meditations on the falling man image, Nørgaard (2009a) begins by considering the first photograph of the falling man in the novel which appears amidst a set of photographs collected in Oskar's scrapbook *Stuff That Happened to Me*. Nørgaard considers the spatial layout of this static image, with the World Trade Center on the left, through Kress and van Leeuwen's (1996) division of layout into given and new on the horizontal axis and real and ideal along the vertical axis. More interestingly for this thesis, she (2009a: 122) continues by relating these to conceptual metaphor, arguing that Kress and van Leeuwen's "categories are supported by evidence from cognitive science that humans in many contexts tend to evaluate 'up' as good and 'down' as bad". Obviously, this is a reference to the related conceptual metaphors good is up and bad is down.

The implication of Nørgaard's use of Conceptual Metaphor Theory works in two ways. Firstly, she seems to be suggesting that if the body occupies the top of the image, Kress and van Leeuwen's (1996) ideal space, it is 'good' while when the body is at the lowest point it is 'bad'. Secondly, when, two paragraphs later, she discusses the flipbook, Nørgaard argues that it enables the reader to "make the man float from Real to Ideal" (2009a: 14). The implication of this, in light of the earlier comparison with conceptual metaphor, is that the movement of the flipbook is a visual-kinaesthetic realisation of good is up. good is up *could* be a cognitive structural model which readers draw on to understand the flipbook images in visual motion. However, as Mandel (2008) points out, the flipbook as a device enables the past (truth) and potential (fictionality) to coexist in the same textual space. That is, readers may actually choose to flip the pages in either direction so that the body falls down through the air or flies upwards in a visual and cognitive recovery of the moment. Although good is up and bad is down are complementary conceptual metaphors and cannot be totally discounted here, I suggest that cognitive negation makes for a more suitable account of both the cognitive processes and multimodal materialisation involved.

Discussed in detail in section 4.2.2 of Chapter 4, negation is a cognitive process that involves conceptualising and comprehending first that which is being negated followed by the negation itself. Applied in this context, regardless of whether the reader actually experiments by flipping the pages to show the body falling downwards as in real time, comprehending the significance of the body travelling upwards can only be understood through its foregrounding of the negated context in which the body fell downward. Gessen's comments implicitly support my application of negation as he sees Foer as "trying to get at the loss by indirection: the relief of its backward respooling suggests the pain of its actual occurrence" (2005). Interestingly, in 'In the Ruins of the Future', DeLillo (2001) philosophically reflects on the impact of 9/11, suggesting that it caused a shift in the conceptualisation of time. Now, in light of the events of September 11, 2001, time cannot be understood as an ongoing linear process since the future is haunted by the past and the past haunted by imagined temporal possibilities or 'counternarratives'. Understanding Foer's flipbook through the process of cognitive negation highlights the way in which it demonstrates such hauntings or temporal interpellations.

Returning briefly to Foer's employment of the past conditional mood, mentioned by Codde (2007), rather than signalling that Oskar's reversal of time is an illusory project in terms of its psychological use-value in the context of resolving trauma, the grammatical mood subtly foreshadows the flipbook's reworking of time. Foer's past conditional mood is created through the use of the epistemic modal auxiliary *would* with its main verb inflected by past tense. How this relates to an interrelating temporality can be uncovered by returning to Langacker's (1991) epistemic model. Like *could, would* points to a distal possible future signifying non-immediate irreality. Past tense, obviously, grounds its meaning in the past or known reality. Consequently, the past conditional mood, sometimes colloquially spoken of as 'future in the past tense', similarly represents time as dual and coexistent. In other words, Oskar's revisioning of time, both in the flipbook and in grammatical mood, 'laminates' (Goffman 1974, 1981) temporal frames, known reality and non-immediate irreality, past temporality and imagined potentiality.

Temporal revisions appear in many narrative texts of/as trauma. Two such examples are Kurt Vonnegut's (1969) *Slaughterhouse-Five* and Martin Amis's (1991) *Time's Arrow*, both of which fictionalise the Second World War. In *Time's Arrow*, Martin Amis (re)structures the entire narrative through a chronological reversal. In comparison, Vonnegut puts this into effect in one scene, though significantly it reverses the bombing of Dresden by American fight planes:

> The formation flew backwards over a German city that was in flames. The bombers opened their bomb bay doors, exerted a miraculous magnetism which shrunk the fires, gathered them into cylindrical steel containers, and lifted the containers into the bellies of the planes. (53)

In *Extremely Loud & Incredibly Close*, Foer (2005a) appears to pay homage to Vonnegut. Not only does Thomas Sr.'s letter 'why i'm not where you are; 4/12/78' narrate his experience of the Dresden bombings. In Oskar's grandmother's final chapter of the novel, she describes a recent dream about 'where she came from', namely, Dresden:

> In my dream, all the collapsed ceilings re-formed above us. The fire went back into the bombs, which rose up and into the bellies of planes where propellers turned backward, like the second hands of the clocks across Dresden, only faster. (306–307)

The device of temporal reversal in texts that narrate trauma can be seen to express an essential desire to undo the wrong doings of the event and put them to right, so to speak.

Revisioning time has an important role in dealing with traumatic memory which, intended or not, these texts put into practice through their readers' literary imaginings. Speaking in interview about the trauma of 9/11 as a major event, Derrida articulates:

> we must question its "chrono-logy," that is, the thought and order of temporalization it seems to imply. We must rethink the temporalization of a traumatism if we want to comprehend in what way "September

11" *looks like* a "major event." For the wound remains open to our terror before the *future* and not only by the past. (Borradori 2003: 96)

Indeed, one of the ways to deal with traumatic memories is through a temporal rethinking of their chronology. 'Visual-Kinaesthetic Dissociation' (Cameron-Bandler 1985; Dietrich 2000; Hossack and Bentall 1996), first suggested by Bandler (1985), is a treatment employed in cases of post-traumatic disorders. As I explained in section 6.3.8, a central experience in individuals with post-traumatic stress suffering from trauma is the psychological repetition of the event or as Kacandes details, "reliving experiences or flashbacks" (2001: 91). To relieve these symptoms of trauma, visual-kinaesthetic dissociation is an imaginative process which subjects are asked to perform cognitively, involving replaying the traumatic memory backwards in what is referred to as 'reverse displacement' (Dietrich 2000). In doing so, "the kinaesthetic (feeling) portion is dissociated from the visual memory" (Cameron-Bandler 1985: 152). Put another way by Dietrich (2000), the goal of visual-kinaesthetic dissociation is to "modify the client's kinaesthetic memory of the trauma so that it no longer holds the same mnemonic associative power".

Vonnegut's (1969) and Amis' (1991) novels evidently invite readers to perform visual-kinaesthetic dissociation in the process of literary imagining. Foer's (2005a) *Extremely Loud & Incredibly Close* also does this, both in its linguistic narrative as well as in the flipbook, the performative dimension of which is crucial to this process since it becomes the way in which the reader controls the process of traumatic replay. Explaining the stages of recovery from trauma, Herman contends, "Given the 'iconic,' visual nature of traumatic memories, creating pictures may represent the most effective initial approach to these 'indelible images'" (1992: 177). Foer himself explicitly recognises the need to treat the visual in handling 9/11: "My experience, and the experience of so many people I know, is wishing that it could be undone. Also, 9/11 is the most visually documented event in human history; those images are how people remember it" (Moggach 2005).

Foer's flipbook is not simply a multimodal gimmick, as some critics have judged it, but rather a deliberate device, which enhances the temporal revisioning of the falling man and 9/11 in the verbal narrative, and is utilised to full advantage in a multimodal text of/as trauma. Discussing 'awakenings' from trauma, Caruth expounds, "an awakening, if it is in some sense still a repetition of the trauma [. . .], is not, however, a simple repetition of the *same* failure and loss" (1996: 106). Rather, it is a "new act that repeats precisely a departure and a difference". At the text-world level, the past conditional mood and the irreality of the flipbook's recovery of the falling man insert a 'newness' into the image of trauma which haunts Oskar and thus represents the start of his awakening and traumatic recovery.

The flipbook itself works to create doubly deictic subjective alignment for the reader with Oskar as well as positioning readers in a figured trans-world. Since the presence of the flipbook at the end of *Extremely Loud & Incredibly Close* directs the reader into the figured trans-world, it is an invitation to the reader, making a call to them for traumatic cowitness and coparticipation to which reader-response is constituted in physical engagement with the flipbook. Finally, the flipbook works to direct readers to perform curative procedures for post-traumatic stress, enabling them to deal with the unforgettable image of the falling man so central to the trauma of 9/11. The flipbook is, therefore, a way for Foer to 'talk' to readers in an incontestable circuit of witness grounded in the discourse-world, literary-historical witnessing.

6.4 CONCLUSION: "EXTREMELY LOUD" AND "INCREDIBLY CLOSE"

The meaning of the title to Foer's novel, *Extremely Loud & Incredibly Close*, is never addressed explicitly within the book. One point of reference for the title's meaning can be found in eye-witness accounts of September 11, 2001. Fink and Mathias (2002) conducted and collected interviews of eighty-one survivors and/or witnesses of 9/11. Many of these make reference to the noise of the event and/or to having been too close to the towers and too close to death. Fire-Officer Joseph Pfeifer's comments are particularly interesting in light of *Extremely Loud & Incredibly Close*'s title and themes: "It was almost like the closer you were, the less you knew" (2002: 20). Pfeifer's words are highly reminiscent of Oskar's feelings in the novel about the image of the falling body: "I started thinking about the pixels in the image of the falling body, and about how the closer you looked, the less you could see" (293). In interview, Foer himself has briefly touched upon the significance of the title: "'Every relationship in the book is built around silence and distance,' Foer said. 'Extremely loud and incredibly close is what no two people are to one another'" (Solomon 2005). Interpreted thus, the title of the novel relates to its themes of the inability to communicate, and specifically, the inability to communicate traumatic memory.

The cognitive-poetic analysis in this chapter has raised insights into how *Extremely Loud & Incredibly Close* can be seen to function as what Kacandes (2001) calls circuit(s) of witnessing. In the process, I have suggested how the novel's stylistic choices and use of multimodal devices position readers in those circuits as well as asking them to participate in the circuit by constituting a 'reply'. Indeed, readers' responses may be conceptual through cowitness in perceiving in the narrative, and particularly in characters, signs of traumatic witness, testimony, or response; they may be personal through a self-implication (Kuiken, Miall, and Sikora 2004) with a second-person pronoun or through doubly deictic subjective alignment; and they can even occur in a more concrete form, when readers take up invitations in the text to enter into figured trans-worlds. This last form of response is particularly relevant to multimodal narratives of/as trauma, as the literary use of multimodality, emphasising the doubling nature of the multimodal literary experience, often prompts embodied action from readers.

An interesting effect of Foer's use of multimodality was its creation of a sense of narrative depth. In the chapter 'WHY I'M NOT WHERE YOU ARE; 4/12/78', multimodal elements, such as colour, resulted in narrative worlds appearing to be layered on top of each other. Building upon the analysis of *House of Leaves* in section 4.2.10 of Chapter 4, whereby a real reader-centred narrative layer was added through the novel's self-conscious recursive narrative structure, this layered chapter of *Extremely Loud & Incredibly Close* was seen to enable a similar additional narrative layer centred upon the reader. Following Herman's (2009a, 2009b) use of Goffman's (1974, 1981) concept of lamination, these narrative layers, superimposed on top of each other, were said to be laminated, a process which enhanced awareness of the 'rim' of literary experience.

Since Foer's (2005a) novel works to involve the reader as cowitness and participant in its narrative and the trauma of 9/11 upon which it focuses, the words of the title, 'extremely loud and incredibly close' could be viewed as metaphorical for the reader's experience of the novel: *Extremely Loud & Incredibly Close* employs stylistic devices such as pronoun selection seen in the novel's opening as well as multimodality to draw the readers closer into its storyworlds and the traumas experienced within them. As section 6.3.7 showed in its discussion of the numerically coded message, readers do not have to step closer, to take up doubly deictic subjective alignment in figured trans-worlds, but can abstain from such involvement. Nevertheless, the stylistic and multimodal strategies of the novel 'talk' to the reader of trauma, the reader whose cognitive and multimodal engagement can 'talk' back. The volume of this talk, how loud the conversation becomes, is in the reader's hands.

7 Cut, Paste, Repair, but Read
Woman's World by Graham Rawle

7.1 INTRODUCTION

Graham Rawle made a name for himself with his early work *Lost Consonants*. The "text and image word play series", as Rawle's own website describes it (www.grahamrawle.com), appeared in the Weekend *Guardian* newspaper for a lengthy period of fifteen years, and was later published as a series of books. *Woman's World* (2005) is Rawle's second novel, and was constructed through a painstaking cut-and-paste process, that is to say the novel is composed of collected words and phrases from 1960s British women's magazines. As such, it is part of a small tradition of collage and/or treated novels, alongside writer-artists such as Eduardo Paolozzi (1966) and Tom Phillips (1970). While the first hardback edition of *Woman's World* features the subtitle 'A Novel', the paperback emphasises the multimodal nature of the book referring to it as 'A Graphic Novel'. Indeed, the text and image combination of *Woman's World* has resulted in it being described as "a virtuoso piece of old-fashioned paste-up" (Poynor 2005) and as looking like "an epic ransom note" (Loeb and Girl, Interrupting 2008). However, the magazine heritage is illustrated by the text both visually and linguistically, a phrase which seeks to dispel the idea that multimodality and/or the inclusion of visuality in literature is a 'low-culture gimmick', as opposed to a serious literary contribution (such comments, for instance, were made by critics about Foer's *Extremely Loud & Incredibly Close*, as discussed in section 6.3.9 of the previous chapter). Interestingly, responding to this very subject in interview, Rawle revealed, "That's the thing that concerned me the most, that people would look at it as a novelty rather than a novel. For me, if the story doesn't work then it's quite a spectacular waste of time" (Doig 2008). Rawle's words, which display his flair for linguistic tomfoolery ('novelty rather than a novel'), typical of his work, are in line with the characterisation of multimodal printed literature taken in this book: the various modal forms of the text work in synthesis, not with one mode seeming ineffectual in comparison to others.

The story of *Woman's World* centres upon the lives and fantasies of Miss Norma Fontaine and her brother Roy Little. The narrative begins just before Roy gets a job as a delivery man for White's Laundry. Norma, the first-person homodiegetic narrator of the novel, is an avid magazine reader, and therefore the tale is frequently interspersed with picture-perfect commentary straight from the women's weeklies. The latter, it must be noted, displays Norma's aspirations to embody the femme ideal, while Roy's knowledge of women's fashion and etiquette comes from buying the magazines for his sister. Although this short synopsis makes the plot seem rather mundane, on the contrary, dark family secrets set a series of events in motion that threaten to disrupt Roy and Norma's simple suburban lives.

Like *Woman's World*, Rawle's first book *Diary of an Amateur Photographer* (1998) is a work of collage. The novel fits neatly into the murder mystery genre, yet its uniqueness stems from its status as a multimodal artefact. It is designed to look like the journal or diary of the narrating character Michael Whittingham. *Diary of an Amateur Photographer* uses images and found text from magazines, while the main narrative is typewritten. Thus in typographical terms (outlined in section 2.3.6 of Chapter 2), *Diary of an Amateur Photographer* carries a great deal of indexical meaning; both the facsimile reproduction of the found text and the typewritten diary entries indicate their source and mode of production.

As a writer and collage artist (and Rawle blends both of these roles in his work, rather than keeping them mutually exclusive), Rawle's employment of multimodality is self-evident. Having said this, his current book project, *The Card* (though according to Rawle's [2008b] blog, it might instead be called *The Card Collector, The Completist*, or *Face Down in the Gutter*) is inspiring online speculation since it may be "a piece of writing rather than collage" (Johnstone 2010). Nevertheless, *Woman's World* provides another case study of printed multimodal literature and importantly, its use of multimodality is dramatically different to *House of Leaves, VAS: An Opera in Flatland*, and *Extremely Loud & Incredibly Close*. Unlike the preceding case studies, *Woman's World*'s cut-and-paste format means that multimodal typographical meaning will be a primary focus of this chapter. Indeed, the *Guardian* newspaper hailed the book as "a typographical rollercoaster" (Phillips 2005). Additionally, the novel's inclusion of images, illustrations, and page layout will be considered in cognitive-poetic analysis. As a final textual analysis in this book, this chapter reinforces the investigations of the preceding chapters and provides empirical evidence to support key arguments put forward in this book about the experience of reading multimodal literature, such as its integrative nature, the process of bistable oscillation, and the permeability of text-world and discourse world contexts. In the next section, I start by considering one of *Woman's World*'s central contextual elements, that of 1960s women's magazines.

7.2 ANALYSIS

Women's magazines, or the women's periodical press, can be traced back to the launch of *The Ladies' Mercury* in 1693, prompting further titles in the eighteenth and nineteenth centuries, with the industry expanding considerably in the early twentieth century (Ferguson 1983; White 1970) with titles such as *Woman's Weekly* (1911). It was in the 1930s, however, that the mass market of women's weeklies was born, with many titles from this period such as *Woman's Own* (1932) and *Woman* (1937) maintaining their popularity for a significant portion of the twentieth century. The latter two, along with the aforementioned *Woman's Weekly*, for instance, are cited by Ferguson (1983: 39) as accruing the largest sales between 1949 and 1974, and all three are still published today by IPC media, whose website boasts that their "print brands alone [reach] almost two thirds of UK women". For *Woman's World* (incidentally also the name of a women's weekly), Rawle uses snippets from many of these publications, taking issues from the early 1960s, to assemble the story of his novel. For instance, several titles can be seen in Figure 7.1, taken from Rawle's own documentation of his production process. Sources can also be gleaned when they appear within the novel. As such, we can be sure that Rawle's corpus consisted of *Woman, Woman's Own, Woman's Realm, Woman's Journal, Wife,* and *House Beautiful,* amongst other titles.

Figure 7.1 The 'making of' *Woman's World*: Graham Rawle's source material.

From this source material, Rawle began to cut fragments of text that he thought could be useful for his literary project. Discussing the evolution of *Woman's World*, Rawle admits, "Early on, I let the narrative be driven by what I was finding. The problem was that it would quickly go off the rails" (Doig 2008). In the initial stages, the source material or found text dictated the development of the story, an approach which impeded comprehensive narrative progression. Consequently, Rawle started over with a new strategy. In the first instance, he wrote the story of the novel, and subsequently exchanged his own words with cuttings from the women's magazines. *Woman's World* was an elaborate project, taking Rawle five years to complete, and so he had to create a system to keep track of the vast number of magazine cuttings. Rawle explains (Doig 2008; Rawle 2008a) that he catalogued cuttings by sticking them (lightly) into scrapbooks, which were page-numbered. He then typed the phrases into a computer database he'd created, including the page number for ease of reference in order to locate the scrapbook page and desired fragment at a later date. Once all of the fragments had been input into the database, Rawle categorised them—"the weather; shopping; light conversation; confrontational conversation; driving; police; medical" (Rawle 2008a)—allowing him to search his database of 1.2 million words in order to find a suitable phrase for the rewrite. Ultimately, the linguistic texture of *Woman's World*, as it is encountered by its readers, is what Rawle describes as "an approximation of what I wanted to say" (Doig 2008), the kitsch language of 1960s women's magazines furnishing the novel with its distinctive narrative tone.

The way in which the source material permeates through into the target location, in this case *Woman's World*, is a crucial part of Rawle's attraction to collage as an artistic and literary medium. Talking about the finished novel, Rawle reflects, "both visually and in terms of the content, the words [a character] uses retain the essence of their original context. It's what I love about collage" (Wigan 2008: 57). Thus, through the transfer of material, moving words and phrases from their women's magazine source into the context of a twenty-first-century novel, the original story of *Woman's World* is reconstructed, transfigured with the inflection of the source material's 1960s bijou voice. The transformative process, however, is not unidirectional but bidirectional. That is, by moving the words of 1960s women's magazines into a new context, fragmenting them and making new sentences and new meanings from them, Rawle's book is rather subversive. The literature on women's magazines (Ballaster et al. 1991; Ferguson 1983; White 1970; Winship 1983, 1987), for instance, considers the form as prescriptive in the message it communicates to its readership, and although the focus of these studies is placed upon thematic and cultural issues, some consistent linguistic techniques do emerge, such as personalised forms of address in editorial and problem-page contexts. Thus, Rawle's renewal of the language of women's magazine through collage in *Woman's World* evokes fresh reflection on the language such publications use, and to what end.

Rawle's use of collage is also at the heart of *Woman's World*'s multimodality. With the font size and type-face of the novel varying relentlessly and the often noticeable outline of the cut-out fragments, it is possible to identify the distinct textual particles, to see the divisions between source texts and thus also the fracture lines in the target. In Matwychuk's (2008) rather poetic words, "each part of the sentence has been sewn together like a Frankenstein monster". Since the textual composition is noticeable to the reader and the 'graphic novel' form of *Woman's World* makes the written text so visual in nature, this chapter has a strong focus upon typography including the way in which it influences readerly attention and narrative experience.

7.2.1 First Impressions

On opening Graham Rawle's novel, readers are greeted by the title page, the words '*Woman's World*' appearing in the traditional upper-centre position. There is a facsimile quality to the page, or to the title at least. In terms of typography, '*Woman's World*' is bold in weight and the letters are disconnected. All in all, '*Woman's World*' has an archaic quality to it; it seems to iconically suggest the era from which the source material is taken. Turning the page, the reader is then greeted by the words '№ 1'. This time, the cut-and-paste outline can be seen, while the superscript setting of the 'o' is visually reminiscent of the logo for *Chanel № 5*, or even the lesser known *Mademoiselle Chanel № 1* which enjoyed a brief distribution between 1942 and 1946. Whatever the source of this cut-out, it is somewhat evocative of the sleek marketing that adorned women's magazines.

The words '№ 1', in fact, mark the start of the novel's opening chapter. Interestingly, all of the book's chapter numbering is fashioned from magazine cuttings, and so every chapter number is different to the last: some are written in word form, some are numerical, and the font constantly changes. The page numbers were created similarly: Rawle remarks, "It was fun trying to find a printed number for every page of the book. A bit of tinkering was often required." For page 209, for instance, "the 209 is intact as part of a telephone number" (Kachka 2008).

Turning the page again, readers encounter the first page of the narrative. The appearance of this page is both typical of *Woman's World* and worlds apart from readers' expectations of how a novel usually looks. Although it does to some extent conform to conventional type-setting in that it contains a block of text that reads from left to right, it may come as a shock to some readers (assuming, of course, that they haven't already flicked through the novel—nevertheless, the 'shock factor' would be applicable to all first encounters with the text).

Discussions about the book on online forums are quite insightful. When *Woman's World* was featured as the book in the 'book of the month club' on the Jezebel.com blog (essentially an online twenty-first-century version of a women's magazine, with monthly issues, that seeks to subvert or at the

Figure 7.2   Rawle (2005) *Woman's World*: 3.

very least go against the branding culture and prescriptive feminine ideal of women's magazines proper), it received mixed comments by the blog's readers (see Website 7 in References). The post showed an image of the book's cover and an accompanying sample image of the book's pages in the form of a double page spread, in this case pages 42–43. In total, Jezebel's readers posted eighty-four comments, fifty of which were either indifferent/unrelated in subject matter to the topic of reading the novel or part of ongoing discussions. (Incidentally, one such thread is about Danielewski's

[2000a] *House of Leaves*, starting as a form of comparison with *Woman's World* and progressing into a subjective discussion of Danielewski's novel. From the perspective of this study, it is interesting to see real readers making genre connections between the two, however fleeting.)

Of the remaining thirty-four comments, thirteen users (38.2 per cent) expressed a keenness to read the novel or said that they enjoyed reading it; one user (2.9 per cent) implied that she was reading the novel but finding it frustrating (I discuss this reader's comments in more detail later in section 7.2.7 of this chapter); eight users (23.5 per cent) commented positively on the book's design but thought it would be difficult to read; eight more users (23.5 per cent) were adamant that they were not going to read it based on the book's design; two users (5.9 per cent) said that they weren't going to read it, but for reasons unrelated to the design; and two users (5.9 per cent), who both posted towards the end of the comments thread, sought to rebuff design concerns by saying the book was not, in fact, difficult to read. It is noteworthy that the design and look of *Woman's World* actively influenced the Jezebel.com blog users' decisions to read the book or not. In particular, those users who opted not to read it or thought it would be difficult to read due to its design total a striking 47 per cent. In the representative comments given below, for instance, blog users frequently suggest it would give them a headache and/or hurt or be hard on their eyes:

"I'm pretty sure I'd need stronger contacts to get through that book." (Petuniacat)

"Wow. I suspect, however, this might give me a headache." (Pinkosaurus)

"That is possibly the coolest thing ever. I've done collage art with found text, but that's taking it to a whole new level. Hard on the eyes, though." (LLB)

"Literally, the most painful book to read, ever. It should come with Excedrin." (Sukie: Sea Gangster)

"Half the designer in me thinks 'kick ass' the other half says 'illegible'." (Twilly)

"I think I may be blind now." (Zivah)

"That hurts my head. And my eyes." (Kittenish)

"I don't think I could read it without getting sick from the layout." (Captain Morgan)

"This is one of those things that I think would be awesome in theory, but might give me a migraine (or just piss me off) actually reading. See also: *House of Leaves* and particularly *Only Revolutions* by Mark Z. Danielewski." (Go Like Hell Machine)

(Website 7 in References; all posted by users February 19, 2008)

Evidently, the multimodality of *Woman's World* has a striking impact on reader's opinions of the book before they even start reading.

Research in cognitive science suggests that the style of printed fonts affects both effort prediction and motivation. In a series of three related experimental studies, Song and Schwarz (2008) presented participants with task instructions in either an easy-to-read font (Arial, 10 point) or a difficult-to-read font (𝓑𝓻𝓾𝓼𝓱, 10 point; 𝓜𝓲𝓼𝓽𝓻𝓪𝓵, 10 point). All three studies signal that participants judge a task to be harder and more time-consuming when it is imparted in the more difficult-to-read type-face. Moreover, participants expressed less willingness to undertake the given exercise in the difficult-to-read font. As such, Song and Schwarz conclude that "people misread the difficulty of processing instructions as indicative of the difficulty of executing the behavior, and that this misperception has down-stream effects on their willingness to engage in that behavior" (2008: 986).

Woman's World is, of course, not a set of task instructions, so transferable inferences from Song and Schwarz's (2008) study to the reading experience of the novel are tentative at best. However, it seems apparent that users of the Jezebel.com blog, who are reticent to read the novel based on its design, are employing similar effort predictions. The potential readers on the Jezebel.com blog are assessing the constantly shifting type-faces in *Woman's World*, transpiring as a result of the collage production, as requiring greater reading processing effort (presumably because the newness of each font attracts and distracts attention), an assessment which is affecting their motivation to read the novel. These readers weren't judging the book by its cover but by its pages, so to speak.

7.2.2   What Is *Your* Idea of a Perfect Home?

For readers undeterred by *Woman's World*'s multimodal design, the novel begins, "What is your idea of a perfect home? Do you long for a gracious way of living that provides comfort without clutter and an atmosphere of charming elegance throughout the whole house?" (3). Here, readers encounter two rhetorical questions, both featuring second-person address. As such, the novel opens in a direct and engaging way, harnessing the affective force of the second-person pronoun along with interrogatives that prompt readers to self-implicate by performing the imaginative task implicitly asked of them by the discourse, envisaging their 'perfect home'. The narrative then continues, "I like things to be just so in my house" (3), thus introducing a first-person narrator.

Following deictic shift theory (see section 3.2.3 of Chapter 3 for a brief introduction), the pronoun change from second to first person would instantiate a deictic shift for the reader, who moves from projecting into the 'you' role of the questions to projecting into the focalising perspective of the 'I' narrator. Discussing the deictic centre and focalisation of narrative, Zubin and Hewitt (1995) advocate:

the unitary nature of experience causes us to construct a deictic centre from which to view the unfolding story events, and we use this deictic center as we would use the "I" of face-to-face interaction to anchor our comprehension of the text. The reader tracks the shifted deixis in the text as if placed in that center. The decoupling of deixis in narrative from the speech situation allows the linguistic realization of the deictic center to be altered from that of face-to-face interaction in a variety of ways, from a fictional "I" to impersonal third-person narration. (131)

Furthermore, Zubin and Hewitt's comments on fictional "I" a few pages later make explicit their opinions on the absolute nature of "I" as a deictic centre into which readers shift. Fictional first-person narratives "offer an illusion like viewing the story world through a movie camera controlled by the narrator; we only see what this person sees" (Zubin and Hewitt 1995: 133). Thus, in the opening to *Woman's World*, the subjective experience of the reader should be one which initially feels addressed by the apostrophic use of the second person, but subsequently shifts into the deictic centre and focalising perspective of the first-person narrator. However, this seems to disregard both the seductive power of textual *you* and the communicative context the novel opens with, generated through the complementary usage of the first- and second-person (interpersonal) pronouns.

In a recent study of embodiment and perspective taking in narrative, Brunyé et al. (2009) examined the role of pronouns in influencing the perspective a reader adopts. To do so, Brunyé et al. carried out two experiments. In the first, they presented readers with pronoun variations of action sentences which followed a pronoun–verb–direct object pattern (e.g. 'I am slicing the tomato', 'You are taping the package', 'He is ironing the pants'), after which readers were shown images of the action from internal (performing) or external (non-performing) perspectives and asked to verify whether the picture matched or mismatched the verbal description. Response times were used as the form of measurement so, as Brunyé et al. put it, "if linguistic information influences the perspective adopted by a reader, then picture response times should be contingent upon the pronoun in the sentence" (2009: 28). The same procedure was used in the second experiment, but short discourse contexts were added prior to the original verbal descriptions, lengthening the verbal narrative from one to three sentences. For instance, 'I am a thirty-year-old deli employee. I am making a vegetable wrap. Right now, I am slicing the tomato'. The purpose of this was to test whether "enriched descriptions might change the perspectives readers use while imagining events" (Brunyé et al. 2009: 30). The first experiment showed that pronoun choice cued corresponding imagined mental representations. Third person cued external perspective, second person cued internal embodied perspective, while first person cued internal embodied perspective but *inconsistently* (I italicise this, since it is a finding that presents a slight anomaly to deictic shift theory as discussed earlier).

The second experiment demonstrated that extended narrative contexts do impact on imaginative projection:

> when character identity is revealed through an extended discourse we find that readers are more likely to adopt an external perspective following first-person pronouns. It could be the case that reiterating pronouns in extended discourse helps readers to disambiguate the actor from the observer and encourages them to play a role as one or the other. In any case, the present results suggest that to imagine oneself in "someone else's shoes" during narrative comprehension, the reader must be directly addressed as the subject of the sentence. (Brunyé et al. 2009: 31)

These findings have dramatic implications for deictic shift theory. They suggest, for instance, that literary genre may be an important variable for the durability of deictic shifts into first-person narrative roles: readers might ultimately be more likely to identify with the 'I' of a short poem than the 'I' of an extended piece of fictional prose. More importantly, Brunyé et al.'s (2009) results seem more in line with a view of deictic projection that is *both embodied and social*, since it implicitly takes account of conversational discourse contexts (where an 'I' speaker talks to a 'you' listener). That is, in ordinary conversation, I am most accustomed to being addressed in the second person, and referring to myself in the first person; correspondingly, when others refer to themselves as 'I', I know they use it in self-reference and do not necessarily take on their perspective. Indeed, Green (1997) notes that a significant "difference between 'I' and other deictics, such as the demonstratives, is that while speakers can instantiate any number of groups, they cannot ordinarily instantiate individual persons to whom they are not identical" (91). For the purposes of this analysis, I'd like to draw attention to Brunyé et al.'s conclusion that the reader must be 'directly addressed' by the text in order to actually take on that role and narrative perspective. Ultimately, Brunyé et al. admit that in the second experiment, they "only found evidence for embodied language comprehension with the second-person pronoun" (Brunyé et al. 2009: 31). As such, in cognising the opening to *Woman's World*, readers are placed in the addressee role. They are in dialogue with the narrator, and the narrator addresses the reader as her listener and confidant. This is a rhetorical strategy utilised by women's magazines, as I go on to discuss in the next section.

7.2.3   Do *You* Long for a Gracious Way of Living..?

The conversational tone that opens *Woman's World* is emblematic of the language and address of the 1960s women's magazines that act as the source material for the novel. As the literature on women's magazines indicates, the editorial section, which fronts the magazine, is written in first person and addresses its readers in the second person, often in the generic style of a friendly letter. Indeed, Winship (1987: 66) suggests that a central purpose of the editorial is to establish "a personal relationship" between the editor and the magazine's readership. She writes, "both in and beyond the editorials the personal tone allows women to feel they are being individually addressed" (1987: 66). Elsewhere, she claims:

> What is specific about that address in all women's magazines is its friendly conversational style of *one woman to another*. The magazine speaks with some degree of intimacy as the concerned *friend* of women readers. Or as *Woman's Own* puts it each week 'Woman's Own—the magazine that cares'. (1983: 24; original emphasis)

In borrowing the language of women's magazines, Rawle's *Woman's World* takes on the very same conversational style, a style made all the more apparent by the direct and apostrophic address of the novel's opening. Interestingly, Winship continues, "the apparent intimate communication between editors and readers contributes to the sense for the reader of entering a 'woman's world' common to the editor and herself alike" (1983: 24). Equally, the opening of *Woman's World* suggests a shared communicative context, or in text-world terms—a textual speech-world, between the first-person narrator and the reader, however illusory and ontologically unstable such a context is in reality.

In the previous section of this chapter, the allure of the second-person pronoun was discussed, leading to the conclusion that readers focalise the narrative from the perspective of the 'you' addressee. However, the degree to which readers will self-implicate and therefore associate with this 'you' enactor is another matter. Section 6.3.4 of Chapter 6 touched upon obstructions to self-implication in second-person fiction in the form of Gavins' (2007b: 86–87) confession to being a resistant reader. Gavins proposes that in second-person literary narratives, where a voice from the text ontologically crosses the 'semipermeable membrane' (McHale 1987: 34–36) between the fictional world and the world of the reader, the author unavoidably makes claims as to the reader's identity. While, in order to follow the narrative, readers necessarily project into the deictic centre of the second-person reference, Gavins asserts that the "closer the resemblance between the life of the text-world enactor and the life of the real reader, the more likely it is the reader will be comfortable inhabiting the new projected text-world persona" (Gavins 2007b: 86). In this section of *Woman's World*, the text does not explicitly dictate the personality of 'you'. However, the language and subject matter that emanate from the 1960s women's magazine cuttings have an implicit ideal reader. Unsurprisingly, this ideal reader is female and has a keen interest in the home and her domestic duties. If this analysis were to take a crude angle here, it might consider that male readers of *Woman's World* are less likely to associate with the 'you' enactor of the text-world, though of course in fact this applies to all readers, regardless of gender, who do not share the implicit domestic interests of the passage.

The identity and subjective appeal of the second-person pronoun in the opening to *Woman's World* is further troubled by the novel's status as a work of collage. While readers necessarily project into the deictic centre of the 'you' role, it can be argued that the apostrophically addressed 'real reader' is not the only referent of the second person here. To claim that s/he were would be to overlook context. In *Story Logic* (2002), Herman discusses what he calls 'contextual anchoring':

> Just as narratives cue interpreters to build temporal and spatial relationships between items and events in the storyworld, and just as they constrain readers, viewers, and listeners to take up perspectives on the items and events at issue, stories trigger recipients to establish a more or less direct or oblique relationship between the stories they are interpreting and the contexts in which they are interpreting them. Or rather, the format of a story can sometimes prompt interpreters to assess the relation between two types of mental models involved in narrative understanding. On the one hand, interpreters build models as part of the process of representing the space-time profile, participant roles, and overall configuration of storyworlds. On the other hand, interpreters rely on analogous, model-based representations of the world(s) in which they are trying to make sense of a given narrative. Contextual anchoring is my name for the process whereby a narrative, in a more or less explicit and reflexive way, asks its interpreters to search for analogies between the representations contained within these two classes of mental models. (331)

In other words, contextual anchoring is a cognitive operation, undertaken by the reader, whereby the boundaries between the space-time parameters of the world of the narrative and the space-time parameters of the world in which reading and interpretation take place are seen as blurred, and therefore seem to coincide. Herman uses his (1994; 2002) conception of doubly deictic *you* (introduced in section 4.2.3 of Chapter 4) as an example of contextual anchoring, whereby "the second-person pronoun grafts the text *more or less* onto its context(s), superimposing the fictional protagonist/addressee *more or less* onto the audience" (Herman 2002: 364). In this book, doubled forms of subjective experience, namely, doubly deictic subjectivity (introduced in section 4.2.9 of Chapter 4, and see also sections 6.3.2, 6.3.3, and 6.3.7 of Chapter 6) and the figured trans-world (see sections 4.2.9 and 4.2.10 of Chapter 4 and section 6.3.7 of Chapter 6), are also instances of contextual anchoring.

The opening to *Woman's World*, "What is your idea of a perfect home? Do you long for a gracious way of living that provides comfort without clutter and an atmosphere of charming elegance throughout the whole house?" (3), can be seen to generate at least two subjective referents through its use of the second person. Primarily, it is the 'real' reader who is apostrophically addressed by the text. In addition, the collage nature of the book, as well as readers' potential knowledge as to the source of the cut-out fragments, works to contextually anchor a further frame of interpretation, that of 1960s women's magazines. If this were in doubt, the words of Amazon.com customer M. A. Lord show just how prevalent this contextual frame can be:

> When I was a child I loved to climb into the window seat behind my grandmother's sofa, draw the curtains so I was hidden from anyone who came into the room, and spend hours pouring over the stack of 1960s *Home Beautiful* and *Woman's Weekly* magazines that resided there. The brittle, yellowing pages held such a visual fascination, with their improbable promises of domestic perfection, and this book transported me right back there. (Website 6 in References)

Clearly, for this reader, there are personal contextual frames being anchored, too. However, it is clear that the cut-and-paste style of *Woman's World* very definitely evokes its 1960s source. Therefore, considering the novel's second-person reference, 'you' addresses at once both the real reader of the text in the twenty-first century and the 1960s women's magazine readership. On one hand, these two referents elicited by the opening address of the novel do not initially appear to be doubly deictic since both 'real' reader and the original 'real' readers of 1960s women's magazines have an actual status, external to the narrative. However, the twenty-first-century reader of *Woman's World* can only access the 1960s readers through the creation of an imagined text-world, triggered by the combination of contextual knowledge and the look and language of the novel. Consequently, a further referent is called forth, in the form of a text-internal *you*, who is a notional enactor of the 1960s female reader and is always implicitly present in the discourse context of *Woman's World*. Figure 7.3 represents the doubly deictic network prompted by the opening address of Rawle's *Woman's World*.

Consequently, I argue that the rhetorical questions that begin *Woman's World* engender double deictic *you*. They emit what Herman describes as an "ontological interference pattern produced by two or more interacting spatio-temporal frames" (2002: 345). As such, the reader's subjective experience of the novel is contrapuntal, or, as Herman phrases it, "In this economy of speech, hearing can no longer be neatly distinguished from overhearing. We are eavesdroppers on the discourse that addresses us and beckoned by discourse addressed to others" (2002: 366). Reading *Woman's World*, we are both addressed by Norma's first-person narrative and privy to the charming rhetoric of women's magazines intended

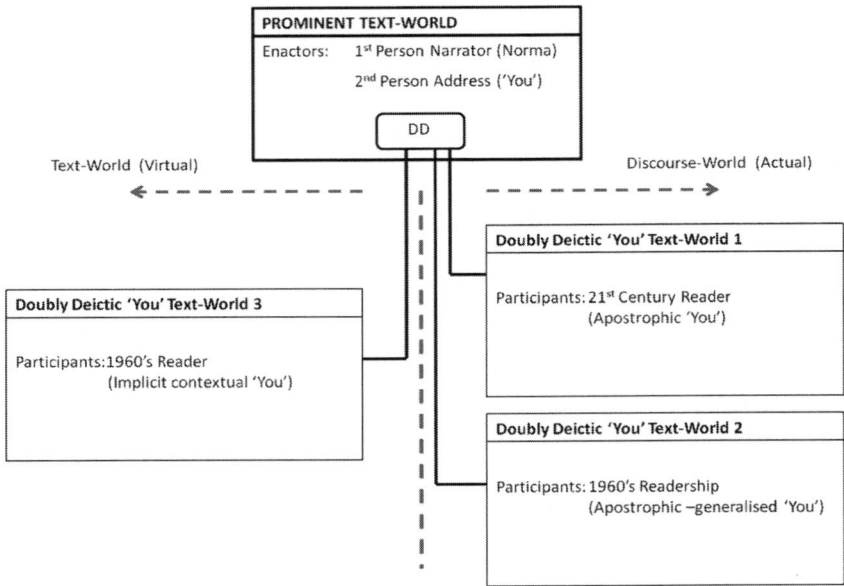

Figure 7.3 Contextual anchoring and double deixis in the opening to *Woman's World*.

for their 1960s readership. Thus, the demarcations between text and context(s) are fuzzy, and the illocutionary force of this discourse is always ontologically multiple.

7.2.4   He Knows How Much I Love My Magazines

The reader of *Woman's World* hears a great deal about Norma's brother Roy, but it is not until the start of Chapter 6 that Norma announces, "ROY *is* HOME" (83). The material realisation of the sentence here does not capture the typographical emphasis with which it is endowed in the novel. 'ROY *is* HOME' takes up a third of the page and uses both capitalisation and italicisation. As such, its meaning is foregrounded and thus loaded, however intentionally, with narrative emphasis. In the chapters prior to Roy's return, Norma goes for a job interview at White's Laundry for the position of delivery man, or delivery *woman* as she tries to advocate. All does not go smoothly, though, as she forgets her proof of identification in the form of her driving license, claiming that it is "in the dresser at home", and arguing that it is unnecessary and of little use, because it is "in my brother's name, though, since he's the one who taught me to drive, it amounts to the same thing. We sort of share it" (43). Norma's liberal views are also affronted, since Mr. White insists he needs a man for the job, causing Norma to feel herself a victim of gender inequality. On her way home, Norma's disappointment is counterbalanced by a chance meeting with an avid photographer called Mr. Hands, with whom she arranges a date to have her portrait taken. This meeting, unfortunately, delays Norma and her late arrival home and lack of success at the interview upset her mother, Mary. Roy's return home is therefore heralded by Norma as a chance to lift Mary's mood and spirits.

Upon his return, Roy goes to interview for the very same job for which he finds himself as successful candidate. It is at the interview that Roy meets Eve, a young woman who becomes the object of his affection. He sees her again a few days later in the local shop where she works. At the time, Roy is in the women's magazine section, absorbed by the latest copy of *Woman's Journal* in which he thinks his sister Norma will be interested:

> "Hallo," she said.
>
> Roy looked up.
>
> It was Eve. Her morning-fresh face was smiling at him from under the row of magazines hanging on a string above her head, and her eyes were alight with that excitement he had seen in them before. To-day she wore a pink cardigan—a soft pink it was, the colour of hedge roses in June, very becoming indeed to Eve's fair skin, to her soft ringed hair that held the warmth of chestnut in its brown. To complete the outfit, she wore a gemstone brooch and the scenes of London scarf I had left in the waiting room. It was the perfect colour combination and I have to admit, even though it was really my scarf that added the finishing touch, that this young woman had an enviable sense of style.
>
> "Hello," said Roy. (102–103)

The importance and attention Roy bestows on Eve is clear from the descriptive detail Rawle presents between their conversational turns, Hallo—Hello. Additionally, the description of Eve is interesting since it is representative of the narrative style of *Woman's World*. Of course, the twee 1960s women's magazine voice is present, romanticising Eve through flowery language, literally in this case since much of Rawle's descriptive prose is underscored with metaphors of nature: 'Her *morning-fresh* face', 'her eyes were *alight*', 'the *colour of hedge roses in June*', 'warmth of *chestnut* in its brown'.

As previously mentioned, Norma is *Woman's World*'s homodiegetic narrator, setting up a dialogue with the reader through recurrent second-person address. Prior to Roy's return, the narrative has been dominated by Norma's internal focalisation. However, as can be seen in the preceding extract, Roy's arrival complicates the singularity of character focalisation. That is, while Norma remains the central narrating character and an internal character-focaliser, she also has an omniscience which enables her to penetrate Roy's consciousness. In the preceding passage, for instance, Roy is clearly the one whom is looking intently at Eve, and yet the language of

1960s women's magazines which is so predominant in the description of Eve is most closely associated with Norma's character. Norma's narratorial influence becomes explicit in the final two sentences of description, mentioning her own scarf and adding the admiring comment, "It was the perfect colour combination and I have to admit, even though it was really my scarf that added the finishing touch, that this young woman had an enviable sense of style". Thus, from a reader's perspective, the focalisation of the narrative seems to shift between Roy and Norma.

A further example shows the intertwining of character consciousness more acutely. A few chapters later, Roy is being questioned by nosey neighbour Mrs. Price about a mysterious young woman Mrs. Price has seen at Roy and Norma's home. This is an altercation Roy is keen to extricate himself from, not enjoying Mrs. Price's gossip-fuelled interrogations. The narration explains:

> Roy stepped inside the house, hoping to terminate the conversation, but Mrs. Price was like a terrier tugging at a bit of rope. How would Marjorie in *Woman's Day* have suggested he handle it? "What a pity I can't invite you in," you must say regretfully. "As you see, I'm just tackling the stair carpet. But you must come one day when I've made some of my special chocolate cakes. What about tea next Friday at four?" No, he couldn't make cakes and he didn't want her there on Friday. He didn't want her there at all. (132)

The extract opens with narrative description, including an amusing metaphorical comparison of Mrs. Price to an overeager terrier. However, it then moves into free indirect thought (How would Marjorie in *Woman's Day* have suggested he handle it?) before representing the imagined advice proffered in women's magazines as direct speech (of which there are two levels—Marjorie's advice to 1960s readers and the words she suggest those readers utter). As is generally accepted in stylistics (Bray 2007; Simpson 2004: 82), such free indirect discourse creates the impression of a dual voice, blurring the clarity of narrator and character. However, this is typically understood to be an external narrator and an internal character, whereas in this instance we have a *character*-narrator and a further character. Moreover, since it is Norma who is the keen magazine reader, it initially seems that this may simply be her narrative interjection, a possibility that may be supported by the use of the simple conditional tense. This possibility, though, is not supported when the narration continues again with a piece of free indirect discourse that leaves no doubt as to the presence of Roy's consciousness ('No, he couldn't make cakes'). As such, the language of *Woman's World* leads to a complex style of narration, not merely shifting between character consciousnesses but presenting moments in which the focalisation seems indistinct, imbruing it with a sense of multiplicity. Thus, just as second-person address was shown, in the previous section of this chapter, to have multiple referents, the first-person narrative voice also seems subjectively insecure.

Having considered the development of *Woman's World*'s focalisation subsequent to Roy's return within the narrative, it seems apparent that the narration of the novel merges the voice and tone of 1960s women's magazines with both Norma as narrator and internal focaliser and Roy as an additional internal focalising character, making *Woman's World* highly polyphonic in nature. Interestingly, this seems in keeping with the culture of the source texts, 1960s women's magazines, since different features would be written by different authors, shaped for different genres and thus use differing rhetorical styles (e.g. letters pages, fashion advice, recipes, fiction); and of course all of these styles feed into the overall voice and tone of each magazine. We might thus think of women's magazines as already containing a 'collage' of voices, but that their collage is in some ways concealed by overall style principles. Moreover, in terms of *Woman's World*, it is possible to suggest a subversive correspondence between the prescriptive yet friendly address of 1960s women's magazines and the blurred focalisation of Rawle's novel. The women's magazine is sold to its readers as an invaluable 'friend', ready to offer advice on all aspect of feminine life. Comparably, Norma's seemingly omniscient presence at this point in the novel, infringing upon focalisation anchored to Roy, constructs her and the 1960s women's magazine speakers as what we might think of as Roy's additional constant companions, with advice and opinions in abundance. In section 7.2.8 of this chapter, I return to the complex focalisation of the novel, showing that it becomes even more involved as the story progresses.

7.2.5   Writing and Reading the Cut-And-Paste Collage

Nearly half-way through the novel, and life is looking up for Roy and Norma: Roy's job at White's Laundry is going well and Norma is looking forward to her photographic debut in a portrait session with Mr. Hands. Norma embarks on this adventure one Friday night. Figure 7.4 shows the opening to Chapter 13, with Norma on Mr. Hands's doorstep. As with each and every page of the novel, page 209 exhibits the shifting typography that characterises *Woman's World*.

Rawle talks about the creation of page 209 in *New York Magazine* (Kachka 2008), explaining his choice of elements and dissecting the page into its various cut-out pieces. Rawle's discussion provides a rare opportunity to compare a writer's intentions with the experience of real readers. With this in mind, I conducted a small-scale pilot study of readers' responses to the text, sourcing volunteers to participate in the study through a social networking site. Volunteers received the documentation for the study via email and were asked to return the completed report in the post. Although some of the initial volunteers did not complete the task, ultimately twenty-five participants did read the extract, annotating it with their immediate responses, before

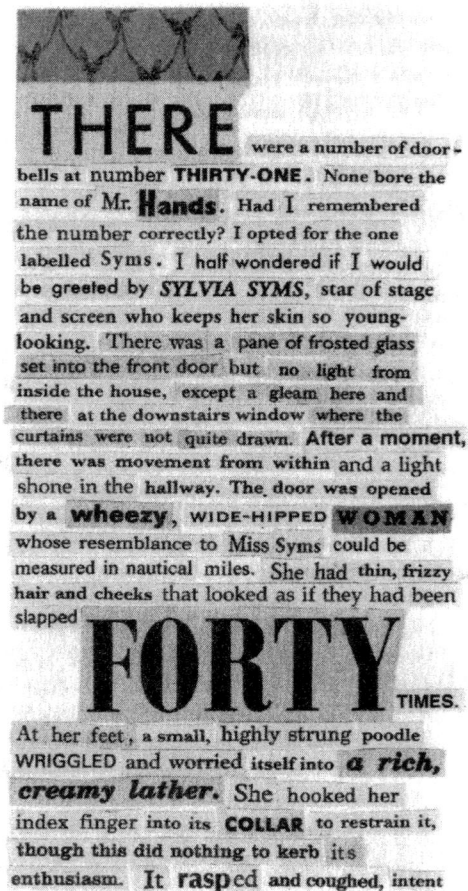

THERE were a number of door-bells at number **THIRTY-ONE**. None bore the name of Mr. **Hands**. Had I remembered the number correctly? I opted for the one labelled Syms. I half wondered if I would be greeted by *SYLVIA SYMS*, star of stage and screen who keeps her skin so young-looking. There was a pane of frosted glass set into the front door but no light from inside the house, except a gleam here and there at the downstairs window where the curtains were not quite drawn. After a moment, there was movement from within and a light shone in the hallway. The door was opened by a **wheezy**, WIDE-HIPPED **WOMAN** whose resemblance to Miss Syms could be measured in nautical miles. She had thin, frizzy hair and cheeks that looked as if they had been slapped **FORTY** TIMES. At her feet, a small, highly strung poodle WRIGGLED and worried itself into *a rich, creamy lather.* She hooked her index finger into its **COLLAR** to restrain it, though this did nothing to kerb its enthusiasm. It **rasp**ed and coughed, intent

209

Figure 7.4 Rawle (2005) *Woman's World*: 209.

answering a short questionnaire. The group of participants was composed of fifteen females (60 per cent) and ten males (40 per cent) with a range of ages: four at twenty-one to twenty-five years (16 per cent), eight at twenty-six to thirty years (32 per cent), six at thirty-one to thirty-five years (24 per cent), three at thirty-six to forty years (12 per cent), one at forty-one to forty-five years (4 per cent), one at forty-six to fifty years (4 per cent), and two over fifty-one years (8 per cent). The group also had diversity of education with 20 per cent holding a bachelor's degree (one in the arts, four in the sciences), 52 per cent holding postgraduate qualifications (ten in the arts, three in the sciences), and 28 per cent having not been to university (see Appendix A for participant profiles). The participants were informed in advanced reading matter that the extract came from Graham Rawle's (2005) *Woman's World* and that it was a collage novel, assembled from 1960s women's magazines. Given the scale of this empirical study, future research is needed to investigate the effects of multimodal literature on the reading experience in greater depth. Nevertheless, while the results presented in this chapter are seen to be by no means conclusive when it comes to reader's encounters of multimodal novels, they do serve to provide an insight into the experiences of real readers of *Woman's World*.

Several readers instantly pointed to the extract's multimodality by either highlighting its cut-out nature as a work of collage (two readers) or by suggesting, as some reviewers have done (Loeb and Girl, Interrupting 2008), that it looks like an anonymous letter or ransom note (four readers). One reader even goes so far as to use the imagistic nature of the text as a basis for making narrative inferences: "gives the impression that it's going to be about a secretive woman who sends anonymous letters (cut-out from newspapers)" (R-19). Clearly the imagistic nature of the text was remarkable to many of the participants.

Rawle's commentary is considered in both this section and the next two sections of this chapter. While Rawle offers nine notes to the text, I will not look at each and everyone one. Rather, two salient points will be examined here, with a further three discussed in section 7.2.6, and another one in section 7.2.7. In *New York Magazine*, Rawle's reflections on the page begin at its opening:

> I think the word *there* was originally part of a title for a feature in [the magazine] *Woman's Own*. Above it was a picture, the lower part of which showed a drab wallpaper background. When cutting out the word, I decided to include a fragment of it because the scene describes such an interior. (Kachka 2008; original emphasis)

Most of the participants did not remark on this aspect of the extract, though one intrigued reader (R-16) did write "What is this!?", an arrow next to which pointed to the wallpaper image. Of the twenty-five participants, only five (20 per cent) related the patterned section of the cut-out to wallpaper, but for these participants the connection seems to have been both clear and strong. They write:

> "This reminds me of wallpaper in a period house." (R-3)

> "Wallpaper? Think of a house/corridor—girly." (R-4)

> "Makes me think of wallpaper, having read the description of the house." (R-9)

> "Makes you think of an old woman's house not decorated since the 40s. Puts you into the frame of mind before you even start reading the text." (R-13)

"Odd to have some wallpaper—give the impression of a 'faded glory' kind of person—someone who wants to be seen as romantic." (R-19)

The responses of Reader 3, Reader 4, and Reader 13 all suggest solid associations are conjured up by the image. Reader 3 and Reader 13, for instance, both connect the wallpaper to a previous era, while Reader 4 calls it 'girly' and Reader 19 uses it to infer characterisation. These responses can be nicely linked to *Woman's World*'s source texts. Additionally, Reader 9's comment, "Makes me think of wallpaper, having read the description of the house", is interesting from the perspective of a study in multimodality, since it shows that the reader is drawing connections between text and image, allowing the linguistic description of a house to trigger a context of understanding for the opening image.

The image itself also appears to play a key role in readers' deictic shift or projection into the world of the text, perhaps not least because it is accompanied by the spatial adverb 'there'. As discussed in section 4.2.1 of Chapter 4, the opening of a novel presents the first boundary across which readers must deictically shift. While this is not the first sentence of *Woman's World*, it is the opening to a chapter, and moreover the first encounter with the text for the participants of this study. As such, their comments enable a consideration of the ways in which multimodal texts may evoke projection as well as create storyworlds. For Reader 4, the image suggests a house or corridor, and these locations can be seen as providing important world-building information. Reader 13's remarks, on the other hand, are rather self-reflexive. Having identified the image (later in his responses, he explicitly talks of it as wallpaper) with a house, he reflects, "Puts you into the frame of mind before you even start reading the text". For this reader, it seems that the image generates a narrative context in the form of a vivid text-world (the old woman's house, mentioned by the reader) from which the succeeding linguistic narrative departs.

In the second half of page 209, the word 'FORTY' is presented in bold capital letters, its font size far larger than any of the surrounding text. Rawle explains rather nonchalantly, "The word *forty* happened to be sitting on the top of my numbers file as I was pasting down the words, so I stuck it in. It also added a nice graphic element to the page" (Kachka 2008; original emphasis). Rawle's decision to use this fragment in particular is made to seem rather arbitrary in his explanation. However, readers found this item of the text to be undeniably eye-catching with eleven readers (44 per cent) signalling it as important. Of these readers, the word 'FORTY' was considered on a merely visual level by two readers; one of whom (R-25) wanted to know why it was so large in size, while the other (R-24) said that when she was reading it, this was the word she "noticed first and it kept standing out". The remaining nine readers linked the visuality of the word to its narrative context. In the extract, the word appears in the sentence, "She had thin, frizzy hair and cheeks that looked as if they had been slapped forty times" (209). Some said that it created emphasis, while others went even further:

"! Adds mock value." (R-6)

"Foregrounded—first word I noticed. [. . .] Very red cheeks?! Wonder why the narrator has chosen the number forty?" (R-9)

"Exaggeration? Size seems to make it implausible." (R-11)

"Large bold type gives emphasis to her very rosy cheeks." (R-12)

"Emphasises the number of slaps by having such a big font." (R-18)

For these readers, the typographical size and style of the word 'forty' work in concert with the narrative, accentuating the description of the woman's cheeks. Reader 9 and Reader 12, for example, specifically attribute colour to the cheeks (red and rosy, respectively), colour not explicitly mentioned in the text, but which the combination of words and image in *Woman's World* has established within their visual imagination. Furthermore, the mentions of 'mock value' by Reader 6 and implausibility by Reader 11 imply that the pictorial quality of words, the way in which typography can be manipulated and designed, can lead to the creation of an inferred narrative tone, here one of irony and perhaps even humour. Indeed, one reader particularly (R-23) found much of the extract to be highly amusing, including the sentence in which the word 'forty' appears next to which he had emphatically scribbled "made me laugh out loud!" (I revisit this reader's engagement with the text in section 7.2.7)

The examination of page 209 thus far draws parallels between Graham Rawle's authorial intentions and decisions and the way in which the text is received by real readers. Three central implications emerge as a result. Firstly, it shows the implicit influence of the 1960s women's magazines upon the reading experience of *Woman's World*. The original contexts infiltrate the new narrative world(s) created by Rawle. This was suggested in sections 7.2.3 and 7.2.4 of this chapter in relation to textual voice (second-person address and focalisation, respectively), but the responses of real readers demonstrate that the source texts' presence is much more pervasive. Thus when reading this novel, the text-worlds encountered by readers are always, to a greater or lesser degree, blended worlds. That is to say that the text-worlds of the novel cannot escape from the underlying source of the 1960s women's magazine fragments, and so the textural experience of the storyworld of *Woman's World* features an inevitable synthesis and layering of worlds and contexts.

Secondly, the responses of real readers evidences that interpretative connections are made between word and image, including the pictorial qualities of words as found in typographical meaning-making, when reading multimodal novels. Connected to this is the third and final implication:

Visual elements in texts may have world-building properties in themselves, a finding that is important for cognitive poetics since Text World Theory as a discourse-processing framework has a linguistic bias. The language of page 209 is the focus of the following section, considering if and how visuality influences linguistic awareness and imaginative process.

7.2.6　Recycled Language and 'Hand-Me-Down' Images

Rawle's *Woman's World* is examined in *if:book*, the thought-provoking blog from the Institute for the Future of the Book. In his consideration of the novel, Visel, a literary scholar and designer, creates a neutral typesetting of one of *Woman's World*'s pages, since he believes "the difference between reading a plain text version of Rawle's story and the collaged version of the same" shows up the complex strata of language. Reading both versions, he claims, shows that "something is lost in my translation" (Visel 2008). Certainly, it would be interesting to see how differences in presentation impact upon reader's enjoyment and engagement with the novel. To this end, I conducted the empirical study outlined above with a further group of eleven participants: eight females (72.7 per cent), three males (27.3 per cent); one at twenty-one to twenty-three years (9.1 per cent), seven at twenty-six to thirty years (63.6 per cent), and three at thirty-one to thirty-five years (27.3 per cent) (see Appendix B for participant profiles). The methodology for this study was identical to the aforementioned study, the only difference was that this group were not told about *Woman's World*'s collage production and were shown instead a mock-up of the same page, presented in a more 'traditional' format. The two versions of page 209 are shown in Figure 7.5. The purpose of the second empirical study, therefore, was to enable a comparison of the reading experience of multimodal literature and literature which has a more conventional appearance.

The starting-point for this comparative analysis is a consideration of Rawle's language. Rawle utilises the advertisements found in women's magazines as well as the magazines' own contents. Indeed, ruminating on his description of Sylvia Syms, Rawle says, "Celebrity endorsed products were common in 1962. I think this bit came from an ad for a moisturizing cream used by British screen actress Sylvia Syms, which said something to the effect of: 'Look over there. Isn't that Sylvia Syms, star of stage and screen who keeps her skin so young-looking?'" (Kachka 2008). Among the readers of the original version of *Woman's World*, three readers (12 per cent) found this description particularly poignant, two of them gesturing towards the advertising quality of the language. The third of these readers, Reader 18, was also fascinated by the visual presentation of the text about Sylvia Syms. Reader 18 annotated the extract saying, "the poster-like presentation of her name makes you feel she must be a 'star'". Additionally, when asked in the questionnaire if she visualised any particular parts of

There were a number of door-bells at number thirty-one. None bore the name of Mr. Hands. Had I remembered the number correctly? I opted for the one labelled Sym. I half wondered if I would be greeted by Sylvia Syms, star of stage and screen who keeps her skin so young-looking. There was a pane of frosted glass set into the front door but no light from inside the house, except a gleam here and there at the downstairs window where the curtains were not quite drawn. After a moment, there was movement from within and a light shone in the hallway. The door was opened by a wheezy, wide-hipped woman whose resemblance to Miss Syms could be measured in nautical miles. She had thin, frizzy hair and cheeks that looked as if they have been slapped forty times.

At her feet, a small, highly strung poodle wriggled and worried itself into a rich, creamy lather. She hooked her index finger into its collar to restrain it, though this did nothing to keb its enthusiasm. It rasped and coughed, intent

209

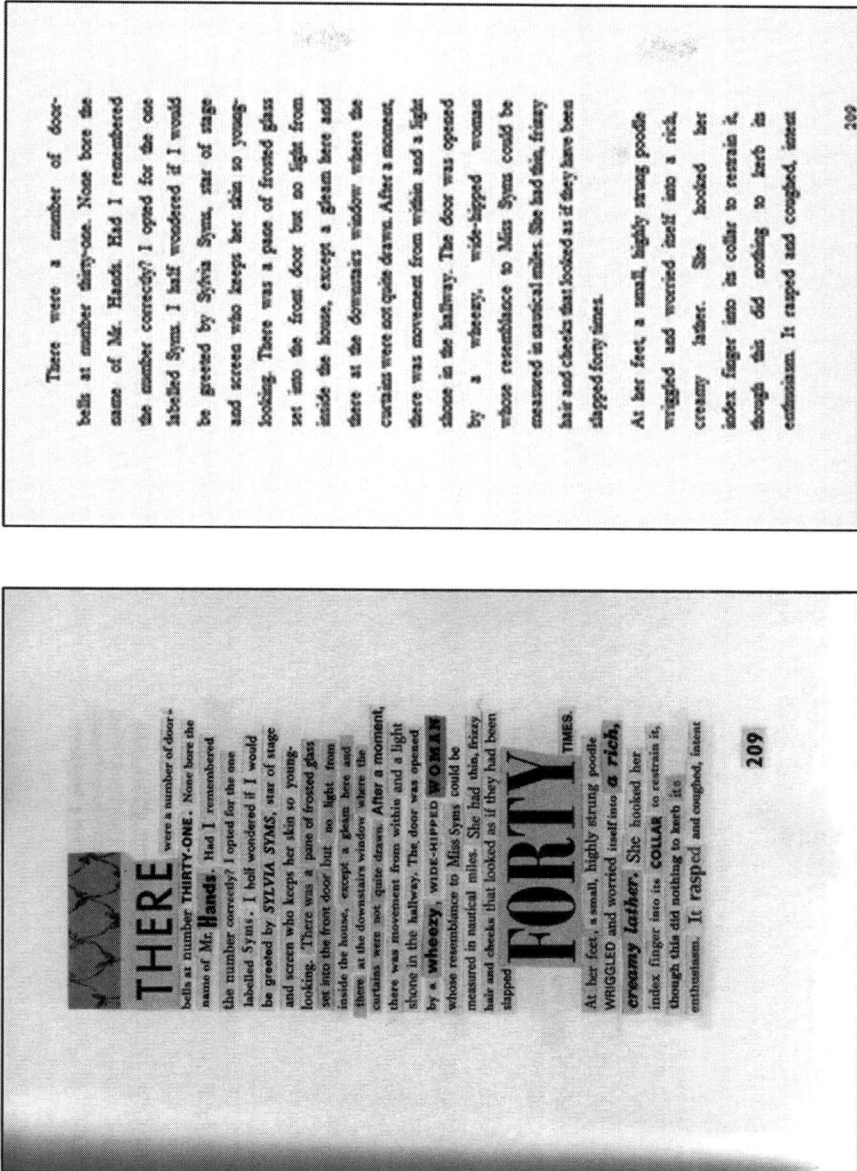

Figure 7.5 Rawle (2005) *Woman's World*: 209 alongside the traditional mock-up.

the extract, Reader 18 commented, "I visualised Sylvia Syms as some kind of poster or placard". Therefore, it seems that the context of the source text, that of an advertisement which drew on the cult of celebrity, filtered into Reader 18's reading experience. Not only does the extract's language and presentation heighten the sense of stardom surrounding the invocation of Sylvia Syms, but, for Reader 18 at least, the nature of the language and presentation, having been sourced from a beauty product advertisement, actually infiltrates the reader's visual experience. Consequently, we might take this as further evidence of the prevalence of blended worlds in reading collage.

Towards the end of page 209 sits the following description: "a highly strung poodle wriggled and worried itself into a rich, creamy lather". Discussing this line, Rawle discloses that the 'rich, creamy lather' is "a phrase I found in an advertisement for beauty soap" (Kachka 2008). Amongst the readers of the traditionally presented mock-up, only two readers (18.18 per cent) linked the description to advertising discourse: Reader B wrote "Like a soap" (R-B), while Reader A identified both the characterisation of the poodle and the earlier description of Sylvia Syms as from a "Soap advert" (R-A). Amongst the readers of the 'true' *Woman's World* extract, we find similar figures, with five readers (16 per cent) pinpointing the specific instances of advertising language, and an additional reader (totalling six readers; 24 per cent) comparing the extract's language more generally to the field of advertising. Indeed, one of these readers had very strong brand associations, saying that the metaphor or the poodle's movement "made me think of imperial leather soap we had as a kid" (R-23). Interestingly, the imaginative visualisation of two of these readers was influenced by the advertising context: Reader 18, as discussed earlier, imagined Sylvia Syms in a poster-like way, while Reader 15, talking about whether she visualised any of the characters, believed that the "Poodle would be white and fluffy as bubble/soap as the 'rich, creamy lather' suggests". Furthermore, it is notable that many of the readers of the original page 209 explicitly saw the visuality of the extract as a trigger for their interpretations of the text's advertising language, as seen in the following explanations:

> "The kind of font that would be used to advertise hot chocolate!" (R-18) [In reference to the description of the poodle]

> "[C]hanged the meaning of the section to one of an advert style or sensationalist style." (R-22) [On the collage presentation of the extract]

Consequently, while there appears to be an approximate correspondence between the percentage of readers in the two participant groups who noticed the advertising language of the text, it is credible to suggest that the multimodal version, by maintaining the original typography of the adverts, enhanced the effect of such language in terms of both readers' imaginative visualisations and the strength of their associations with brands and product types.

In the *New York Magazine* feature, Rawle considers the way in which the process of creating the text metamorphoses his original words into the final linguistic eccentricities of *Woman's World*:

> The line I had in mind ended with something like, " . . . ; whose resemblance to Sylvia Syms was extremely remote." Having previously categorized my found material into specific subjects, I searched my "measuring and distance" category for the word *remote* but instead found the phrase ". . . could be measured in nautical miles." Much better. (Kachka 2008)

In his commentary, Rawle offers a positive value judgement, an appreciation of the verbal art of the original source material. As he expounds in an interview with Doig (2008), the process of creating the text "forced me to be more inventive in the way I constructed sentences. It's one of those truisms that's always true of the creative process: if you place rigid restrictions on it, it enables you to kick against it". As such, the corpus of reader-responses was examined in order to observe the extent to which the different groups of readers found the linguistic peculiarity of the phrase '. . . could be measured in nautical miles' noteworthy. Six out of eleven of the readers (55.6 per cent) who read the traditional mock-up of page 209 marked the word out in some way (underlining, circling, etc.), with one reader going so far as to comment in the margin, "I love the entirely unnecessary use of 'nautical'" (R-A). Certainly, it is phrases such as this that lead Poyner (2005) to marvel, "In his inspired use of simile, [Rawle] is a kitchen-sink surrealist". In contrast with the readers of the mock-up, within the group of participants who read the original version of page 209, only three readers (12 per cent) mark out the phrase '. . . could be measured in nautical miles', one of whom also writes in the margin "Funny" (R-20). In consequence, it is possible to deduce that for readers of the extract as it appears in *Woman's World*, the multimodality of the text offers a barrage of stimuli and as such, the distinctiveness of the phrase '. . . could be measured in nautical miles' is less apparent.

On one hand, it might appear that the comparisons of readers' responses to advertising language and linguistic idiosyncrasy throw up an anomaly, in that the readers of the original *Woman's World* extract were more observant when it came to noticing the advertising language of the extract but less mindful of the passage's linguistic eccentricities. At the core of this seeming incongruity, though, is the correlation between the words and imagistic dimensions of the text. In Chapter 5's discussion of bistable oscillation when reading Steve Tomasula's (2002) *VAS: An Opera in Flatland* (section 5.2.8 through to the conclusion), it was suggested that when imagistic representations complemented linguistic content narrative immersion was aided, while divergences between word and image had the potential to impede such immersion. A similar phenomenon appears to be occurring with readers' language awareness. Marketing and advertising make great use of the visual facets of writing in creating brand identities and for communicating brand messages. To put it another way, they exploit the iconic meaning of typography. As culturally exposed beings, readers are accustomed to encountering writing in this format and interpreting the synthesis of word and image in typography appropriately, thus the same process is at work for readers of the *Woman's World* extract. In contrast, amidst the multimodality of the original version of page 209, the typographical style of 'could be measured in nautical miles' does not enhance its meaning, nor does it play on the nautical theme. Moreover, in *Woman's World*, 'could be measured in nautical miles' is presented in a less visually arresting way to surrounding text, thus explaining its reduced figural attraction. Within the traditional mock-up, however, there are fewer visual distractions and the phrase's linguistic oddity makes it a good textual attractor, matching Stockwell's figure-creating category of 'aesthetic distance from the norm' (2009: 25). The context within which textual elements appear, the intensity of the possible textual attractors around them, must therefore influence readers' attention and depth of processing.

7.2.7　Collage's Surreal Sounds and Visions across Oscillating Worlds

In terms of comparing the reading experience of traditional and multimodal literature, a key question given to participants was 'Do you think the way the novel is presented affected your reading?' Strikingly, nine of the readers (81.9 per cent) of the traditional text answered yes, while the remaining two readers (18.1 per cent) simply answered that they didn't know. The responses given by these readers unanimously said that they found the text easy to read. There were varying reasons for this—"typesetting of a narrow column" (R-B), "larger text and space" (R-E), "the text being well spaced out on the page" (R-J)—but the verdict is undeniable. Unsurprisingly, the readers of the multimodal version similarly deemed the presentation of the text as important, with twenty-four readers (96 per cent) answering yes and the remaining reader (4 per cent) answering no. However, this group of readers had a much more varied response when asked to elaborate. In line with the Jezebel.com blog readers' initial reactions, discussed in section 7.2.1 of this chapter, ten readers (40 per cent) of the multimodal extract found the typography "distracting" (a variant of this word appears six times in the corpus of responses) or said that it made their reading feel "disjointed" (a variant of this word appears twice in the corpus).

The corpus of responses of real readers of *Woman's World* did, though, reveal further nuances in the form of the following readers' comments:

"Although reading in my head, the type face, size of characters etc. made me read the text differently, putting emphasis on different words and seeing their significance differently." (R-3)

"The size of the typing made me hear the words like they would be spoken e.g. larger was louder." (R-11)

"The way the whole paragraph has been written feels very disjointed, almost emphasising it not being spoken by the same person, i.e. phrases/ words taken from the different articles and put together to form the above paragraph." (R-13)

"The narrator's voice in my head conformed to the contours of the text, so that words such as 'wheezy' and 'woman' were heavily emphasised." (R-16)

Interestingly, three of the four readers quoted above refer specifically to cognitive process; Reader 3 and Reader 16 are highly aware of what's going on 'in my head', while Reader 11 talks about hearing the words 'like they would be spoken'. In section 3.4.1 of Chapter 3, I introduced the concept of multisensory perception, that is, the way in which our brain processes differing sensory stimuli in an integrative manner with the combination of incoming stimuli resulting in enhanced neurological responses. From this, I suggested that the combination of modes in multimodal literature may engender more intense narrative experiences. Arguably, this claim is borne out by the confessions of these readers as to their enhanced awareness of their cognitive and perceptual experience of the text.

From these readers' comments, we may also deduce that typographical design, changes in type-face, and font size impact upon a reader's experience of the text, and in particular their sense of the 'voice' of the narrative. These readers' insights indicate two related effects of the varying typography. The first is one of the three semiotic principles of typographical meaning as outlined in section 2.3.6 of Chapter 2 (see also Nørgaard 2009b; van Leeuwen 2006): iconicity, whereby type-face visually resembles its meaning. In her investigation of the semiotics of typography in literary texts, Nørgaard analysed the way in which capitalisation in character speech can function to indicate shouting while italics may comparably construct a mocking tone or suggest whispering (2009b: 150–151). Obviously, the iconic meaning of type is somewhat dependent on narrative context, yet Nørgaard uses her examples to deftly suggest a parallel between visual salience and perceived sonic salience. Readers of *Woman's World* are reporting a similar phenomenon, except without a narrative context to support such iconic meaning. Nevertheless, the typographical emphasis in the extract of page 209 in the form of capitalisation, emboldened words, and larger font style is evoking sonic salience in the perception of the narrator's voice (or delivery of voice, if you will) for Reader 3, Reader 11, and Reader 16. As such, since there is no justifiable narrative context for the visual to sonic salience experienced by these readers, their comments reveal the power of connection between aspects of typography and certain forms of iconic meaning.

The second effect of the varying typography is the perception of textual polyphony, briefly discussed in section 7.2.4 of this chapter. You may recall that in section 7.2.1, I mentioned a Jezebel.com blog reader who, having embarked upon reading *Woman's World*, claimed to be finding it frustrating. In fact, the reason behind her frustration is directly related to the readerly perception of narrative voice. She exclaims, "AHHH it's driving me crazy! I feel like I have a million different loud voices in my head: 'WELLLL miss fontaine take THE TEAcup and WE'LL have a CHAT OKAY!!?!?!?'" (missgolightly 2008, Website 7; original emphasis). Interestingly, missgolightly (as she calls herself online) uses the very technique that has led to her annoyance to depict the words of the novel as well as place emphasis on her own frustrated outburst. For both missgolightly and for Reader 13, the differing type-faces have corresponding differing vocal qualities, again a form of typographical iconic meaning-making. Moreover, Reader 13 relates the polyvocal nature of the text to its mode of production, providing further evidence of the influence of the 1960s women's magazines upon the reading experience of *Woman's World*.

Another remarkable difference between the two participant groups relates to their capacity for visualisation when reading the extract. When asked, "Do you visualise any particular parts of the scene?", all eleven readers (100 per cent) in the traditional mock-up study answered yes and were able to provide details (who, what, and how) of their imaginative visions. While many such imaginative visualisations were not out of the ordinary, two of these readers had very striking responses. In elaborating on his visualisations, in this section of the questionnaire, Reader C discloses, "Nautical Miles—pictured a whale". For this reader, the semantics of the premodifying adjective 'nautical' is having a profound influence on his imaginative visualisation. Moreover, both Reader C and Reader H had bizarre imaginative reactions to the character of Mr. Hands. In *New York Magazine*, Rawle justifies the name for the character of Mr. Hands, saying:

> One of the problems with using only found fragments to assemble my story was finding multiples of people's names, which were repeated many times throughout the novel. I decided on Mr. Hands for my antagonist because the word *hands* is easy to come by in adverts for nail polish, soap powders, and the like. The name also describes his licentious, groping nature. (Kachka 2008; original emphasis)

For Reader H, Mr. Hands' 'licentious, groping nature' is implicit in her visualisation. In the margin next to his name, she wrote, "Urgh—lots of hands—creepy" (R-H). Similarly, for Reader C, the mention of Mr. Hands conjures up "a face made up of hands, like in the film *Labyrinth*" (R-C). Other readers saw Mr. Hands as mysterious and/or sinister, but these two readers have an almost surreal imaginative construal of Mr. Hands, a visualisation that, judging by their comments, seems lucid, vivid, and emotionally affecting.

A slight difference can be seen in the responses of the readers of the multimodal original extract, with twenty-one readers (84 per cent) answering yes and four readers (16 per cent) answering no. Moreover, in this group, while readers did admit to having the sorts of visual imagery one would expect with reading (e.g. what characters look like), some of the visualisations they describe are clearly inflected by the imagistic quality of the extract they read: for example, the archaic look of the house stems from the wallpaper cut-out (discussed in section 7.2.5); the advertising language and typography embedding their advert contexts into readers' imaginative reconstructions (discussed in the previous section). The comparative survey presented here is, of course, exploratory and far from extensive. However, the differences in readers' reports of their visualisations suggest that the experience of reading traditional and multimodal literature is not equivalent. Multimodality palpably impacts upon the nature of readers' literary visualisation and the ways in which they experience imagined worlds.

Having considered the responses of the two groups of readers to both the concrete presentation of the text and their capacity to visualise the scene, it seems a logical analytical move to return to the question of the experience of reading and imagining text-worlds in the form of bistable oscillation. Bistable oscillation, developed in section 5.2.8 through to the conclusion of Chapter 5, is the cognitive and perceptual process by which a reader's experience of the text shifts from the surface of the page (the at level) to the narrative world(s) (the through level), and vice versa. The responses of the participants who read the original collage version of page 209 appear to offer support for bistable oscillation in reading multimodal texts. Three readers provide particularly fascinating reflections on their reading of the extract. Reader 23's annotations are quite telling. You may recall in section 7.2.5, Reader 23 was mentioned because he found the text rather amusing: his marginalia indicated that he laughed out loud at the description of the woman who looked as if her cheeks 'had been slapped forty times', as well as at Rawle's description of the poodle. Such visceral reactions show that he is engaging with the extract on a cognitive level. He also claims within the questionnaire to have experienced visualisations of the scene—soap (presumably invoked by the metaphor), the dog and its actions, the woman opening the door (who incidentally apparently looked like someone he knew!). However, Reader 23's cognitive and perceptual attention cannot have been consistently focused within an imagined text-world, since early on in his annotations of page 209 he writes, "Started to notice where cut-and-paste had been done and tried to work out where the 'breaks' were" (R-23). Then again at the end of the extract, he jots, "noticed join here"

(R-23) with an arrow pointing to the word 'rasped' which is noticeably (through typography as well as paper cutting) composed of two different textual particles, the free morpheme 'rasp' and the inflectional morpheme '-ed'. Indeed, using second person self-reflexively, Matwychuk (2008) muses "every sentence become unusually compelling—you can't help marvelling at how cleverly he'll take words of clauses from two, three, four, even five different sources and link them into a brand new sentence that makes grammatical and literary sense". The combination of imaginative visualisation and attention to the surface of the page within Reader 23's account of his reading experience tenders support for bistable oscillation. Further verification can be found in Reader 4's observations as to how he thought the collage presentation affected his reading: "Had to concentrate a bit more + gave me a physical feeling as well as imagination involved with reading" (R-4). Here, Reader 4 cites both the physical *and* imaginative elements of his reading experience.

Although the comments of Reader 4 and Reader 23 proffer support enough for bistable oscillation, I also want to look at the remarks of Reader 16, since his response is slightly different. When asked if he visualised any particular aspects of the scene, Reader 16 offered the followed response:

> Yes, but it's all a little bit abstract. Influenced by the materiality of the text, and words such as 'labelled' or phrases that were obviously from elsewhere—'star of stage and screen who keeps her skin so young looking'—I couldn't help but visualise a rather strange papery world! (R-16)

In his reference to the 'materiality of the text' and pinpointing of specific parts, it seems implicit that during his reading of page 209, Reader 16 did experience certain moments in which his attention was focused upon the at/surface of the text. Moreover, the fact that he can pinpoint particular moments suggests that this surface-level focus was not consistent, thus we may suppose that at times his perceptual capacities had moved through and into imagined text-worlds. What is really fascinating about Reader 16's remark, though, is his admission to visualising 'a rather strange papery world'. In section 5.2.10 of Chapter 5, I related the process of bistable oscillation to Gavins' (2007b) conception of the blended world, a text-world space which mergers pre- and/or coexisting text-worlds. I suggest that Reader 16's vision of a 'a rather strange papery world' can be seen as a blended world in itself, featuring a synthesis of the textual surface of the page that catches his attention as well as the content of the imagined text-world created by the linguistic narrative.

Since section 7.2.5, I have been looking at the responses of real readers to page 209 of Graham's Rawle's *Woman's World*, and in this section specifically I have considered readers' concrete engagement with the text, their experience of narrative voice and visualisation, finally linking these to the process of bistable oscillation. In his review of *Woman's World*, Poynor (2005) touches on many of these issues when he asks:

Would *Woman's World* be as engaging if Rawle had presented it as an unwrinkled text in a single type style? Probably not. The changes of typeface allow you to see how he has fashioned each sentence and this adds to the pleasure. Early digital typographers liked to talk about 'activating' text and allowing it to speak in a more complex array of typographic voices. It has rarely been done so wittily. The different typefaces, type sizes and degrees of emphasis become an inseparable part of the prose's texture and tone, while evoking the printed sources with great vividness.

I am not inclined to disagree with Poynor when it comes to the virtuosity of *Woman's World*. He does, nevertheless, ask a provocative question, and one which I hope to have addressed in sections 7.2.5, 7.2.6, and 7.2.7 of this chapter. Based on the two exploratory empirical studies of real readers, it has been shown that there are differences in the ways in which readers engage with traditional-looking texts and *Woman's World* as a work of collage. In multimodal novels, word and image often act as polar attractors bringing about bistable oscillation. Then again and in tandem with bistable oscillation, word and image may also work in synthesis to create imagined text-worlds, many of which are inescapably blended worlds, blends that arise from the at and through layers of the narrative and/or from the source and target domains of the collage.

7.2.8 Make-Up, Repair, and Split

Norma's portrait session with Mr. Hands, beginning on page 209, does not go as she had hoped. In fact, it is worlds away from the glamour and sophistication she imagined. Mr. Hands, it turns out, has lured her there under false pretences, and instead has a far cruder purpose. Norma, with eyes closed to more fully enjoy the compliments Mr. Hands is paying her, opens her eyes to find Mr. Hands standing over her in what she describes as a "mood-changing moment". In that moment, she sees "what he had been fiddling with. Man's sausage meat" (221). Norma's horror combined with Mr. Hands's zealous desire leads to a struggle which culminates in Norma hitting Mr. Hands over the head forcefully with the heel of her Cinderella shoe (275). Thinking she has killed Mr. Hands, who now lies motionless on the floor, Norma checks his camera for film (it is empty) and flees the scene, returning home tattered and a mess:

> I was hunched over the sink, washing the make-up from my face when a knock on the door startled me. Outside, on the other side of the door, Mary stood on the landing, her dressing gown pulled tight around her. She knocked again, and there was silence inside the room. She knocked once more, very loudly, and rattled the door-handle as if to disturb the silence. After a moment, the key turned in the lock, the door opened and there stood Roy in his dressing gown. His face bore traces of

make-up, which was streaked as if he had been crying. Why do men dislike make-up so much? It isn't that men really dislike make-up; it's that they *think* they dislike it. (244–245; original emphasis)

Over the course of this passage, which obviously looks rather different on the pages of *Woman's World*, a significant narrative admission takes place. The passage opens with Norma 'hunched over the sink' in the bathroom, occupying the focus of the reader's attention as her character takes the subject role of the sentence. However, attentional focus is soon shifted onto a new grammatical attractor in the form of the 'knock on the door' while Norma moves to the object position of the clause. The most dramatic shift, though, occurs with the start of the second sentence in the form of the spatial deictic adverb 'outside'. There is a cinematic quality to this, in that as readers our imaginative focus seems to shift from within the bathroom to the door (the boundary) to outside of the bathroom and onto the new grammatical subject Mary. The focalising perspective is originally Norma's, with 'outside' and the embedded locative clause 'on the other side of the door' projected from her deictic centre. The focalisation becomes progressively omniscient here though since Norma, from within the bathroom, cannot possibly see through the door; thus her narrating consciousness appears to withdraw. Instead, Rawle skilfully places readers in Mary's shoes, by keeping her as the narrative focus through description and her repeated action ('She knocked . . .') which is foregrounded as a result. Rawle then heightens anticipation, zooming attention onto the key turning in the lock of the door, before panning back outwards.

Most of the passage is focalised through Mary's viewpoint so that readers witness the dramatic moment through her eyes. Finally, on the other side of the open door, 'there stood Roy' (note the distance denoted by the spatial deictic adverb 'there'). Even without the description of him 'in his dressing gown', the 'traces of make-up', the 'crying' presumably from the emotional uproar of the evening with Mr. Hands, readers would put two and two together: Norma and Roy are not individual characters but rather two different personas of one and the same character. Roy cross-dresses *as* Norma. Moreover, multimodality works to highlight the transformation, the shift from Norma to Roy. The passage occurs across a double page spread. On the left-hand page, the passage's opening words 'I WAS' are capitalised and emboldened and by far the largest words on the page. As the passage continues on the right-hand page with the words 'opened and there stood ROY', 'ROY' is also capitalised and is in a larger type than the surrounded text. As readers' discussions of the word 'FORTY' in section 7.2.5 demonstrate, type size has considerable attentional attraction. Rawle uses the multimodality of typography to foreground the characters of Norma and Roy, consequently also emphasising the metamorphosis that has taken place.

Oddly, the linguistic text of *Woman's World* does not linger on the significance of the narrative event. Norma's voice, and along with it the wisdom of 1960s women's magazines, immediately chimes back in with a rhetorical question and condescending retort: 'Why do men dislike make-up so much? It isn't that men really dislike make-up; it's that they *think* they dislike it'. Notably, Norma's first-person narration isn't explicit here. Rather it is implied through the recourse to the 1960s editorial voice, once again showing up the complex blend of character voice and vision. Speaking in interview, Rawle makes an interesting connection between *Woman's World*'s plot and the reasoning behind the novel's form:

> If you look at women's magazines from that time, they're very prescriptive. They're kind of an instruction manual for how to be a woman. So you imagine yourself as a transvestite reading it, and it's like, this is how you do it, this is how you walk without flashing your stockings, and stuff like that. The idea was that he composes himself as a woman through these magazines. (Doig 2008)

Rawle's comments also serve to elucidate upon the blurred narrative consciousness employed in the novel. Not only are Roy's and Norma's consciousnesses intertwined *because* they are in fact fractured psyches of the same character, but the 1960s women's magazine voice penetrates both since it is, in essence, a precious collaborator in the masquerade.

The revelation that Norma is Roy's alter ego is not entirely out of the blue for readers of *Woman's World*. In many ways, while writing this chapter I have been carefully attempting not to accidentally expose this detail through either my own analytical comments or by providing too many textual clues; and the clues are certainly there. The novel opens with Norma as the homodiegetic narrator in direct address with the reader, though narrative events offer small suggestions that all is not as it seems. After Roy's return at the start of Chapter 6, it becomes harder and harder for Rawle to conceal the situation (if indeed he even intends to). The strange focalisation and blurring of character consciousness, discussed in section 7.2.4 of this chapter, of course offers a trace of the fictional truth. In addition, when Mrs. Price interrogates Roy about the identity of the woman she has seen (also discussed in section 7.2.4), readers are more than likely to have at least an inkling of doubt concerning the distinction between Norma's and Roy's respective selfhoods (as the episode continues, Mary deters Mrs. Price by claiming this woman is Roy's cousin and when Mary berates Roy, he responds "I'll make sure Norma stays indoors" [137]). For some readers, this may even be the moment in which the penny drops. A friend of mine who has read the novel, for instance, identifies this as the pivotal moment in his realisation. Similarly, avid reader Chazz W., on his Word-Press blog, talks about his reading experience, admitting, "It wasn't until Chapter Six (of 24) that I began to suspect that all is not what it seems (in the Shakespearean sense), and began to assemble to puzzle. It wasn't until Chapter Fourteen that the author comes clean about the true identities of some players" (Chazz W. 2010). Undoubtedly though, the passage analysed at the start of this section is the 'reveal' moment.

At whatever point in the novel readers apprehend the truth about Norma and Roy, a world-repair will inevitably be required. In Text World Theory, the term 'world-repair' is used to describe the cognitive process performed by a reader when new information in the text causes a text-world to be reinterpreted (see Gavins 2007b: 141–142). Discussing the process of world-repair in relation to Alex Garland's (2004) *The Coma*, Gavins argues, "The damage caused to the reader's mental representation of the novel may be so extensive, in fact, that world-replacement may be necessary before the discourse process can continue" (2007b: 142). World-replacement is rather more radical than word-repair. In the former, the new information contradicts or disrupts the text-worlds to such an extent that it needs to be completely replaced. In *Woman's World*, whether a world-repair or world-replacement is necessary will depend entirely on the individual reader and how far into the novel they have read before making the discovery about Norma and Roy's combined identity.

One might think that once the narrative has 'come clean' so to speak about Roy and Norma being split selves of the same consciousness, the novel's strange focalisation (discussed in section 7.2.4) would be redressed. This is not the case. In many ways, it simply gets stranger still. Roy, believing he has murdered Mr. Hands, vows never to dress as Norma again. He cannot, however, bring himself to dispose of or destroy Norma's clothes, and so he stores them at Eve's house, his relationship with whom has over the course of the novel turned into a rather serious love affair. At first, the solution seems to be working: the police have not paid Roy a visit, his relationship with Eve is on such good terms that he intends to propose, and Norma is no more. Mr. Hands, however, is not dead, and upon discovering the 'ugly truth' about Roy's cross-dressing habits, threatens to tell Eve. Roy refuses to respond to Mr. Hands's blackmailing with the money he demands, so Mr. Hands lets the family secret out. Roy rushes over to Eve's flat in an attempt to prevent the inevitable: Eve isn't there, but it is apparent that she knows all. Emotionally exhausted, Roy passes out on Eve's bed, and on waking, notices he has got one of Eve's pillows dirty so goes to wash it in the sink:

> He stripped the pillow of its case and submerged it in the soapy solution. Looking up then, he caught his reflection in the mirror.
> "Oh, hello," he said, surprised. "I thought you were in Scotland."
> But it was not himself he was talking to, it was me.
> I must have come down unexpectedly on the Flying Scotsman because there I was, in all my glory, a little dishevelled from the journey, I'll admit, but otherwise looking like my wonderfully familiar self. (416–417)

The opening of this extract positions Roy as a third-person character, in line with the narration throughout the novel. Things start getting complicated, though, when he looks up and says to his reflection, "I thought you were in Scotland". The reference to Scotland cues readers, through the process of frame recall (Emmott 1994, 1997), to draw on existing knowledge of the text (namely, that Roy has told Eve that his sister has gone to Scotland) and thus deduce that the second-person reference of his articulation is meant to signal Norma. This interpretation is then confirmed by Norma's own interjection, 'it was me'. Emmott (2002) undertakes a cognitive-stylistic account of split selves in narrative fiction and in real medical case studies. Drawing on Lakoff's (1996) study of conceptual metaphor and selfhood, she suggests that one such approach to the identification and analysis of split selves is through recourse to the pronoun system and co-referentiality. Lakoff (1996: 99, 107) uses the phrase "Sorry, I'm not myself today" to suggest a disjunction between the self-referential pronouns 'I' and 'myself', which if taken literally to signify a single and unitary selfhood would be nonsensical. As Emmott explains, "In cases such as this, Lakoff argues that co-referential terms such as 'I', 'me', 'myself' (and the corresponding second and third person expressions) actually denote different sets of properties rather than signalling identical notions" (2002: 156). Such co-referential forms can be seen in Norma's comment about Roy, with the negated 'it was not *himself he* was talking to' (emphasis mine).

Stylistically, it is the final paragraph of the extract that is most fascinating. In modal terms, the sentence features epistemic modality. The modal phrase 'must have' along with the adverb 'unexpectedly' suggests a high degree of uncertainty and, since the action of the main verb (come down, e.g. to travel) is usually considered to be a wilful material process, also a lack of self-awareness. Emmott (2002: 163–167) also considers the split self as a demarcation of mind and body through the container metaphor, that is, the body as a container of the mind. The container metaphor is not in use here, but there does appear to be an implicit discongruity between body and consciousness: Norma is unaware of how she *physically* arrived at the scene. The third-person pronoun would, in fact, sit more comfortably in this sentence: '*She* must have come down unexpectedly on the Flying Scotsman . . .' Indeed, the only part of the sentence that could not be altered in this way is 'I'll admit', since it is a mental process in Systemic Functional terms (Halliday 1978, 2004) and because the tense of the verb 'admit' would need to be back-shifted into the past. Because the pronouns in this sentence ('I', 'my') do not match up with the knowledge levels of the corresponding character (Norma), the deictic centre here is hard to locate. Rather, it seems distorted, which in turn impacts upon literary interpretation by making the character seem confused. Crucially, Emmott introduces her study by saying that the theme of the split self "can be found in a wide range of fictional and non-fictional narratives, since it commonly occurs at times of personal crisis" (2002: 153). For Roy and Norma, this is a point in the narrative in which they have indeed found themselves in a moment of personal crisis, and this manifests itself linguistically in three ways: the perceptual deictic division of Roy and Norma ('I' and 'you' respectively), even though they are in fact one character; Roy's own fragmented sense of selfhood as suggested through co-referentiality ('himself', 'he'); and Norma's seeming cognitive estrangement from what ought to be her own physical action(s). Consequently, the split self can therefore be identified as a central theme of *Woman's World*, while the narration's increasingly nomadic deictic centre is a symptom of Roy and Norma's deteriorating mental state.

7.2.9 THE (Happy) END.

As she leaves Eve's flat, Norma rushes past Eve on the landing, and Eve, bewildered, can only utter a dismayed "Roy?" (423). Roy, dressed as Norma, makes his way home, but when he sees the house from the other side of the street, he is horrified to spy Mr. Hands through the window: "In a frantic panic I took to my heels and made for the house, fearful of what he might be doing there. As I stepped out on to the road, there was the sound of a horn, and I turned too late to see the van coming towards me at breakneck speed" (432–433). This is from the final chapter of the novel and the narration at this point is, as can be seen, in first person, though in order to understand the magnitude of the narrative event, readers must cognitively blend the characters of Norma and Roy. Indeed, since the discovery of Roy's cross-dressing habits, the effect of a reader's world-repair is likely to have been the creation of a new character-construct who is already a blend of the two, Norma and Roy. Readers' comments about the closure of the novel show up their affective responses to the narrative. For example, a reader who calls him/herself 'Dr in the house' posted a review of the book on Amazon.co.uk, saying, "The plot is much more surprising than I anticipated as I reckoned I'd cracked the story very early on but was intrigued by the nuances of the story itself and was not prepared for the end of the novel" (see Website 5 in References). Dr in the house's claim that s/he 'was not prepared for the end of the novel' suggests that the act of Roy/Norma being hit by the van came as a shock. Similarly, Tia Lowe on Amazon.com describes *Woman's World* as a "story which first intrigues, then surprises and finally has one holding one's breath" (see Website 6 in References), presumably as to the outcome—whether Roy/Norma lives or dies.

As Roy/Norma (written in Norma's homodiegetic voice) begins to lose consciousness, there is a touching moment as Mary arrives at her offspring's side:

> "I didn't see it coming, mum. It's my own fault."
> "It's nobody's fault, love. It was an accident. No one is to blame."
> She hadn't called me 'love' since I was little. (434)

Norma subsequently begins to fantasise about the time she will have to commit to feminine tasks (such as cooking, cleaning, dressmaking, and decorating) as she recovers from the accident. She concludes, "And, of course, it would be the perfect opportunity to work on my scrapbook. Mary would take care of things. No ambulance—simply carried home in the arms of forgiveness and laid to rest in my room" (434–435). The reference to the 'scrapbook' here functions as a textual deictic marker, drawing attention to the pages of the book which, with their cut-and-paste character, bear resemblance to the scrapbook medium. Norma's certainty of her future well-being is presented through the epistemic modal auxiliary 'would', yet the phrase 'laid to rest' does not sit easily alongside such an interpretation since it holds connotations of death and finality, of burial. This is, in fact, the last a reader hears of Norma's plight and so, although Rawle never provides a definitive resolution to Norma's fate, readers are left to assume that Norma/Roy dies there on the tarmac, head resting "in a pothole in the surface of the road" (433).

The narrative, however, continues for a few more pages, resuming, "Back at the little flat above the post office, Eve would be waiting eagerly for her beloved Roy, brimming over with compassion and forgiveness" (435). (Note: the repeated use of the word 'forgiveness'—Mary forgiving Roy/Norma in the extract discussed earlier and Eve forgiving Roy here). The adverbial phrase 'Back at the little flat above the post office' signals a marked deictic shift in terms of spatial location. The sentence also maintains the use of the epistemic modal 'would'. In this context, it is used within the verb phrase 'would be waiting', therefore indicating the progressive conditional tense. As such, modality and tense serve to construct the text-world currently set in Eve's flat as hypothetical, focusing on the possibility and progress of Roy's journey back to Eve. In this way, the ending to *Woman's World* can be likened to the ending to Jonathan Safran Foer's (2005a) *Extremely Loud & Incredibly Close*, which, as discussed in section 6.3.9 of the previous chapter, uses the past conditional tense. Both *Woman's World* and *Extremely Loud & Incredibly Close* employ the conditional mood in their conclusions as a form of wish-fulfilment on the part of their main characters.

Returning to the extract from *Woman's World* in question, the narrative then moves into the simple conditional with the phrase "He'd take her in his arms" (435). A few paragraphs later, there is another tense shift with a switch into simple past tense, which, without the inclusion of epistemic modals, makes the events appear as more of a fictional reality than fantasy: "And then he was there—right there in the beautiful moment. He pulled her closer to him" (436). In its final lines (436–438), the novel concludes:

> All at once, their lips were joined together in holy matrimony. The kiss
> was a poem, and the poem was bordered with dainty crayon flowers

in pastel shades and headed by a blue angel, complete with hovering wings and bare celestial feet.

Lost in the depth of her sweet embrace, Roy felt himself slipping into a heavenly reverie where the future seemed to stretch before them like a rosy dream. In that moment of mutual surrender, bliss touched them with a sweet and gentle hand as they learned from one another the unselfishness of true love.

THE END

●

The ending of *Woman's World* is as beautiful and beguiling as it is disturbing and contrary. For my part as both critic and reader, I particularly like the phrase, 'The kiss was a poem, and the poem was bordered with dainty crayon flowers', which initially uses a simile to abstract the physical act of kissing into an intangible artistic craft, before returning the figurative to the realm of the concrete through the reference to hand-drawn decoration that (as with the mention of scrapbooks discussed earlier) triggers textual deictic consideration.

The focus of this final chapter has gradually shifted from Norma to Roy and Eve. The reader, of course, knows that such a shift is in fact illusory: Norma and Roy are split selves of the same character, and therefore Roy's fate is inevitably intertwined with Norma's. Indeed, while Roy's consciousness is faintly present in the closing passage through free indirect discourse, Norma's seems to have faded from view; yet, paradoxically, the very phrase which signals the presence of Roy's consciousness also suggests his demise: '*He felt himself* slipping into a *heavenly reverie*' (emphases mine). The semantic field of death, spirituality, and the afterlife is brought to mind through the words 'heavenly reverie' as well as the afore-written 'blue angel' and 'hovering wings and bare celestial feet'. Note, too, the co-referential pronouns in the passage which, following Lakoff's (1996) and Emmott's (2002) conceptions of pronouns and split selves (as discussed in the previous section), imply a division between the Roy who is experiencing the romantic encounter with Eve ('He') and a counterpart Roy who is 'slipping into the heavenly reverie' ('himself'). Arguably, this may add weight to the interpretation that the experiencing Roy, the Roy whom is very much alive and present in the scene, is in fact a fantasy.

Fantasy is also conjured by the language of the passage. Drawing heavily on its source text medium of women's magazines, the closing lines of *Woman's World* feature lexis and phrases related to marriage and the overblown conceptions of romantic love: 'holy matrimony', 'mutual surrender', 'bliss', 'unselfishness of true love'. Discussing the dominant messages of women's magazines between 1949 and 1974, Ferguson (1983) identifies one such central theme, or as she calls it "the theme of themes", as "Getting and Keeping your Man" (1983: 44). In doing so, she talks of "romance with a capital R—and the fantasy delights suggested by glittering scenarios" (48). One of the chief ways in which this theme is communicated is, unsurprisingly, through the magazines' serials and short stories. Winship (1987) also connects fiction to the ideological goal of marriage, stating that in serials "the romantic myth of marriage as the 'fairy story come true' prevails" (1987: 90). Indeed, Winship brands such writing as "the stirring stuff of daydreams and the experience of moments" (90), a rather poignant phrase in light of the fantastic invocation of Roy's romantic desire as well as the repeated use of the word 'moment' in the conclusion to *Woman's World*. Ferguson explains that there are many reasons why serials and stories are so key in identifying the ideology of women's magazines, such as "the editorial importance attached to serials and short stories, the audience response that they are believed to evoke, the sameness of many fiction plots and the tight conceptual corset placed upon writers briefed 'to order'" (1983: 42–43). To evidence the 'tight conceptual corset' (a fitting feminist metaphor) placed upon the women's magazine fiction, Ferguson produces a 'fiction specification' used by one such British weekly magazine, and although it comes from as late as the mid-1970s, it still instructs writers that stories must have a "Romantic central theme, involving, especially in serials, some central conflict that is not resolved until the end" (1983: 43).

Fascinatingly, Rawle uses the very structure of the romantic fiction of 1960s women's magazines to end *Woman's World*. He offers up a happy ending for Roy and Eve, who are united in their love for each other. However, Rawle's happy ending is a discernible delusion, a flight of Roy/Norma's imagination in the final moments. As suggested in section 7.2 of this chapter, Rawle's use of collage is subversive since it promotes a discursive interaction between source text and target text, 1960s women's magazines and *Woman's World*. Throughout this chapter (and particularly throughout the analysis of page 209 in sections 7.2.5, 7.2.6, 7.2.7), I have made the claim that Rawle's collage technique generates blended worlds between source and target text(s). As such, a conceptual integration takes place. In line with the revised understanding of conceptual integration presented in section 5.2.5 of Chapter 5, therefore, not only do the source and target texts interanimate (Stockwell 1999) to create the blended worlds of the novel, they are also involved in the process of retrospective projection (Coulson 2001) so that the reader reconsiders both in light of each other (see Figure 5.5 in Chapter 5). In *Woman's World*, it is the very process of retrospective projection that is responsible for the reader's subversive interpretation. In relation to women's magazines, Winship articulates:

What is important to grasp here is that as a reader you are never simply a passive consumer, who can choose or choose not to digest what the text offers. You are forced, for a start, actively to engage with the text in order to make sense of it and, having done that, you are implicated in its verbal and visual representations. As a result, the text cannot fail to affect you in some way, emotionally and ideologically. (1983: 60)

Parallel claims could indeed by made about *Woman's World*, particularly in terms of its emotional and ideological affect. The novel's conclusion not only features deep pathos as to Roy/Norma's fate, its 'happy ending' exposes the prescriptive ideology of 1960s women's magazines and their obsessive insistence of a particular kind of romantic love.

7.3   CONCLUSION

Graham Rawle's (2005) *Woman's World* is a work of collage, a work whose visual form sometimes deters readers from delving into its pages, yet it is not a book which privileges form over content. On the contrary, Rawle even claims, "the most important thing for me is to ensure that the story works; if readers aren't asking what happens next, they won't turn to the next page, however pretty or interesting it might look" (Wigan 2008: 57). Rather, the form and content, the imagistic quality of the text and its linguistic narrative, work in synthesis, as with all multimodal novels, and it is this synthesis that creates the peculiar sensation of reading this text. *Woman's World* is a world in which the visual and the verbal coalesce, a contemporary narrative collides with the language and ideology of 1960s women's magazines.

   This chapter has, in many ways, functioned to consolidate many of the ideas and advancements made in the preceding chapters of this book. Specifically, it has explored the reading experience of *Woman's World* by looking at the responses of real readers in both online forums (section 7.2.1) and as part of two related empirical studies (sections 7.2.5 through 7.2.7). The latter yielded confirmation for the integrative nature of the multimodal reading experience. It also offered an avenue for the exploration of readers' perceptual and attentional engagements, providing evidence for bistable oscillation and blended worlds within readers' reported experiences of the text.

   In the final chapter of the novel, before the fatal accident, Norma cheerfully muses over her hobbies:

   I really must think about starting a scrapbook. My dressing room is piled high with all the women's magazines I have saved over the years. Wouldn't it be wonderful to collect together my favourite fashion features, all the hints and tips on glamour and etiquette that I have found especially useful, and keep them together in one big book? It would be my own edited highlights, as if I had written the articles myself. And through them I could tell my own personal story. (429)

This is a clear example of textual deixis, and a fitting description of *Woman's World* itself. Written in free direct speech, Norma is evidently narrating, yet in light of the very nature of the novel, the textual deixis is so marked that within the first-person 'I' there is also a sense of Rawle's own presence. Five years in the making, *Woman's World* is a scrapbook, at least of sorts, and its multimodality offers traces of Rawle as its writer/ designer and the journey of the book as a creative project. It is also a multimodal object that manages to tell both the fictional story of Roy/Norma's personal life and tribulations as well as the stories of many women in the 1960s—what their lives were like or rather what they were 'told' their lives should be like. It is the strange ontological permutations of voice and vision, such as this, that led critics to speak of the novel as "an addictive, zigzagging narrative as beautiful as it is demented" (Doig 2008). Beautiful, yes; demented, yes. Reading *Woman's World* opens up a world in which first impressions are illusory; a world from which authority and subversion speak in the same tongue; and a world which seduces and sabotages in equal measure.

8 Conclusion

8.1 INTRODUCTION

In the introduction to this book, I argued that existing accounts of word and image in fiction were inadequate and neglected to consider how such works affect literary reading experiences. My approach has drawn centrally upon cognitive poetics and multimodality studies, as defined in Chapter 2 and Chapter 3. The potential for understanding multimodal printed literature in light of cognitive process and reader experience was explored in the case studies presented in Chapters 4, 5, 6, and 7. Here, detailed cognitive-poetic analyses of four multimodal texts were undertaken, namely, Mark Z. Dan-ielewski's (2000a) *House of Leaves*; *VAS: An Opera in Flatland* (2002), by Steve Tomasula with art and design by Stephen Farrell; Jonathan Safran Foer's (2005a) *Extremely Loud & Incredibly Close*; and Graham Rawle's (2005) *Woman's World*. In this conclusion, I consider the principal implications that have emerged from these analytical investigations. Further to this, I evaluate the advantages and disadvantages of the multimodal cognitive poetics put forward in this book and suggest future directions for research in this field.

8.2 THE MULTIPLICITY AND/OR DUPLICITY OF MULTIMODAL NOVELS

In each of the analyses performed in this book, a multiplicity, or at least a doubling, was persistently found to be a prominent and essential feature of both multimodal printed narratives and the literary experiences they entail. The phenomena and frameworks of this study that are related to such dou-bling and/or multiplicity are reviewed in this section.

8.2.1 Bistable Oscillation

The visual designs of multimodal fiction, their graphic elements and strik-ing compositions, obstruct sustained engagement with the imagined con-tent of the narrative. Instead, they promote bistable reading strategies, whereby the surface and texture of a book's pages also become a significant dimension of literary meaning. In Chapter 5, this aspect of multimodal literary experience was explored in detail, showing that literary multimodality results in shifting perceptual awareness of the AT and THROUGH of narrative communication. This process of toggling between conceptual and corporeal layers constitutes bistable oscillation.

Although Lanham (1993) named and noted this dynamic fluctuation in reading perception, bistable oscillation was a theoretical observation rather than a phenomenon that had been verified by rigorous analytical treatment or tracked by such a framework. To this end, my analysis employed Text World Theory (e.g. Gavins 2007b; Werth 1999). This facilitated a greater understanding of the multimodal mechanisms that enabled or impeded narrative immersion and three central inferences were suggested as a result. The first two can be quickly summarised. In section 5.2.11, it was suggested that both images with what Kress and van Leeuwen call a 'naturalistic coding orientation' (1996: 170) and imagistic elements that support rather than contradict the linguistic content and narrative events are more likely to assist immersion. A significant inference leads on from this. Narrative immersion or expulsion can be seen to align with deictic pushes and pops (Galbraith 1995; Stockwell 2002a), respectively. In my analysis of *VAS*, for instance, images that corresponded to character viewpoint, thus impelling readers to project into the deictic centre of a character, and deictic factors such as usage of the present tense were found to be mechanisms of immersion. Continued applications of Text World Theory to multimodal texts are obviously needed to bear out these conjectures into more decisive conclusions. However, this initial study of bistable oscillation, aligning multimodal textual cues with forms of deictic shift, shows promise by suggesting ways in which the analyst may track the perceptual focus of readers in the reading process.

In the final analytical chapter of this book, an exploratory study of Graham Rawle's *Woman's World* yielded empirical evidence of bistable oscillation in the reading of multimodal texts. This is an important advancement for a cognitive understanding of multimodality.

8.2.2 Double Situatedness

The multimodal novels examined in this book all encourage double situatedness. For Ensslin (2009), critical awareness of double situatedness means attending to both the psychological and physical aspects of narrative experiences. In her paper on double situatedness in cybertexts, Ensslin considers how readers are at once embodied users of the cybertext and also "re-embodied through feedback which they experience in represented form, e.g. through visible or invisible avatars (third-person or first-person graphic or typographic representations on screen)" (2009: 158). Ensslin's exploration is engaging, yet there are points of ambiguity. Since her initial definition uses the phrase 'in represented form', double situatedness therefore seems to include an extensive range of psychological involvements. In section 5.2.1 of Chapter 5, I suggested this could include self-implication (Kuiken, Miall, and Sikora 2004; Gavins

2007b: 86); projection (Gerrig 1993) and deictic shift (Galbraith 1995; Segal 1995; Zubin and Hewitt 1995); as well as forms of identification such as those with characters or counterparts (Lahey 2005) or with the narrative (Miall and Kuiken 2002). I believe that using the term in this broad sense is justified since Ensslin's qualification, focusing on the reader-user's connection with the characters of cybertexts, is an example of double situatedness and not a delimitation.

In her analysis, Ensslin (2009) fleshes out her example of double situatedness as character alignment. Conversely, in doing so, she does not make clear if shifting engagements are possible, that is, whether this form of double situatedness with an avatar is isolated to a single and central entity in the cybertext that is sustained or whether such re-embodiment can occur more dynamically and/or capriciously. Nor does Ensslin explain why in her definition, she rules out second-person avatars. In treating character subjectivities, my own work stemmed from Herman's (1994, 2002) concept of doubly deictic 'you' since this provided a rigorous and linguistically grounded point of departure (reviewed in section 8.2.3). Understanding the multiple ways in which multimodal novels position the reader in a relationship of double situatedness to the text, it is also important to recognise that such forms do not necessarily require readers to feel a sense of identification with a character.

8.2.3   Doubly Deictic Subjectivity

Doubly deictic subjectivity has been proposed in this book as a term for the way in which subjective resonances can occur between readers in the discourse-world and characters within the text-world. Herman's work on what he calls the doubly deictic you (1994, 2002) provided the linguistically driven impetus. As in Herman's original conception, doubly deictic subjectivity relies upon the superimposition of fictional character and actual reader. Herman's doubly deictic you is an eloquent and replicable framework since it is linguistically founded in pronominal polysemous reference. To ensure systematic analytical precision was maintained, I established my conception of doubly deictic subjectivity in section 4.2.9 by grounding it in multimodal imposition, that is, the graphic designs of multimodal printed literature created parallel relations between reader(s) and character(s).

The notion of doubly deictic subjectivity was extended in sections 6.3.2, 6.3.3, and 6.3.7 of Chapter 6 on *Extremely Loud & Incredibly Close*, which showed that doubly deictic subjectivity can occur in moments of literary experience that are not explicitly multimodal, for instance, with the reader's imaginative relocation superimposed onto Oskar's escapist imaginings. As such, doubly deictic subjectivity is appropriate to, and can be found in, all forms of literary experience, multimodal and more traditional. Finally, in section 7.2.3 of Chapter 7, I considered the doubly deictic network of *Woman's World*'s opening rhetorical address. As such, my analyses of multimodal printed narratives argue that multimodal design, often evoking performative engagement from the reader, accentuates the experience.

8.2.4   Figured Trans-Worlds

In sections 4.2.9 and 4.2.10 of Chapter 4 and section 6.3.7 of Chapter 6, it was seen that in multimodal printed novels, concrete poetic layouts, codes to decipher, and other devices of graphic design result in the reader interacting with the book in an overtly physical manner. However, when such physical interaction occurs in a way that positions the reader doubly deictically through a subjective resonance with a character, this enactive engagement does not simply promote greater awareness of the book as textual artefact. Rather, when analysing *House of Leaves*, I argued in section 4.2.9 that the reader is required and/or directed by the text into a performative role, a role that calls upon corporeal activity and insinuates, to greater or lesser extent, active reader involvement in the narrative. Subjective resonance with characters encouraged trans-world projection relations. However, enactive performance forges a concretised form of trans-world projection for the reader, an embodied connection between participant and enactor. It was also shown in section 6.3.7 of Chapter 6 in relation to *Extremely Loud & Incredibly Close* that readers can choose not to act in a figured trans-world by not taking up the directive of the text to actively participate in the narrative.

To account for how this works in cognitive terms, I proposed the figured trans-world as an advance on Text World Theory in section 4.2.9 of Chapter 4. The figured trans-world necessarily involves doubly deictic subjectivity, due to concretised trans-world projection. Advancing Text World Theory in respect to the figured trans-world initially caused some complications, principally due to the fact that Text World Theory, as a discourse framework, is founded on rigorous ontological distinction between worlds, and particularly between text-worlds and the discourse-world. Ultimately, the strength of this distinction was useful since it highlighted the distinct blurring of the ontological boundary found in the relationship signalled by the figured trans-world.

Many fictional genres, such as the multimodal novels at the centre of this book and of course postmodernist fiction (McHale 1987) and metafiction, play with ontological boundaries, often deliberately disrupting the divides between ontological narrative levels. My proposal of the figured trans-world has endeavoured to treat the ontological separation of text-worlds and discourse-world with sensitivity, suggesting that the worlds do not merge but instead the boundaries between these worlds are obscured somewhat in the reader's experience of the text. In doing so, it has taken a progressive step towards enhancing Text World Theory with regards to texts that exhibit ontological instability.

In its application to the multimodal novels of this book, the figured trans-world has been a successful augmentation to Text World Theory, casting light on this dynamic aspect of multimodal literary experience. Continued examination of multimodal novels using the figured trans-world classification will enable further assessment of its value, as will the application of the figured trans-world to other literary forms, such as metafiction and postmodernist fiction noted earlier as well as fictional genres such as hypertext and cybertext

(Bell 2006, 2010; Ensslin 2009) since these fundamentally rely upon a reader-user. In my own work (forthcoming), I begin to explore this possibility in relation to Steve Tomasula's (2009) new media novel *TOC*.

In addition, I suspect that the figured trans-world may have value in understanding cognitive and phenomenological understanding beyond literary experience. In particular I am thinking of computer games, and most pertinently the games of interactive consoles such as the Nintendo Wii, which demands its players to engage in physical activity in order to control the game's avatars. An obstacle in this latter proposal may be the fact that the movements of players are not identical to the movement of characters (and their real-world equivalencies). Even so, this is a possibility for future exploration.

8.3   ONTOLOGY AND NARRATOLOGY

In the preceding discussion of the figured trans-world, I began to engage with the issue of ontology and how ontological uncertainties in multimodal printed narratives can complicate a cognitive approach. This is principally because multimodal literature foregrounds the role of the reader in relation to the book as object, to narrative progression and world-creation, and to literary experience. In this section, I discuss issues of ontology and narratology, namely, McHale's (1987) notion of semipermeable membranes, additional narrative layers that encapsulate the reader, and Herman's (2009a, 2009b) employment of the concept of lamination.

8.3.1   Semipermeability

McHale (1987) in regard to postmodernist fiction and Bell (2006, 2007) in relation to hypertext fiction both suggest that when there is a transgression of the boundaries between discourse-world and text-world, for instance, in the use of second-person direct address, semipermeation serves to foreground the ontological distinctions between these worlds. All of the aspects of multimodal experience, as reviewed in section 8.1, foreground the role of the actual reader and thus show up and gesture toward the interconnected nature of the reader with the narrative. Semipermeation was explored explicitly in my analysis of *House of Leaves*, but left implicit in Chapters 5, 6, and 7, in order to further develop multimodal cognitive poetics. This conclusion provides a suitable forum for explicating the effects of semipermeable membranes in multimodal literature.

Some forms of semipermeation in multimodal novels support McHale's (1987) and Bell's (2006, 2007) views. In *VAS* for instance, the diagram for page-turning as instruction acts like direct address to the reader and then causes the narrative effect of the lovers in copulation (see my discussion in Chapter 5, section 5.2.2). The workings of multimodal fiction manifest semipermeation in this example and, therefore, to quote Bell, "draw our attention to the ontological game in which, as readers, we normally passively partake" (2006: 267). In the example from *VAS*, the reader's bodily actions in the discourse-world are utilised for narrative effect while maintaining autonomy. As such, processes such as this are congruent with hypertextual and postmodernist strategies of semipermeation. They emphasise the reader's role in relation to the text but in a way that insists on the reader's separation from that text.

My analysis of *House of Leaves* in Chapter 4 was framed by an explicit interest in the semipermeability of discourse-world and text-worlds. While I see no issue in McHale's or Bell's stance on semipermeation, ontological instability found in *House of Leaves* did not result in a similar foregrounding of the boundary. Indeed, rather than reinforce the division between discourse-world and text-world, Danielewski's novel sought most often to conceal such distinction. The creation of a figured trans-world is the principal device in which this concealment is achieved. I believe that this is an original perspective on the semipermeable membrane and, as such, it shows up the intricacies of ontological obscurity.

8.3.2   The World of the Reader in the Narrative

In both *House of Leaves* and *Extremely Loud & Incredibly Close*, figured involvement was seen to entail overt acknowledgement of the reader in relation to the novels' narratological structures. *House of Leaves* is narratologically complex, formed chiefly through recursive narrative structures consisting of embedded worlds. Many of the worlds of *House of Leaves'* narrative centre upon an author figure; Zampanò wrote the central commentary on "The Navidson Record", Truant penned notes and an introduction, Pelafina wrote letters, and so forth. Thus, both the figured trans-world in which the reader decodes Pelafina's ciphered letter and more generally any scribblings the reader makes upon their copy of the text take on greater semantic value (see section 4.2.10 of Chapter 4). Rather than simply being the reader's notes to self, so to speak, these scrawls construct a further narrative encasing dramatised through doubly deictic subjectivity with the fictional writers (most centrally Truant) and the figured trans-world which the indelible act of writing manifests. A comparable occurrence was noted in my analysis of *Extremely Loud & Incredibly Close*, when attending to the letter chapter 'why i'm not where you are; 4/12/78' (see section 6.3.6 of Chapter 6). The red circling, another form of writing, causes enhanced attention to both the textual surface and the act of writing so that if readers pen notes to this chapter on its pages, again, a narrative level with the reader is exposed.

Despite the multimodality of both *House of Leaves* and *Extremely Loud & Incredibly Close* resulting in the inclusion of a reader-centred narrative layer, the narrative levels of the two novels were not synonymous. Both could be described as outermost layers, but where in *House of Leaves* this level was a form of narrative encasing, in *Extremely Loud & Incredibly Close* it was a narrative stratum in a tier of layers. The differences here suggest that while the foregrounding of the reader's inscriptions on the book can result in the exposure of a reader-centric narrative level, the form this narrative level takes will be dictated by the existing narratological structure of the fiction or the fictional episode.

8.3.3   Lamination

The recognition of a reader-centred narrative layer in the letter chapter 'why i'm not where you are; 4/12/78' of *Extremely Loud & Incredibly Close* led to a further narratological effect in the form of lamination. The concept of lamination stems from Goffman's (1974, 1981) work in social interaction and has been suggested as an account of literary narrative by Herman (2009a, 2009b). Herman proposes that "one set of space-time parameters can be 'laminated' within another" (2009b: 106; 2009a: 131). In section 6.3.6 of Chapter 6, I took up Herman's suggestion, showing how the reader's experience of certain episodes of the text led to the lamination of the reader's world parameters onto the parameters of the text-world. Specifically, in 'why i'm not where you are; 4/12/78', the tiered narrative structure including the reader-centred narrative layer entailed multiple laminations, each world laminated on top of the next, an effect achieved primarily through Foer's use of multimodality.

In this conclusion, it is important to consider how lamination fits with the other frameworks that have emerged in the analyses of this book, in particular doubly deictic subjectivity and the figured trans-world. Doubly deictic subjectivity, either singularly or as part of a figured trans-world, is founded on a vital superimposition of reader and character, as in Herman's (1994, 2002) original formulation of doubly deictic you. As such, this superimposition suitably corresponds to the lamination of space-time parameters at the narrative level, showing that where either or both doubly deictic subjectivity and the figured trans-world occur, so too does lamination. This is a consistent conclusion since in the process of lamination, the rim of literary experience is accentuated as is the case with all modes of double situatedness inherent in multimodal literary experience. Lamination also has a transformative effect, since the superimposition of higher layers causes the lower layers to be (re)considered in light of the layer above.

8.4   REVIEW

Sections 8.2 and 8.3 of this chapter reviewed some of the advances of the book, including proposed new terminology and categories with regards to the experience of multimodal printed novels and the ontological and narratological implications of these experiences. Somewhat inevitably, some of these concepts exhibit interconnectivity. In order to provide further clarity on the interrelatedness of terms and the experiential aspect of multimodal literature, I provide a diagrammatic review. This can be seen in Figure 8.1 overleaf. The purpose of Figure 8.1 is twofold. Firstly, it recaps the conclusions of this book about the nature of multimodal literary experience. Secondly, in relation to those concepts that can occur either simultaneously or separately, the diagram makes clear the possible occurrence combinations, as suggested by my analyses.

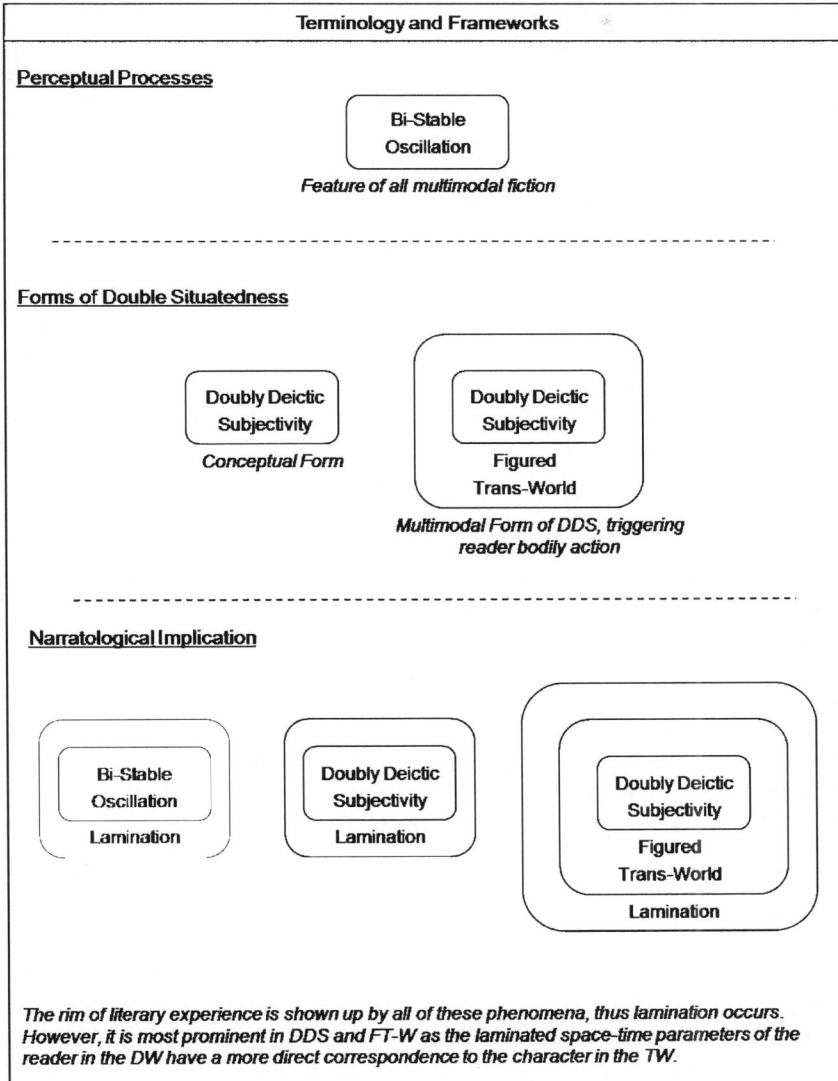

Figure 8.1 Terminology and frameworks: A diagrammatical review.

8.5   TOWARDS A MULTIMODAL
COGNITIVE POETICS . . . REVISITED

The analytical case studies performed in this book successfully demonstrate that a cognitive-poetic approach to multimodal printed novels is both possible and more significantly productive. In my own analytical endeavours, some of the tools of traditional multimodal studies were disregarded since the reliance upon linguistic structures was believed to run the risk of enacting monomodal criticism of multimodal texts. However, the tools I did use in my multimodal cognitive poetics, such as cluster analysis, vectors, and reading paths were shown to be compatible. An additional tool of multimodal study that became useful was Kress and van Leeuwen's (1996) aspects of coding orientation of images (1996: 168–176). Although these were not employed exactly in accord with Kress and van Leeuwen's original intent to understand the imagistic depiction of modality (in the linguistic sense of the word), they were useful in considering the semantic impact of certain images and the way in which images worked within the process of bi-stable oscillation.

I preferred to consider colour, a seemingly typical element for multimodal tools, through a cognitive perspective. When understanding the contribution of colour to literary meaning-making, I drew on experimental results in cognitive psychology. Colour psychology is a branch of cognitive science that still needs to refine its techniques in order to reach more decisive conclusions. However, my employment of certain findings demonstrated that a cognitive rather than semiotic approach to colour provided a more useful account of reader literary interpretation and experience.

Multimodal cognitive poetics stands as a replicable approach to multimodal literary texts, through the integrated use of components from cognitive poetics (figure and ground, cognitive deixis, cognitive grammar, conceptual metaphor and integration, text-world analysis) and multimodality studies (cluster analysis, vectors, reading paths). This is also true of newly incorporated components, such as my employment of cognitive narratology in the form of double deixis. Identifying double deixis is a case of looking for parallel relations between reader and character created by the text, either through linguistic elements such as the second-person pronoun or through multimodal design in which the reader's movements or point of view match a character's.

In terms of advancements to existing cognitive frameworks, I believe that this book makes essential contributions to cognitive poetics in five key fields: Text World Theory, Negation, Conceptual Metaphor Theory and Conceptual Integration Theory, and Deictic Shift Theory. Since I have dealt with the advances to Text World Theory, both in its handling of bistable oscillation and in the proposed inclusion of the figured transworld, I will not repeat discussion of it here. In sections 8.5.1, 8.5.2, and 8.5.3. I will recapitulate how this book has engaged with the remaining four frameworks.

8.5.1 Negation

The opening to Danielewski's *House of Leaves*, "This is not for you" (2000a: ix), launched an enquiry into some of the cognitive effects of the use of negation in a direct address to the reader. Negation was understood as a complex cognitive operation with a foregrounding effect. In section 4.2.2 of Chapter 4, it was suggested that due to the nature and context of the proposition, this particular instance of negation also caused readers to experience cognitive dissonance and reactance. These concepts from cognitive behavioural psychology have not previously been considered in relation to literary understanding and interpretation. My account suggests that in creating the text-worlds of "This is not for you", readers seeking to overcome dissonance react to the inferred meaning of the proposition. In doing so, they manipulate the referential ambiguity of the second-person pronoun in order to self-implicate into the 'you' role and provoke the enhanced foregrounding of the negative text-world. Since what was being charted here is a cognitive operation of the reader stemming from behavioural psychology, it regrettably cannot be wholly evidenced using the stylistic details of the text. However, I believe that careful employment of the insights of behavioural psychology led to suggestions regarding the potential impact of these responses in text-world construction and negotiation. Nevertheless, the consideration of reader reactance in literary experiences would certainly be improved through empirical investigations.

Foer's flipbook section at the end of *Extremely Loud & Incredibly Close* demonstrated that negation was not just found in linguistic constructions but could be achieved through images, including the cognitive processes negation entails. In the rising image of the falling man, my analysis in section 6.3.9 of Chapter 6 successfully argued such imagistic reversal involved negation since the understanding of the body's upwards motion foregrounded the event as it occurred on September 11, 2001. This is a significant critical offering, demonstrating the way in which some cognitive operations are consistent across modes of expression and communication.

8.5.2 Conceptual Metaphor and Conceptual Integration

Throughout the analyses in this book, I have shown that both conceptual metaphor and conceptual integration can be realised multimodally. Central accounts of conceptual metaphor (Johnson 1987; Lakoff and Johnson 1980, 1999; Lakoff and Turner 1989; Turner 2000 [1987]) have consistently used verbal linguistic constructions to substantiate conceptual metaphors as underlying patterns of human thought. There are two weaknesses in this, as Forceville acknowledges (2006: 381). Firstly, there is the potential for research to be closed off to other manifestations of conceptual metaphor. Secondly, it risks circular reasoning, using language to understanding the mind, and then refracting that understanding back onto the study of language. The identification of what I see as multimodal metaphors (recall that I do not follow Forceville in his distinction of source and target being realised in different modes) makes an initial contribution to studying conceptual metaphors, alongside existing work on multimodal metaphor (see section 2.3.5), and to studying conceptual blends in their multimodal forms.

Chapter 5 on *VAS: An Opera in Flatland* examined multimodal conceptual metaphor and conceptual integration in detail. Exploring the two as complementary frameworks and cognitive processes, in section 5.2.3 of Chapter 5 I considered the Invariance Hypothesis (Lakoff 1990; Lakoff and Turner 1989; Murphy 1996; Turner 1990; Stockwell 1999). Studying the extended conceptual metaphor and integration of book and body, in section 5.2.6 of Chapter 5 I proposed that this be revised. Following Stockwell (1999), I see the two domains not as locked in an asymmetrical mapping but as interanimating. Furthermore, in a conceptual blend, this causes a cognitive refraction, a revision of both domains in light of not just their interanimation, but also of the blended meaning itself. To account for this latter process, I refined Coulson's (2001) usage of the term *retrospective projections*.

In my exploration of multimodal conceptual metaphor and conceptual integration, it is evident that a greater clarity of understanding needs to be realised in relation to the way in which the original domains are understood in light of both metaphorical relation and emergent blended meaning. Indeed, this is not a new issue within these fields of study, but it is one that the cognitive analysis of multimodal texts shows up as requiring further investigation. I believe that the solution I have proposed is satisfactory. Nevertheless, these terms and processes should continue to be tested across multimodal genres and modes of expression.

8.5.3 Deictic Shift Theory

The contribution this book makes to the continued development of Deictic Shift Theory can be found in section 7.2.2 of Chapter 7, and is by no means limited to deixis as it works in multimodal contexts. In considering the reader's self-implication with the second-person pronoun in the opening to *Woman's World*, I pointed towards an empirical study from the journal *Psychological Science*. The article in question by Brunyé et al. (2009) considers the interconnections between pronoun use, embodiment, and perspective taking. Ultimately, Brunyé et al. find evidence that the second-person pronoun 'you' is the only pronoun which consistently provokes embodied language comprehension and perspective taking. As such, the findings by Brunyé et al. suggest that some of the founding conceptions of Deictic Shift Theory, namely, that of perceptual projection, are simplifications of the complexity of the human cognitive system. Specifically, the first-person pronoun 'I' does not always trigger a perceptual shift into the first-person perspective on the part of the reader. Deictic projection is thus revealed to be both embodied and social, taking account of discursive context. By highlighting and using Brunyé et al.'s findings in cognitive-poetic analysis, I hope to have suggested two key points to fellow cognitive poeticists and any scholars interested in deictic projection relations. Firstly, that the intricacies of deictic shift need further empirical investigation, and, secondly, that context (that all important term for cognitive poetics) is crucial in understanding how cognition and self-implication work.

8.6 EMPIRICAL RESEARCH

One of the strongest criticisms of existing approaches to multimodality is the lack of empirical testing behind them. On the whole, my own project is semi-empirical in that it has sought to draw on empirical evidence from across disciplines (cognitive psychology, cognitive linguistics, cognitive science, and cognitive neuroscience) in order to substantiate some of the claims it makes for multimodal literary experience. Nevertheless, such findings cannot be transferred into a new context, that of literature, with absolute accuracy. The final chapter of this book featured a small-scale empirical investigation into the experiences of readers of *Woman's World*. While such an exploratory study cannot be held up as definitive, it represents an important step towards redressing the empirical balance. In doing so, the study offered some support for claims made earlier in the book. The most significant finding to emerge from the empirical data came in the form of evidence of the process of bistable oscillation occurring in the perceptual experiences of real readers. The study also indicated that there is a difference in the reading experiences of multimodal and so-called traditional literature, particularly in terms of attention, sonic imagination, and visualisation.

More research-specific empirical testing, of course, needs to be carried out. Cognitive psychological experiments of literary experience often focus upon readers' emotion responses and personal engagements with narrative (Gerrig 1993; Kuiken, Miall, and Sikora 2004; Miall and Kuiken 2002). Emmott, Sanford, and Morrow (2006) have begun to perform cognitive psychological testing of literary elements with a more multimodal dimension. In 'Capturing the Attention of Readers?', for instance, they examine the attention-capturing potential of sentence fragments and mini-paragraphs. Such elements have a multimodal dimension, since it is in part their visual separation from surrounding text that has the potential to suggest their significance to readers. Emmott, Sanford, and Morrow's findings are encouraging, endorsing my own analytical take on multimodal novels, as they conclude that such fragments do capture attention "just as we have generally been assuming in the stylistic analysis" (2006: 23).

With multimodal novels, the use of eye-tracking experiments obviously poses another potential route in which to take empirical research. By using an eye-tracking device, reading paths and vectors could be charted, particularly with the purpose of confirming or falsifying if these devices work in the way proposed in multimodal studies. Holsanova, Rahm, and Holmqvist (2006) in fact test some of the ideas of traditional multimodal study. In their eye-tracking analysis of newspaper spreads, Holsanova, Rahm, and Holmqvist's study had mixed results. While the top-down—ideal-real dialect seemed to be supported, the left-right—given-new dialectic was in fact falsified. Additionally, their results seem to offer support for the visually salient aspects evoking attention (figure and ground) and for the directive power of vectors. However, as they acknowledge, eye-tracking devices cannot take into account the goals of readers. Therefore, although eye-tracking experimentation still needs further development, using eye-tracking studies alongside multimodal analysis "can be mutually beneficial" (Holsanova, Rahm, and Holmqvist 2006: 89).

8.7 FUTURE DIRECTIONS

The purpose of this book has been to advance understanding of multimodal printed novels and to develop cognitive poetics for such a purpose. Based on the results of my analyses, I now propose future directions for further research into multimodal cognitive poetics.

8.7.1 Continued Analysis of Multimodal Printed Novels

The cognitive-poetic approach to multimodal printed novels employed in this book has established the foundations for precise, systematic, and replicable analytical methods. However, continued and repeated application of multimodal cognitive poetics to additional multimodal fiction is required in order to strengthen the approach and test both its successes and its limitations. In doing so, additional multimodal novels by the authors used in this study, such as Danielewski's (2006) *Only Revolutions*, Tomasula's (2006) *The Book of Portraiture*, and Rawle's (1998) *Diary of an Amateur Photographer*. Another novel that would fit the cultural and historical parameters of the fiction used in this book is Steven Hall's (2007) *The Raw Shark Texts*.

Each of these four books exhibits points of similarity with the novels discussed as well as points of departure. *The Raw Shark Texts*, for instance, has a flipbook section; the image to be flipped is a concrete poetic shark that appears to move towards the reader as the pages move. Although a flipbook then, the cognitive experience of this section will differ from that associated with the flipbook in *Extremely Loud*

& Incredibly Close. In this example, the shark is preparing to attack. This, therefore, may evoke a form of doubly deictic subjectivity with Eric Sanderson, the central character, though this would need proper analytical engagement to substantiate. Since flipbooks are a feature of many multimodal novels, Foer's (2005a) and Hall's (2007) included, it would also be interesting to see what the effect of operating flipbooks is in a more general sense. In my research for this book, I had hoped to find empirical studies in terms of both visual perception and embodiment which explored flipbooks. Regrettably, these seem not to exist. However, this lack presents opportunity for original investigation.

Flipbooks are highly physical objects. Another novel which foregrounds physical form is Jonathan Safran Foer's (2010) *Tree of Codes*. The novel is, in many ways, more of a sculptural object in that Foer has cut into and out of Bruno Schulz's *The Street of Crocodiles*. The physicality of the book presents another form of multimodality deserving of attention. In particular, I would be keen to seek responses from real readers about their experience of a book such as this which challenges the material boundaries of its own being.

Repeated application to texts such as those suggested here and to more and less extreme manifestations of multimodality in literary contexts will help to build on existing frameworks, establish and confirm frameworks proposed by this book, as well as to develop multimodal cognitive poetics in hitherto unforeseen ways. For more on the analysis of multimodal literature, see Gibbons (2012) and Nørgaard (2009a).

8.7.2 Analysis of Other Printed Genres

Multimodal cognitive poetics could also be applied to other multimodal literary forms. The most obvious examples are concrete poetry, children's picturebooks, and graphic novels. Danielewski's (2000a) novel and Tomasula and Farrell's (2002) book both frequently arrange linguistic text on the page in a way comparable to concrete poetry. Extending the analytical achievements of concrete poetic sections in this book into the domain of concrete poetry proper therefore seems a sensible progression. Such research would build on work by Hiraga (2005), who brings a conceptual integration perspective to iconicity in poetry, as well as other stylistic and semiotic accounts of concrete poetry (van Peer 1993).

Critical attention to children's picturebooks is well established, with studies seeking to explore children's picturebooks from a semiotic perspective that can be seen as related to traditional multimodal study or from a more literary-critical stance that often seeks to align features of such works with literary movements, such as postmodernism (Hall 2008). It is envisaged that a cognitive approach to such texts would be productive. Such an approach could be paired with multimodal studies of children's literacy (Jewitt 2005; Jewitt and Kress 2003; Kress 2003;

Kress et al. 2001). Moreover, since some of the originating concepts which have been drawn on in this book, such as the figured world and lamination, have been used to explore children's social and educational interaction and development (Buchbinder 2008; Jurow 2005), my development of multimodal cognitive poetics should fit with an existing critical climate.

Considering the latter suggestion of graphic novels, Herman (2009a) presents a cognitive narratological perspective on Daniel Clowes' (1997) graphic novel *Ghost World*, examining how scenes are construed and how vantage points are created through visual perspective. Additionally, Kukkonen (2008) is taking tentative steps towards developing cognitive accounts of graphic novels, with a particular interest in Text World Theory. While neither of these accounts is fully developed, each represents a promising direction in which to take multimodal cognitive poetics.

I also believe it would be productive to revisit more traditional forms of printed literature, in light of the achievements of multimodal cognitive poetics. A multimodal cognitive poetics could therefore be used to create more complete analysis of novels which include illustration (images which are clearly and consistently partitioned off from the text), such as Alex Garland's (2004) *The Coma* and Marisha Pessl's (2006) *Special Topics in Calamity Physics*, as well as genres which exhibit similar characteristics, such as postmodernist fiction and metafiction, as previously mentioned. In metafiction, for instance, the repeated use of metafictive comment, a form of textual deictic expression, "foregrounds the textuality of the text" (Stockwell 2002a: 46), and, thus, despite lacking overt multimodality involves unmistakable bistable reading. It is expected that by revisiting traditional forms of printed fictional narratives, multimodal literary experience can be shown not to be wholly unique but as an accentuation of many of the processes involved in conventionalised literary reading.

8.7.3 Analysis of Other Multimodal Genres

More ambitious and progressive applications of multimodal cognitive poetics hold the potential to develop an even better account of multimodal experience across narrative. Hypertext and cybertext fictions (Bell 2006, 2010; Ensslin 2009), particularly those that are multimodal and multimedia works, are a prospective avenue for continued application. So too could the analysis of dramatic and televisual mediums. Notably, McIntyre (2006) has developed a cognitive stylistic approach to such forms, as well as taking steps toward integrating multimodal analysis into his approach (McIntyre 2007). Similarly, Lahey and Cruickshank (2010) have applied Text World Theory to theatrical texts.

A final suggestion for the development of multimodal cognitive poetics is to use it in the analysis of pictorial billboard posters and television commercials. In the process of developing his theory of pictorial and multimodal metaphor, Forceville has already expressed interest in using these for analytical material (1994, 1995, 1996, 2007). Hidalgo Downing (2003) has similarly used Text World Theory to look at television commercials. A cognitive-poetic approach to the multimodal strategies of the marketing industry may have three advantages. Firstly, it could enable a greater understanding of multimodal textual structures; second, a cognitive approach to multimodal marketing could provide powerful insight into both the cognitive processes that are fundamental in creating consumer interest (e.g. reactance) and what evokes them; and, thirdly, since marketing has a very specific purpose, it can be used alongside a consideration of the designer's motivations. Furthermore, given the current academic climate in which research projects are often supported by, or sometimes even driven by, financial support, including governmental funding bodies, applying multimodal cognitive poetics to the advertising industry may even ensure that it becomes a research thrust with market value (for further research on marketing strategy and rhetoric, see Sinha and Foscht 2007).

8.7.4 Emotion Research

In 'Writingandreading: The future of Cognitive Poetics', Oatley suggests that cognitive poetics must develop its understanding of the personal dimension of literary experience, and particularly emotion response (2003: 167–170). He articulates:

> Emotions are centres of considerable density of meaning in texts. For the writerandreader, they are places of personal significance, not necessarily the same as the emotions in the text. The effects are achieved not only because emotions are signals that some event has impinged on an important goal or aspiration, but because emotions are touchstones of our deeply held values, both those that are known to us, and those that may only be guessed at. (168)

Evidently, emotion is an essential issue for cognitive science and cognitive poetics alike. Oatley is right to identify this as a direction in which cognitive poetics should move. Literary experiences have the potential to make readers cry, laugh, reflect. In short, literary encounters can evoke powerful feelings.

Cognitive disciplines have begun to take strides toward understanding the emotional implications of linguistic comprehension (Havas and Glenberg 2007) and literary experiences (Miall and Kuiken 2002). Two studies on emotion of particular interest. The first is a recent doctoral thesis that develops Text World Theory (Whiteley 2010). By drawing on emotion theories from cognitive and social psychology as well as considering the responses of other readers, Whiteley conducts Text World Theory analyses on three novels by Kazuo Ishiguro. The combination of empirical study in the form of reader-responses, psychological theory, and text-world analysis enables Whiteley to shed light on the emotional effects of literary texts on readers' narrative experiences.

The second significant study, by Burke (2001), considers the emotional affect of stylistic iconicity. Iconicity is defined as the "specific relation between the form of a linguistic sign and the concept to which that sign refers in a person's understanding of his or her physical world" (Burke 2001: 33). What distinguishes Burke's stylistic account of emotion is his decision to analyse a poem not just in terms of linguistic iconicity but also in terms of graphological iconicity. Burke convincingly finds evidence of the latter form at the micro level in the form of lexical compounds and on a macro level in terms of the overall composition of the poem.

I believe that any account of emotional responses to literature, and especially to multimodal literature, must take the embodied nature of cognition into account. Gibbs (2006: 239–274) reviews cognitive investigations of emotion and embodiment. In doing so, he reports a broad sweep of evidence for the dynamic relationship between emotion and corporeality. For instance, "particular body movement may induce specific emotions" (Gibbs 2006: 253). The relationship between emotion and corporeality is complex and it seems that academic consensus on this relationship has not yet been reached, but it is clear that the interconnection holds implications for the emphasised enactive reading strategies of multimodal fiction.

As knowledge of the dynamic interconnection of body and emotion develops, this can be integrated into multimodal cognitive poetics and utilised in the analysis of multimodal printed novels. Briefly, I'd like to return to Burke's (2001) article of the iconicity of emotion. Leech and Short's (2007 [1981]) seminal book *Style in Fiction* is a point of departure for Burke's work. Burke (2001: 32) quotes the following passage:

> The iconic force in language produces an ENACTMENT of the fictional reality through the form of the text. This brings realistic illusion to life in a new dimension: as readers, we do not merely receive a report of the fictional world; we enter into it iconically, as a dramatic performance, through the experience of reading. (Leech and Short 2007 [1981]: 189–190; original emphasis)

The notion of enactment that Leech and Short bring to bear on iconicity is highly beneficial for the purposes of integrating embodied emotion into multimodal cognitive poetics. I have suggested throughout the analyses of this book that performative engagement is a significant feature of multimodal novels and that this enactive dimension of the reading experience leads to the development of figured trans-worlds, in which the reader feels a concretised form of trans-world projection while their own role in the reading process is also dramatised by the text. With this in mind, it is interesting that Burke concludes, "it has been my intention to show how we, as readers, might enter into a fictional world as an emotive, dramatic performance" (2001: 46). Burke's article therefore appears to confirm my own research and furthermore suggests that it may be possible both to pinpoint stylistic features related to emotion and to successfully integrate embodied emotion into multimodal cognitive poetics.

8.8   CENTRAL ACCOMPLISHMENTS OF THIS BOOK

In this conclusion, I have reviewed the specific advancements of the book in terms of the identification of perceptual processes, advances made to existing frameworks, and proposed new terminology. I have also suggested the potentialities for future research that stem from the exploration of cognitive poetics and multimodality. More generally, the central accomplishments of this book can be seen to exist in a two-way dynamic in which the principal disciplines, multimodality studies and cognitive poetics, have been revealed not only as critically compatible when combined in the way this book suggests, but also as capable of enhancing each other's value. Indeed, there is much to gain from such a critical venture.

This book has developed the study of multimodality through rigorous investigation of a hitherto neglected genre, multimodal printed literature. Furthermore, I have shown that a cognitive-poetic account of multimodality can add insight into both traditional and multimodal literary experience, for example, in the forms of bistable oscillation, doubly deictic subjectivity, and the figured trans-world. Advances have also been made to some of the frameworks of cognitive poetics, namely, Text World Theory, Deictic Shift Theory, Conceptual Metaphor Theory, and Conceptual Integration Theory, and to the study of negation. These developments help to prepare cognitive poetics as a discipline for further analytical explorations beyond linguistic and verbal forms.

Cognitive poetics has been the driving force for the analytical investigations of this study. If this relatively young discipline wishes to sustain its current momentum, it must demonstrate its significance not only in advancing cognitive understanding of literary and artistic forms, but also beyond that, across the humanities, and to general human experience. This study has made an initial contribution to the cognitive-poetic movement by applying it to challenging (multimodal) texts. Indeed, tackling analytical challenges is the principal way to explore, develop, and refine analytical tools and frameworks. In doing so, cognitive poetics will verify its status as an invaluable approach to the study of experience, both textual and otherwise. A multimodal cognitive poetics, by extending the boundaries and proving cognitive poetics' applicability and pliability, stands to gain practical and theoretical resilience.

Appendix A
Reading *Woman's World*

PARTICIPANT PROFILES

Reader 1

Female, thirty-one to thirty-five years
Education: has a postgraduate qualification in the arts/humanities
Reading habits: reads fiction regularly for work

Reader 2

Female, twenty-one to twenty-five years
Education: has a BSC in the sciences
Reading habits: rarely reads fiction

Reader 3

Female, twenty-six to thirty years
Education: has a postgraduate qualification in the arts/humanities
Reading habits: reads fiction regularly for pleasure

Reader 4

Male, twenty-six to thirty years
Education: has a postgraduate qualification in the arts/humanities
Reading habits: reads fiction regularly for pleasure

Reader 5

Female, fifty-one-plus years
Education: has a postgraduate qualification in the arts/humanities
Reading habits: rarely reads fiction

Reader 6

Female, twenty-six to thirty years
Education: has a postgraduate qualification in the arts/humanities
Reading habits: reads fiction regularly for pleasure

Reader 7

Male, twenty-one to twenty-five years
Education: has a BSC in the sciences
Reading habits: reads fiction regularly for pleasure

Reader 8

Female, twenty-six to thirty years
Education: has a BA in the arts/humanities
Reading habits: reads fiction regularly for pleasure

Reader 9

Female, twenty-one to twenty-five years
Education: has a postgraduate qualification in the arts/humanities
Reading habits: reads fiction regularly for pleasure

Reader 10

Female, forty-one to forty-five years
Education: did not go to university
Reading habits: reads fiction regularly for pleasure

Reader 11

Male, twenty-six to thirty years
Education: has a BA in the arts/humanities
Reading habits: reads fiction regularly for pleasure

Reader 12

Male, thirty-one to thirty-five years
Education: has a BSC in the sciences
Reading habits: rarely reads fiction

Reader 13

Male, thirty-one to thirty-five years
Education: has a BSC in the sciences
Reading habits: rarely reads fiction

Reader 14

Male, thirty-six to forty years
Education: did not go to university
Reading habits: reads fiction regularly for pleasure

Reader 15

Female, twenty-six to thirty years
Education: did not go to university
Reading habits: reads fiction regularly for pleasure

Reader 16

Male, thirty-one to thirty-five years
Education: has a postgraduate qualification in the arts/humanities
Reading habits: reads fiction regularly for work

Reader 17

Male, thirty-one to thirty-five years
Education: did not go to university
Reading habits: reads fiction regularly for pleasure

Reader 18

Female, twenty-one to twenty-five years
Education: has a BSC in the sciences
Reading habits: reads fiction regularly for pleasure

Reader 19

Female, forty-six to fifty years
Education: has a postgraduate qualification in the arts/humanities
Reading habits: reads fiction regularly for work

Reader 20

Female, thirty-six to forty years
Education: did not go to university
Reading habits: reads fiction regularly for pleasure

Reader 21

Male, thirty-one to thirty-five years
Education: has a postgraduate qualification in the sciences
Reading habits: reads fiction regularly for pleasure

Reader 22

Female, thirty-six to forty years
Education: has a BA in the arts/humanities
Reading habits: reads fiction regularly for pleasure

Reader 23

Male, twenty-six to thirty years
Education: has a postgraduate qualification in the sciences
Reading habits: rarely reads fiction

Reader 24

Female, twenty-six to thirty years
Education: did not go to university
Reading habits: reads fiction regularly for pleasure

Reader 25

Female, fifty-one-plus years
Education: did not go to university
Reading habits: rarely reads fiction

Appendix B
Reading the Mock-Up

Reader A

Male, thirty-one to thirty-five years
Education: has a postgraduate qualification in the sciences
Reading habits: reads fiction regularly for pleasure

Reader B

Female, thirty-one to thirty-five years
Education: has a postgraduate qualification in arts/humanities
Reading habits: reads fiction regularly for pleasure

Reader C

Male, thirty-one to thirty-five years
Education: has a BA in arts/humanities
Reading habits: reads fiction regularly for pleasure

Reader D

Female, twenty-six to thirty years
Education: has a BA in arts/humanities
Reading habits: reads fiction regularly for pleasure

Reader E

Female, twenty-six to thirty years
Education: has a BSC in the sciences
Reading habits: reads fiction regularly for pleasure

Reader F

Female, twenty-six to thirty years
Education: has a postgraduate qualification in arts/humanities
Reading habits: rarely reads fiction

Reader G

Female, twenty-six to thirty years
Education: has a BSC in the sciences
Reading habits: reads fiction regularly for pleasure

Reader H

Female, twenty-six to thirty years
Education: has a postgraduate qualification in arts/humanities
Reading habits: reads fiction regularly for work

Reader I

Female, twenty-one to twenty-five years
Education: has a postgraduate qualification in arts/humanities
Reading habits: reads fiction regularly for pleasure

Reader J

Female, twenty-six to thirty years
Education: has a postgraduate qualification in arts/humanities
Reading habits: reads fiction regularly for pleasure

Reader K

Male, twenty-six to thirty years
Education: has a BA in arts/humanities
Reading habits: rarely reads fiction

References

LITERARY WORKS

Abbott, E. A. (1998 [1884]) *Flatland: A Romance of Many Dimensions by A. Square*, New York; London: Penguin Books.

Amis, M. (1991) *Time's Arrow or the Nature of the Offence*, London: Vintage Books.

Beigbeder, F. (2004) *Windows on the World*, London: Fourth Estate.

Clowes, D. (1997). *Ghost World*, Seattle: Fantagraphics Books.

Danielewski, M. Z. (2000a) *House of Leaves by Zampanò with Introduction and Notes by Johnny Truant*, London; New York: Doubleday.

Danielewski, M. Z. (2000b) *The Whalestoe Letters*, New York: Pantheon Books.

Danielewski, M. Z. (2005) *The Fifty Year Sword*, Amsterdam: De Bezige Bij.

Danielewski, M. Z. (2006) *Only Revolutions*, London; New York: Doubleday.

DeLillo, D. (2007) *Falling Man*, London: Picador.

Foer, J. S. (2002a) 'About the typefaces not used in this edition', *The Guardian*, December 2.

Foer, J. S. (2002b) *Everything Is Illuminated*, London; New York: Penguin.

Foer, J. S. (2002c) 'A primer for the punctuation of heart disease', *New Yorker*, June 10.

Foer, J. S. (2005a) *Extremely Loud & Incredibly Close*, London; New York: Penguin.

Foer, J. S. (2005b) 'My life as a dog', *New York Times*, November 27.

Foer, J. S. (2006) *A Convergence of Birds: Original Fiction and Poetry Inspired by Joseph Cornell*, London: Hamish Hamilton.

Foer, J. S. (2010) *Tree of Codes*, London: Visual Editions.

Gaiman, N. (2005) *Anansi Boys*, London: Headline Book Publishing.

Garland, A. (2004) *The Coma*, London: Faber and Faber.

Gibson, W. (2003) *Pattern Recognition*, London: Penguin Books.

Hall, S. (2007) *The Raw Shark Texts*, Edinburgh: Canongate.

Joyce, J. (1967 [1914]) *Dubliners*, New York: Penguin Books.

Kalfus, K. (2006) *A Disorder Peculiar to the Country*, New York: Ecco.

McEwan, I. (2005) *Saturday*, London: Jonathan Cape.

McInerney, J. (2006) *The Good Life*, Leicester: Charnwood.

Messud, C. (2006) *The Emperor's Children*, London: Picador.

Paolozzi, E. (1966) *Kex*, Chicago: William and Noma Copley Foundation.

Pessl, M. (2006) *Special Topics in Calamity Physics*, London: Viking.

Phillips, T. (1970) *A Humument: A Treated Victorian Novel*, London: Tetrad Press.

Radcliffe, A. (1966 [1794]) *The Mysteries of Udolpho*, ed. B. Dobree, Oxford: Oxford University Press.
Rawle, G. (1991) *Lost Consonants*, London: 4ᵗʰ Estate.
Rawle, G. (1992) *More Lost Consonants*, London: 4ᵗʰ Estate.
Rawle, G. (1993) *Lost Consonants 3*, London: 4ᵗʰ Estate.
Rawle, G. (1994) *Lost Consonants 4*, London: 4ᵗʰ Estate.
Rawle, G. (1995) *Lost Consonants 5*, London: 4ᵗʰ Estate.
Rawle, G. (1996) *Lost Consonants 6*, London: 4ᵗʰ Estate.
Rawle, G. (1997) *Lost Consonants 7*, London: 4ᵗʰ Estate.
Rawle, G. (1998) *Diary of an Amateur Photographer: A Mystery*, London; Basingstoke: Picador.
Rawle, G. (1999) *Return of Lost Consonants*, London: Boxtree.
Rawle, G. (2005) *Woman's World: A Novel*, London: Atlantic Books.
Siegel, L. (1999) *Love in a Dead Language: A Romance*, Chicago; London: University of Chicago Press.
Sterne, L. (1967 [1759–1767]) *The Life and Opinions of Tristram Shandy, Gentleman*, London: Penguin.
Sterne, L. (2010 [1759–1767]) *The Life and Times of Tristram Shandy, Gentleman*, London: C & C Offset Printing Co.; Visual Editions.
Tomasula, S. (2002) *VAS: An Opera in Flatland*, art and design by Stephen Farrell, Chicago: University of Chicago Press.
Tomasula, S. (2003) *In&Oz*, Madison, WI: Ministry of Whimsy Press.
Tomasula, S. (2006) *The Book of Portraiture*, Tallahassee, FL: Fiction Collective Two.
Tomasula, S. (2009) *TOC: A New Media Novel*, Tallahassee, FL: Fiction Collective Two.
Tomasula, S. and Farrell, S. (1996) 'TOC', *Émigré* 37 (no pagination).
Vonnegut, K. (1969) *Slaughterhouse-Five or the Children's Crusade*, London: Vintage.
Winterson, J. (1992) *Written on the Body*, Chatham: Quality Paperbacks Direct.

CRITICAL WORKS

9/11: The Falling Man, March 16, 2006, Channel 4.
Adolphs, S. and Carter, R. (2007) 'Beyond the word: New challenges in analysing corpora of spoken English', *European Journal of English Studies* 11(2): 114–128.
Andrade, J. and May, J. (2004) *Cognitive Psychology*, London: BIOS Scientific Publishers.
Austin, J. L. (1962) *How to Do Things with Words: The William James Lectures Delivered at Harvard University in 1955*, ed. J.O. Urmson and M. Sbisa, Oxford: Oxford University Press.
Bakhtin, M. M. (1981) *The Dialogic Imagination: Four Essays*, trans. C. Emerson and M. Holquist, ed. M. Holquist, Austin: University of Texas Press.
Bakhtin, M. M. (1984) *Problems of Dostoyevsky's Poetics*, ed. and trans. C. Emerson, Manchester: Manchester University Press.
Baldry, A. (ed.) (2000) *Multimodality and Multimedia in the Distance Learning Age*, Campobasso: Palladino.
Baldry, A. (2005) *Multimodal Approach to Text Studies in English: The Role of MCA in Multimodal Concordancing and Multimodal Corpus Linguistics*, Campobasso: Palladino.
Baldry, A. (2007) 'The role of multimodal concordancers in multimodal corpus linguistics', in Royce, T. D. and Bowcher, W. L. (eds.) *New Directions in the*

Analysis of Multimodal Discourse, Mahwah, NJ; London: Lawrence Erlbaum Associates, pp. 173–193.

Baldry, A. P. and Taylor, C. (2004) 'Multimodal concordancing and subtitles with MCA', in Partington, A., Morley, J., and Haarman, L. (eds.) *Corpora and Discourse*, Bern: Peter Lang, pp. 57–70.

Baldry, A. and Thibault, P. J. (2001) 'Towards multimodal corpora', in Aston, G. and Burnard, L. (eds.) *Corpora in the Description and Teaching of English*, Bologna: CLUEB, pp. 87–102.

Baldry, A. and Thibault, P. J. (2006) *Multimodal Transcription and Text Analysis: A Multimedia Toolkit and Coursebook*, London: Equinox.

Ballaster, R., Beetham, M., Frazer, E., and Hebron, S. (1991) *Women's Worlds: Ideology, Femininity and the Women's Magazine*, Basingstoke: Macmillan.

Bandler, R. (1985) *Using Your Brain for a Change*, Moab, UT: Real People Press.

Barbash, T. (2005) 'Mysterious key sends boy sifting through his life's wreckage after 9/11', *San Francisco Chronicle*, April 3 (no pagination), Online, retrieved March 12, 2008, from http://www.sfgate.com/cgi-bin/article.cgi?f=/c/a/2005/04/03/RVG8RBUL551.DTL.

Baron, R. A. and Byrne, D. (2003) *Social Psychology*, tenth edition, Boston; London: Allyn and Bacon.

Barringer, F. and Fabrikant, G. (2001) 'A day of terror: the media; as an attack unfolds, a struggle to provide images to homes', *New York Times*, September 12 (no pagination), Online, retrieved March 15, 2008, from http://query.nytimes.com/gst/fullpage.html?res=9903E7DC1238F931A2575AC0A9679C8B63&scp=1&sq=as+an+attack+unfolds&st=nyt.

Barthes, R. (1977 [1964]) 'Rhetoric of the image', *Communications* 4 (1964). Reprint, *Image-Music-Text*, trans. Stephen Heath, London: Fontana Press.

Barthes, R. (1977 [1968]), 'The death of the author', *Matéla* V (1968). Reprint, *Image-Music-Text*, trans. Stephen Heath, London: Fontana Press.

Bateman, J. A. (2008) *Multimodality and Genre: A Foundation for the Systematic Analysis of Multimodal Documents*, Basingstoke: Palgrave Macmillan.

Bateson, G. (1972) *Steps to an Ecology of Mind: Collected Essays in Anthropology, Psychiatry, Evolution, and Epistemology*, San Francisco: Chandler Publishing.

Baudrillard, J. (2001) *Selected Writings*, ed. Mark Poster, Cambridge: Polity.

Beardslee, D. C. and Wertheimer, M. (eds.) (1958) *Readings in Perception*, Princeton, NJ: Van Nostrand.

Bell, A. (2006) *The Possible Worlds of Hypertext Fiction*, unpublished PhD thesis, University of Sheffield.

Bell, A. (2007) 'Do you want to hear about it? Exploring possible worlds in Michael Joyce's hyperfiction, *Afternoon, A Story*', in Lambrou, M. and Stockwell, P. (eds.) *Contemporary Stylistics*, London; New York: Continuum, pp. 43–55.

Bell, A. (2010) *The Possible Worlds of Hypertext Fiction*, Basingstoke: Palgrave-Macmillan.

Bennett R. L., Steinhaus, K. A., Uhrich, S. B., O'Sullivan, C. K., Resta, R. G., Lochner-Doyle, D., Markel, D. S., Vincent, V., and Hamanishi, J. (1995) 'Recommendations for standardized human pedigree nomenclature', *American Journal of Human Genetics* 56(3): 745–752.

Bertamini, M. (2002) 'Representational momentum, internalised dynamics, and perceptual adaptation', *Visual Cognition* 9(1/2): 195–216.

Bertelson, P. and De Gelder, B. (2004) 'The psychology of multimodal perception', in Spence, C. and Driver, J. (eds.) *Crossmodal Space and Crossmodal Attention*, Oxford; New York: Oxford University Press, pp. 141–177.

Bird, B. (2007) 'History, emotion, and the body: Mourning in post-9/11 fiction', *Literature Compass* 4(3): 561–575.

Birren, F. (1961 [1950]) *Color Psychology and Color Therapy: A Factual Study of the Influence of Color on Human Life*, New York: University Books.

Black, M. (1962) *Models and Metaphors: Studies in Language and Philosophy*, Ithaca, NY: Cornell University Press.

Black, M. (1979) 'More about metaphor', in Ortony, A. (ed.) *Metaphor and Thought*, Cambridge: Cambridge University Press, pp. 19–43.

Bolter, J. D. and Grusin, R. (1999) *Remediation: Understanding New Media*, Cambridge, MA: MIT Press.

Booth, W. C. (1983) *The Rhetoric of Fiction*, Chicago: University of Chicago Press.

Borradori, G. (2003) 'Autoimmunity: Real and symbolic suicides: A dialogue with Jacques Derrida', in *Philosophy in a Time of Terror: Dialogues with Jürgen Habermas and Jacques Derrida*, Chicago; London: University of Chicago Press, pp. 85–136.

Boxall, P. (2006) *1001 Books: You Must Read before You Die*, New York: Universe.

Brandt, L. and Brandt, P. A. (2005) 'Making sense of a blend: A cognitive-semiotic approach to metaphor', *Annual Review of Cognitive Linguistics* 5: 216–249.

Brauner, D. (2007) *Philip Roth, Contemporary American and Canadian Novelists Series*, Manchester: Manchester University Press.

Bray, J. (2007) 'The "dual voice" of free indirect discourse: A reading experiment', *Language and Literature* 16(1): 37–52.

Brehm, J. W. (1966) *A Theory of Psychological Reactance*, New York; London: Academic Press.

Brick, M. (2004) 'Blueprint(s): Rubric for a deconstructed age in *House of Leaves*', *Philament* 2 (no pagination), Online, retrieved August 16, 2006, from http://www.arts.usyd.edu.au/publications/philament/issue2_Critique_Brick.htm.

Brunyé, T. T., Ditman, T., Mahoney, C. R., Augustyn, J. S. and Taylor, H. A. (2009) 'When you and I share perspectives: Pronouns modulate perspective taking during narrative comprehension', *Psychological Science* 20(1): 27–32.

Buchbinder, M. H. (2008) '"You're still sick!" Framing, footing, and participation in children's medical play', *Discourse Studies* 10(2): 139–159.

Budson, A. E., Simons J. S., Sullivan, A. L., Beier, J. S., Solomon, P. R., Scinto, L. F., Daffner, K. R., and Schacter, D. L. (2004) 'Memory and emotions for the September 11, 2001, terrorist attacks in patients with Alzheimer's disease, patients with mild cognitive impairment, and healthy older adults', *Neuropsychology* 18(2): 315–327.

Burke, M. (2001) 'Iconicity and literary emotion', *European Journal of Literary Studies* 5(1): 31–46.

Burn, A. and Parker, D. (2003) *Analysing Media Texts*, London; New York: Continuum.

Cameron-Bandler, L. (1985) *Solutions*, San Rafael: Future Pace.

Carlsson, M. A., Løland, A., and Malmgren, G. (eds.) (2005) *Multimodality: Text, Culture and Use, Proceedings of the Second International Conference on Multimodality*, Kristiansand: Agder University College/Norwegian Academic Press.

Caruth, C. (1993) 'Violence and time: Traumatic survivals', *Assemblage* 20: 24–25.

Caruth, C. (1995) 'Introduction', in Caruth, C. (ed.) *Trauma: Explorations in Memory*, Baltimore, MD: The Johns Hopkins University Press, pp. 3–12.

Caruth, C. (1996) *Unclaimed Experience: Trauma, Narrative, and History*, Baltimore, MD; London: The Johns Hopkins University Press.

Chazz W. (2010) '*Woman's World*—Graham Rawle', weblog post, January 4, 2010, WordPress.com weblogs (no pagination), Online, retrieved February 15, 2010, from http://chazzw.wordpress.com/2010/01/04/womans-world-graham-rawle/.

Clark, H. H. and Clark, E. V. (1977) *Psychology and Language: An Introduction to Psycholinguistics*, New York: Harcourt Brace Jovanovich.

Coates, J. (1983) *The Semantics of the Modal Auxiliaries*, London: Longman.

Codde, P. (2007) 'Philomela Revised: Traumatic iconicity in Jonathan Safran Foer's *Extremely Loud & Incredible Close*', *Studies in American Fiction* 35(2): 241–254.

Cottrell, S. (no date) 'Bold type interview: A conversation with Mark Z. Danielewski', *Bold Type* (no pagination), Online, retrieved September 2007, from http://www.randomhouse.com/boldtype/0400/danielewski/interview.html.

Coulson, S. (2001) *Semantic Leaps: Frame-Shifting and Conceptual Blending in Meaning Construction*, Cambridge: Cambridge University Press.

Cranny-Francis, A. (2005) *Multimedia: Texts and Contexts*, London: Sage.

Crawford, M. T., McConnell, A. R., Lewis, A. C., and Sherman, S. J. (2002) 'Reactance, compliance, and anticipated regret', *Journal of Experimental Social Psychology* 38: 56–63.

Crisp, P. (2003) 'Conceptual metaphor and its expressions', in Gavins, J. and Steen, G. (eds.) *Cognitive Poetics in Practice*, London; New York: Routledge, pp. 99–113.

Dancygier, B. (2006) 'What can blending do for you?' *Language and Literature* 15(1): 5–15.

Dawkins, R. (2004) *The Ancestor's Tale: A Pilgrimage to the Dawn of Life*, additional research by Yan Wong, London: Wiedenfield and Nicolson.

de Certeau, M. (1984) *The Practice of Everyday Life*, trans. Steven Rendall, Berkeley; London: University of California Press.

DeLillo, D. (2001) 'In the ruins of the future', *The Guardian*, December 22 (no pagination), Online, retrieved March 16, 2004, from http://books.guardian.co.uk/departments/generalfiction/story/0,6000,623732,00.html.

de Vega, M., Robertson, D. A., Glenberg, A. M., Kaschak, M. P. and Rinck, M. (2004) 'On doing two things at once: Temporal constrains on actions in language comprehension', *Memory & Cognition* 32(7): 1033–1043.

Dietrich, A. M. (2000) 'A review of visual/kinesthetic disassociation in the treatment of posttraumatic disorders: Theory, efficacy and practice recommendations', *Traumatology* 6(2): Article 3 (no pagination), Online, retrieved March 3, 2004, from http://www.fsu.edu/~trauma/v6i2a3.html.

Doig, W. (2008) 'Cover girl: A new novel composed entirely of women's-magazines blurs the line between form and content', interview with Graham Rawle, *Nerve*, March 18 (no pagination), Online, retrieved January 15, 2010, from http://www.nerve.com/content/cover-girl.

Duchan, J. F., Bruder, G. A., and Hewitt, L. E. (eds.) (1995) *Deixis in Narrative: A Cognitive Science Perspective*, Hillsdale, NJ: Lawrence Erlbaum.

Eggertsson, G. T., and Forceville, C. (2009) 'Multimodal expressions of the HUMAN VICTIM IS AN ANIMAL metaphor in horror films', in Forceville, C. and Urios-Aparisi, E. (eds.) *Multimodal Metaphor,* Berlin; New York: Mouton de Gruyter, pp. 429–449.

Elleström, L. (2010) (ed.) *Media Borders, Multimodality and Intermediality*, Basingstoke: Palgrave Macmillan.

Elliot, A. J., Maier, M. A., Moller, A. C., Friedman, R., and Meinhart, J. (2007) 'Color and psychological functioning: The effect of red on performance attainment', *Journal of Experimental Psychology: General* 136(1): 154–168.

Emmott, C. (1994) 'Frames of reference: Contextual monitoring and narrative discourse', in Coulthard, R. M. (ed.) *Advances in Written Text Analysis*, London: Routledge, pp. 157–166.

Emmott, C. (1997) *Narrative Comprehension: A Discourse Perspective*, Oxford: Clarendon Press.

Emmott, C. (2002) '"Split selves" in fiction and in medical "life stories"', in Semino, E. and Culpeper, J. (eds.) *Cognitive Stylistics: Language and Cognition in Text Analysis*, Philadelphia: John Benjamins, pp. 153–181.

Emmott, C., Sanford, A. J., and Morrow, L. I. (2006) 'Capturing the attention of readers? Stylistic and psychological perspectives on the use and effect of text fragmentation in narratives', *Journal of Literary Semantics* 35: 1–30.

Ensslin, A. (2009) 'Respiratory narrative and cybertextual de-intentionalisation: Kate Pullinger's *The Breathing Wall*', in Page, R. (ed.) *Narrative and Multimodality: New Perspectives and Practices*, London; New York: Routledge, pp. 154–165.

Evans, V. and Green, M. (2006) *Cognitive Linguistics: An Introduction*, Edinburgh: Edinburgh University Press.

Faber, M. (2005) 'A tower of babble', *The Guardian*, June 4 (no pagination), Online, retrieved March 12, 2008, from http://books.guardian.co.uk/reviews/generalfiction/0,6121,1498494,00.html.

Fahie, J. J. (1903) *Galileo: His Life and Works*, London: John Murray.

Farrell, S. (1999) 'Body language in the paper theatre', *Electronic Book Review: A Gathering of Threads* 9 (no pagination), Online, retrieved November 15, 2006, from http://www.altx.com/ebr/ebr9/index.html.

Fauconnier, G. and Turner, M. (2002) *The Way We Think: Conceptual Blending and the Mind's Hidden Complexities*, New York: Basic Books.

Felman, S. and Laub, D. (1992) *Testimony: Crises of Witnessing in Literature, Psychoanalysis, and History*, New York: Routledge.

Ferguson, M. (1983) *Forever Feminine: Women's Magazines and the Cult of Femininity*, Aldershot; Vermont: Gower.

Festinger, L. (1957) *A Theory of Cognitive Dissonance*, Stanford: Stanford University Press.

Fillmore, C. (1977) 'Scenes-and-frames semantics', in Zampoli, A. (ed.) *Linguistic Structure Processing*, Amsterdam: North Holland, pp. 55–82.

Fillmore, C. (1982a) 'Frame semantics', in Linguistic Society of Korea (ed.) *Linguistics in the Morning Calm*, Seoul: Hanshin Publishing, pp. 111–137.

Fillmore, C. (1982b) 'Towards a descriptive framework for spatial deixis', in Jarvella, R. J. and Klein, W. (eds.) *Speech, Place, and Action*, London: John Wiley, pp. 31–59.

Fillmore, C. (1985) 'Frames and the semantic of understanding', *Quaderni di Semantica* 6(2): 222–254.

Fink, M. and Mathias, L. (2002) *Never Forget: An Oral History of September 11, 2001*, New York: Regan Books.

Fisher, J. (1997) 'Relational sense: Towards a haptic aesthetic', *Parachute* 87: 4–11.

Fludernik, M. (1995) 'Pronouns of address and "odd" third person forms: The mechanics of involvement in fiction', in Green, K. (ed.) *New Essays in Deixis: Discourse, Narrative, Literature*, Amsterdam: Rodopi, pp. 99–129.

Forceville, C. (1994) 'Pictorial metaphor in advertisements', *Metaphor and Symbolic Activity* 9: 1–29.

Forceville, C. (1995) 'IBM is a tuning fork: Degrees of freedom in the interpretation of pictorial metaphors', *Poetics* 23: 189–218.

Forceville, C. (1996) Pictorial Metaphor in Advertising, London; New York: Routledge.

Forceville, C. (1999) 'Review: "Educating the eye? Kress and Van Leeuwen's *Reading Images: The Grammar of Visual Design* (1996)",' *Language and Literature* 8(2): 163–178.

Forceville, C. (2000) 'Compasses, beauty queens and other PCs: Pictorial metaphors in computer advertisements', *HERMES: Journal of Linguistics* 24: 31–55.

Forceville, C. (2002) 'The identification of target and source in pictorial metaphors', *Journal of Pragmatics* 34: 1–14.

Forceville, C. (2006) 'Non-verbal and multimodal metaphor in a cognitivist frame-work: Agendas for research', in Kristiansen, G., Achard, M., Dirren, R. and Ibáñez, F. J. R. d. M. (eds.) *Cognitive Linguistics: Current Applications and Future Perspectives*, Berlin; New York: Mouton de Gruyter, pp. 379–402.

Forceville, C. (2007) 'Pictorial and multimodal metaphor in commercials', in McQuarrie, E. F. and Phillips, B. J. (eds.) Go Figure! New Directions in Adver-tising Rhetoric, Armonk, NY: M. E. Sharpe, pp. 178–204.

Forceville, C. (2009) 'Non-verbal and multimodal metaphor in a cognitivist frame-work: Agendas for research', in Forceville, C. and Urios-Aparisi, E. (eds.) *Multi-modal Metaphor*, Berlin; New York: Mouton de Gruyter, pp.19–42.

Forceville, C. and Urios-Aparisi, E. (eds.) (2009) *Multimodal Metaphor*, Berlin; New York: Mouton de Gruyter.

Fordham, F. (2002) 'Novels as underworlds: James Joyce's *Finnegan's Wake*, David Foster Wallace's *Infinite Jest*, Don De Lillo's *Underworld* and Mark Z. Dan-ielewski's *House of Leaves*', in Bazarnik, K. (ed.) *From Joyce to Literature*, Krakow: Universitas, pp.139–168.

Foucault, M. (1977) *Discipline and Punish: The Birth of The Prison*, London: Allen and Unwin.

Galbraith, M. (1995) 'Deictic shift theory and the poetics of involvement in nar-rative', in Duchan, J. F., Bruder, G. A., and Hewitt, L. E. (eds.) *Deixis in Nar-rative: A Cognitive Science Perspective*, Hillsdale, NJ: Lawrence Erlbaum, pp. 19–59.

Gallese, V. and Lakoff, G. (2005) 'The brain's concepts: The role of the sensory-motor system in conceptual knowledge', *Cognitive Neuropsychology* 22(3/4): 455–479.

Gavins, J. (2000) 'Absurd tricks with bicycle frames in the text-world of *The Third Policeman*', *Nottingham Linguistic Circular* 15: 18–33.

Gavins, J. (2005a) '(Re)thinking modality: A text-world perspective', *Journal of Literary Semantics* 34(2): 79–93.

Gavins, J. (2005b) 'Text world theory in literary practice', in Pettersson, B., Polvinen, M., and Veivo, H. (eds.) *Cognition in Literary Interpretation and Practice*, Helsinki: University of Helsinki Press, pp. 89–104.

Gavins, J. (2007a) '"And everyone and I stopped breathing": Familiarity and ambigu-ity in the text world of "The day lady died"', in Lambrou, M. and Stockwell, P. (eds.) *Contemporary Stylistics*, London; New York: Continuum, pp. 133–143.

Gavins, J. (2007b) *Text World Theory: An Introduction*, Edinburgh: Edinburgh University Press.

Gavins, J. and Steen, G. (eds.) (2003a) *Cognitive Poetics in Practice*, London: Routledge.

Gavins, J. and Steen, G. (2003b) 'Contextualising cognitive poetics', in Gavins, J. and Steen, G. (eds.) *Cognitive Poetics in Practice*, London: Routledge, pp. 1–12.

Genette, G. (1997 [1987]) *Paratexts: Thresholds of Interpretation*, trans. Jane E. Lewin, Cambridge: Cambridge University Press.

Gerber, A. and Triggs, T. (2006) 'Acrobat reader', *Print* 60(4): 62–67.

Gerrig, R. (1993) *Experiencing Narrative Worlds: On the Psychological Activities of Reading*, New Haven, CT: Yale University Press.

Gessen, K. (2005) 'Horror tour', *New York Review of Books* 52(14): 68–72, Sep-tember 22, Online, retrieved March 12, 2008, from http://www.nybooks.com/articles/18267.

Ghazanfar, A. A. and Schroeder, C. E. (2006) 'Is neocortex essentially multisen-sory?', *Trends in Cognitive Science* 10(6): 278–285.

Gibbons, A. (2009) '"I Contain Multitudes": Narrative multimodality and the book that bleeds', in Page, R. (ed.) *New Perspectives on Narrative and Multi-modality*, London; New York: Routledge, pp. 99–114.

Gibbons, A. (2010) 'Narrative worlds and multimodal figures in *House of Leaves*: "Find your own words; I have no more"', in Grishakova, M. and Ryan, M-L (eds.) *Intermediality and Storytelling*, Berlin: Walter de Gruyter, pp. 285–311.

Gibbons, A. (2011) '*Mulitmodal Metaphor* by Charles, J. Forceville and Eduardo, Urios-Apansi (eds.) 2009. Berlin and New York: Mouton de Gruyter, pp. 470', [Review Article] *Language and Literature* 20(1): 78–81.

Gibbons, A. (2012) 'Multimodal literature', in Bray, J., Gibbons, A., and McHale, B. (eds.) *Routledge Companion to Experimental Literature*, London; New York: Routledge.

Gibbons, A. (forthcoming) '"You've never experienced a novel like this": Time and interaction when reading *TOC*', *Electronic Book Review*, special festschrift edition on Steve Tomasula.

Gibbs, R. W. (2005) 'Embodiment in metaphorical imagination', in Pecher, D. and Zwaan, R. A. (eds.) *Grounding Cognition: The Role of Perception and Action in Memory, Language, and Thinking*, Cambridge: Cambridge University Press, pp. 65–92.

Gibbs, R. W. (2006) *Embodiment and Cognitive Science*, Cambridge: Cambridge University Press.

Gibson, J. J. (1966) *The Senses Considered as Perceptual Systems*, London: George Allen and Unwin.

Givón, T. (1979) *On Understanding Grammar*, New York: Academic Press.

Givón, T. (1993) *English Grammar: A Function-Based Introduction*, Amsterdam: John Benjamins.

Glenberg, A. M. (2007) 'Language and action: Creating sensible combinations of ideas', in Gaskell, G. (ed.) *Oxford Handbook of Psycholinguistics*, Oxford: Oxford University Press, pp. 361–370.

Glenberg, A. M. (2008) 'Embodiment for education', in Calvo, P. and Gomila, A. (eds.) *Handbook of Cognitive Science: An Embodied Approach*, Amsterdam: Elsevier, pp. 355–372.

Glenberg, A. M. and Gutierrez, T. (2004) 'Activity and imagined activity can enhance young children's reading comprehension', *Journal of Educational Psychology* 96(1): 424–436.

Glenberg, A. M., Jaworrski, B., and Rischal, M. (2007) 'What brains are for: Action, meaning, and reading comprehension', in McNamara, D. (ed.) *Reading Comprehension Strategies: Theories, Interventions, and Technologies*, Mahwah, NJ: Psychology Press, pp. 221–240.

Glenberg, A. M. and Kaschak, M. P. (2002) 'Grounding language in action', *Psychonomic Bulletin & Review* 9(3): 558–565.

Goffman, E. (1961) *Encounters: Two Studies in the Sociology of Interaction*, Indianapolis, IN: Bobbs-Merrill.

Goffman, E. (1974) *Frame Analysis: An Essay on the Organization of Experience*, New York: Harper.

Goffman, E. (1981) *Forms of Talk*, Philadelphia, PA: University of Philadelphia Press.

Gordon, I. E. (1997) *Theories of Visual Perception*, West Sussex: John Wiley and Sons.

Grady, J. E., Oakley, T., and Coulson, S. (1999) 'Blending and metaphor', in Gibbs, R. W. and Steen, G. J. (eds.) *Metaphor in Cognitive Linguistics*, Amsterdam; Philadelphia, PA: John Benjamins Publishing Company, pp. 101–124.

Green, K. (1997) 'The shifting *origo* and the deictic centre of orientation', in Simms, K. (ed.) *Language and the Subject*, Amsterdam: Rodopi, pp. 87–93.

Gregory, R. L. (1970) *The Intelligent Eye*, London: Weidenfield and Nicolson.

Guernica. (2005) 'The distance between us: An interview with Jonathan Safran Foer', *Guernica: A Magazine of Art & Politics*, August (no pagination), Online,

retrieved March 12, 2008, from http://www.guernicamag.com/interviews/73/
the_distance_between_us/.

Haber, R. N. and Hershensen, M. (1973) *The Psychology of Visual Perception*,
New York; London: Holt, Rinehart, and Winston.

Hall, C. (2008) 'Imagination and multimodality: Reading, picturebooks and anxieties
about childhood', in Sipes, L. and Pantaleo, S. (eds.) *Postmodern Picturebooks: Play,
Parody, and Self-Referentiality*, New York; London: Routledge, pp. 130–146.

Halliday, M. A. K. (1978) *Language as Social Semiotic: The Social Interpretation
of Language and Meaning*, London: Edward Arnold.

Halliday, M. A. K. (1979) 'Modes of meaning and modes of expression: Types
of grammatical structure and their determiner by different semiotic functions',
in Allerton, D., Carney, E., and Holdcroft, D. (eds.) *Function and Context in
Linguistic Analysis: A Festschrift for William Haas*, Cambridge: Cambridge
University Press, pp. 57–79.

Halliday, M. A. K. (2004) *An Introduction to Functional Grammar*, third edition
with C. M. I. M. Matthiessen, London: Arnold.

Hanks, J. (2008) Personal correspondence on behalf of Jonathan Safran Foer (email
communication), December 12, 2006.

Hansen, M. B. (2006) *Bodies in Code: Interfaces with Digital Media*, New York;
London: Routledge.

Hauk, O., Johnsrude, I., and Pulvermüller, F. (2004) 'Somatopic representation of
action words in human motor and premotor cortex', *Neuron* 41: 301–307.

Hayles, N. K. (2002a) 'Saving the subject: Remediation in *House of Leaves*', *American Literature* 74(4): 779–806.

Hayles, N. K. (2002b) *Writing Machines*, Cambridge, MA: MIT Press.

Head, D. (2008) *The State of the Novel*, Malden, MA; Oxford: Blackwell.

Henrikson, E. (2006) 'Jonathan Safran Foer: *Extremely long and incredibly
detailed*', interview with Jonathan Safran Foer, *Portland Mercury* (no pagination), Online, retrieved March 12, 2008, from http://www.portlandmercury.com/portland/Content?oid=38717&category=34029.

Herman, D. (1994) 'Textual you and double deixis in Edna O'Brien's *A Pagan
Place*', *Style* 28(3): 378–410.

Herman, D. (2002) *Story Logic: Problems and Possibilities of Narrative*, Lincoln;
London: University of Nebraska Press.

Herman, D. (2004) 'Towards a transmedial narratology', in Ryan, M-L. (ed.)
Narrative across Media: The Languages of Storytelling, Lincoln: University of
Nebraska Press, pp. 47–75.

Herman, D. (2009a) 'Beyond voice and vision: Cognitive Grammar and Focalization', in Hühn, P., Schmid, W., and Schönert, J. (eds.) *Point of View, Perspective, and Focalization: Modeling Mediation in Narrative*, Berlin; New York:
Walter de Gruyter, pp. 119–142.

Herman, D. (2009b) 'Cognitive approaches to narrative analysis', in Brône, G. and
Vandaele, J. (eds.) *Cognitive Poetics: Goals, Gains and Gaps*, Berlin: Mouton
de Gruyter, pp. 79–118.

Herman, D. (2009c) 'Word-image/utterance-gesture: Case studies in multimodal
storytelling', in Page, R. (ed.) *Narrative and Multimodality: New Perspectives
and Practices*, London: Routledge, pp. 78–98.

Herman, J. L. (1992) *Trauma and Recovery: From Domestic Abuse to Political
Terror*, London: Pandora.

Hidalgo Downing, L. (2000) *Negation, Text Worlds, and Discourse: The Pragmatics of Fiction*, Stamford: Ablex Publishing Corporation.

Hidalgo Downing, L. (2003) 'Text world creation in advertising discourse', *CLAC*
13 (no pagination), Online, retrieved January 23, 2006, from http://www.ucm.
es/info/circulo/no13/hidalgo.htm.

Hiraga, M. K. (2005) *Metaphor and Iconicity: A Cognitive Approach to Analysing Texts*, Basingstoke; New York: Palgrave Macmillan.

Holland, D., Lachicotte Jr., W., Skinner, D., and Cain, C. (1998) *Identity and Agency in Cultural Worlds*, Cambridge, MA; London: Harvard University Press.

Holsanova, J. Rahm, H., and Holmquist, K. (2006) 'Entry points and reading paths on newspaper spreads: company semiotic analysis with eye-tracking measurements', *Visual Communication* 5(1): 65–93.

Hossack, A. and Bentall, R. P. (1996) 'Elimination of posttraumatic symptomology by relaxation and visual-kinesthetic dissociation', *Journal of Traumatic Stress* 9(1): 99–110.

Iser, W. (1974) *The Implied Reader: Patterns in Communication in Prose Fiction from Bunyan to Beckett*. Baltimore: Johns Hopkins University Press.

Jewitt, C. (2005) *Technology, Literacy, Learning: A Multimodal Approach*, London: Routledge.

Jewitt, C. (2009a) 'Different approaches to multimodality', in Jewitt, C. (ed.) *The Routledge Handbook to Multimodal Analysis*, London; New York: Routledge, pp. 28–39.

Jewitt, C. (2009b) 'Introduction: Handbook rationale, scope and structure', in Jewitt, C. (ed.) *The Routledge Handbook to Multimodal Analysis*, London; New York: Routledge, pp. 1–7.

Jewitt, C. (2009c) 'An introduction to multimodality', in Jewitt, C. (ed.) *The Routledge Handbook to Multimodal Analysis*, London; New York: Routledge, pp. 14–27.

Jewitt, C. (ed.) (2009d) *The Routledge Handbook to Multimodal Analysis*, London; New York: Routledge.

Jewitt, C. and Kress, G. (eds.) (2003) *Multimodal Literacy*, New York; Oxford: Peter Lang.

Johansen Mange, E. and Mange, A. P. (1999) *Basic Human Genetics*, second edition, Sunderland, MA: Sinauer Associates.

Johnson, M. (1987) *The Body in the Mind: The Bodily Basis of Meaning, Imagination and Reason*, Chicago: University of Chicago Press.

Johnstone, A. (2010) 'The untamed tiger: Falmouth illustration open forum', weblog post, March 17, 2010, Glynn, C., Humphries, T., and Johnstone, A. (2009–2010) *2010 Illustration, Cardiff School of Art and Design* Weblog (no pagination), Online, retrieved March 29, 2010, from http://illustrationcardiff.wordpress.com/2010/03/17/the-untamed-tiger-falmouth-illustration-open-forum/.

Junod, T. (2007) 'The falling man', *Esquire*, September 11 (no pagination), Online, retrieved March 12, 2008, from http://www.esquire.com/features/ESQ0903–SEP_FALLINGMAN.

Jurow, A. S. (2005) 'Shifting engagements in figured worlds: Middle school mathematics students' participation in an architectural design project', *Journal of the Learning Sciences* 14(1): 35–67.

Kacandes, I. (1994a) 'Narrative apostrophe: Reading, rhetoric, resistance in Michel Butor's *La Modification* and Julio Cortazar's "Graffiti"', *Style* 28(3): 329–349.

Kacandes, I. (1994b) '"You who live safe in your warm houses": Your role in the production of Holocaust testimony', in Lorenz, D. and Weinberger, G. (eds.) *Insiders and Outsiders: Jewish and Gentile Culture in Germany and Austria*, Detroit, MI: Wayne State University Press, pp. 189–213.

Kacandes, I. (2001) *Talk Fiction: Literature and the Talk Explosion*, Lincoln; London: University of Nebraska Press.

Kachka, B. (2008) 40,000 Not-Very-Easy Pieces', *New York Magazine*, March 24 (no pagination), Online, retrieved January 15, 2010, from http://nymag.com/arts/process/45309/.

Khateb, A., Pegna, A. J., Michel C. M., Landis, T., and Annoni, J-M (2002) 'Dynamics of brain activation during an explicit word and image recognition task: An electrophysiological study', *Brain Topography* 14(3): 197–213.

Klatzy, R. L. and Lederman, S. J. (2000) 'Modality specificity in cognition: The case of touch', in Roediger, H. L., Nairne, J. S., Neath, I., and Suprenant, A. M. (eds.) *The Nature of Remembering: Essays in Honor of Robert G. Crowder*, Washington, DC: American Psychological Association Press, pp .233–245.

Knight, D., and Adolphs, S. (2008) 'Multi-modal corpus pragmatics: The case of active listenership', in Romero-Trillo, J. (ed.) *Pragmatics and Corpus Linguistics: A Mutualistic Entente*, Berlin; New York: Mouton de Gruyter. Online, retrieved June 5, 2008, from http://www.mrl.nott.ac.uk/~axc/DReSS_Outputs/Corpus_&_Pragmatics_2007.pdf.

Koffka, K. (1935) *Principles of Gestalt Psychology*, New York: Harcourt-Brace.

Köhler, W. (1947) *Gestalt Psychology*, Liverpool: Liveright.

Kourtzi, Z. and Kanwisher, N. (2000) 'Activation in human MT/MST by static images with implied movement', *Journal of Cognitive Neuroscience* 12(1): 48–55.

Kress, G. (2003) *Literacy in the New Media Age*, London; New York: Routledge.

Kress, G. (2009) 'What is mode?' in Jewitt, C. (ed.) *The Routledge Handbook to Multimodal Analysis*, London; New York: Routledge, pp. 54–67.

Kress, G. (2010) *Multimodality: A Social Semiotic Approach to Contemporary Communication*, London; New York: Routledge.

Kress, G., Jewitt, C., Ogborn, J., and Tsatsarelis, C. (2001) *Multimodal Teaching and Learning: The Rhetorics of the Science Classroom*, London: Continuum.

Kress, G. and van Leeuwen, T. (1996) *Reading Images: The Grammar of Visual Design*, London: Routledge.

Kress, G. and van Leeuwen, T. (2001) *Multimodal Discourse: The Modes and Media of Contemporary Communication*, London: Arnold.

Kress, G. and van Leeuwen, T. (2006 [1996]) *Reading Images: The Grammar of Visual Design*, second edition, London: Routledge.

Kristeva, J. (1986) 'Word, dialogue and novel', in Moi, T, (ed.) *The Kristeva Reader*, Oxford: Basil Blackwell, pp. 35–61.

Kuiken, D., Miall, D. S., and Sikora, S. (2004) 'Forms of self-implication in literary reading', *Poetics Today* 25(2): 53–74.

Kukkonen, K. (2008) 'Textworlds and metareference', unpublished paper presented at *Metareference in the Arts and Media* International Symposium at the Faculty of Humanities, Karl-Franzens-Universität Graz, May 22, 2008.

Lahey, E. (2004) 'All the world's a subworld: Direct speech and subworld creation in "After" by Norman MacCraig', *Nottingham Linguistic Circular* 18: 21–28.

Lahey, E. (2005) *text-world Landscapes and English-Canadian National Identity in the Poetry of Al Purdy, Milton Acorn and Alden Nowlan*, unpublished PhD thesis, University of Nottingham.

Lahey, E. (2006) '(Re)thinking world-building: Locating the text-worlds of Canadian lyric poetry', *Journal of Literary Semantics* 35: 145–164.

Lahey, E. and Cruickshank, T. (2010) 'Building the stages of drama: Towards a text-world Theory account of dramatic play-texts', *Journal of Literary Semantics* 39(1): 67–91.

Lakoff, G. (1982) *Categories and Cognitive Models*, Trier: Linguistics Agency, University of Trier.

Lakoff, G, (1987) *Women, Fire, and Dangerous Things: What Categories Reveal about the Mind*, Chicago: University of Chicago Press.

Lakoff, G. (1990) 'The invariance hypothesis: Is abstract reason based on image-schemas?' *Cognitive Linguistics* 1(1): 19–74.

Lakoff, G. (1996) 'Sorry, I'm not myself today: The metaphor system for conceptualizing the self', in Fauconnier, G. and Sweetser, E. (eds.) *Spaces, Worlds, and Grammar*, Chicago: University of Chicago Press, pp. 91–123.

Lakoff, G. (2006) 'The neuroscience of form in art', in Turner, M. (ed.) *The Artful Mind: Cognitive Science and the Riddle of Human Creativity*, Oxford: Oxford University Press, pp. 153–169.

Lakoff, G. and Johnson, M. (1980) *Metaphors We Live By*, Chicago; London: University of Chicago Press.

Lakoff, G. and Johnson, M. (1999) *Philosophy in the Flesh: The Embodied Mind and its Challenge to Western Thought*, New York: Basic Books.

Lakoff, G. and Turner, M. (1989) *More than Cool Reason: A Field Guide to Poetic Metaphor*, Chicago; London: University of Chicago Press.

Lander, B. (2005) 'Graphic novels as history: Representing and reliving the past', *Left History* 10(2): 113–126.

Langacker, R. (1987) *Foundations of Cognitive Grammar: Volume I Theoretical Prerequisites*, Stanford, CA: Stanford University Press.

Langacker, R. (1991) *Foundations of Cognitive Grammar: Volume II Descriptive Application*, Stanford, CA: Stanford University Press.

Langacker, R. (1999) *Grammar and Conceptualisation*, Berlin: Mouton de Gruyter.

Langacker, R. (2002 [1991]) *Concept, Image, Symbol: The Cognitive Basis of Grammar*, second edition, Berlin: Mouton de Gruyter.

Langacker, R. (2002) 'Deixis and subjectivity', in Brisard, F. (ed.) *Grounding: The Epistemic Footing of Deixis and Reference*, Berlin: Mouton de Gruyter, pp. 1–28.

Langacker, R. (2008) *Cognitive Grammar: A Basic Introduction*, Oxford: Oxford University Press.

Lanham, R. (1993) *The Electronic Word: Democracy, Technology and the Arts*, Chicago: University of Chicago Press.

Laub, D. (1992) 'An event without a witness: truth, testimony and survival', in Felman, S. and Laub, D. (eds.) *Testimony: Crises of Witnessing in Literature, Psychoanalysis, and History*, New York: Routledge, pp. 57–74.

Lederman, S. J. and Klatzy, R. L. (2001) 'Designing haptic and multimodal interfaces: A cognitive scientist's perspective', in Farber, G. and Hoogen, J. (eds.) *Proceedings of Collaborative Research Centre 453*, Munich: Technical University of Munich, pp. 71–80.

Lee, D. (2001) *Cognitive Linguistics: An Introduction*, Oxford: Oxford University Press.

Leech, G. N., and Short, M. (2007 [1981]) *Style in Fiction: A Linguistic Introduction to English Fictional Prose*, second edition, Harlow: Pearson.

Lester, P. M. (2000) *Visual Communication: Images with Messages*, second edition, Belmont: Wadsworth.

Levine, P. and Scollon, R. (eds.) (2004) *Discourse and Technology: Multimodal Discourse Analysis*, Washington, DC: Georgetown University Press.

Loeb, W. and Girl, Interrupting (2008) 'Cut and paste', *Bookslut*, February (no pagination), Online, retrieved January 15, 2010, from http://www.bookslut.com/girl_interrupting/2008_02_012374.php.

Lyons, J. (1977) *Semantics*, Cambridge: Cambridge University Press.

Machin, D. (2007) *Introduction to Multimodal Analysis*, London: Hodder Arnold.

Mandel, N. (2008) 'Being nomadic with the truth: J. S. Foer's postmodern parables', unpublished paper presented at the International Conference on Narrative, Annual Conference of the Society for the Study of Narrative Literature, the University of Texas, Austin, May 1–4.

Manguel, A. (1997) *A History of Reading*, London: Flamingo.

Marchessault, J. (2000) 'David Suzuki's *The Secret of Life*: Informatics and the popular discourse of the life code', in Marchessault, J. and Sawchuk, K. (eds.)

Wild Science: Reading Feminism, Medicine and the Media, London: Routledge, pp. 55–64.

Margolin, U. (1984) 'Narrative and indexicality: A tentative framework', *Journal of Literary Semantics* 13: 181–204.

Margolin, U. (1986–1987) 'Dispersing/voiding the subject: A narratological perspective', *Texte* 5/6: 181–210.

Marks, L. (2002) *Touch: Sensuous Theory and Multisensory Media*, Minneapolis; London: University of Minnesota Press.

Marr, A. (2007) 'Curling up with a good ebook', *The Guardian*, May 11 (no pagination), Online, retrieved 16 May 2007, from http://technology.guardian.co.uk/news/story/0,,2077278,00.html?gusrc=rss&feed=20.

Marsh, J. (2005) 'Ritual, performance and identity construction: Young children's engagement with popular culture and media texts', in Marsh, J. (ed.) *Popular Culture, New Media and Digital Literacy in Early Childhood*, London; New York: Routledge, pp. 28–50.

Matwychuk, P. (2008) 'A cut-and-paste-masterpiece', *See Magazine*, July 24 (no pagination), Online, retrieved January 15, 2010, from http://www.seemagazine.com/article/arts/books/cut-and-paste-masterpiece/.

McCaffery, L. and Gregory, S. (2003) 'Haunted house—an interview with Mark Z. Danielewski', *Critique* 44(2): 99–135.

McGlothlin, E. (2003) 'No time like the present: Narrative and time in Art Spiegelman's *Maus*', *NARRATIVE* 11(2): 177–198.

McHale, B. (1987) *Postmodernist Fiction*, London; New York: Routledge.

McInerney, J. (2005) 'The uses of invention', *The Guardian*, September 17 (no pagination), Online, retrieved March 28, 2008, from http://books.guardian.co.uk/review/story/0,12084,1570906,00.html.

McIntyre, D. (2006) *Point of View in Plays: A Cognitive Stylistic Approach to Viewpoint in Drama and Other Text-Types*, Amsterdam; Philadelphia: John Benjamins.

McIntyre, D. (2007) 'Deixis, cognition, and the construction of viewpoint', in Lambrou, M. and Stockwell, P. (eds.) *Contemporary Stylistics*, London; New York: Continuum, pp. 118–130.

Merleau-Ponty, M. (1962) *Phenomenology of Perception*, trans. Colin Smith, London; Henley: Routledge and Kegan Paul.

Miall, D. S., and Kuiken, D. (2002) 'A feeling for fiction: becoming what we behold', *Poetics* 30: 221–241.

Miller, A. (2006) 'Revolutionary: *House of Leaves* author Mark Z. Danielewski returns with an epic poem/novel that travels across the American landscape', *Los Angeles City Beat*, September 21 (no pagination), Online, retrieved October 15, 2006, from www.onlyrevolutions.com.

Moggach, L. (2005) 'If there was ever something emotional', interview with Jonathan Safran Foer, *Financial Times Weekend—LIVING*, June 11 (no pagination), Online, retrieved March 12, 2008, from http://www.ft.com/cms/s/0/654e6f68-da14-11d9-b071-00000e2511c8.html?nclick_check=1.

Mukařovský, J. (1976) *On Poetic Language*, trans. and ed. John Burbank and Peter Steiner, Lisse: Peter deRidder.

Mukařovský, J. (1977) *The Word and Verbal Art: Selected Essays*, trans. and ed. John Burbank and Peter Steiner, New Haven, CT; London: Yale University Press.

Murphy, G. (1996) 'On metaphorical representation', *Cognition* 60: 173–204.

Næss, A. (2005) *Galileo Galileo—When the World Stood Still*, New York: Springer.

Nørgaard, N. (2007) 'Disordered collarettes and uncovered tables: Negative polarity as a stylistic device in Joyce's "Two Gallants"', *Journal of Literary Semantics* 36: 35–52.

Nørgaard, N. (2009a) 'Multimodality and the literary text: Making sense of Safran Foer's *Extremely Loud and Incredibly Close*', in Page, R. (ed.) *New Perspectives on Narrative and Multimodality*, London; New York: Routledge, pp. 115–126.

Nørgaard, N. (2009b) 'The semiotics of typography in literary texts: A multimodal approach', *Orbis Litterarum* 64(2): 141–160.

Norris, S. (2004) *Analyzing Multimodal Interaction*, New York; London: Routledge.

Norris, S. (2009) 'Multimodal density and modal configurations: Multimodal actions', in Jewitt, C. (ed.) *The Routledge Handbook to Multimodal Analysis*, London; New York: Routledge, pp. 78–90.

Nowottny, W. (1962) *The Language Poets Use*, London: Athlone Press.

Oatley, K. (2003) 'Writingandreading: The future of cognitive poetics', in Gavins, J. and Steen, G. (eds.) *Cognitive Poetics in Practice*, London: Routledge, pp. 161–173.

O'Halloran, K. L. (1999) 'Towards a systemic functional analysis of multisemiotic mathematical texts', *Semiotica* 241(1/2): 1–29.

O'Halloran, K. L. (2000) Classroom discourse in mathematics: A multisemiotic analysis', *Linguistics and Education* 10(3): 359–388.

O'Halloran, K. L. (ed.) (2004) *Multimodal Discourse Analysis: Systemic Functional Perspectives*, London; New York: Continuum.

O'Halloran, K. L. (2005) *Mathematical Discourse: Language, Symbolism, and Visual Images*, London: Continuum.

Olalquiaga, C. (1992) *Megalopolis: Contemporary Cultural Sensibilities*, Minneapolis: University of Minnesota Press.

Olsen, L. (2004) 'Notes toward the musicality of creative disjunction, or: Fiction by collage', *Symploke* 12(1/2): 130–135.

O'Toole, M. (1994) *The Language of Displayed Art*, London: Leicester University Press.

O'Toole, M. (2004) 'Opera Ludentes: The Sydney Opera House at work and play', in O'Halloran, K. (ed.) *Multimodal Discourse Analysis*, London: Continuum, pp. 11–27.

Page, R. (2009a) 'Introduction', in Page, R. (ed.) *New Perspectives on Narrative and Multimodality*, London; New York: Routledge, pp. 1–13.

Page, R. (ed.) (2009b) *New Perspectives on Narrative and Multimodality*, London; New York: Routledge.

Palmer, F. R. (1986) *Mood and Modality*, Cambridge: Cambridge University Press.

Pavani, G., Murray, M. M., and Schroeder, C. E. (2006) 'Rethinking mind, brain and behaviour through a multisensory perspective', *Neuropsychologia* 45(3): 467–468.

Peirce, C. S. (1940) 'Logic as semiotic: The theory of signs', in Buchler, J. (ed.) *The Philosophy of Peirce: Selected Writings*, London: Kegan Paul, Trench, Trubner and Co., pp. 98–119.

Perkins, M. R. (1983) *Modal Expressions in English*, London: Pinter.

Pezdek, K. (2003) 'Event memory and autobiographical memory for the events of September 11, 2001', *Applied Cognitive Psychology* 17: 1033–1045.

Phillips, T. (2005) 'Powder and Paste', *The Guardian*, October 15 (no pagination), Online, retrieved January 15, 2010, from http://www.guardian.co.uk/books/2005/oct/15/featuresreviews.guardianreview15.

Posner, M. I. and Raichle, M. E. (1997) *Images of Mind*, New York: Scientific American Library.

Poynor, Rick (2003) 'Evolutionary tales', *Eye* 49(31) (no pagination), Online, retrieved February 2, 2007, from http://www.eyemagazine.com/critique.php?cid=242.

Poyner, R. (2005) 'Paste up ladies', *Eye Magazine*, October 31 (no pagination), Online, retrieved January 15, 2010, from http://www.eyemagazine.com/critique.php?cid=314.

Pressman, J. (2006) '*House of Leaves*: Reading the networked novel', *Studies in American Fiction* 34(1): 107–127. Online, retrieved February 2007 from http://gateway.proquest.com/openurl?ctx_ver=Z39.88–2003&xri:pqil:res_ver=0.2&res_id=xri:lion&rft_id=xri:lion:ft:abell:R03944197:0.

Pulvermüller, F. (2005) 'Brain mechanisms linking language and action', *Neuroscience* 6: 576–582.

Pulvermüller, F., Hauk, O., Nikulin, V. V., and Ilmoniemi, R. J. (2005) 'Functional links between motor and language systems', *European Journal of Neuroscience* 21: 793–797.

Rauh, G. (1983) 'Aspects of deixis', in Rauh, G. (ed.) *Essays on Deixis*, Türbingen: Gunter Nair Verlag, pp. 9–60.

Rawle, G. (2008a) 'Frequently asked questions no.19', weblog post, September 13, Rawle, G. (2008–2010) Graham Rawle News-Blog (no pagination), Online, retrieved January 15, 2010, from http://www.grahamrawle.blogspot.com/.

Rawle, G. (2008b) 'Night Waves BBC Radio 3', weblog post, December 24, Rawle, G. (2008–2010) Graham Rawle News-Blog (no pagination), Online, retrieved January 15, 2010, from http://www.grahamrawle.blogspot.com/.

Rizzolatti, G. and Arbib, M. A. (1998) 'Language within our grasp', *Trends in Neuroscience* 21(5): 188–194.

Rizzolatti, G. and Craighero, L. (2004) 'The mirror-neuron system', *Annual Review of Neuroscience* 27: 169–192.

Royce, T. D. and Bowcher, W. L. (eds.) (2007) *New Directions in the Analysis of Multimodal Discourse*, Mahwah, NJ; London: Lawrence Erlbaum.

Rubin, E. (1958 [1915]) 'Figure and ground', in Beardslee, D. C. and Wertheimer, M. (eds.) *Readings in Perception*, Princeton, NJ: D. Van Nostrand, pp. 194–203.

Russell, P. J. (2002) *Genetics*, San Francisco, CA: Benjamin Cummings.

Ryan, M-L. (1991) *Possible Worlds, Artificial Intelligence, and Narrative Theory*, Bloomington: Indiana University Press.

Saraceni, M. (2003) *The Language of Comics*, London: Routledge.

Scarry, E. (2001) *Dreaming by the Book*, Princeton, NJ: Princeton University Press.

Schiffrin, D. (2006) *In Other Words: Variation in Reference and Narrative*, Cambridge: Cambridge University Press.

Schuster, M. A., Stein, B. D., Jaycox, L. H., Collins, R. L., Marshall, G. N., Elliott, M. N., Zhou, A. J., Kanouse, D. E., Morrison, J. A., and Berry, S. H. (2001) 'A national survey of stress reactions after the September 11, 2001, terrorist attacks', *New England Journal of Medicine* 345(20): 1507–1512.

Scollon, R. and Scollon, S. (2003) *Discourses in Place: Language in the Material World*, London; New York: Routledge.

Segal, E. M. (1995b) 'A cognitive-phenomenological theory of fictional narrative', in Duchan, J. F., Bruder, G. A., and Hewitt, L. E. (eds.) *Deixis in Narrative: A Cognitive Science Perspective*, Hillsdale, NJ: Lawrence Erlbaum, pp. 61–78.

Semino, E. and Short, M. (2004) *Corpus Stylistics: Speech, Writing and Thought Presentation in a Corpus of English Writing*, London: Routledge.

Shen, Y. and Cohen, M. (1998) 'How come silence is sweet but sweetness is not silent: A cognitive account of directionality in poetic synaesthesia', *Language and Literature* 7(2): 123–140.

Shen, Y. and Cohen, M. (2008) '"Heard melodies are sweet, but those unheard are sweeter": Synaesthetic metaphors and cognition', *Language and Literature* 17(2): 107–121.

Shenk, J. W. (2005) 'Arts: Living to tell the tale', interview with Jonathan Safran Foer, *Mother Jones*, May/June (no pagination), Online, retrieved March 12, 2008, from http://www.motherjones.com/arts/qa/2005/05/Safran_Foer.html.

Simpson, P. (1993) *Language, Ideology, and Point of View*, London: Routledge.

Simpson, P. (2004) *Stylistics: A Resource Book for Students*, London; New York: Routledge.

Sinha, I., and Foscht, T. (2007) *Reverse Psychology Marketing: The Death of Traditional Marketing and the Rise of the New "Pull" Game*, Basingstoke; New York: Palgrave Macmillan.

Slocombe, W. (2005) '"This is not for you": Nihilism and the house that Jacques built', *Modern Fiction Studies* 51(1): 88–109.

Smith, M. C., Bibi, U., and Sheard, D. E. (2003) 'Evidence for the differential impact of time and emotion on personal and event memories for September 11, 2001', *Applied Cognitive Psychology* 17: 1047–1055.

Solomon, D. (2005) 'The rescue artist', interview with Jonathan Safran Foer, *New York Times*, February 27 (no pagination), Online, retrieved March 12, 2008, from http://www.nytimes.com/2005/02/27/magazine/27FOER.html?pagewanted=print&position.

Song, H. and Schwarz, N. (2008) 'If it's hard to read, it's hard to do: Processing fluency affects effort prediction and motivation', *Psychological Science* 19(10): 986–988.

Stafford, T. and Webb, M. (2005) *Mind Hacks: Tips & Tools for Using Your Brain*, Sebastopol, CA: O'Reilly.

Steen, G. (1994) *Understanding Metaphor in Literature*, London: Routledge.

Stockwell, P. (1999) 'The inflexibility of invariance', *Language and Literature* 8(2): 125–142.

Stockwell, P. (2002a) *Cognitive Poetics: An Introduction*, London: Routledge.

Stockwell, P. (2002b) 'Miltonic texture and the feeling of reading', in Semino, E. and Culpeper, J. (eds.) *Cognitive Stylistics: Language and Cognition in Text Analysis*, Philadelphia, PA: John Benjamins Publishing Company, pp. 73–94.

Stockwell, P. (2003) 'Surreal figures', in Gavins, J and Steen, G. (eds.) *Cognitive Poetics in Practice*, London: Routledge, pp. 13–25.

Stockwell, P. (2004) 'Paying attention', unpublished keynote lecture at the APAC conference, University of Barcelona, March.

Stockwell, P. (2005) 'On cognitive poetics and stylistics', in Veivo, H., Pettersson, B., and Polvinen, M. (eds.) *Cognition and Literary Interpretation in Practice*, Helsinki: Yliopistopaino Helsinki University Press, pp. 267–282.

Stockwell, P. (2008) 'Faultlines: The value of English studies', inaugural lecture for the Chair in Literary Linguistics, University of Nottingham.

Stockwell, P. (2009) *Texture: A Cognitive Aesthetics of Reading*, Edinburgh: Edinburgh University Press.

Styles, E. (1997) *The Psychology of Perception*, Hove: Psychology Press.

Sweetser, E. (1990) *From Etymology to Pragmatics: The Mind–Body Metaphor in Semantic Structure and Semantic Change*, New York: Cambridge University Press.

Szollosy, M. (2002) '"If my mouth could marry a hurt like that!": Reading auto-mutilation, auto-biography in the work of Christopher Bollas and Sylvia Plath', in Scalia, J. (ed.) *The Vitality of Objects: Exploring the Word of Christopher Bollas, Disseminations: Psychoanalysis in Contexts Series*, London; New York: Continuum, pp. 139–157.

Tettamanti, M., Buccino, G., Saccuman, M. C., Gallese, V., Danna, M., Scifo, P., Fazio, F., Rizzolati, G., Cappa, S. F., and Perani, D. (2005) 'Listening to action-related sentences activated fronto-parietal motor circuits', *Journal of Cognitive Neuroscience* 17(2): 273–281.

Thacker, E. (2006) '*VAS: An Opera in Flatland* (Review)', *Leonardo* 39(2): 166.

Thesen, T., Vibell, J. F., Calvert, G. A., and Österbauer, R. A. (2004) 'Neuroimaging of multisensory processing in vision, audition, touch, and olfaction', *Cognitive Processes* 5: 84–93.

Thomas, B. (2011) 'Trickster authors and tricky readers on the MZD forums', in Bray, J. and Gibbons, A. (eds.) *Mark Z. Danielewski*, Manchester: Manchester University Press, pp. 86–102.

Thompson, A. and Thompson, J. O. (1987) *Shakespeare: Meaning & Metaphor*, Brighton: Harvester.

Thompson, A. and Thompson, J. O. (2005) 'Meaning, "seeing", printing', in Brooks, D. A. (ed.) *Printing and Parenting in Early Modern England*, Aldershot: Ashgate, pp. 59–86.

Tomasula, S. (1996) 'Three axioms for projecting a line (or why it will continue to be hard to write a title sans slashes or parenthesis)', *Review of Contemporary Fiction* 16(1): 100–108.

Turner, M. (1990) 'Aspects of the invariance hypothesis', *Cognitive Linguistics* 1(2): 247–255.

Turner, M. (2002) 'The cognitive study of art, language, and literature', *Poetics Today* 23(1): 9–20.

Turner, M. (2000 [1987]) *Death is the Mother of Beauty: Mind, Metaphor, Criticism*, Christchurch: Cybereditions.

Turner, M. (ed.) (2006) *The Artful Mind: Cognitive Science and the Riddle of Human Creativity*, Oxford: Oxford University Press.

Tyler, A. and Evans, V. (2003) *The Semantics of English Prepositions: Spatial Scenes, Embodied Meaning and Cognition*, Cambridge: Cambridge University Press.

Ungerer, F. and Schmid, H. J. (1996) *An Introduction to Cognitive Linguistics*, Edinburgh: Longman.

Updike, J. (2005) 'Mixes messages: Extremely loud and incredibly close', *New Yorker*, March 14 (no pagination), Online, retrieved January 1, 2007, from http://www.newyorker.com/archive/2005/03/14/050314crbo_books1?currentPage=all.

Valdez, P. and Mehrabian, A. (1994) 'Effects of color on emotions', *Journal of Experimental Psychology: General* 123(4): 394–409.

van Dijk, J. (2000) 'The language and literature of life: Popular metaphors in genome research', in Marchessault, J. and Sawchuk, K. (eds.) *Wild Science: Reading Feminism, Medicine and the Media*, London: Routledge, pp. 66–79.

van Leeuwen, T. (2005) 'Typographic Meaning', *Visual Communication* 4(2): 137–143.

van Leeuwen, T. (2006) 'Towards a semiotics of typography', *Information Design Journal & Document Design* 14(2): 139–155.

van Leeuwen, T. and Jewitt, C. (eds.) (2001) *Handbook of Visual Analysis*, London: Sage.

van Peer, W. (1986) *Stylistics and Psychology: Investigations of Foregrounding*, London: Croom Helm.

van Peer, W. (1993) 'Typographical Foregrounding', *Language and Literature* 2(1): 49–61.

Ventola, E., Charles, C., and Kaltenbacher, M. (eds.) (2004) *Perspectives on Multimodality*, First International Congress on Multimodality, Amsterdam; Philadelphia, PA: John Benjamins Publishing Company.

Verdonk, P. (2005) 'Painting, poetry, parallelism: Ekphrasis, stylistics and cognitive poetics', *Language and Literature* 14(3): 231–244.

Visel, D. (2008) 'He do the police in different voices', weblog post, February 23, *if:book*—blog project of The Institute of the Future of the Book (no pagination), Online, retrieved January 15, 2010, from http://www.futureofthebook.org/blog/archives/2008/02/he_do_the_police_in_different_1.html.

Vygotsky, L. (1978) *Mind in Society: The Development of Higher Psychological Processes*, Cambridge, MA: Harvard University Press.

Wales, K. (1996) *Personal Pronouns in Present-Day English*, Cambridge: Cambridge University Press.

Wales, K. (2001 [1991]) *A Dictionary of Stylistics*, Second Edition, Harlow: Longman.

Walton, K. (1990) *Mimesis as Make Believe: On the Foundations of the Representational Arts*, Cambridge, MA; London: Harvard University Press.

Website 1. Amazon.co.uk, customer reviews for *House of Leaves*, Online, 'Obsessive House of Horrors', by Laura A., Retrieved May 15, 2008, from http://www.amazon.com/review/product/038560310X/ref=cm_cr_pr_link_3?_encoding=UTF8&pageNumber=3&sortBy=bySubmissionDateDescending.

Website 2. *Exploration Z: A ~~Haunted~~ House of Leaves Alternative Universe*, unofficial fansite, Online, retrieved July 10, 2008, from http://markzdanielewski.info/holgen.html.

Website 3. *House of Leaves by Mark Z. Danielewski*, unofficial fansite, Online, retrieved July 10, 2008, from http://www.geocities.com/run_rom_run/houseofleaves.html.

Website 4. *Z, Official House of Leaves* forum, Online, retrieved May 15, 2008, from http://www.houseofleaves.com/forum/.

Website 5. Amazon.co.uk, customer reviews for *Woman's World*, Online, 'Woman's World—A Novel' by A Customer, December 11, 2005; 'Perfect read and also a great bookclub choice!' by D. S. Webster, November 13, 2006; 'Metafiction at its best', by Dr in the house, April 12, 2008; and 'A little distracting. . .' by Paperback. Writer, February 11, 2009. Retrieved February 15, 2010, from http://www.amazon.co.uk/product-reviews/1843543680/ref=cm_cr_dp_all_helpful?ie=UTF8&coliid=&showViewpoints=1&colid=&sortBy=bySubmissionDateDescending.

Website 6. Amazon.com, customer reviews for *Woman's World*, Online, 'More than just reading' by M. A. Lord, June 10, 2008; 'Amazing' by Tia Lowe, February 11, 2010. Retrieved February 15, 2010, from http://www.amazon.com/Womans-World-Novel-Graham-Rawle/product-reviews/1582434638/ref=cm_cr_dp_all_helpful?ie=UTF8&showViewpoints=1&sortBy=bySubmissionDateDescending.

Website 7. Jezebel.com, reader comments for *Woman's World*, Online, retrieved January 15, 2010. from http://jezebel.com/358256/book-of-the-month#comments.

Weich, D. (2006) 'Unlocking Jonathan Safran Foer', interview with Jonathan Safran Foer, *Powells.com*, April 13 (no pagination), Online, retrieved March 12, 2008, from http://www.powells.com/interviews/foer.html.

Werth, P. (1977) 'The linguistics of double-vision', *Journal of Literary Semantics* 6: 3–38.

Werth, P. (1994) 'Extended metaphor—a text-world account', *Language and Literature* 3(2): 77–103.

Werth, P. (1995) 'HOW TO BUILD A WORLD (in a lot less than six days, and using only what's in your head)', in Green, K. (ed.) *New Essays in Deixis: Discourse, Narrative, Literature*, Amsterdam: Rodopi, pp. 49–80.

Werth, P. (1999) *Text Worlds: Representing Conceptual Space in Discourse*, London: Longman.

Wertheimer, A. (1958 [1923]) 'Principles of perceptual organisation', in Beardslee, D. C. and Wertheimer, M. (eds.) (1958) *Readings in Perception*, Princeton, NJ: D. Van Nostrand, pp. 115–135.

White, C. (1970) *Women's Magazines: 1963–1968*, London: Michael Joseph.

White, G. (2005) *Reading the Graphic Surface: The Presence of the Book in Prose Fiction*, Manchester: Manchester University Press.

Whiteley, S. (2010) *Text World Theory and the Emotional Experience of Literary Discourse*, unpublished PhD thesis, University of Sheffield.

Wigan, M. (2008) *Text and Image*, Switzerland: AVA Publishing.

Wilson, N., and Gibbs, R. (2007) 'Real and imagined body movement primes metaphor comprehension', *Cognitive Science* 3(4): 721–731.

Winship, J. (1983) 'Unit 6—Femininity and Women's Magazines: A case study of *Woman's Own*—"First in Britain for Women"', in *The Changing Experience of Women*, Milton Keynes: Open University Press, pp. 1–73.

Winship, J. (1987) *Inside Women's Magazines*, London; New York: Pandora.

Young, K. G. (1987) *Taleworlds and storyrealms: The phenomenology of narrative,* Hingham, MA: Kluwer.

Zubin, D. A. and Hewitt, L. E. (1995) 'The deictic center: A theory of deixis in narrative', in Duchan, J. F., Bruder, G. A., and Hewitt, L. E. (eds.) *Deixis in Narrative: A Cognitive Science Perspective*, Hillsdale, NJ: Lawrence Erlbaum, pp. 129–155.

Zwaan, R. A., Madden, C. J., Yaxley, R. H., and Aveyard, M. E. (2004) 'Moving words: Dynamic representations in language comprehension', *Cognitive Science* 28: 611–619.

Zwaan, R. A. and Taylor, L. J. (2006) 'Seeing, acting, understanding: Motor resonance in language comprehension', *Journal of Experimental Psychology: General* 135(1): 1–11.

Index